The First Vietnam War

The First Vietnam War

COLONIAL CONFLICT AND COLD WAR CRISIS

◆　◆　◆

Edited by

Mark Atwood Lawrence

Fredrik Logevall

HARVARD UNIVERSITY PRESS

Cambridge, Massachusetts

London, England

2007

Library of Congress Cataloging-in-Publication Data
The First Vietnam War : colonial conflict and Cold War crisis / edited by Mark Atwood
Lawrence, Fredrik Logevall.
p. cm.
Includes bibliographical references and index.
ISBN-13: 978-0-674-02371-0 (cloth : alk. paper)
ISBN-10: 0-674-02371-4 (cloth : alk. paper)
ISBN-13: 978-0-674-02392-5 (pbk. : alk. paper)
ISBN-10: 0-674-02392-7 (pbk. : alk. paper)
1. Indochinese War, 1946–1954. I. Lawrence, Mark Atwood. II. Logevall, Fredrik.
III. Title: 1st Vietnam War.
DS553.1.F48 2007
959.704'1—dc22
2006046496

Contents

Acknowledgments

LIKE MANY BOOKS, this one grew from a simple idea that bubbled to the surface at an unlikely moment—between courses, if memory serves, of a particularly tasty Indian meal in Austin, Texas, in the spring of 2001. Wouldn't it be great, we brainstormed, if we could gather together in one place—and in one book—a group of leading scholars to reexamine the First Vietnam War, the conflict between France and Vietnamese nationalists that ran its course between 1945 and 1954? The second war, the one that directly involved the United States, had received intense scholarly attention. But the earlier conflict had received relatively little in-depth scrutiny in recent years. Given the profound significance of the Franco-Vietnamese conflict in Southeast Asian, European, and indeed global history, the time seemed right to take another look.

Our idea would have remained just that—an idea—without the generous support and encouragement of many individuals and organizations who shared our enthusiasm for exploring the prehistory of America's war in Vietnam. Most important, the Lyndon Baines Johnson Presidential Library and the Lyndon Baines Johnson Foundation offered us the opportunity to bring a "dream team" of scholars from around the world to a conference that took place at the LBJ library in November 2002. Harry Middleton, the former director of the library, approved the idea, and then Betty Sue Flowers, his successor, presided over the organization and execution of an enormously successful event. We are deeply grateful to them both and to many members of the library staff who helped us at every step of the way. Tina Houston and Larry Reed played particularly important roles.

It is no surprise, of course, that the LBJ Library was able to pull off the event with such skill. Over the years the library has hosted a series of landmark conferences devoted to the history of the Vietnam wars. Under the guidance of Ted Gittinger and Lloyd Gardner, these events have not only drawn top scholars but have also resulted in publication of important books reflecting the latest research on various aspects of the origins and course of America's involvement in Southeast Asia. We are indebted to Ted and Lloyd for sharing their wisdom, and we hope that this volume lives up to the high standards they set. We also benefited from the advice and encouragement of five other outstanding scholars of the Cold War—Bill Brands, Frank Gavin, Chris Goscha, Jim Hershberg, and Ed Miller—who contributed to this project in various ways. Our thanks go as well to Lieu-Hang T. Nguyen for sharing her expertise in the Vietnamese language.

At Harvard University Press, we owe a sincere debt of gratitude to Kathleen McDermott, who provided a perfect blend of enthusiasm and patience as we passed through the various stages of cat-herding that inevitably go into an edited collection of this sort. Kathleen helped shape this project every step of the way, and we could imagine no better guide in bringing it to completion. We also wish to thank Kathleen Drummy for her invaluable assistance along the way and to acknowledge the vital contribution of two anonymous reviewers, whose advice pushed us to make innumerable improvements to the manuscript.

Acronyms

CGT	Conféderation générale du travail
CIA	Central Intelligence Agency
DRV	Democratic Republic of Vietnam
EDC	European Defense Community
ICP	Indochinese Communist Party
MRP	Mouvement républicain populaire
NATO	North Atlantic Treaty Organization
NSC	National Security Council
PCF	Parti communiste français
PRC	People's Republic of China
SEAC	South East Asia Command
SEATO	Southeast Asia Treaty Organization
SFIO	Section française de l'internationale ouvrière
STEM	Special Technical and Economic Mission
UDSR	Union démocratique et socialiste de la résistance
VWP	Vietnamese Workers' Party

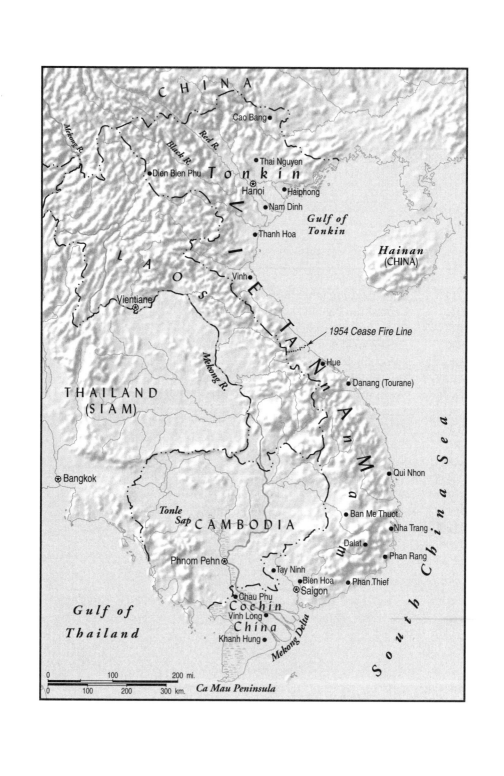

CHINA

LAOS

Cao Bang

• Thai Nguyen

Red R.

Black R.

• Dien Bien Phu

Tonkin

Hanoi ⊗ • Haiphong

• Nam Dinh

Mekong R.

• Thanh Hoa

Gulf of
Tonkin

Hainan
(CHINA)

• Vinh

Vientiane ⊗

L
a
o
s

V
I
E
T
N
A
M

1954 Cease Fire Line

Mekong R.

• Hue

THAILAND
(SIAM)

• Danang (Tourane)

An

⊗ Bangkok

• Qui Nhon

Tonle
Sap

CAMBODIA

a
m

• Ban Me Thuot

• Nha Trang

Dalat •

Phnom Pehn ⊗

• Tay Ninh

• Phan Rang

Bien Hoa •
⊗ Saigon

• Phan Thief

South China Sea

Chau Phu •

Cochin

Gulf of
Thailand

Vinh Long •

China

Khanh Hung •

Mekong Delta

0   100   200 mi.

0   100   200   300 km.

Ca Mau Peninsula

ONE

* * *

Introduction

MARK ATWOOD LAWRENCE

FREDRIK LOGEVALL

AS THE BATTLE of Dien Bien Phu reached its climax in early May 1954, the *New York Times* pointed to a paradox. Just a few months earlier, Dien Bien Phu had been merely "an unheard-of point in a far-away valley in the jungles of Southeast Asia," the newspaper observed in an editorial. Even after fighting had broken out in March, the place seemed to hold only minor strategic significance to the decade-old struggle between Vietnamese revolutionaries and the French military. "It is not even a decisive battle in the war for Indo-China," the *Times* pointed out. And yet the fight had assumed overwhelming importance. "Today," asserted the editorial, "Dienbienphu rings around the world as one of the epic battles of history."[1]

The *Times* was not exaggerating. All over the globe, policymakers and media invested the battle raging in remote jungles of northwestern Vietnam with enormous symbolic value. Nothing less than Indochina's political destiny seemed to be at stake. In France, political leaders and public opinion alike viewed the battle as the final test of their country's ability to keep Indochina within the French empire. In the United States, the Eisenhower administration considered the fight a last stand against communist expansion into Southeast Asia. In China and the Soviet Union, meanwhile, communist leaders saw the clash as an opportunity to score a major propaganda victory and to weaken the Western position in East-West talks due to open imminently in Geneva. In India, Algeria, Egypt, and other "third world" countries making the transition from colonialism to independence, nationalists regarded the battle of Dien Bien Phu as a key moment in the global struggle against European domination.[2]

1

Governments around the world had, in fact, increasingly fastened their attention on Vietnam ever since French and Viet Minh forces had first clashed in 1945, nearly a decade before "Dien Bien Phu" entered the global lexicon. To be sure, the Franco–Viet Minh War—or First Vietnam War—captured banner headlines and became the focus of sustained international negotiation only in 1954. But over the preceding years the conflict had steadily drawn interest as it acquired meanings that far transcended the political, economic, or geostrategic significance of a small territory on the eastern rim of the Southeast Asian peninsula. For France, the war amounted to a test of national will following the humiliations of World War II. In the United States, policymakers had come to see the fighting as part of a worldwide struggle against communism, a calculation that would lead to direct U.S. intervention in a new Vietnam conflict in later years. For the communist powers, especially after 1949, the war generated an opportunity to drain the Western powers politically and militarily, to demonstrate commitment to revolution in the third world, and, in the best case, to incorporate parts of Southeast Asia into the Eastern bloc.[3]

Persistent efforts by foreign powers to influence events within Vietnam had enormous consequences for the various Vietnamese factions that struggled to shape their country's political order in the 1940s and 1950s. While Vietnamese nationalism sprang from indigenous roots, it had to adjust constantly to opportunities and constraints created by foreign interference. Most notably, Ho Chi Minh's Democratic Republic of Vietnam repeatedly tacked before foreign winds, variously accommodating, resisting, or redirecting pressures from abroad. Ho's partial triumph in 1954 and the ultimate victory of his cause in 1975 owed a great deal to his remarkable ability—in contrast to his rivals for power—to maneuver adroitly within a complicated, rapidly changing international environment in the years after World War II. To understand the course and outcome of the Vietnam wars, it is essential to appreciate the connections between political-military events within Vietnam and the geopolitical currents in the wider world that gave those events meaning among the governments that possessed the power to influence Southeast Asia's postwar order.

This book explores those interconnections through a series of essays that examine various dimensions of the First Vietnam War, the conflict between France and Vietnamese revolutionaries that began in 1945, accelerated into open warfare at the end of 1946, and reached its climax at Dien Bien Phu eight years later. The collection naturally includes some discussion of the United States. Washington played a crucial role in Indochina between 1945 and 1954 and laid the groundwork in this period for its own full-blown embroilment in Vietnam in later years. Some of the essays that follow strive to shed fresh interpretive light on U.S. calculations during the French war. Unlike much of the vast scholarship on Vietnam's twentieth-century wars, however, this book ranges far beyond the matter of how Washington policymakers understood and responded to crisis in Southeast Asia.

Taking advantage of archival material in several nations, the volume's contributors strive to examine the First Vietnam War from the vantage point of several other nations, especially China, France, and Great Britain, all of which contributed in crucial ways to the transformation of the Vietnam conflict from a colonial skirmish to a major Cold War crisis. Moreover, some essays draw on newly available Vietnamese sources to explore the development of the political and military apparatus that successfully challenged the French and, later, American empires. In doing all this, we aspire to build on existing scholarship by setting the Franco-Vietnamese war within a broad global context and to seek new insight into the war—and into the international history of the twentieth century more generally.

Scholars of international affairs have insisted for many years on the need for studies of this sort.[4] Too often, they have complained, authors have explored international topics from the vantage point of a single government, usually the United States in the case of historians writing about the Cold War. The problems with such an approach are plain. Studies risk perpetuating policymakers' misperceptions and validating, rather than critiquing, their views. Only by examining the input of multiple states can we gain a critical perspective on policymakers' assumptions, evaluate their perceptions of threats and opportunities, and determine whether and how governments influenced each other. Only with a multinational approach, in short, can we write good international history.

Advocates of "international history" have, of course, been preaching to the choir. It has been common practice for many years among historians of foreign affairs to conduct research in multiple countries and to write studies that capture policymaking deliberations within multiple governments. Some ambitious scholars have drawn on archives from half a dozen or more countries.[5] Others have gone still further,

especially in recent years, by considering not just multiple governments but also nongovernmental bodies that helped shape international
affairs—multinational institutions, liberation movements, citizen groups,
media, lobbying organizations, and the like.[6] All this innovative work
has given rise to an extraordinary body of scholarship reflecting more
completely than ever before the complexity of international relations.

And yet substantial barriers remain for would-be practitioners of international history. For one thing, vital archives in many parts of the
world remain wholly or partially closed to scholars. As a result, it is impossible to gain satisfactory access to the kinds of materials that would
enable a scholar to explore policymaking in many countries, particularly third world nations and some members of the former communist
bloc. The need to master multiple languages poses another formidable
problem and can lead otherwise intrepid researchers to rein in their
ambitions, as can the cost and difficulty of traveling to various parts of the
world for research. Finally, there is the problem of sheer complexity.
Historians often have their hands full trying to master the decision-
making dynamics of a single country. To attempt to explore the experiences of several may lie beyond the grasp of a single scholar or, more
likely, may mean compromising analytical depth and nuance—not
necessarily a price worth paying.

Despite these problems, several scholars of the Franco–Viet Minh
War have succeeded over the years in producing helpful studies that
have explored decision-making in multiple nations. Ralph B. Smith,
Lloyd C. Gardner, Christopher Thorne, Robert J. McMahon, and Walter LaFeber, to name just a few, have drawn skillfully on non-American
sources, especially those of Great Britain, to set U.S. decision-making
within a larger frame.[7] Anyone taking up the challenge of writing
about the First Vietnam War these days necessarily stands on the shoul-
ders of these giants. Still, innumerable opportunities have remained
for new scholarship—opportunities that historians have recently begun seizing, thanks largely to the partial opening of archives within the
former communist bloc. Limited access to Vietnamese sources has fundamentally altered the study of the Vietnam wars by enabling scholars
to begin writing with unprecedented confidence about decision-
making in Hanoi and Saigon.[8] The partial opening of Chinese and Soviet sources, meanwhile, has enabled others to explore the wars with
new rigor from the standpoint of the communist superpowers.[9] Furthermore, the more complete opening of Western archival materials in the

last decade—and the new possibility of considering these sources in light of discoveries made in places like Vietnam and China—has permitted reappraisals of decision-making in places more familiar to Western scholars: Washington, London, and Paris.[10]

This book aims to showcase some of the best of this pathbreaking research and to make at least three contributions to the study of the First Vietnam War. First and most simply, the book, by drawing on newly available sources, helps us understand what happened and why. Several of the essays reach into relatively familiar U.S. and British sources to uncover new stories or new lines of inquiry. Others draw on new research in France, exposing fresh dimensions of French decision-making. Still others mine Chinese or Vietnamese archives to explore the motives and actions of Asian decision-makers whose behavior was, until recently, largely a matter of speculation. It is important to stress that access remains limited and that conclusions about Chinese or Vietnamese decision-making must remain tentative pending the availability of additional material. Yet sufficient evidence has come to light to enable scholars to assemble accounts of Chinese and Vietnamese policy-making that are much more complete than in the past. The pages that follow offer new accounts of Chinese calculations around the time of the Geneva Conference and of Vietnamese deliberations about how to wage war against France.

Second, this book illuminates the complex patterns of influence and causation that characterized the First Vietnam War and, by extension, the Cold War in the third world during the 1940s and 1950s. Taken together, the essays demonstrate in particular that many actors helped to shape events in Southeast Asia. Most important, we see that the Vietnamese revolutionaries themselves, while depending on foreign assistance, retained a striking degree of autonomy and sometimes succeeded in shaping foreign ideas and assistance to their own purposes. The essays show, too, that the great powers, in making policy toward Vietnam, acted on the basis of a complicated brew of domestic and international pressures that made clear-cut policy choices extraordinarily difficult. Each of the main powers in the Vietnam conflict was forced to weigh competing interests and to craft policies that took careful account of the attitudes of several other governments. Only by understanding the vexed relationships among the key participants—a central objective of some of the essays in this collection—can we better understand the origins, course, and outcome of the First Vietnam War.

Third, this volume argues for the crucial significance of the First Vietnam War in the history of the twentieth century. The war's chronological span, straddling the century's midpoint, suggests a deeper reality: Vietnam sat at a crossroads of most of the grand political forces that drove human affairs across the century. In part, of course, Vietnam's experience belongs to the story of the coming of the Cold War in the first years after 1945. Indeed, a central problem for historians of the war lies in explaining how it was that so small and impoverished a place as Vietnam became a major cockpit of tensions among the great world powers by the 1950s. But Vietnam's experience between 1945 and 1954 is part of another story, too—the story of European colonialism and the emergence of anticolonial nationalism throughout the developing world. While the First Vietnam War was partly an East-West conflict, it was also a "North-South" conflict pitting imperialism against the two principal competitors that gained traction by mid-century—communist-inspired revolutionary nationalism and U.S.-sponsored liberal internationalism.

Close examination of the First Vietnam War helps to reveal the ways in which the Cold War drama and the colonial drama intermingled with and distorted each other, producing a complicated blend that heightened passions on all sides and inhibited a negotiated settlement. In showing this interplay, the Vietnam struggle offers a microcosm of processes that unfolded across much of the globe after 1945 as anti-colonial nationalism surged and the great powers, concerned largely with gaining advantage in the Cold War, struggled to harness it to their purposes or, failing that, to dampen its challenge. Similar trends played out across Asia, Africa, and Latin America in the years that followed. Vietnam deserves especially careful attention because it was one of the first places where one can see this destructive dynamic in action. But Vietnam also merits careful analysis because of the particularly great political, material, and, above all, human cost that would result from the tensions unleashed by World War II.

The roots of the Franco–Viet Minh War go back to the early days of the French colonial period in Indochina and the rise of a multifaceted Vietnamese nationalist movement in the first decades of the twentieth century. In a more immediate sense they go back to the early 1930s, when Vietnamese nationalists first engaged in armed resistance to French rule. The Indochinese Communist Party (ICP), organized in 1930 under Nguyen Ai Quoc, the future Ho Chi Minh, led unsuccessful uprisings in northern Annam and Tonkin in 1930 and 1931. Nationalist agitation continued in the years thereafter but could not overcome the repression of the French colonial authorities. After the fall of France to the Nazis in the spring of 1940, Japan gradually assumed control of Indochina, but French authorities were allowed to continue to administer the colony until the Japanese ousted them in March 1945. The ICP-led Viet Minh, with limited aid from a U.S. intelligence unit, in short order began to systematically harass the new colonial master. When Japan surrendered in mid-August, the Viet Minh swiftly seized the initiative, proclaiming power in Hanoi. On August 29, the Viet Minh formed a national government they called the Provisional Government of the Democratic Republic of Vietnam (DRV), with its capital in Hanoi and Ho Chi Minh as its leader.[11]

As Ho well understood, however, the struggle had only begun. French leaders were determined to reassert control over Indochina. At stake, they believed, was their status as a great power. Under a plan agreed to at the Potsdam Conference, British troops entered the southern part of Vietnam to disarm the defeated Japanese while Chinese Nationalist forces arrived in the north to perform the same function. The British, concerned about losing their own colonies and not wanting Vietnam to set any precedents, released and rearmed interned French soldiers, who promptly clashed with Viet Minh forces. New French units landed to reassert France's authority in the south.[12]

Ho Chi Minh saw no option but to negotiate. In the spring of 1946 he offered concessions to the French, agreeing to permit them to return to the north to displace the Chinese. He also agreed to affiliate an autonomous Vietnam with the French Union, a loose federation of states linked to France. In return, French negotiator Jean Sainteny pledged that there would be a national referendum to determine whether Cochinchina, the southern part of Vietnam, would rejoin Annam and Tonkin in a reunited Vietnamese state or remain a separate French territory. Inconclusive negotiations continued over the summer at Fontainebleau near Paris, while both sides bolstered their forces. In September Ho Chi Minh left Paris for the last time, resigned to the reality that diplomacy had failed. The French had not granted independence; now, he realized, he very likely would have to fight for it. The war began in earnest in December 1946, following the late-November shelling of the port of Haiphong by a French cruiser.[13]

Viet Minh forces under General Vo Nguyen Giap benefited from fighting experience won during the last phases of the Japanese occupation and had the added advantage of operating in a region where much of the population was on their side. Initially, however, French troops scored successes, taking Hanoi and forcing the Viet Minh to retreat into the countryside. Paris leaders exulted, but privately some military leaders harbored doubts that the Viet Minh, a formidable adversary with bona fide nationalist credentials, could be subdued for long. General Jean Philippe Leclerc, for example, who commanded French forces until mid-1946, came to have doubts that there could be any kind of lasting military solution in Indochina and told his superiors that France should seek a negotiated settlement.

Leclerc's skepticism, it soon became clear, was amply justified. His French forces had a massive superiority in weapons and could take and hold any area they wanted. The Viet Minh, however, being far better able to recruit soldiers locally, held a considerable edge in manpower. In military terms the war soon became stalemated, a low-scale affair of patrols, ambushes, and small-unit actions. The French held most cities and major towns while the Viet Minh dominated mountainous and remote areas. In political terms, though, the French lost more and more ground. Absent the transfer of major executive and legislative authority to the Vietnamese government, there could be little hope of an early resolution to the conflict, and France was unwilling to yield more than a titular independence. Real power would remain in French hands.[14]

Yet Paris officials grasped that it would be important to make a nod in the direction of greater Vietnamese autonomy. Accordingly, the French in 1948 formed a government, the "State of Vietnam," in opposition to Ho Chi Minh's DRV. Widely perceived as a puppet regime, the government won little support, even among those Vietnamese who were opposed to the Viet Minh. Under a March 1949 agreement with former emperor Bao Dai, Vietnam was given "independence" as an "associated state" within the French Union. Vietnam now had two rival governments—one bent on achieving independence before regulating its relations with France by treaty, the other counting on the attainment of independence by gradual means through close association with France. Unfortunately for Bao Dai, however, his government continued to lack broad popularity and depended on French support for its day-to-day survival.[15]

The monarchs of Laos and Cambodia, meanwhile, who granted constitutions to their people and held elections in 1947, agreed to bring their countries into the French Union in 1948. Almost immediately they learned that the Paris government would continue to control their diplomacy and armed forces, and that even in domestic affairs French representatives in Vientiane and Phnom Penh would still wield a great deal of power. Nevertheless, representatives of both governments entered into agreements with France in 1949. The status of Laos and Cambodia as Associated States within the French Union was confirmed on July 19 and November 8, respectively.

In Laos especially the agreement generated internal dissension. "Free Laotian" leaders in exile, believing that independence would come quickly, voluntarily disbanded the Lao Issarak nationalist movement, and two of three dissident princes returned from Bangkok with their followers. Prince Souvanna Phouma announced that he would cooperate with French authorities during the remainder of the transition period to true independence; in due course he became prime minister. But another leader, Prince Souphanouvong, remained dubious about French intentions and later placed himself at the head of a revived dissident movement under the name of Pathet Lao, which owed part of its strength to the proximity of its headquarters to Viet Minh strongholds neighboring in Vietnam.

The March 1949 agreement with Bao Dai and the agreements of July and November with Laos and Cambodia did not have the galvanizing effect on the war effort that French leaders hoped. On the contrary, the conflict in Indochina now entered a new, more international—and more dangerous—phase. The victory of the Chinese communists over Chiang Kai-shek in 1949, followed by the decision of the Mao Zedong government to support the Viet Minh with arms, advisers, and training, had a major impact on the fighting in Indochina. Giap launched a Viet Minh offensive that overwhelmed the French garrisons in and around Cao Bang along the Chinese border in October 1950. Believing the French to be on the ropes, Giap attacked the Red River delta in 1951 but was repulsed by French forces under Jean de Lattre de Tassigny.[16]

At about the same time that China stepped up its involvement in the Indochina war, another great power also increased its role: the United States. In 1948 and 1949, U.S. officials watched with growing concern as insurgencies erupted in Burma and Malaya and as Mao's armies gained ground in China. In February 1950 the Truman administration granted diplomatic recognition to the Bao Dai government, and in early May the administration pledged to furnish France with military and economic assistance for the war effort. The outbreak of the Korean War in late June, together with concern about the intentions of the Chinese communists, solidified Washington's commitment. From 1950 onward, the Franco–Viet Minh War was simultaneously a colonial conflict and a Cold War confrontation—a Sino-U.S. war-by-proxy with the potential to escalate into a direct military confrontation.[17]

The American aid decision came at a pivotal time and contributed to some tactical French successes under de Lattre, whose forces included not only French and Indochinese but also Moroccans, Algerians, Senegalese, and French Foreign Legionnaires (among them a sizable number of ex-Nazis). The overall strategic situation, however, still favored the Viet Minh, notwithstanding the fact that Washington provided far more aid to the French war effort than Beijing gave to the Viet Minh. By early 1953, French forces were suffering from low morale, lack of mobility and air power, and a shortage of officers. Total French casualties reached 150,000, and even with American aid the war consumed one-half of the country's defense expenditures. More and more, proposals could be heard in Paris—from various points on the political spectrum—for a withdrawal from Indochina. The proposals were rejected. The government insisted (at least publicly) that its policy of holding on in Indochina was working and that the war-weary Vietnamese were bound sooner or later to accept an arrangement that promised a stable regime and security. The Vietnamese would rally to Bao Dai, Paris officials predicted, if the communists could only be held back by military action a little longer.[18]

And so the fighting raged on, while the United States kept raising the level of its material aid until, by the spring of 1954, American taxpayers were carrying more than two-thirds of the financial cost of the French effort. A steady stream of bombers, cargo planes, trucks, tanks, naval craft, automatic weapons, small arms and ammunition, radios, hospital and engineering equipment, plus financial aid flowed to the French war effort. Between 1950 and 1954 U.S. investment in the war in Indochina reached a total of approximately $3 billion.

In mid-1953, French commander Henri Navarre, feeling pressure from Washington to show aggressiveness in the field, announced plans for a "general counteroffensive." The press in France and the United States gave much coverage to this so-called Navarre Plan. Though its details were always sketchy, in essence it called for sending an additional ten French battalions to Indochina and boosting significantly the Vietnamese segment of the armed forces. By 1955, this larger army would be ready to mount a major offensive to drive the Viet Minh from their strongholds in the north and the south. Privately, though, Navarre expressed misgivings and repeated Leclerc's doubts from the early days of the fighting that a military victory was possible. The best that could be hoped for, he said, was a draw *(coup nul)*. Still, he pressed ahead with his plan.[19]

General Giap, meanwhile, made preparations to mount a major operation in the highlands of northwest Tonkin. He wanted to force the French to disperse their forces and also sought to prepare the ground for a possible invasion of northern Laos. Giap reasoned that the French would feel compelled—for political as well as military reasons—to try to beat back such an invasion, which would lead them to stretch long supply lines across Viet Minh-dominated territory. Giap further calculated that with control of northern Laos he could more easily join up with Viet Minh forces in southern Vietnam for an assault on Saigon. Navarre chose to block the Viet Minh at Dien Bien Phu, a remote outpost two hundred air miles west of Hanoi near the Laotian border. The Frenchman conceded the high ground surrounding Dien Bien Phu to Giap, but he hoped to draw enemy forces into a set-piece conventional battle and overcome them with French artillery and air power. Giap, however, equipped his men with artillery provided by China (as well as tens of thousands of Russian Skoda rifles), and they succeeded in trapping the French garrison on the valley floor.[20]

Desperate Paris officials tried in early 1954 to secure direct American air intervention to relieve the beleaguered French garrison. Washington leaders, aware that a French defeat at Dien Bien Phu might lead to a French withdrawal from Indochina, faced the uncomfortable fact that only U.S. intervention might save the day. Indochina's strategic importance remained a given: virtually no one questioned that communist domination of Vietnam would weaken noncommunist governments throughout Southeast Asia, with far-reaching ramifications. At a press conference on April 7, President Dwight D. Eisenhower gave public expression to these concerns in what was to become one of the most frequently cited justifications for U.S. involvement in Vietnam in the decade that followed—the so-called domino theory which suggested that the fall of one country in the region to communism would cause others to tumble swiftly as well. Knock over one domino and the rest would soon follow.[21]

Accordingly, Eisenhower and his secretary of state, John Foster Dulles, seriously considered military intervention, asking Congress in April for authority to use, if necessary, U.S. troops to save France's position. The lawmakers refused to go along unless the British also joined and furthermore insisted that France had to pledge to move swiftly to grant Vietnam independence. This congressional attitude effectively left the matter in the hands of Winston Churchill's government in London, which declined to participate on the ground that the intervention might precipitate a disastrous war with communist China if not with the Soviet Union too. British officials were dubious in any case that limited military intervention had any real hope of salvaging the French position and accordingly pinned their hopes on a negotiated settlement.[22]

On May 7, 1954, Giap's troops overran the French garrison at Dien Bien Phu. The next day an international conference already in session in Geneva began to discuss a basis for a cease-fire in the war. Notwithstanding the ongoing fighting and the Viet Minh leadership's vow to secure a total victory, hopes ran high that a diplomatic solution might be possible. The Soviet Union sought such a settlement as part of its plan to reduce East-West tension. China saw an opportunity to establish its great-power credentials by helping to secure an agreement and also wanted to avoid indefinitely matching in Indochina the stepped-up pace of U.S. military aid, with the attendant risk of a general war. Beijing leaders apparently believed, moreover, that the Viet Minh hold on Indochina was already strong enough to ensure that communist interests would be well served there in the future. France itself was losing the will to continue a war it obviously could not win. Several NATO powers thought Paris should cut its losses in Southeast Asia and concentrate its attention instead on the reorganization of Europe, while among neutralist Asian states there was a strong desire to end a conflict that many saw as retarding the development of newly independent countries in South and Southeast Asia.[23]

The Viet Minh and the Americans were more skeptical. DRV leaders were reluctant to agree to a compromise settlement when military victory seemed within reach, but they were pressured by Moscow and Beijing to accept a settlement that left them in control of only a part of the country. Take one-half of the loaf now, the communist giants in effect told them, and count on getting the other in the not-too-distant future. The Eisenhower administration, for its part, had grave misgivings about the negotiations and advised the French to continue the struggle in Indochina in the interest of the "free world." The French refused, and after ten weeks a peace settlement was signed. Vietnam was partitioned at the seventeenth parallel pending nationwide elections in 1956, after which the residual French presence would be terminated and Vietnam would be reunited and independent under—in all probability— Ho Chi Minh and the Viet Minh.

The essays in this volume bring new evidence and new analysis to bear on this story. In Chapters two and three the subject is not so much the war itself as the ways in which historians have understood it over the years. Mark Philip Bradley surveys English- and French-language studies and points out that a new generation of scholars—several of whom are included in this volume—has brought unprecedented subtlety to the study of the war. In contrast to older studies that situated the war rigidly within narratives of decolonization or the coming of the Cold War, Bradley argues, the new scholarship has emphasized the contingency and fluidity that characterized decision-making during the conflict. Lien-Hang T. Nguyen examines scholarship about the war emanating from Vietnamese universities and publishing houses, demonstrating that Vietnamese scholars have crafted and recrafted the story of the French war to suit the state's needs at various points in its development.

Chapters four through seven explore how key actors in the United States, the Democratic Republic of Vietnam, Britain, and France responded to the end of the Pacific war and the emergence of a new conflict in Vietnam as a restored French republic made plain its intention to restore its colonial rule. First, Stein Tønnesson offers a revisionist interpretation of President Franklin Roosevelt's behavior with respect to the Indochina problem, especially by challenging the widely held view that FDR abandoned his opposition to French rule in the last weeks of his life. Rather, Tønnesson argues, American bureaucrats, ultimately backed by President Harry S. Truman, made the crucial decisions that led to U.S. toleration for the restoration of French colonialism. David G. Marr shifts the focus to Vietnam, examining the process by which the nascent Democratic Republic of Vietnam overcame massive material disadvantages and created a military force capable of challenging the French army. In the third essay, Mark Atwood Lawrence explores growing unease in the British Empire as fighting mounted in Vietnam. Lawrence argues that skittish British officials, worried that their country risked implication in French colonial repression, pulled back from deep involvement in Vietnam and sought to shift the burden of supporting the French onto the United States. Finally, Martin Thomas analyzes the roles of the major French political parties in launching and sustaining the war against the Viet Minh. Thomas demonstrates especially how peculiarities of the Fourth Republic militated against a negotiated settlement.

Chapters eight through ten depict how tensions over resurgent French colonialism became inextricably intertwined with Cold War tensions, especially in the years after 1949. First, William J. Duiker explores the complicated relationship between Ho Chi Minh and Mao Zedong's China. Duiker argues above all that Ho borrowed liberally from Maoist ideas of "people's war" but deserves credit for adroitly bending those ideas to suit his own purposes and the particular Vietnamese circumstances. In the second essay, Laurent Cesari explores French decision-making as Cold War priorities in Europe and Southeast Asia increasingly competed for limited French resources. By the early 1950s, Cesari argues, the war in Vietnam constituted a debilitating drain on France and could no longer be considered worth the price. In the third essay, Marilyn B. Young examines the vexed Franco-American partnership after 1949, calling attention to the severe tensions that emerged between U.S. officials, who focused on fighting communism, and their French counterparts, who were waging war on a more complicated blend of motives.

Chapters eleven through fourteen examine the final phase of the First Indochina War. First, John Prados analyzes the French defeat at Dien Bien Phu, asking especially what significance the battle had for the U.S. policymakers who would confront a renewed Vietnam problem in later years. In his contribution Chen Jian explores the crucial role played by the Chinese government at Geneva. As the chapter makes clear, the Chinese delegation adroitly adjusted its negotiating strategy as the conference proceeded and, at a pivotal moment, placed decisive pressure on the DRV delegation to compromise by accepting the division of their country. The final two essays reach beyond 1954 and draw connections between the Franco–Viet Minh War and later events in Vietnam. First, Kathryn C. Statler analyzes tensions between the United States and France as the two competed for influence in the new quasi-state of South Vietnam. Statler demonstrates not only how the United States gradually supplanted France as the key Western actor in Vietnam but also how France managed to retain a considerable cultural and political presence. Finally, Andrew J. Rotter illuminates the striking parallels and continuities between the first and second Vietnam wars.

TWO

❖   ❖   ❖

Making Sense of the French War

*The Postcolonial Moment and the
First Vietnam War, 1945–1954*

MARK PHILIP BRADLEY

A SHARED SENSE of misgiving and discomfort hovered over the meanings that French, American, and Vietnamese observers accorded to the first year of the French war. After war broke out in Hanoi in December 1946 between the French and the Ho Chi Minh government, the conflict produced considerable ambivalence in France itself. When asked about the future of French policy in Indochina by the Institut Française d'Opinion Publique in January 1947, 37 percent of respondents supported the reestablishment of colonial order. But an equal number favored a negotiated settlement or immediate end to French colonialism in the area. More than 20 percent expressed indifference.[1]

A month later, U.S. secretary of state George Marshall wrote to the American embassy in Paris to express "increasing concern over the situation as it is developing in Indochina." While Marshall acknowledged that the United States had "fully recognized France's sovereign position" in the area, he could not understand "the continued existence of an outmoded colonial outlook" and the inability of the French to recognize the realities of a postcolonial future. Equally concerned by Ho Chi Minh's internationalist connections, Marshall also argued it "should be obvious that we [are] not interested in seeing colonial empire administrations supplanted by a philosophy emanating from and controlled by the Kremlin." Confounded by the perceived impossibilities of choosing between a radical political regime and an archaic colonial one, Marshall could offer no clear American policy toward the French war.[2]

At the end of December 1947, as the first year of the war came to a close, the poet Nguyen Dinh Thi gave voice to the soul-searching dilemmas facing many patriotic northern Vietnamese intellectuals who supported the Ho Chi Minh government. Deeply sympathetic to the state's calls to use their talents to represent the struggles of peasants, soldiers, and workers in the war against the French, Thi and other patriotic intellectuals found it difficult to know how to place their art in the service of politics and the state and at the same time maintain a sense of themselves as independent creative artists. In an essay titled "Nhan Duong" (Finding the Way), Nguyen Dinh Thi argued that the revolutionary imperatives of the anticolonial war against the French meant that literature should work to "change the lives of the reader—*creating man,* pushing toward a new life that formerly we could only stand observing from afar." Yet at the same time he drew vivid attention to what he called "the often aching doubts of a shedding of a skin" to express the dilemmas of meeting the artistic and political transformations pressed on him by the Vietnamese state.[3]

Why draw attention to these episodes? They are not, after all, a central part of the standard historiography of the French war. Here the focus has been on explaining events that appear to mark moments of clarity and decisiveness: the outbreak of the war in 1946, American and Chinese intervention in 1950, and the climactic battle of Dien Bien Phu in 1954. In them, the meanings of the war are often subsumed into a variety of more familiar metanarratives of the post-1945 world. Much of the existing Western-language historiography on the French war views it as a chapter in the history of increasingly untenable French and British efforts to manage the global phenomenon of decolonization after 1945, an incident in the emerging Soviet-American Cold War struggle, or a prelude (and sometimes a cautionary tale) to what is usually seen as the more important American war in Vietnam. In the officially sanctioned histories of the Vietnamese state, the French war serves as the template for a narrative of sacred war *(chien tranh than thanh)* that sought to give the Vietnamese past and present a unified revolutionary history and to foreground the power of the socialist state in shaping Vietnam's postcolonial future.

The ambiguous and hesitant voices of French public opinion, George Marshall, and Nguyen Dinh Thi, however, occupy a critical place in a new scholarship on the French war that complicates these standard interpretations. The work of a younger generation of international historians has begun to reshape our understanding of French,

British, Soviet, Chinese, American, and Vietnamese state perceptions and policies toward the war in ways that emphasize the fragility of state efforts to manage the construction of postcolonial Vietnam. At the same time, a complementary body of new scholarship in cultural history and literary studies points to the multiplicity of meanings that a variety of nonstate participants in the French war ascribed to the events that unfolded around them and their uneasy relationships with the increasing rigidity of state visions of Vietnam's postcolonial future.

In this essay I explore the ways in which this new scholarship opens up the historical possibilities of what we call the French war. This Vietnam war, like the larger rupture of decolonization throughout the colonized world after 1945 of which it was a part, emerges in these works overall as a remarkably fluid site of contestation in which both state and nonstate actors imagined a highly contingent postcolonial future. In analyzing these works, I suggest the potentialities of recovering this remarkable era in which the postcolonial remained very much in the process of becoming. In addition, I explore the wider implications for writing about the French war and the international history of the last century.

Western Decision-Making

The year 1950 occupies a pivotal space in much of the standard historiography on the French war. In January both the Soviet Union and Mao's China extended formal diplomatic recognition to the Ho Chi Minh–led Democratic Republic of Vietnam (DRV). Within weeks, diplomatic recognition of the Vietnamese state came from the governments of Poland, Romania, Czechoslovakia, Hungary, Bulgaria, Albania, and Yugoslavia. With Chinese recognition also came military advisers and substantial amounts of military equipment and supplies for the Vietnamese state's war against the French. The U.S. response was swift. In early February the Truman administration announced its recognition of the French-backed Associated State of Vietnam led by former Vietnamese emperor Bao Dai. In May the administration allocated $15 million in military and economic aid to the French and the Bao Dai government; the figure had increased to $100 million by the end of the year.

Much of the previous work by American diplomatic historians views the significance of this period largely through the prism of the Cold War and the later American war in Vietnam. For them, the dramatic events of 1950 mark the moment in which the growing primacy of America's concerns with the Cold War and the containment of international communism intersects with Vietnam. George Herring's *America's Longest War,* perhaps the leading account of American intervention in Vietnam, opens with a brief analysis of the events of 1950 to underscore his larger argument that the U.S. commitment to Vietnam "was a logical, if not inevitable, outgrowth of a world view and a policy—the policy of containment—that Americans in and out of government accepted without serious question for more than two decades."[4] Other scholars have focused on efforts to promote the postwar economic recovery of Japan and the domestic politics of fending off partisan attacks after the communist victory in China as critical factors behind the Truman administration's decision to extend its policy of containment to Vietnam.[5] Whether analyzed in terms of geopolitics, economics, or domestic imperatives, however, the coming of the Cold War in Vietnam in 1950 often appears overdetermined, lending a sense of inevitability to Harry S. Truman's support of the French war effort.

Scholarship on U.S. decision-making is not alone in attaching great significance to the events of 1950. As Lien-Hang T. Nguyen suggests in her essay in this volume, Vietnamese historiography on the French war has viewed 1950 as a defining moment for political and military efforts to move toward a general counteroffensive against the French. Historians of French policy have made similar claims for the significance of 1950 in shaping French tactics and strategy against the Vietnamese. An older, and somewhat polemical, Western-language historiography of Vietnamese abilities and intentions argues that the Sino-Vietnamese embrace of 1950 put the Vietnamese state well on the way to becoming a "model satellite" of the Soviets and the Chinese.[6]

The new history of the French war does not so much displace 1950 as a watershed event as considerably deepen and complicate our understanding of its larger significance. By employing novel interpretative frameworks to carefully unpack developments both before and after 1950 it suggests that a focus on the war's critical decision-making moments, whether they be 1950 or 1946 or 1954, can significantly obscure the broader uncertainties and ambiguities through which contemporary state and nonstate actors viewed the French war. This new historiography emphasizes the tensions and contradictions of French, British, and American policies toward the war as well as the ways in which the approaches of these states to it were mutually constituted. It also concentrates on the complicated roles of the Soviets and the Chinese in the war and their frequently quite fractious relations with the Vietnamese state. And while the complexities of the Vietnamese experiences of the war remain significantly understudied, aspects of this new scholarship reveal the iconoclastic approaches of the Vietnamese state to its war against the French and the brittleness of the state's effort to manage and shape the meanings of the war and Vietnam's postcolonial future. Moreover, the attention scholars accord to nonstate actors who were participants in or observers of the French war, and their complex relationships to state perceptions and policies, both expands the range of voices that have served as the traditional subjects of narratives of the war.

One seminal work in this new scholarship is Mark Lawrence's *Assuming the Burden*, which most explicitly questions the utility of valorizing 1950 as a landmark moment for Western policy toward the French war in Vietnam.[7] Lawrence argues that Truman's policy in 1950 cannot be understood without reference to a broader chronological and transnational framework that foregrounds the contingent nature of the critical decisions of 1950. Lawrence suggests that Marshall's anguished musings in 1947, quoted at the outset of this essay, captured a powerful and persisting current of uncertainty in U.S. policy toward Vietnam. Could or should the emerging Cold War trump the colonial dimension of the French war in Vietnam, both the restorative efforts of the French and the decolonizing sensibilities of the Vietnamese, for American perceptions and policies toward Vietnam? In casting his interpretative net beyond American policy, Lawrence explores not only the dilemmas these questions posed in Washington but the complex and unstable forces shaping attitudes in London and France toward colonialism and decolonization in Vietnam. Ultimately, Lawrence views U.S. policy toward Vietnam between 1945 and 1950 as part of a complex transnational negotiation in which like-minded French, British, and American policymakers increasingly, and eventually successfully, sought to construct a postcolonial Vietnam under Bao Dai that could overcome the seemingly intractable problems that support for the French in Vietnam posed to Marshall and other Americans.

In some ways other scholars have anticipated the arguments Lawrence makes for the value of a more expansive frame for appreciating the American decisions of 1950. Stein Tønnesson's multiarchival and globally inflected studies of the early years of the war reveal the

overlapping and intertwined ways in which the French, Americans, and
Vietnamese shaped the nature of the Vietnamese revolution and the
outbreak of the French war.[8] In my own *Imagining Vietnam and America,*
I have emphasized the broader continuities of American attitudes
toward race in shaping increasingly unfavorable American perceptions
of Vietnam in the late 1940s. In this case, derisive American dismissals
of the Vietnamese capability to build an independent postcolonial
state, whose genealogy rested on long-standing Euro-American racism
toward nonwhite peoples at home and abroad, prompted deepening
suspicions by Truman administration policymakers that the Ho Chi
Minh government could be little more than a puppet of Moscow or
Beijing.[9]

Lawrence also builds in part upon an existing scholarly literature
that has explored the internal divisions among Truman administration
Vietnam policymakers. In his *The United States' Emergence as a Southeast
Asian Power,* Gary R. Hess explored the differences of approach by
Americans on postcolonial Vietnam and policy toward the French
war.[10] For Asianists in the Truman State Department in the late 1940s,
Hess argued, aggressive French policy, if unchecked and supported by
the United States, could produce a potentially destabilizing climate
throughout the region and embitter and estrange America's potential
future allies in Vietnam and the decolonizing world. At the same time,
the Europeanist wing of the State Department stressed the overriding
importance of the place of France in the construction of a stable postwar strategic and economic order. Throughout the early years of the
French war, as both Hess and Lawrence argue, proponents of these
competing visions intensely jockeyed to make their views official policy.
American policymakers like Secretary Marshall in much of this period
remained unable to resolve these competing visions of America's Vietnam policy.

But by simultaneously exploring British and French perceptions and
policy, Lawrence deepens our appreciation of the complexities and
hesitancy that marked French, British, and American thinking about
Vietnam and the increasingly transnational nature of policy toward
the French war among the Western powers. The first English-language
scholar to draw fully on the French archival record, Lawrence's account of French policy is particularly revealing.[11] Lawrence makes
clear the French desire to return to Vietnam rested on efforts to restore the *grandeur* and Great Power status of the *metropole* after the

wartime devastations and humiliations experienced by France during World War II and the economic role Vietnam could play in its domestic recovery. His account also reveals the highly contentious and divisive discourse on French postwar colonial policy, in part reflecting the broader instabilities of the Fourth Republic itself and the tenuous base of domestic political support for war against the DRV. On one side were Gaullist, center-right political groupings (notably the Mouvement républicain populaire), right-leaning members of the Socialist Party, and military and colonial administrators in Saigon who defended French sovereignty over its empire and believed France should fight to return to the status quo ante in Vietnam. The hardliners were opposed by left-leaning Socialist Party and French Communist Party reformers who advocated negotiation and liberalization of French rule in Vietnam; although the Communist Party initially kept a low profile on colonial issues in an effort to build domestic political legitimacy, its withdrawal from the governing coalition in May 1947 brought increasingly vocal denunciations of hardline French policy.

British policymaking toward Vietnam, Lawrence suggests, displayed similarly complex motivations in this period. Scholars have directed some attention to British policy, most notably Andrew Rotter, who contends in his *Path to Vietnam* that a shared concern among British and American policymakers over postwar British economic recovery, particularly the necessity for the British of unimpeded access to rubber and tin in Malaya, prompted American interest in defeating communist movements throughout Southeast Asia, including Vietnam.[12] But Lawrence points out that while Clement Attlee's British Labour Party government was broadly supportive of the restoration of French colonial control in Vietnam, it was nonetheless constrained by domestic politics and the attitudes of its own colonial subjects. The Labour Party itself was divided on foreign policy issues. A substantial number of Labour back-benchers in Parliament, who were advocates of colonial self-determination, expressed sharp criticism of British support for the French war in Vietnam, effectively muting official Labour support for the French. Moreover, considerable hostility among nationalist groups in South and Southeast Asia to French suppression of Vietnamese nationalism further complicated British policymaking as the Labour government grew fearful of upsetting Asian nationalists while Britain was negotiating transfers of power in India and Burma.

Much of Lawrence's *Assuming the Burden* focuses on the ways in which these ambiguities were eventually subsumed in a transnational dialogue between like-minded conservative elites in Paris, London, and Washington. The eventual American embrace of the French-crafted Bao Dai solution, he suggests, paved the way for more aggressive U.S. support of the French war beginning in 1950. Without the sustained efforts of the French and British to construct a postcolonial Vietnamese alternative to Ho Chi Minh's government compelling to the Americans, Lawrence questions whether the U.S. commitment to the French war would ever have been made.

The nature of French, British, and American policy in the last years of the French war has yet to receive sustained scholarly attention.[13] But a plausible, if necessarily provisional, argument can be made that French, British, and American policy in the final years of war exhibited the same remarkable fragility within the Western alliance and the persistence of the doubts and uncertainties through which the three states had initially apprehended the postcolonial moment in Vietnam. Within months of the Truman administration's decision to recognize the Bao Dai government, tensions quickly emerged over the political, economic, and social construction of the new Vietnamese state. In the fall of 1950 Americans began to voice doubts about the capabilities of "the Vietnamese Govt and its leadership to inspire support." A National Intelligence Estimate prepared by the Central Intelligence Agency somewhat drily suggested that Bao Dai's "qualities of leadership" were "hereto unrevealed." American policymakers also expressed dissatisfaction with the French, including "deficient French generalship" and colonial controls of the economy that deprived Vietnam of its "economic liberty."[14] But a larger problem, most American agreed, was that "concessions to nationalist sentiment, leading to full sovereignty for the Bao Dai government, have been forthcoming so slowly and with such seeming reluctance on the part of the French" that the government had not "won a strong nationalist following in any quarter."[15]

Persistent dissatisfaction with the Bao Dai government and French policies toward Vietnam continued to animate U.S. discussion of Vietnam after 1950, echoing the kinds of qualms and debates that had infused American official debates throughout the 1940s. As increasing amounts of U.S. military and economic aid entered Vietnam, American scorn for French colonial methods also intensified and provoked bitter disputes between French and American officials over how U.S. aid dollars in Vietnam would be spent. The organization and command of the Vietnamese army was a particular source of concern for many American officials who supported Vietnamese control of it against strong French opposition. From the U.S. perspective, French efforts to control the Vietnamese army prevented it from acting to instill notions of political community and citizenship that Americans believed essential for the construction of a viable postcolonial state.[16]

The Communist World

New work on the Chinese and Soviet relationship with Ho Chi Minh's Democratic Republic of Vietnam during the French war, drawing for the first time on Chinese and Soviet primary materials, suggests the ambiguities and problems in the Western alliance found significant parallels in the international communist world. Qiang Zhai and Chen Jian's studies of Sino-Vietnamese relations[17] highlight the significant contributions Mao's China made to the Vietnamese war effort against the French beginning in 1950, including substantial numbers of Chinese military and political advisers who worked closely with their Vietnamese counterparts and provided large quantities of supplies. But their work also reveals the tremendous strains that emerged in Sino-Vietnamese relations. Again, some of this discussion is not entirely new. Since the Sino-Vietnamese border war of 1979 and the publication of the Vietnamese white paper, Vietnamese retrospective displeasure at what they perceived as undue Chinese pressure to make concessions at the Geneva Conference of 1954 has been clear. Similarly, Chinese and Vietnamese disputes over the importance of Chinese support in the Vietnamese victory in the battle of Dien Bien Phu became a very public point of contention after 1979, as did Vietnamese accusations of Chinese culpability in the disastrous Vietnamese land reform campaign of the mid-1950s.[18]

The deeper tensions and ambiguities underlying these polemical exchanges, however, emerge more fully in the densely textured accounts of Qiang Zhai and Chen Jian. Qiang Zhai in particular makes brilliant use of the diary of General Chen Geng, who served as the first senior Chinese military adviser in Vietnam and was closely involved in the successful border campaign against the French in 1950, to illustrate the frictions in the relationship. Intensely critical of he what he termed the "deficiencies" of the Vietnamese, Chen Geng in his diary conveys numerous instances in which he confronts the Vietnamese leadership, in-

cluding Vo Nguyen Giap, who led the Vietnamese army, about their in-
adequacies. Tellingly, he also conveys his great surprise that the Vietnamese often appeared resistant to his critiques. As Qiang Zhai
suggests, the relationship between Chinese advisers and the Vietnamese troops was not always characterized by cordiality and trust.
In his diary, Chen Geng described Giap as "slippery and not very up-
right and honest." According to Chen Jian, Giap once complained to
Chen Geng about Luo Guibo's (head of the Chinese political advisory
mission in Vietnam) criticism of him, but in Luo's presence Giap always showed intimacy and warmth. "The greatest shortcoming of the
Vietnamese communists," Chen Geng wrote, "was their fear of let-
ting other people know their weaknesses. They lacked Bolsevik self-
criticism."[19]

The tensions and uncertainties through which the Chinese viewed
their Vietnamese allies also emerge in new work on Soviet-Vietnamese
relations by Ilya Gaiduk and Mari Olsen.[20] In characterizing a somewhat later period, Gaiduk argues, "The secretiveness and duplicity of
the Vietnamese comrades was experienced by all Soviets who worked
in the DRV... They lived in an atmosphere of mistrust and suspicion."[21] Soviet skepticism of the Vietnamese, Gaiduk has more recently
argued, was rooted in Stalin's unfavorable perception of Ho Chi Minh:

> Stalin suspected Ho Chi Minh of becoming too independent and na-
> tionalist oriented to be a loyal follower of Moscow's political line . . .
> The leader of the French Communists, Maurice Thorez, once confided
> to his Hungarian comrades that "Stalin was somewhat distrustful of Ho
> and his group." Thorez said Stalin thought that Ho Chi Minh had gone
> too far in his contacts with U.S. and British intelligence. Furthermore,
> Stalin was annoyed by Ho's unwillingness to seek his advice and consent
> prior to taking action. As an example, Thorez mentioned the dissolu-
> tion of the Indochinese Communist Party in 1945, and complained that
> he had a hard time convincing Stalin that it was just a tactical step in or-
> der to win support of Vietnamese nationalists.[22]

Sophie Quinn-Judge's *Ho Chi Minh: The Missing Years*,[23] which draws
upon newly available sources from the Comintern archives, suggests
that Stalin's suspicions of Ho had an even deeper genealogy. During
his stay in Moscow from 1934 to 1938 Ho Chi Minh underwent severe
criticism for his alleged nationalist proclivities and his purported sympathy with the bourgeoisie. His Comintern minder in Moscow re-

ported, "We feel that in the coming two years he must apply himself se-riously to his studies and will not be able to handle anything else." A June 1938 letter from Ho to the Comintern suggests the depth of his eclipse from communist party politics in Vietnam: "Use me in whatever way you judge useful. What I am requesting is that you not let me live too long without activity, outside the party." Reports that Ho was put on trial while he was in Moscow remain unconfirmed without access to KGB archives, but Quinn-Judge argues that some sort of tribunal would not have been impossible in a time of widespread Stalinist paranoia and terror.[24] Stalin's lasting distrust of Ho Chi Minh, along with the low priority he ascribed to developments after 1945 in the colonial world compared with Europe, Gaiduk argues, meant that "Moscow did al-most nothing to help in any material way" to support the Vietnamese in their war against the French beyond public rhetoric in support of the anti-imperialist cause.[25]

Recent accounts of Soviet-Vietnamese and Sino-Soviet relations also reveal the ways in which national and geostrategic interests often pre-vailed over fraternal ideological ties and shaped the fragile contours of the Vietnamese relationship with international communism during the French war. Qiang Zhai argues that fears of an American-led invasion into southern China were a primary motive in Chinese support of the Vietnamese during the French war. These national interests could pro-mote cooperation with and support of the Vietnamese, but they could also prompt policies inimical to Vietnamese state interests. China's ef-forts to seek "peaceful coexistence" with the West and push the Viet-namese toward compromise at Geneva, Zhai suggests, is one important illustration of how Chinese national interests could trump ideological solidarity. Similarly, Chinese suspicions that Vietnam sought regional dominance in Cambodia and Laos, areas that the Chinese sought to control to protect their own state interests, strained Sino-Vietnamese re-lations during the French war and in its aftermath.[26] Gaiduk also em-phasizes the importance of national interests in shaping Soviet policy toward Vietnam. If Stalin was both suspicious of Ho Chi Minh and in-clined to let the Chinese deal directly with the Vietnamese during the early years of the French war, Soviet policy toward Vietnam remained ambiguous after Stalin's death. In urging a compromise position at Geneva and promoting a cautious policy of socialist development in North Vietnam in the immediate post-Geneva period, Soviet policy was designed "to eliminate the Vietnamese problems from the Soviet foreign policy agenda" so they were not "an impediment to the solution of other issues of primary importance to the Kremlin—Soviet-U.S. relations and détente with the West," argues Gaiduk.[27] The emerging Sino-Soviet split and Chinese support for higher levels of military confrontation in Vietnam only reinforced Soviet hesitancy and prompted appeals to the Vietnamese for moderation.

The Vietnamese Dimension

The Vietnamese dimensions of the French war remain the least studied of any aspect of the conflict. We know comparatively little about the Vietnamese state's prosecution of the war, the development of the party, state, and military apparatus during the period of the war, and the ways in which individual Vietnamese apprehended their experiences of war. The vitality and depth that has long characterized the historiography on Vietnam under French colonial rule in the interwar period stands in sharp contrast to a prevailing static conception of the post-1945 period, one which has often emphasized purported continuities between Vietnamese Marxism and Confucianism and elided the contingent and contested processes of revolution and state-making in the postcolonial era. In part, the reticence of the Vietnamese state to open its archives has inhibited the development of Western-language scholarship on the French war period. Vietnamese-language historiography has also been limited by archival restrictions as well as its often wooden official character. However, the past decade or so has brought a gradual loosening of state control over the form and content of Vietnamese historiography and a greater, if still constrained, willingness to open the official record. At the same time a broader turn in Vietnamese studies in the West to more critically interrogating narratives of the Vietnamese past has begun to produce a richer and suppler account of postcolonial Vietnam.[28]

Severe source limitations do remain. For instance, Vietnamese diplomatic, military, and party archives on Chinese relations during the French war remain largely closed, in part because of the continuing sensitivity of Sino-Vietnamese relations for the Vietnamese state. These restrictions make it impossible to explore such critical aspects of the period as the political and military advisory relationship and the problematics of Sino-Vietnamese diplomacy at Geneva in the penetrating and textured ways Qiang Zhai and Chen Jian have accomplished on the Chinese side. Nonetheless, a gradual and salutary archival and interpretative opening up is taking place. Western scholars have begun to take advantage of it, as David Marr's essay in chapter 5 of this volume powerfully suggests, and for the first time a provisional sense of Vietnamese perceptions and policies during the period of the French war is beginning to emerge. Significantly, these new works on the Vietnamese dimension of the French war reveal the same kinds of ambiguities, tensions, and strains that emerge in recent accounts of American, British, French, Soviet, and Chinese policy.

Along with Marr's pathbreaking work on the early Vietnamese state apparatus, several works grounded in newly available Vietnamese primary source materials reveal many of the challenges faced by the nascent Vietnamese state during the French war and the experimental and iconoclastic ways in which they were met. The isolation of the Vietnamese state in the early years of the war and its varied domestic and international approaches to transcending the problems posed by it emerge in Greg Lockhart's *Nation in Arms,* Christopher Goscha's *Thailand and the Southeast Asian Networks of the Vietnamese Revolution,* and my own work on this period.[29] Although the Ho Chi Minh government retained loose control over rural northern Vietnam after the outbreak of the French war, the fragile state apparatus constructed in 1945 and 1946 largely ceased to function. As one contemporary critic in the government argued, "plans were slow in coming out" and "orders and instructions were not complete." Each rural community, this critic continued, "simply followed its own developments concerning tactics and organization. At the same time the way our cadres worked was also poor so that each time an order to set something in motion needed coordination it seemed to be too difficult."[30] Communication beyond northern Vietnam was even more challenging. Some use was made of wireless radios, but more commonly, governmental decisions were transmitted by couriers who made the two- to three-month trip between Hanoi and Saigon partly by boat and partly on foot. The crisis faced by the state in this period was compounded by Vietnam's isolation from its potential allies in the communist world; there is little evidence of sustained contact or of financial or technical assistance from the Chinese communists, the Soviet Union, or the French Communist Party in the initial years of the war.[31]

In part, the state sought to meet these challenges by looking inward. In April 1947 a central party cadre conference issued a directive calling for an immediate shift to guerrilla tactics to meet the increasingly fierce French military challenge. As part of this shift, villages were instructed to establish self-defense militia units, and sustained training in guerrilla warfare began in liberated areas of the north. Domestic weapons manufacturing also increased with the establishment of several major factories and numerous local arms workshops to produce bazookas, grenades, pistols, rifles, and machine guns. At the same time, the state sought to sustain and build popular support through renewed efforts at moderate land reform and intensified literacy campaigns.[32] But the state also looked to regional diplomacy in an effort to capitalize on the widespread professions of moral support the Vietnamese had received from nationalist leaders in India and Southeast Asia who opposed French efforts to regain its colonial control in the area. Through its diplomatic mission in Bangkok and later in Rangoon, the Vietnamese state sought to establish closer ties with Thailand, Burma, Indonesia, India, and the Philippines as well as more informal ties with radical nationalists in Malaya. Vietnamese diplomats were active in the 1947 Asian Relations Conference in India and the establishment of the Southeast Asia League, which aimed to formalize networks of nationalist regional cooperation. They also launched an initiative in the spring and summer of 1947 with American diplomats and intelligence operatives in Bangkok to win U.S. political and economic assistance and support for mediation of the war with the French.[33]

Although these efforts brought few immediate material rewards, they served to foster ties of nationalism and anticolonialism in the region that made possible the organization of clandestine networks to obtain arms, military supplies, and medicines needed for the war against the French. Bangkok initially served as the center for an underground network that sent arms and supplies into Vietnam, though eventually this was expanded to include clandestine arrangements with sellers in Burma, Singapore, and the Philippines and arms purchases from nationalist Chinese military commanders in northern Vietnam. While available evidence makes it difficult to draw precise conclusions about the larger significance of this arms traffic, Vietnamese documents captured by the French in this period suggest it was vital to the Vietnamese war effort. With the exception of weapons produced in local armament factories and those captured from the French, the Vietnamese state's regional arms networks were the only major source of military equipment and supplies until the Chinese communists opened up a new source of military assistance in 1950. Even when these new Chinese weapons began to arrive, transport difficulties slowed their delivery and distribution, and the continuing fragility of the government and military infrastructures hampered their effective use by the Vietnamese state and its army until mid-1952.[34]

New works that focus on the Vietnamese state and society during the French war and its immediate aftermath have also begun to explore the coercive mechanisms through which the state sought to impose its increasingly rigid postwar vision on Vietnamese society and the often highly ambiguous responses of Vietnamese intellectual elites to the state construction of postcolonial Vietnam. Their claims usefully complicate our understanding of the ideational place of the Cold War in Vietnamese political and cultural discourse. Patricia Pelley's *Postcolonial Vietnam: New Histories of the National Past* focuses on the processes of history writing itself in the period immediately following the French war.[35] She is the first scholar to critically examine the officially sanctioned histories of the Vietnamese state in which the French war served as a kind of template.

Pelley explores the state project to recast the Vietnamese past through an analysis of the Party Central Committee's research committee, which began its work at the moment of the French defeat in the climactic battle of the French war at Dien Bien Phu. Keenly sensitive to French colonial scholarship that had viewed the Vietnamese in racially derisive terms and seen Vietnam as a lesser and inferior China, she argues the committee turned in part to Stalin's *Marxism and the National Question* and his five-stage model of history—an evolutionary line from primitive communism to slavery to feudalism to capitalism and finally to communism—to normalize and universalize the contours of the Vietnamese past. At the same time, however, the committee sought to recover what they saw as uniquely and timelessly Vietnamese in an effort to give official meaning and legitimacy to the state's war against the French and the postwar emergence of the socialist state. Here their narratives focused on uncovering a national soul *(quoc hon)* or essence and valorizing the "fighting spirit of the Vietnamese" *(tinh than tranh dau)* against foreign aggression throughout Vietnam's history in ways that resonated with the claims of shared national and anticolonial sentiment.

Pelley's account pays close attention to the tensions and contradictions that marked these efforts, illustrating both the complexities of the translingual practices through which members of the committee as agents of the state made the vocabularies of Marxism-Leninism their own and the kinds of internal divisions the tropes of national unity sought to mask. She draws attention, for instance, to the conscious and unconscious ironies of employing Stalin's antinational text for national purposes:

> Stalin defined the nation in order to censure it; he linked nationalism with counterrevolutionary agendas and condemned the "obfuscation" and "lying propaganda" carried out on its behalf. Vietnamese revolutionaries, on the other hand, celebrated the idea of the nation, but because they were also obliged to demonstrate the proper reverence for Stalin, they converted his condemnation of nationalism into a value-neutral set of conditions that Vietnam . . . happily satisfied.[36]

Pelley also emphasizes the prescriptive and mythical rather than normative character of the oft-expressed "tradition of unity against foreign aggression," convincingly suggesting that the historical instances in which Vietnamese historians invoked the phrase, including during the French war, were often those moments in which the Vietnamese were in fact most "cataclysmically divided" among themselves.[37]

Pelley highlights the fragility of state efforts to supervise the rewriting of the Vietnamese past and the struggles even among members of the research committee itself to resist the state's totalizing vision. For example, some twenty years passed between the inception and publication of the first volume of the official *History of Vietnam;* volume two was thirty years in the making. Why, she asks, was the production of a new canonical history of Vietnam so much delayed, given the urgency and significance the state accorded to the project? Among the contributing factors, she argues, was the reticence of members of the research committee themselves to complete their own work. Though foot-dragging resulted in part from a very real fear of purges, she also suggests that "the stalling functioned as an oblique form of protest—a protest against the intrusiveness of the state and a comment on the pointlessness of scholarship that is driven by decrees."[38]

Kim N. B. Ninh's *A World Transformed: The Politics of Culture in Revolutionary Vietnam* is centrally concerned with the contested construction of cultural policies by the socialist state in northern Vietnam.[39] Her work combines an analysis of top-down institutional efforts aimed at radical reforms of art, literature, and education with a nuanced examination of the complex societal reactions to the state's revolutionary cultural vision. The first part of Ninh's study examines the French war itself. It concentrates on efforts by the Vietnamese state to define the ways in which culture could serve as a weapon in the struggle for national liberation and socialist revolution. Ninh's exploration of the critical 1949 Conference of Debates is particularly valuable. She persuasively demonstrates how the conference, although virtually ignored in the existing Western-language literature, brought artists, writers, and agents of the state together in ways that reflected the state's increasing embrace of hierarchical and class-based conceptions of culture and nationalism and the deepening anxieties of many intellectuals who had been committed to the revolutionary cause.

In the second half of her book, focusing on the period between the French and American wars, Ninh directs significant attention to the mid-1950s Nhan Van Giai Pham affair in which writers and artists raised the banner of "art for art's sake" against official state cultural policies. Although it has received attention in some of the existing literature as the most important single expression of open intellectual dissent against the North Vietnamese state in the postcolonial period, the affair has often been portrayed in a somewhat isolated context.[40] Ninh's account helps us to see it in a broader context as one of a number of instantiations of the contestation between the state and civil society in the immediate postwar period as the state heightened its efforts to shape and control culture. Using archival materials from the Ministries of Culture and Education, her analysis of state projects to introduce socialist culture at the village level and to establish a reformed educational system designed to produce new socialist men and women reveals the state's ambitious agenda of social engineering. But it also draws attention to how often state initiatives appear to have encountered resistance at the local level that frustrated the realization of larger aims.

The culture house project was designed to provide a focus for the florescence of class-based socialist culture in individual villages; the state envisioned the establishment of cultural houses in villages throughout northern Vietnam. But these ambitious efforts at local socialist transformation, a Ministry of Culture report from 1956 suggested, were largely unsuccessful:

> Activities are very haphazard and content is poor. There are even localities that built cultural houses worth more than a million piastres, only

to close them down, such as the cultural houses of Vu Lac in Thai Binh province and a cultural house in Son Tay in which buffaloes and cows were allowed to sleep . . . In Vinh Linh the cultural house was built, and then there was no one in charge so that books were scattered . . . Where there are activities, they are mainly focused on books and newspapers, with the audience being mostly students and very few people from the working class.[41]

Similarly, Ninh's discussion of education reform is deeply revealing of the contestations within the state itself between a desire to create a new class of politically pure intellectuals and the problematics of maintaining the professional standards necessary for economic and social development. As one Ministry of Education report argued,

Almost all the preferential targets tend to be weak students. Having failed the entrance examinations, they are not viewed by the schools in more comprehensive ways in the selection process. Currently there is the opinion among the people that children of soldiers, cadres, and those who have done much for the resistance do not get into the universities [while] children of those who contribute nothing, children of capitalists and the exploiting classes, are selected by the universities, attend this or that school.[42]

Ninh's discussion of the problematics of Vietnamese state development during and after the French war is also accompanied by an extended analysis of nonstate Vietnamese actors and their responses to the war. She explores the ambivalent reactions to these state projects of intellectuals, such as the author Nguyen Dinh Thi discussed at the outset of this essay, many of whom were eager to contribute to the national struggle but were suspicious of the increasingly narrow, utilitarian, and class-based conceptions of art and literature endorsed by the state. Ninh's efforts to recover a number of key literary works from this period, and her discussion of the ways in which they shaped emerging differences in the meanings accorded to revolutionary culture, reinforce a sense of the provisional and often painful nature of Vietnamese responses to the French war and the coming of the postcolonial moment.

Among the leading literary and artistic figures Ninh considers in some detail are the painter To Ngoc Van and the writer Tran Dan, whose wartime situations are particularly revealing of the anguished struggles of some Vietnamese intellectuals as they faced increasing pressure from the state to service its cultural and revolutionary imperatives. To Ngoc Van, one of the most prominent prewar Vietnamese painters, enthusiastically joined the revolution and the war effort. He oversaw the establishment of the state's school for the arts in Viet Minh-controlled territory during the French war. Teaching both drawing and the fundamentals of Marxism-Leninism, the school and its artists produced paintings, posters, stamps, and other visual emblems for the Vietnamese state and its war against the French. To Ngoc Van, who died in 1954 of injuries he suffered at the battle of Dien Bien Phu, was honored by the state as a revolutionary hero and martyr. But despite his prominence and work as an agent of the state's cultural production, To Ngoc Van repeatedly expressed deep concern about official efforts to define wartime art through its effectiveness in serving the goals of national independence and socialist revolution. In a 1947 essay, "Propaganda Art and Art" *(Tranh tuyen truyen va hoi hoa),* Van argued "propaganda art is not art because it expresses a political purpose, raises political slogans, delineates a political path for the people to follow" while art was an expression of "an individual soul, an attitude of an individual toward things, telling his feelings more than philosophy about any issue." Two years later, Van was no closer to resolving the tensions between the state's politicization of art and his capacity as a creative artist. In a 1949 essay "Study or Not?" *(Hoc hay khong hoc?),* he wrote: "Here lies the principal point, the torment of my soul: how to make the self that serves the nation and the masses and the self that serves art—the artist of course cannot forget this responsibility—not come into conflict or even, worse, betray one another."[43]

Ultimately in his art To Ngoc Van appeared to resolve his own creative dilemmas in ways that satisfied both himself and the state. His 1954 watercolor *Militia Woman* suggests the ways in which Van navigated these competing state and private demands. On the one hand, the mood of the watercolor and its gentle representation of a woman who served the state in the French war followed the state's preference for depicting the wartime sacrifices of ordinary people and what the state's cultural czar Truong Chinh called "correctly expressing the feelings of the masses that are pure, sincere and exceedingly warm."[44] At the same time, however, its flowing lines, the delicacy of the central figure, and its gendered subject also recall his prerevolutionary work in the 1930s and early 1940s, which often depicted bourgeois women and female beauty in very similar ways. Indeed, the parallels between his

1944 oil *Two Young Girls and a Child,* representative of his prerevolutionary work, and *Militia Woman* are quite striking. If the social class of the woman in Van's wartime painting more fully fit state demands, its sensibility betrays clear echoes of Van's larger, and very personal, artistic vision.[45]

A recent essay by the art historian Nora Taylor,[46] suggests that other artists who shared Van's unease were less able to comfortably resolve the dilemmas Van posed in his writings. For instance, the painter Nguyen Sang, who was a participant in the Nhan Van Giai Pham affair, found his work rejected by the state arts association. Among these rejected paintings was his 1954 oil *The Enemy Burned My Village.* In this work, a Vietnamese woman who has fled her village with her family after an attack by French forces seeks the help of a soldier from the Vietnamese state's army. As Taylor argues, the overall mood of the painting is one of fear and unease with little sense of connection or empathy between the two figures. This and other works like it from the period were banned from exhibition by the state because they were too harsh and did not properly depict the revolutionary virtues of heroism and solidarity.

Kim Ninh's discussion of the writer Tran Dan reflects similar tensions and the doubleness that often characterized the responses of Vietnamese intellectuals to the war and the state project to control representations of it.[47] On the one hand, Tran Dan might be viewed as an agent of the state's cultural policies toward the war. Tran Dan joined the Vietnamese army and the communist party in 1948, was trained in Chinese thought reform techniques, and led rectification courses in 1951 for fellow intellectuals and performing arts troupes on how better to support the state's war against the French. In the spring of 1955, his novel *Men upon Men, Wave upon Wave (Nguoi nguoi lop lop)* appeared in Hanoi to great official and popular acclaim. The first major novel published in northern Vietnam after the end of the French war, it told the story of the battle of Dien Bien Phu in which Vietnamese victory, seemingly against overwhelming odds, brought the end of more than eighty years of French colonial rule in Vietnam. Tran Dan's novel was less concerned with the formal military dimensions of the battle than capturing the heroic voluntarism of ordinary Vietnamese from all walks of life who contributed to the Vietnamese victory over the French. In the wake of the novel's success, Tran Dan was invited by the state to write the narrative for a commemorative film on Dien Bien Phu that would later be widely disseminated throughout northern Vietnam. Like Tran Dan's novel, the film portrayed the battle as a didactic lesson of the necessity of collective self-sacrifice to achieve national liberation and socialist revolution.

By 1956, however, Tran Dan had been arrested as a reactionary, and he attempted suicide while imprisoned. Always a risk-taker and iconoclast, Tran Dan's relationship with the state and its emerging strictures on cultural production was a complicated one throughout the French war. During the war he clashed with General Nguyen Chi Thanh, the head of the army's political department, over demands for creative freedom. He also incurred the displeasure of the army, which had the right to approve marriages, over his choice of a bride: a Catholic businesswoman who, as Ninh argues, "was an amalgam of everything that was suspicious, dangerous and corrupting to the pure revolutionary army." At the same time as the publication of his war novel, Tran Dan voiced increasingly public critiques of literature and poetry that had received official approval for its depiction of the war. His arrest was ultimately provoked by the publication of a long poem in one of the periodicals associated with the Nhan Van Giai Pham movement. Titled "We Must Win," it expressed his ambivalence over the meanings of the war and the immediate postwar period. The doubts and uncertainties of the poem's refrain mark a sharp contrast to the official postwar optimism of the Vietnamese state:

> I walk on
>> seeing no street
>>> seeing no house
>> Only rain falling
>>> upon the red flag.[48]

The cases of Nguyen Sang and Tran Dan were not anomalies. In the years following the French war, the Vietnamese state increasingly sought to marginalize and silence those who viewed the war in ways that contradicted or challenged the state's vision of it. Although we know even less about northern Vietnamese society during the period of the American war than we do about the French war era, there is evidence of an active underground intellectual elite in Hanoi during the 1960s and 1970s whose sensibilities had been shaped by the dissenting visions of the French war period. They met in clandestine coffee houses, which were officially banned by the state, and discussed works of art and literature whose form and content departed sharply from those mandated by cultural authorities. The works of the painter Bui Xuan Phai—desolate gray and brown streetscapes of wartime Hanoi—illustrate the power and persistence of contrapuntal articulations of society even at the moment of high socialism in Vietnam. As Nora Taylor argues,

> When Hanoians recall the urban atmosphere during those years, their picture often resembles a painting by Bui Xuan Phai . . . Like Hanoi at the time, Bui Xuan Phai's paintings are empty of colorful markets, street stall vendors, and motorcycles. The only signs of modernity are his ubiquitous electrical poles that stand at each street corner as if to mock the government's campaign to develop industry in the city. In one painting, the only sign above a doorway read *nuoc soi,* or "boiled water," as if the artist were reacting against the heroism of wartime depicted in official art and making a statement about the deprivation of the population instead.[49]

The tensions between official efforts to construct a hegemonic meaning for the French war and the myriad private and competing responses to it were not limited to the Vietnamese. Recent cultural histories of Marguerite Duras's 1950 *Un Barrage contre le Pacifique* and Graham Greene's 1955 *The Quiet American,* and the receptions these works received in France and the United States respectively, reveal how increasingly unsympathetic both societies were to narratives that challenged dominant constructions of the war's meaning. In the case of Duras's novel, as Jane Bradley Winston's *Postcolonial Duras* suggests, French critics sought to mute the clear anticolonial tone of the work in what Winston sees as part of a larger and conscious official French effort at containing competing interpretations of the French war at a time when French public opinion remained deeply ambivalent.[50] Duras herself called *Un Barrage* a "book denouncing the colonial state." Through an allegoric story of a mother, son, and daughter from a French settler family in French colonial Cambodia, Duras sought to create what she termed a "word-hole" which would eat through the veil of French colonial ideology and promote revolution in the midst of the French effort at reconquest. Contemporary French critics, Winston suggests, consciously sought to depoliticize the work, displacing its indictment of French colonialism and effacing its social and historical specificity. Instead, critics rendered the novel as a tale of universal human misery, a feminized example of pulp and exotic fiction or a psychological drama of a plucky French heroine who had fallen on hard times but sought to prevail. The 1958 film version of *Un Barrage contre le Pacifique* by French director René Clément completed this inversion; as Winston argues, "it recast the family's suffering, which Duras roots in western patriarchal colonial relations, as the result of one woman's emotional manipulation and mental weakness."[51] Ultimately, critical reception of the film remembered Duras's novel only to forget its strong critique of French policy in Vietnam.

Graham Greene's *The Quiet American,* which was often read in the 1960s and later as a cautionary tale about the perils of increasing American involvement in Vietnam, also encountered significant critical resistance in the 1950s. American literary critics on the left and the right, however, were less concerned with containing Greene's message than fiercely denouncing it. As the cultural historian Stephen Whitfield argues in a recent essay, Greene's "subtle and morally complicated fiction" was often unrecognizable in the critical ire directed at Greene's portrayal of his American protagonist Alden Pyle for daring to criticize American ideals and policy in Vietnam.[52] Representative were the views of the influential liberal critic Diana Trilling, who condemned the novel in a 1956 issue of *Commentary* as a "large and intended lie," "palpably hostile in purpose," and an "assault" and "affront to America."[53] Not only was Greene's novel dismissed by many American critics, Whitfield suggests, but its message was radically altered for the 1958 film version of it. Like the film of *Un Barrage,* Joseph L. Mankiewicz's film of *The Quiet American* almost completely inverts the main lines of the story: the narrator Fowler, who articulates Greene's critique of American actions in Vietnam, becomes the villain and a communist dupe, whereas Pyle, whose efforts in the novel as a CIA operative result in a bombing that kills innocent civilians, emerges as a praiseworthy and tragically martyred victim of the Vietnamese communists.

French and American critical reactions to *Un Barrage* and *The Quiet American,* along with the silencing of Vietnamese contrapuntal narratives of the French war by the Vietnamese state, suggest a transnational rather than national hardening of communist and anticommunist orthodoxies in the period immediately following the French war. As Michael Adas has recently argued, the ideological differences between Cold War liberal capitalism and state socialism too often obscure the shared faith in the rational manipulation of human societies and the natural world that joined American, Soviet, and Chinese Cold War visions of socioeconomic and cultural development at home and abroad.[54] It is a larger phenomenon deserving of further study if we are to move beyond rigid nationally inflected colonial and Cold War interpretative frames toward more fluid and supple apprehensions of the early postcolonial period in Vietnam. The critiques offered by Duras and Greene and the divided and painful articulations of To Ngoc Van, Nguyen Sang, and Tran Dan usefully remind us that beneath the veil of official orthodoxies lies a heterodox if submerged vision of the war with the potential to reveal the multiplicity of meanings through which Vietnamese, European, and American actors sought to make sense of the postcolonial moment in Vietnam.

Conclusion

In his *Provincializing Europe,* Dipesh Chakrabarty uses the image of a waiting room to convey one critical dimension of how colonialism felt for colonized peoples. "Not yet," Chakrabarty argues, was the response of the Euro-American colonial powers to demands by the colonized for self-rule: since they were not yet civilized enough to rule themselves, a period of "development and civilization (colonial rule and education to be precise) had to elapse . . . in history's waiting room . . . before they could be considered prepared for such a task."[55] The new scholarship on the French war reveals the complex reactions of the colonizers and the colonized as the doors to the waiting room burst open in 1945 and 1946 and the emancipatory challenges and potentialities of the postcolonial world began to come into being. Recognizing the struggles of state and nonstate actors to give meaning to the French war and the postcolonial moment in Vietnam helps us transcend more familiar imperial and Cold War narratives. The result is an admittedly messier picture, though probably one truer to the period itself, and one that captures the uncertainty, hestitations, and contestations among and between states and peoples as they sought to make sense of the powerful ruptures that the global turn toward decolonization after 1945 posed for Vietnam.

In thinking about these works together, one might argue that the major parties to the French war sought to manage the unleashing of historical time at a moment when decolonization in Vietnam and much of the colonized world produced a sense among both the colonized and the colonizers of time rushing forward. If the French would have preferred to arrest completely the temporal movement toward decolonization, the British, Americans, Soviets, and Chinese appeared keen to retard the passage of time to wrest control of the fragmentary, transient, and chaotic character of the period in order to reassert the centrality of rational and orderly, albeit sometimes radically different, paths for Vietnam's future development. And if the Vietnamese were perhaps alone in their enthusiastic embrace of the quickening of time and release from history's waiting room, the state and at least some of its members clearly did not always view the passage toward the post-colonial future in quite the same ways.

The ambiguities that emerge in the new scholarship on the French war suggest the necessity of a more capacious framework for approaching the multiple meanings state and nonstate actors gave to the French war. One promising path in this regard emerges in Matthew Connelly's recent study of the Algerian war.[56] His depictions of the tensions between forces of political, economic, and sociocultural fragmentation and integration in the Algerian conflict closely parallel what the new historiography under consideration here reveals of the French war. But Connelly goes further to suggest the wider processes of decolonization were made up of forces—among them population growth, environmental scarcities, international institutions, new media, and the conscious agency of colonized peoples to promote radical systemic change—that severely weakened the Cold War international system even at the height of superpower confrontation and ultimately gave shape to the post–Cold War world. If Connelly is right, and I suspect he is, the new scholarship on the French war not only promises to recast our understanding of the thirty years war in Vietnam but also to begin to reshape how we think about the place of the colonial and the post-colonial in the construction of world order in the twentieth and twenty-first centuries.

THREE

◆ ◆ ◆

Vietnamese Historians and the
First Indochina War

LIEN-HANG T. NGUYEN

ANALYZING VIETNAMESE SCHOLARSHIP on the French war is a much-needed but difficult endeavor.[1] To a certain extent, Vietnam's decolonization struggle is the intellectual and political property of the government. The act of historicizing and remembering the French war plays an ever-present role in the formation of state-sponsored memory and political legitimization.[2] Sensing that Vietnamese writing is, more or less, official propaganda rather than serious scholarship, Western scholars have generally ignored works coming out of the Socialist Republic of Vietnam. Westerners certainly have a point: Vietnamese literature on the French war reveals as much about the country's development after the conflict as about the actual war. The country's successive military engagements and economic liberalization policies have heavily influenced the study of Vietnam's struggle against colonialism. Though this teleology and lack of objectivity are not unique to Vietnamese historiography—one has only to look to U.S. scholarship on its own Vietnam War—the lack of overt debate in Vietnamese universities, media, and publishing houses is indeed an obstacle to presenting an analytical survey of the literature.

Despite these problems, this chapter explores the trends and patterns of postcolonial Vietnamese historiography in an effort to draw more scholarly attention to Vietnamese writing on the French war. Rather than concentrate on the historical narrative or offer an exhaustive bibliographic review, this chapter will contextualize the writing of history on the French war within the broader development of communist party politics after 1954.[3] Dividing the chapter into two sections, I

41

will first discuss how Vietnamese historians have understood the war and describe the main area of debate that has animated their writing. In the second section, I will suggest an alternative way of understanding the development of Vietnamese historiography of the French war.

It is essential to offer a brief note about the types of Vietnamese scholarship that I have consulted for this chapter.[4] On the whole, I found that journal articles were more interpretive and analytical than books, which tended to offer merely straightforward narratives. *Nghien Cuu Lich Su* (Historical Research, or NCLS) and *Lich Su Quan Su* (Military History, or LSQS) were particularly important in helping me understand the development of the scholarship since they constitute the leading journals on general history and military history, respectively. To mark anniversaries of key battles and other noteworthy events, these journals have published useful commemorative issues with contributions by leading scholars in the field. In addition, textbooks were also instructive since they represent the "official voice." Offering detailed narratives, these textbooks include sections on "lessons learned" that ostensibly still guide current policy. Lastly, I made use of provincial studies as well as monographs concerning specific battles and campaigns.[5] These sources not only provided detailed narratives of key regions and pivotal battles, but they also utilized provincial archives and specialized collections that were not present in textbooks or nationwide studies.

The Great Debate

Given the symbiotic relationship between government and academe, there are no conflicting schools of interpretation in Vietnamese historiography of the French war. Over the past four decades, the only real point of uncertainty in the literature has centered on the three-stage military strategy that the Viet Nam Doc Lap Dong Minh (League for Vietnamese Independence, or Viet Minh) ostensibly followed in waging war against French colonial forces: the progression from the "defensive" phase *(phong ngu),* to the "equilibrium" or "holding back" phase *(cam cu),* and finally to the "general counteroffensive" phase *(tong phan cong).*[6] Although factionalization plagued the Viet Minh leadership particularly during the early years of fighting, the Indochinese Communist Party (ICP) clearly dominated decision-making during the French war.[7] According to the party's application of the Maoist model of warfare, the insurgents intended to hold a defensive posture in the initial phase in order to build up their forces in the face of superior enemy strength. In the "equilibrium" phase, the Viet Minh sought to establish a military balance that would prevent the enemy from launching any large-scale attacks while enabling the resistance to prepare its own general counteroffensive. In the last phase, the resistance aimed to launch a large-scale offensive that would ultimately lead to victory.

Although the debate over the evolution of the Viet Minh war effort touched on theoretical as well as technical aspects of military strategy, it also spoke to the question of periodization, a key element in presenting the French war to Vietnamese readers. After the Geneva Accords, the precarious situation in North and South Vietnam prevented the study of the French war from becoming a rarefied academic pursuit. The Hanoi Politburo recognized that the legacy of the French war constituted a powerful weapon that could bolster party leadership in Vietnam and justify the continuation of the revolution. In order for Hanoi leaders to capitalize on the success of the French war, scholars needed to study the evolution of the Viet Minh's war strategy. To instill confidence in the Politburo leadership's ability to guide the Vietnamese people to complete liberation and reunification after 1954, then, scholars had to present the narrative of the French war in a manner that vindicated the party's war strategy against French colonial forces from 1945 onwards.

A very brief summary of the debate shows that historians concur that the defensive phase began when fighting broke out after the failure of negotiations and lasted until late 1947, when the resistance undertook the Viet Bac campaign that shattered French hopes of an early victory in Indochina. Starting in 1948, the Viet Minh began to wrest the initiative away from the French culminating in the 1950 Border Campaign victory for the resistance that marked a major turning point in the war. At this point, however, scholars disagree over the Viet Minh's progression to the final phase of the war. The initial view that emerged in the immediate aftermath of the war held that the resistance entered its final phase following the 1950 victory. This view accords with the official aim declared at the Third National Party Conference convened in late January to early February 1950.[8]

In a 1957 article, however, the North Vietnamese official-cum-historian Tran Huy Lieu challenged the initial view by urging scholars not to adhere to strict dates since the stages merged at various points.[9]

As a senior communist member, Lieu's article commanded the attention of not only the academic community, but more importantly, the party. Lieu's "revisionist"[10] interpretation disputed the contention that the Viet Minh unwaveringly held the initiative after 1950 in order to explain the failure of the 1951 and 1952 campaigns to turn the war in the DRV's favor.[11] Instead, the campaigns aimed to prevent a massive offensive on the part of the French colonial forces and thus did not constitute genuine attempts at a general counteroffensive. According to Lieu, the Viet Minh war effort never completed the final stage since the conflict ended before the fruits of the general counteroffensive at Dien Bien Phu could be realized. He concluded that the Geneva Accords, then, could only deliver peace but not total liberation and reunification for Vietnam.[12]

At the commemoration of the fiftieth anniversary of the start of the French war in 1996, the Politburo, leading military brass, and the scholarly establishment collaborated in writing the official history of the conflict entitled *Summary of the Resistance War against Colonial France,* that finally laid to rest the contentious issue.[13] The 1996 official survey held that though there were indeed three phases to the French war, they should no longer be connected to the three-stage strategy. Instead, the collaborative study offered a new paradigm to conceptualize the stages of the French war based on historical events rather than military theory and strategy. Following roughly the initial periodization but recognizing the concerns raised by the "revisionist" interpretation for the 1951 to 1952 period, the 1996 survey could be labeled as "post-revisionist."[14] According to this view, the first phase of the French war began in September 1945 and lasted until December 1947, with scholars emphasizing the importance of the August Revolution, the period of negotiations, the total mobilization of the entire country behind the war, and the Viet Bac victory in late 1947. The second phase from the beginning of 1948 to the fall and winter of 1950 included the acceleration of Vietnam's guerrilla war, the defeat of France's strategy of using Vietnamese to fight Vietnamese, and the preparation for and initiation of the Viet Minh's first large-scale northern offensive. The third phase from 1951 to the signing of the Geneva Accords in 1954 is characterized by Vietnam's ability to maintain the initiative through military operations in 1951 and 1952, followed by the sound defeat of the French offensive at Dien Bien Phu that ended the war and brought down the old colonial order in Indochina. Concentrating on the events themselves, the "post-revisionist" interpretation freed scholars from the burdensome responsibility of forcing the historical progression of the conflict to fit the three-stage process of war. In doing so, the narrative of Vietnam's French war became less didactic and overtly polemical.

History and Its Many Uses

In the early 1960s, the esteemed historian Lieu challenged the field once again in an influential article entitled "On the subject of writing the history of the Resistance," in which he confronted the problem of approaching the war against France as history.[15] By 1962, Lieu argued that sufficient primary materials and local studies had been made available for scholars to write narratives of the French war. In fact, the amount of material available on strategy and guerrilla warfare was potentially "suffocating," but what was missing, Lieu contended, were "syntheses of value."[16] Not only was it necessary to integrate provincial studies into the national history of the French war, but it was also important to address the economic, social, and cultural aspects of the decolonization struggle. According to Lieu, since the conflict with France was a total war for the Vietnamese, researching the "homefront" should be of comparable value to studying the "battlefront." Although he conceded that the political climate was not conducive to "dispassionate" history, Lieu was the first to raise the problem of how to historicize the French war.[17]

Over the 40 years since the appearance of Lieu's article, his exhortation has not fallen on deaf ears, but the extension of the state into academia has resulted in heavy censorship and government control over the universities, research centers, and publishing houses of Hanoi and Ho Chi Minh City. As a result, there exists no historiographical essay or bibliographic survey on the French war in Vietnam to facilitate the mapping of the immense terrain of Vietnamese scholarship. In deciding what to include, when to start, and how to organize my survey, I followed Lieu's line of argument by limiting my survey to works written from the 1960s to the present. Departing from the 1996 official study, I have opted not to structure the survey based on the "stages debate." Instead, I propose a different method to analyze Vietnamese scholarship—by dividing the literature based on major events in Vietnam following the French war that have influenced the writing of its history: the Vietnamese-American War, the Sino-Khmer-Vietnamese conflict, and the *Doi Moi* (Renovation) reforms. These three developments after 1954 greatly influenced the writing of the decolonization struggle.

The studies produced in the first two generations attempted to locate the origins of the Second and Third Indochina Wars in the first. In addition, the demands of carrying out successive wars in the immediate aftermath of the French war necessitated that the victorious example of the decolonization struggle be used to strengthen the peoples' confidence in the Hanoi leadership. The third generation of scholarship, written in the post–*Doi Moi* era, finally treats the French war on its own terms and not as a preface to or justification for other conflicts. By the end of the decade, with the last soldiers returning from Cambodia, history no longer had to "mobilize the masses" for war. With the 1986 reforms, history was further freed—but not entirely released—from political needs of the moment. On the whole, though, scholars are now better able to study the French war as history, exploring issues that were previously ignored or untouchable. Recent literature on the French war portrays Vietnam's struggle for decolonization to instill patriotism in peacetime as national history and also to reflect Vietnam's reintegration into the global community as international history.

Phase 1: The American War

The first generation of historical scholarship on the French war appeared during the period of direct American intervention. Due to the "loss of China" in 1949 and the beginning of the Korean War in 1950, the United States became France's largest patron, ultimately funding 78 percent of the French war effort in Indochina.[18] At the end of the war, American advisors replaced French administrators, and, after a stint of failed nation-building, American soldiers appeared on the same battlegrounds south of the seventeenth parallel that French soldiers had evacuated more than a decade before. Given the temporal proximity and similar nature of the French and American involvements in Vietnam, it is logical that the studies written during this period placed heavy emphasis on the U.S. role during the French war while also aiming to strengthen the people's support for the party's leadership of the war effort.

The phrase *"can thiep My"* (U.S. intervention) first appeared in the descriptions of the final phase of the French war from 1950 to 1954 as American involvement in Vietnam's affairs become increasingly direct in the early 1960s. In fact, by the time of the Americanization of the ground war, Vietnamese scholars described the war against France not only as a fight against colonialism *(thuc dan Phap)* but also as the beginning of the struggle against American imperialism *(de quoc My)*. In the opening pages of a collaborative study written in 1963 entitled *The French-American Imperialist Plot during the Dien Bien Phu Victory,* the authors state: "To research the Dien Bien Phu victory is not a matter of history but has deep ramifications for today . . . for one half of our country still must rise up in total resistance against the invasion of the imperialist Americans."[19]

Historical studies of the French war attempted to offer answers to how and why the United States was able to stay and wage a second conflict in Vietnam. By emphasizing the continuity of American involvement in both wars, historians argued that the French war constituted only the first part of the long struggle for liberation and reunification of Vietnam. Dividing the world into two camps at the end of the Second World War, Vietnamese scholarship pitted the old order of Western imperialism, supported by U.S. capitalism, against the colonized people's movement for liberation, supported by Soviet socialism. In 1971, the editors of *Nghien Cuu Lich Su* printed an article commemorating the twenty-fifth anniversary of the French war that underlined this global struggle:

> It has been twenty five years and so looking back [at the French war] now, it makes the American War all the more clearer: Socialism in Asia, Africa, and Latin America has defeated colonialism and imperialism in all of the old colonies. Our forces are getting stronger while theirs are weakening.[20]

Another aspect of the literature during this period served as propaganda for the communist leadership in the war effort. With growing U.S. involvement and particularly in what Hanoi painted as the transition from America's "special war" to its "local war," domestic opposition to the militant Politburo leadership increased in the DRV. In 1967, a major purge of party leaders, government officials, and Hanoi professionals in the "Revisionist Anti-Party Affair" induced hardliners to produce numerous articles and speeches calling for ideological correctness. The arrests targeted mainly pro-Soviet members who opposed armed conflict and prefered peaceful coexistence but also included elements critical of the handling of the war by the Le Duan–Le Duc Tho faction. In a 1968 article about the role of the political and intellectual factors in the French war, historian Pham Quang Toan argued that communist ideology guided the Vietnamese revolutionaries to victory against the European colonialists and would ensure victory for the resistance against the American imperialists.[21] Vietnamese scholars argued that full support of all Vietnamese people was integral to the success of the resistance.[22] Moreover, historical studies during the American war emphasized the victorious nature of the people's protracted war against the French in order to justify exacting mobilization drives in the on-going struggle against the United States.[23]

Phase 2: Sino-Vietnamese Tension

The second wave of studies on the French war emerged during the breakdown of the Asian internationalist alliance in the late 1970s. Sino-Vietnamese and Khmer-Vietnamese relations showed signs of unraveling well before the end of the Second Indochina War.[24] Sino-American rapprochement under the Nixon administration fatally weakened Sino-Vietnamese relations in the 1970s. With the removal of the U.S. threat to the region, the fragile alliance further broke down over ownership of the Spratly and Paracel Islands, oil drilling rights, and the treatment of Chinese émigrés in Vietnam. Khmer-Vietnamese relations also soured in the 1970s with the rise of the Khmer Rouge in the Cambodian communist movement. Ardently anti-Vietnamese, Pol Pot and his followers waged a secret war against Vietnamese-trained Khmer revolutionaries and made minimal effort during the American war to mask their animosity or hide their designs to reclaim Khmer Krom territory in southern Vietnam. By 1978, Cambodian aggression against neighboring Vietnamese villages turned into all-out attacks on the western border of Vietnam. As Vietnamese forces attempted to drive the Khmer Rouge from Phnom Penh, Chinese troops marched south across the Sino-Vietnamese border on February 19, 1979.[25]

Studies of the French war written in this period revised the entire role the PRC played during the decolonization struggle, with particular focus on Chinese "perfidy" from Dien Bien Phu to Geneva. In addition, these studies emphasized the fraternal relations among the Indochinese nations, particularly following the Second National Congress in 1951, in order to counter claims of Vietnam's "hegemonic" designs over Cambodia and Laos.

Although Chinese military and economic aid played a crucial role in

Vietnam's war against the French, the literature written during the height of the Sino-Vietnamese conflict contended that the China's support may not have been either generous or selfless. In an article written in 1983, scholar Nguyen Anh Thai argued that Beijing was in a position to give greater aid to Vietnam in the final phase of the resistance but refused to increase assistance because the Chinese did not want the Vietnamese to "win big."[26] In other words, the Vietnamese believed that their larger ally gave enough to enable the Viet Minh to avoid losing at Dien Bien Phu but not enough to score a major victory that would leave the Vietnamese communists in a position to lead all of Indochina.

The most vitriolic condemnation of the communist China, however, did not concern Chinese aid, or lack thereof, at Dien Bien Phu. Rather, it involved Chinese machinations surrounding the Geneva conference. According to Vietnamese scholarship at the time, the Chinese used Vietnam's struggle against the French to elevate their position on the world stage. In the fall of 1953, the Chinese leaders began to make public statements that their country should play an indispensable role in finding an international settlement to the Indochina conflict.[27] According to Vietnamese scholarship written in the late 1970s and early 1980s, China increased aid for the Vietnamese offensive at Dien Bien Phu because a moderate victory against the French could serve as a bargaining chip for the Chinese at Geneva. At the conference, Vietnamese observers reported that the Chinese were more concerned with proving themselves as a big power than in finding peace.[28] According to Thai, the Chinese owed their great power status and the improvement of Chinese relations with the West to the Vietnamese victory over the French.

Thai argued that the Chinese delegation in Geneva benefited from the Vietnamese struggle in four ways. First, the West began to view China as a great power due to the supposed influence Beijing claimed over the Viet Minh. Second, China gained recognition by Western nations following Geneva. Third, China's southern borders were safe after the Viet Minh victory over the French and the establishment of a cease-fire. Fourth, the Geneva conference provided the Chinese a foothold in Indochinese affairs with the ultimate aim of establishing supremacy in the region.[29] In 1979, Vietnam's Foreign Ministry released a white paper entitled "The Truth About Vietnam-China Relations over the Last Thirty Years." In the publication, the Vietnamese government provided the exact details of China's maneuverings at

Geneva.[30] On May 3–5, Chou En Lai met with Ho Chi Minh in order to force the Vietnamese leader to accept partition at the seventeenth parallel, rather than the sixteenth, and elections leading to reunification in two years rather than in six months. In addition, the Chinese leaders promised the great powers at the conference that they could persuade Vietnam to withdraw its troops from Laos and Cambodia. In June, the Chinese recognized the royal governments of Laos and Cambodia and thus refused to support Vietnam's request that the Khmer Issarak and the Pathet Lao be allowed to participate in the conference. Vietnamese scholars argued that the Chinese carried out a grand plot at the conference to sell out the Indochinese revolutions so that Beijing could maintain control over the region.

Another aim of the literature during the period of Sino-Vietnamese tensions was not only to forge a feeling of unity among the Indochinese nations against China but also to rebut claims of expansionist intentions on the part of Vietnam.[31] As the war expanded to all of Indochina, the Viet Minh immediately took the initiative to strengthen the resistance in Cambodia and Laos in order to strengthen its war against the French. At the Second Party Congress that began in February 1951, the Vietnam Workers' Party (VWP) re-established the overt role of the party in the DRV. By March, the Viet Minh, Khmer Issarak, and Lao Issara formalized their alliance against the French colonialist forces in the mountains of North Vietnam. After the historic meeting, Vietnamese volunteer cadres and soldiers began arriving in Laos and Cambodia out of internationalist duty to help their Indochinese brethren with their war efforts.[32] When the Khmer People's Revolutionary Party was founded in 1951 and the Lao People's Revolutionary Party was created the following year, Vietnamese membership dominated these organizations. More than thirty years later, studies compiled during Vietnam's military presence in Cambodia following the ousting of Pol Pot placed heavy emphasis on the consensual nature of the Indochinese alliance during the French war. Vietnamese historians claimed Khmer and Laotian allies invited Viet Minh advisors into their respective countries and, in return, the Vietnamese helped the Khmer Issarak and Lao Issara to expand their liberated areas and to double the free population in both countries.[33] To quell the international outcry over Vietnamese aggression against Cambodia in the late 1970s, these studies attempted to counter the claims that the Vietnamese unilaterally planted advisors during the French war to control the revolutions in Cambodia and Laos with the ultimate goal of mastery in all of Indochina.

Phase 3: *Doi Moi*

In 1986, Vietnam launched its economic liberalization plan called *Doi Moi*, which essentially marked the shift from central planning to a more market-based economy in an effort to "catch up" to the more-developed countries within Southeast Asia. With the death of Le Duan in April 1986, acting Secretary General Truong Chinh was replaced by Nguyen Van Linh at the Sixth Party Congress in 1986, signifying the changing of the guard.[34] However, in 1989 with the fall of communism in Eastern Europe and the events at Tiananmen Square, Vietnamese *glasnost* came to an abrupt halt as Hanoi leaders reneged on promised political and social reforms. Party leaders once again adopted a Marxist-Leninist world view, citing imperialist forces (United States) as the number one enemy to socialism and reached out to ideological allies (China) with the fall of the Soviet Union. However, the backlash did not result in a return to the same national security strategy of the Cold War. As Vietnam entered the 1990s, the modernizing current of *Doi Moi* resulted in major economic gains with the dampening of hyperinflation and increase in foreign investment connecting Vietnam to the global economy. Over the past two decades, Politburo leaders aimed for equilibrium between the desire to modernize the country through promoting technological progress, liberalizing the economy, and embracing globalization and the need to maintain power by demanding ideological loyalty and political devotion to the party.

Since *Doi Moi*, Vietnam's scholarship on the French war reflects this balancing policy. The third generation of literature on the French war has been influenced heavily by Vietnam's reintergration into the global community with the normalization of relations with its former enemies as well as the party's emphasis on ideological perseverance for the maintainence of domestic power in the post-Cold War era. On the whole, peace has afforded scholars more freedom and less restriction from government control and censors. However, given the volatility of party politics over Vietnam's development and foreign policy, the history of the French war is still not entirely divorced from presentist needs.

The scholarship on the French war written after 1986 is more subdued and balanced in tone with respect to Vietnam's former enemies, China and the United States. In the early 1990s, Vietnam began to reach out to China with the fall of the Soviet Union in order to offset what it viewed as imperialist attempts to erase socialism. To reflect the normalization of relations between Hanoi and Bejing in November 1991, historical accounts of China's role during the Geneva conference omit any trace of bitterness and argue that the West forced Vietnam to accept the terms of the 1954 settlement. Historians describe China as merely advising Vietnam with the latter's best interests in mind.[35] Vietnamese scholars list Chinese military, economic, and moral support among the key factors that led the resistance to victory against the French.[36] With regard to the United States, the revision is less thorough. With the lifting of economic sanctions and the normalization of U.S.-Vietnamese relations in the mid-1990s, Vietnamese scholarship finally acknowledged the history of Ho Chi Minh's relations with the OSS during World War II and the significance of the American Declaration of Independence to Ho's Ba Dinh speech.[37] Prior to that point, there was little mention of cooperation or goodwill between the Vietnamese communists and the American capitalists. However, the literature does not try to rewrite history by diminishing the role that American military and economic support played in the French war effort from 1950 onwards.

During the American War, Vietnamese scholars spoke in Cold War terms of East versus West as American imperialism threatened to block reunification indefinitely.[38] With the breakdown of Asian internationalism in the late 1970s, historians doggedly looked to the past to expose perennial aggression from Vietnam's neighbor to the north. In the post–*Doi Moi* era, although historical literature still must underline the glorious achievements of the party leadership, scholars are now able to explore aspects of the French war that were hitherto deemed unimportant or even forbidden—a reflection of the fact that diplomacy and economic growth, rather than war, drive government policies. Indeed, the power struggle in the party over the exact path to modernization given international developments cannot and does not invoke the same urgency to control history as during wartime. In taking advantage of this new latitude, the literature today attempts to contextualize Vietnam's struggle in the larger field of international history. In particular, recent literature addresses the impact of Vietnam's struggle on the international decolonization movement and the farsightedness of Vietnamese foreign relations.

With regard to the French Empire, Vietnamese scholars have begun to study the linkages between Vietnam and North Africa, exploring in particular the transformation of Maghreb soldiers who fought for France in Indochina into revolutionary insurgents in their struggles against the French.[39] Vietnamese scholars cite the "perpetual" subversive activities of France's colonial troops, who allegedly turned over their weapons and their loyalty to the resistance.[40] In an article entitled "The Historical Meaning of the Resistance Struggle against Colonial France," historian Cao Van Luong argues that the Viet Minh victory proved to the colonized nations of Africa that a small and poor nation could rise up and defeat a great colonial power.[41] Beyond the French colonies, Luong argues that the Vietnamese example acted as a catalyst for wars of liberation and decolonization in Latin America, Africa, and Asia after 1954. Giving hope to the "dispossessed" nations of the world, the Vietnamese defeat of the French and later the Americans brought down not only colonialism but (neo)imperialism as well.

Reflecting Vietnam's interests in joining the global community, studies have also begun to privilege the diplomatic struggle in the French war and especially the party's adept public relations campaign around the world. For example, Ho Chi Minh's negotiating efforts from 1945 to 1946, which had been criticized in earlier times, have been lauded as setting Vietnamese diplomacy on the right path for the remainder of the 30-year war.[42] In a 2001 study entitled *Modern Vietnamese Diplomacy,* the emphasis on Vietnam's ability to garner support from the nations of South and Southeast Asia against the French reflects Vietnam's improvement of relations with the nations of ASEAN and the importance accorded to Southeast Asia in Hanoi's foreign economic policies.[43] Not only did Hanoi's regional and world relations campaign prove an integral factor in attaining ultimate victory, but the new spate of studies also credit Hanoi's propaganda machinery with turning French domestic opinion against its "dirty colonial war." The images and reports originating from the DRV's press offices in Southeast Asia and later Europe won over the French people to the Viet Minh struggle and forced French leaders to abandon their war in Indochina.[44]

The latest generation of Vietnamese literature on the French war can be considered the first generation of real historical scholarship.

Prior to *Doi Moi,* scholars used the history of the French war to suit the purposes of Hanoi's efforts during the Second and Third Indochina Wars. However, in doing so, the studies were more ideological and propagandistic than analytical and objective. As peace came to Vietnam, the leaders in Hanoi no longer needed to use the history of the French war to justify further military engagements. Although the need to maintain political legitimacy in light of momentous economic change drives the party to keep a watchful eye over the writing of history, Vietnam's political situation is steadily improving to allow scholars to explore wider issues associated with the war for decolonization. The result is an improvement in the quality and quantity of scholarship on the French war.

Conclusion

In an article entitled "The Vietnamese Peoples' Resistance against Colonial France in Western Textbooks," historian Phan Ngoc Lien surveys scholarship on the war published in France, Britain, and the United States.[45] Lien concludes that much of the literature has a capitalist slant because Western historians have placed the First Indochina War within the larger theme of the emerging Cold War. In doing so, the "international movement of the colonized people" for liberation has been submerged under the superpower East-West conflict. When scholars in the West do address the Vietnamese resistance, they falsely accuse the party of "hijacking" the struggle from the true patriots, Lien argues. In a further attempt to discredit the ideological commitment of the Viet Minh resistance, Lien contends that Western scholars suffer from orientalist blinkers:

> Moreover, some capitalist scholars affirm another wrong: Asia was foremost an experiment. This continent accepts and adopts Western culture; therefore, in the people's movement for liberation, the Vietnamese could not help but be influence by some ideology or another given to them by Western colonial education. This is the cause for some capitalist scholars to divide the people, between patriots and communists, and prove the latter's reliance on the force and aid of larger powers.[46]

Although Lien's survey is not exhaustive, it reveals that Vietnamese scholars have paid attention to the secondary literature in the West, if only to debunk what the studies have to say.[47]

In contrast, Western scholarship on the First Indochina War, on the whole, has refused to consult Vietnamese scholarship. Given the vast improvement of the quality of Vietnamese scholarship in the last few years, there is no longer an excuse to ignore publications coming out of Hanoi and Ho Chi Minh City. Not only is government control loosening but more archival materials and official documents from the period of the French war are now becoming available. Although there is much room for improvement, as there is in any field of historical study, the secondary literature needs to be taken seriously by historians in the West working on the First Indochina War.

FOUR

◆ ◆ ◆

Franklin Roosevelt, Trusteeship, and Indochina

A Reassessment

STEIN TØNNESSON

ALTHOUGH PRESIDENT FRANKLIN D. ROOSEVELT knew little about Indochina, one of his principal war aims in Asia was to liberate the French colony. His enemy in this case was not just Japan but also the local French regime, which had allowed Japan to use the colony as a stepping-stone for its invasion of Southeast Asia in 1941 and 1942. Roosevelt intended to detach Indochina from both Japan and France and place it under an international trusteeship in which China would have a role.

The present essay summarizes the scholarship on Roosevelt's Indochina policy and argues against the widespread contention that he gave up his opposition to French colonial rule toward the end of his life. Roosevelt came under pressure to do so when Japan launched a coup against the local French regime and some French troops resisted. Still, Roosevelt did not yield. Only after he died on April 12, 1945, did a group of top-level officials in Washington revise U.S. policy in a pro-French direction, while pretending that they pursued Roosevelt's policy. And it was only in June that the U.S. ambassador to China and the commander of U.S. forces there complained to President Harry S. Truman that the current policy conflicted with directives they had received from Roosevelt. Truman was forced to define his own policy. He then endorsed the pro-French line of his Europe-oriented advisers.[1]

Historiography

Historians agree that Roosevelt displayed a surprising interest in French Indochina, which he intended to take away from France and place under an international trusteeship.[2] There is disagreement, however, as to whether Roosevelt abandoned his Indochina policy before he died. At first, historians generally assumed that the trusteeship policy died with Roosevelt.[3] This view was challenged in *The Pentagon Papers,* which argued that Roosevelt had merely paid "lip service to trusteeship and anti-colonialism" and had not translated it into "factual policy."[4] In 1970 historian Edward R. Drachman took the same view. He found that Roosevelt had been compelled to drop his trusteeship plan for Indochina prior to the Dumbarton Oaks Conference, which started in August 1944. Drachman asserts that Roosevelt had decided that "Indo-China would be placed under trusteeship only with the permission of France, which was highly improbable."[5]

Other scholars found it difficult to accept that Roosevelt gave up his policy so early since he continued to speak about it. Gary R. Hess pointed to such evidence and ascribed the nonimplementation of the trusteeship plan to a lack of presidential willpower. "As was frequently true in his diplomacy, Roosevelt was seeking to achieve political goals without paying the necessary price," writes Hess. "The trusteeship plan deserved more thoughtful consideration by the Allies and more vigorous advocacy by Roosevelt than it received."[6]

Authors such as Hess tended to see Roosevelt's policy as a well-intentioned plan, a lost opportunity that could have saved both France and the United States much agony. However, they failed to see the policy in the light of U.S. military strategy, and they also did not see its connection to the U.S. policy toward China. Contributions by Christopher Thorne, William Roger Louis, and Walter LaFeber overcame these weaknesses. From his British perspective, Thorne scornfully remarked that Indochina was one of a good many foreign policy issues for which Roosevelt "provided little solution beyond brave talk and bonhomie."[7] Louis ascribed Roosevelt's Indochina policy to his anticolonialism, his "low esteem" for France, and his "abiding distrust" of de Gaulle. Shortly before his death in 1945, Louis claimed, Roosevelt "conceded that Indo-China and other French colonies should be restored to France." Louis saw three reasons for this change: reduced optimism about establishing a world with "four policemen" (the United States, Britain, the Soviet Union, and China) because of China's weakness, the practical problem of preventing de Gaulle from reestablishing French control, and the hope that France would agree to decolonize.[8] The Indochina trusteeship plan, wrote Walter LaFeber, was based on the assumption that China could replace France as a great power in Asia. As early as May 1944, however, it became clear that China was too weak to assume such a role. By the time Roosevelt recognized de Gaulle's French government in October 1944, it was no longer possible to implement the trusteeship plan. Roosevelt therefore "agreed to turn his head while the French moved back into Indochina."[9] Thus the opportunity was lost long before Roosevelt's death, not because of a lack of will, but due to changes on the ground.

It is necessary to point out that Roosevelt could not know how soon the war would end and, in fact, continued to look for ways of reinforcing China. LaFeber also failed to appreciate the fact that the French colonial administration, which had remained loyal to Vichy, remained in control of the Japanese-occupied colony even after the establishment of de Gaulle's government in Paris. Only on March 9, 1945, did the Japanese topple the French colonial regime. Thus, although developments in the war made it difficult to realize Roosevelt's war aims on the larger strategic level, on the ground inside Indochina the Japanese actually dealt a blow to French colonialism from which it never recovered.

In 1976, Russell H. Fifield drew the connection between Roosevelt's policy and the March 9 coup, which transformed French colonial forces who managed to avoid capture from "collaborators" to "resisters." Hence, asserted Fifield, "Roosevelt's attitude toward the French resistance became crucial." Even in this situation, when the French and British appealed for help to fight Japan, Roosevelt was not ready to accept French sovereignty in Indochina. The trusteeship concept "definitely died," asserted Fifield, "but the circumstances of its decease are not fully clear. It is doubtful if there was a formal decision in the White House to drop Roosevelt's concept. Rather, no person in the highest circles of the government pushed the trusteeship idea." Fifield adds that President Truman himself probably did not know about it when he assumed office.[10]

In 1977, George C. Herring suggested that a high-level decision had been made in May 1945 to abandon the trusteeship policy. The change was "well underway" at the time of the president's death and was "quickly consummated" by the Truman administration as a result of "a decision, made by several top State Department officials in May 1945, to accept the French sovereignty in Indochina as a means of enlisting French cooperation in the San Francisco Conference and in opposing Soviet expansionism in Europe."[11] This analysis was on target. The decision was "under way" in the sense that top officials wanted to change Roosevelt's policy, but they refrained from arguing with the president, probably because they knew how strongly he felt about the issue but also because of his frail health. In addition, Indochina was hardly the most important issue on the U.S. agenda. Once Roosevelt had died, they simply implemented their policy without calling Truman's attention to the change. Unfortunately, Herring later moved closer to LaFeber's position by pushing the abandonment of the trusteeship policy back to the Yalta Conference. "At Yalta in February 1945," wrote Herring, "the President watered down his policy by endorsing a proposal under which colonies would be placed in trusteeship only with the approval of the mother country. In view of France's announced intention to return to its former colony, this plan implicitly precluded a trusteeship for Indochina."[12]

By the late 1970s most American scholars shared the view that Roosevelt had backed down. It became a near-truism that he had buried the trusteeship concept and accepted that Indochina would be restored to France.[13] Gary R. Hess, however, remained in doubt. If Roosevelt had backed away, why did he tell Stalin at Yalta on February 7, 1945, that he "had in mind" a trusteeship for Indochina?[14] This comment indicates that Roosevelt still thought his aim was attainable. After his return to Washington, he "appeared to be searching for an alternative means of assuring a commitment to Indochina's independence," asserted Hess.[15] After Roosevelt's death, however, the White House lost interest in Indochina and left implementation of U.S. policy to the State Department and the military decision-makers. Hess's analysis was close to Herring's initial position: a new policy was not adopted by the U.S. administration until after Roosevelt's death.

Lloyd Gardner stated a similar view in 1988. Like Hess, he read the minutes of the Yalta Conference closely and found in Roosevelt's anti-French remarks to Stalin "a chancy last-ditch scheme" to realize his trusteeship proposal. Gardner felt that Roosevelt's "curious discussion with Stalin at Yalta, when he might have said nothing and let the issue drop, suggested that even when none of the pieces had fallen into place, he still held out a hope that an atmosphere could be created that would help move things along to a more decent world order than had prevailed before the war."[16]

Despite Hess and Gardner's somewhat differing views, the accepted wisdom may be summarized in two points: First, Franklin D. Roosevelt abandoned or watered down his Indochina policy before he died. Second, the Truman administration built upon Roosevelt's policy revision by endorsing the French return to Indochina. Both points will be challenged in the following pages, which argue that Roosevelt, though he was under pressure to abandon his policy, did not yield before he died. He continued to look for ways to bolster China, and he probably expected Indochina to be detached from Japan by U.S.-advised Chinese forces. In such an eventuality, it would have been possible either to prevent a French return or to set strict conditions for that outcome. It was only after Roosevelt's death that U.S. policy changed. To substantiate these claims it is necessary to look at the role Roosevelt imagined for China in the war against Japan, relate the March 9 coup to his policy, and examine how trusteeship was abandoned after his death.

Roosevelt, China, and Indochina

Roosevelt was a juggler, China a potential partner, and Indochina a ball. By keeping the ball in the air and out of de Gaulle's reach, Roosevelt hoped to get Chiang Kai-shek into play. Unlike Woodrow Wilson, Roosevelt did not base his vision of world order on the concept of "collective security." The postwar peace would depend on stable relations between a limited number of powers. Thus FDR developed the concept of the "four policemen," an idea that he discussed with Stalin at Teheran in 1943. The United States, the Soviet Union, Great Britain, and China were to police the world together.[17] FDR proposed that the planned United Nations Security Council should have four permanent members. One of them would be a strong, pro-American China, and France did not belong. How could the detachment of Indochina from France contribute to strengthening China? In Roosevelt's mind it would help by giving China a role in the military occupation of Indochina and by making China one of Indochina's postwar trustees. Thus, Roosevelt's China and Indochina policies were closely connected. When he failed to build up China as a great power, his Indochina policy suffered.[18]

Unfortunately for Roosevelt, few of his advisers shared his interest in Indochina, and by 1944 most of them had lost faith in China's military capabilities. Asia-oriented postwar planners viewed the trusteeship idea with sympathy, but even they started arguing in 1944 that perhaps France should be allowed to retain a role.[19] The prevailing view in the European office of the State Department was that in order to prevent France from moving closer to the Soviet Union, Washington should not offend French pride. On the military side, the Joint Chiefs of Staff disliked any projects that could interfere with their main strategy for the defeat of Japan. Their intention was to conquer islands, construct air bases as close as possible to the Japanese homeland, and bomb Japan's industrial centers. Resources should not be diverted to either China or Indochina. All this provided for a curious decision-making process on the Allied side: most British and American services wanted to exploit the continued existence of the French administration in Indochina as a source of intelligence but did not foresee major military operations in the country. Roosevelt wanted to draw Indochina into the war but refused to accept any cooperation with French forces either inside or outside the colony. He also blocked all requests for ships to send Free French forces eastward.

By October 1944, Japan was making plans for a coup against the French but intended to carry it out only if there were a real danger of an Allied invasion. The Japanese knew that if U.S. forces invaded, the French colonial army would assist them. As long as Indochina was not a battlefront, however, it was preferable to leave administrative matters to the French. An invasion from the north was not a major worry. China remained weak, and a Chinese invasion would most likely meet French resistance.

Roosevelt's interlocutor, Stalin, had no Indochina policy. He assured both de Gaulle and Roosevelt of support, while retaining diplomatic relations with Japan. In Britain there was a general wish to help the French, but Churchill vetoed proposals to put pressure on Roosevelt because he knew how strong the president's convictions were.[20] Most decision-makers in Washington shared the British wish to adjust U.S. policy in a direction more favorable to France but hesitated to press their view for the same reason as Churchill. Roosevelt himself was probably hoping to see a change in the military situation that would strengthen China and make it possible to realize his trusteeship proposal. He requested a plan for the invasion of Indochina.

Roosevelt's Invasion Plan

In 1943 and early 1944, Washington policymakers assumed that U.S. forces would invade Taiwan before the final onslaught against Japan. In September 1944, however, U.S. military planners decided to bypass Taiwan and invade Okinawa, where they could build an air base much closer to Japan.[21] This plan left China almost irrelevant to the U.S. strategy. Tokyo, however, had to consider the possibility that General Douglas MacArthur's invasion of the Philippines would be followed up by attacks against the Chinese coast, Taiwan, Hainan, or Indochina. These apprehensions matched Roosevelt's dreams. The president continued to have China's interests in mind and was unhappy with strategies that bypassed China. In a renewed attempt to realize his ambitions for a strong China, he invited his military commanders in October 1944 to come up with an invasion plan for Tonkin, the northern part of Indochina, in order to open a transport route to China. Accordingly, a detailed plan was drawn up.[22] However, planners insisted that the operation would divert resources from the invasion of Okinawa.[23]

Roosevelt received this disappointing advice just after he had grudgingly recognized de Gaulle's French government and yielded to the decision of the Dumbarton Oaks Conference to add a fifth permanent seat for France in the planned United Nations Security Council. But Roosevelt could still hope to deny France a say in Asian affairs. Plans were now drawn up for occupying Hainan Island in preparation for the invasion of Tonkin. Meanwhile, Roosevelt entrenched his administration in a "do-nothing" attitude concerning Indochina.

What was Roosevelt's motive for requesting the invasion plan? He may have thought it was an astute strategic option overlooked by his chiefs of staff. An invasion of Tonkin might simultaneously strengthen Chiang Kai-shek, create a U.S. base area on the continent, eliminate the need for air transport to China from Burma, and liberate Indochina from France. It is also possible that Roosevelt realized the plan was impractical. What would then have been his motives? By October-November 1944, Nationalist China was on the verge of collapse. Roosevelt may have wanted to take an initiative allowing him to say later that he had done his best to save China. Another purpose might have been to mislead Japan. Perhaps Roosevelt meant the plan seriously at first and later used it for deception. In Washington there was considerable confusion in late 1944 about the president's Indochina policy. On New Year's Day he issued a directive declaring, "I still do not want to get mixed up in any Indochina decision. It is a matter for post-war."[24]

At Yalta five weeks later, the United States, the Soviet Union, and Britain agreed to set up a system of international trusteeships. It would be applicable to three kinds of territories: "a) existing mandates of the League of Nations; b) territories detached from the enemy as a result of the present war; c) any other territory which might voluntarily be placed under trusteeship."[25] Since Indochina was not a mandate of the League of Nations, since it was never detached from the enemy as a result of the war, and since there was little hope that France would voluntarily place it under trusteeship, Roosevelt's approval of these clauses has been interpreted as proof that he had given up on the Indochina trusteeship.[26] However, the only change made in the trusteeship system at Yalta was the addition of the third "voluntary" category. The first two had already been defined at the Dumbarton Oaks Conference in August-October 1944. Hence, if the Yalta trusteeship formula were to prove that Roosevelt had backed down, we would have to argue that he had done so much earlier.

This possibility conflicts with other evidence. Could Roosevelt have imagined that Indochina would fit into one or the other of the categories? If yes, he must either have expected Indochina to come under category "b"—territories detached from the enemy as a result of the war—or have intended to compel France voluntarily to accept a trusteeship. The most important territory to be included under category "b" was Korea, a Japanese colony. Indochina had been under Japanese occupation since 1941, and it must have been considered likely that the territory would sooner or later be detached from the enemy by Chinese, U.S., British—or possibly new French—forces.

The Yalta Conference decided that there should be "no discussion of actual territories." Rather, this would be a matter for later agreement.[27] Still, Roosevelt did raise the question of specific territories in his private chat with Stalin on February 7. He "had in mind for Korea a trusteeship," he said, and "he also had in mind a trusteeship for Indochina." Since Korea would definitely belong to category "b" and Roosevelt mentioned the two territories in the same vein, he also probably thought of Indochina as belonging to that category. Roosevelt told Stalin that de Gaulle had requested ships to transport French forces to Indochina. Stalin inquired where de Gaulle was going to get the troops, to which Roosevelt replied that de Gaulle had said he would find the troops as soon as the president found the ships, but up to the present he "had been unable to find the ships."[28]

From Yalta, also on February 7, General George C. Marshall cabled MacArthur, asking him to consider seizing Hainan Island at the entry to the Gulf of Tonkin.[29] MacArthur opposed the idea, and the Joint Planners in Washington stated that the Hainan operation "should not be further considered at this time."[30] All of this indicates, however, that Roosevelt had neither abandoned nor watered down his trusteeship idea by the time of the Yalta conference. His policy had little support among other decision-makers in the U.S. and British governments, but Roosevelt kept looking for ways to carry it out.

What Did Roosevelt Know?

Roosevelt knew next to nothing about conditions inside Indochina. It is unlikely that he had ever heard of the Viet Minh, the national liberation front formed in 1941 by the communist leader Ho Chi Minh. Roosevelt had little faith in the ability of the Indochinese to govern themselves. At Yalta he told Stalin that the Indochinese were "people of small stature, like the Javanese and Burmese" and that they were "not warlike."[31] In a recent contribution to the scholarship on U.S. policy toward Indochina, Mark Philip Bradley unearthed a wealth of evidence showing that Roosevelt's patriarchal perception of the Indochinese population was typical of American decision-makers, including those who were more familiar with the French colony. U.S. attitudes toward the Indochinese populations were no less prejudiced or patriarchal than the French.

What, then, did Roosevelt know? He knew the role French Indochina had played in the run-up to Pearl Harbor. The French colony had bowed to Japanese pressure to cut the flow of supplies to nationalist China and had allowed the Japanese army and navy to establish a staging area for their invasion of Southeast Asia. Roosevelt was also probably aware that the French administration remained in place in early 1945. His aim could have been to prevent de Gaulle from taking over an intact colonial regime the way he had done in North Africa. If such was Roosevelt's aim, then, ironically, Japan realized it for him by its March 9 coup. The French colonial regime was then replaced by a power vacuum. Japan and native elites had little capacity for setting up a new administration, and the north-central coastal area was hit by a terrible famine. The Viet Minh filled the vacuum in the August revolution immediately after the Japanese surrender. Thus de Gaulle could not take over an intact colonial administration but had to conquer Indochina from the revolutionary Democratic Republic of Vietnam.

Did Roosevelt have advance knowledge of the March 9 coup? It is more than likely that he did. U.S. signal intelligence analysts had long since broken the Japanese diplomatic and military codes. Roosevelt had been an avid reader of "Magic" intercepts—decoded Japanese communications—since the early phase of the war.[32] In late 1944 and early 1945, it took an average of forty-eight hours for intercepted raw material to get back to Washington,[33] where an army of translators and analysts processed it and produced summaries of the main developments. Through such intelligence, Washington could follow in detail how Japan was preparing the coup. Toward the end of 1944, Japanese dispatches indicated a crisis in the relationship between the Japanese army and the French administration. The Japanese seriously feared a U.S. invasion and did not trust that the French would remain loyal or neutral.[34] These fears increased drastically when a U.S. carrier force under the command of Admiral William F. Halsey launched devastating raids along the Indochinese coast on January 12.[35] A Japanese navy message was intercepted on January 17 stating as a "fact that landings in Indo-China by Allied forces are imminent."[36]

On February 11, a U.S. summary of intercepted Japanese diplomatic messages noted that "the Japanese have become increasingly concerned over the possibility of Allied landings in Indo-China and have been taking various measures—and thinking about others."[37] Radio messages intercepted the previous day discussed the possibility of "inventing" some pretext for a coup against the French.[38] On February 21, a summary of Magic intercepts reported a decision in the Japanese Supreme War Council on February 1 to take military control of Indochina and to inform relevant authorities of the timing after February 20. Through these intercepts, U.S. services learned of the Japanese intention to give the governor general of French Indochina two hours to consider an ultimatum before taking action. On February 22, a Japanese official in Saigon advised Tokyo that, although the local military believed the likelihood of an Allied attack to have diminished considerably, they would go ahead with their plans "as scheduled."[39] On March 3, the Japanese foreign minister informed Japanese diplomats abroad that "we have decided to resort to force of arms" in French Indochina. On March 5, another summary of intelligence confirmed that the Japanese Supreme War Council on March 1 had "made the final decision to take control of French Indo-China."[40] Through its intercepts, U.S. services were able to quote the whole text of the ultimatum that the Japanese commander in Indochina was going to hand over to the French governor general.[41] The heading for the Magic summary on March 9, 1945, was "Showdown in Indo-China expected today."[42]

It is not known if any of this was communicated to President Roosevelt while he was away on the USS *Quincy* at Malta and Yalta (January 23 to February 28, 1945). However, after his return, it seems unlikely that he would have been kept in the dark. Still, there is no indication that anything was done to warn de Gaulle of what was about to happen.

On March 8, the day before the Japanese struck against the French, Roosevelt gave separate audiences in the White House to his ambassador to China, Patrick Hurley; the commander of the China theatre forces, General Albert C. Wedemeyer; and Admiral William F. Halsey, who had raided the Indochina coast on January 12.[43] Hurley spoke about the Kuomintang-Communist conflict in China, but Roosevelt's mind seemed elsewhere. When he answered, it was not about China, but Indochina. When General Wedemeyer entered, the president ordered him not to hand over supplies—any supplies at all—to French forces operating in Asia. He and Stalin had agreed that Indochina required a trusteeship, not colonization, he said. National independence was the wave of the future—not empires, not spheres of influence.[44] During his conversation with Halsey, the president made a number of comments that Halsey later told his biographer were "so secret that I would have preferred not to know them." One was Russia's pledge to declare war on Japan; the others, said Halsey, "are still secret."[45]

The March 9 coup changed the fate of Indochina. Most of the French troops capitulated. But some fought, and some fled into China. They requested American support. At first these requests went unheeded, but after a while, the Fourteenth Air Force of U.S. general Claire L. Chennault was authorized to provide some token support. Both the British Foreign Office and the U.S. State Department feared that the lack of Allied support for the French resistance would lead to violent outbursts from de Gaulle. In this situation, Roosevelt had a conversation with his Caribbean affairs adviser Charles Taussig on March 14 and made an oft-cited equivocal statement. First, he said that French Indochina and New Caledonia should be taken from France and put under trusteeship. On closer reflection, he added: "Well, if we can get the proper pledge from France to assume for herself the obligations of a trustee, then I would agree to France retaining these colonies," but only "with the proviso that independence was the ultimate goal."[46]

Does this mean Roosevelt had revised his Indochina policy? He had hinted that France might itself assume the role as trustee if Indochina were promised independence as the ultimate goal. He had reluctantly allowed some aid to be given to the French forces fighting Japan. Was this a change of policy? On March 23, this question was raised at a meeting of the Far Eastern subcommittee of the State-War-Navy Coordinating Committee. The answer was that the authorization to provide assistance to the fighting French forces "in itself was not a change in policy inasmuch as it indicated only the effort to keep the door open for a change in policy which may take place in the near future."[47] Thus by March 22, Roosevelt had not changed his policy but was under pressure—and maybe considering—to do so. He remained undecided and perhaps kept looking for new ways to realize his aims.

On March 23, the president held a second meeting with Wedemeyer. According to one account, the president wanted to know what Wedemeyer could do to arm local resistance groups opposed to French rule.[48] Two months after the meeting, Wedemeyer stated in a cable from China, "When talking to the President on my last visit he explained the United States policy for FIC [French Indochina] and told me that I must watch carefully to prevent British and French political activities in the area and that I should give only such support to the British and French as would be required in direct operations against the Japanese."[49] Hurley later told President Truman that during his last conference with Roosevelt he had asked for a written directive on Indochina. Roosevelt had answered that at the forthcoming San Francisco Conference a United Nations trusteeship would be set up which would ensure the right of colonized people to choose their own form of government as soon as they, in the opinion of the United Nations, were qualified for independence.[50] Thus Roosevelt's last statements to Hurley and Wedemeyer do not substantiate the contention that Roosevelt had given up or watered down his Indochina policy.

By late March 1945, the British Foreign Office was thoroughly displeased with the belated and reluctant support for the French forces fighting Japan in Indochina. A strongly worded telegram was drafted for the prime minister to send to the president: "It would look very bad in history if we failed to support isolated French forces in their resistance to the Japanese to the best of our ability, or, if we excluded the French from participation in our councils as regards Indo-China," the missive asserted.[51] Churchill pondered the draft but did not sign at first. "I am a little shy of over-burdening the President at this moment," protested Churchill. "I hear he is very hard-pressed, and I like to keep him as much as possible for the biggest things."[52] On April 3, however, Churchill decided he would "bring this before the President."[53] The telegram was dispatched on April 11, the day before Roosevelt died.[54] When a reply finally reached Churchill, it bore the signature of Harry S. Truman. There was nothing in this reply to indicate that any decision had been taken to change U.S. policy.

Truman's Decision

Shortly after Truman had been sworn in, some U.S. policymakers discussed the need to ask the new president to consider a more positive approach to France. Still, it was important for Truman to convey an impression of complete loyalty to Roosevelt's legacy, and presidential military adviser Admiral William H. Leahy seems to have preferred to avoid calling Truman's attention to the tortuous Indochina proposals. The French had little patience, however, and intensified their requests for material assistance.[55] The upcoming San Francisco Conference also seemed to make it necessary to reach a conclusion on the trusteeship plan. If Paris were not reassured of future French sovereignty in Indochina, U.S. officials warned, de Gaulle might react strongly and disturb U.S.-British relations.

Washington's handling of the Indochina issue from mid-April to early June 1945 constitutes an eloquent example of how a bureaucracy can exploit a change at the top to carry out its own long-subdued wishes. The State Department decided to present Truman, who had scarcely been involved in decision-making while he was vice president, with an inexact version of Roosevelt's policy towards France and Indochina. A "policy manual" given to Truman on April 16 pretended to summarize Roosevelt's policies but in fact insisted on the need for a pro-French policy: The French government and people, it stated, were "exceptionally sensitive to questions involving their national prestige." It was therefore in the interest of the United States to "treat France in all respects on the basis of its potential power and influence rather than on the basis of its present temporarily depleted strength." The manual failed to mention Roosevelt's Indochina trusteeship proposal. It mentioned none of his prohibitions against supporting the French in Indochina, pointing out only that on April 4, 1945, U.S. air forces in China had been "authorized, in aid of the French, to undertake operations against the Japanese in Indochina."[56] According to a later statement by the head of the State Department's South East Asia Division, Abbot Low Moffat, the European office deliberately left out background information on Roosevelt's policy in order to sell its point of view to Truman.[57]

On April 20, an official in the European office completed a candid memorandum to Truman suggesting "re-examination of American policy with respect to Indo-China." It challenged "the negative policy so far pursued by this Government with respect to Indo-China," which had "aroused French suspicions concerning our intentions" and had "a harmful effect on American relations with the French government and people." The paper recommended that the U.S. government should neither oppose the restoration of Indochina to France, with or without a program of international accountability, nor take any action toward French overseas possessions that it was not prepared to take or suggest with regard to the colonial possessions of other Allies. This memorandum was completed six days before the opening of the San Francisco Conference. Still it was not forwarded to Truman because the Far Eastern office in the State Department objected. The memorandum made a tour of the Washington civilian and military bureaucracy but never reached the president's desk.[58] Thus no new U.S. policy was formulated, either because government officials were unable to agree among themselves, or because someone did not want to draw Truman's attention to the Indochina tangle.

Still, something had to be said to the French. At San Francisco, Secretary of State Edward Stettinius Jr. found an ingenious way of reassuring them while avoiding admission of a policy change. Upon his arrival, French Foreign Minister Georges Bidault stated emphatically that "territories such as Indo-China, which are not mandated and which have not been taken away from the enemy, are excluded from the discussion and will so remain."[59] On May 8, Stettinius met Bidault, who asked the secretary of state about rumors that a special status had been reserved for French Indochina. Stettinius replied that the record was "entirely innocent of any official statement of this government questioning, even by implication, French sovereignty over Indo-China."[60] Formally this was true, since Roosevelt had only made unofficial statements about Indochina, but Stettinius could not have made this statement if Roosevelt had still been alive. Bidault was much relieved.

At San Francisco, U.S. officials thus declared Roosevelt's Indochina trusteeship plan nonexistent. Truman may not even have been aware of what happened. It was Hurley and Wedemeyer who forced Truman to take a stand. Patrick Hurley, Roosevelt's handpicked ambassador to China, had strong anticolonial feelings. A businessman of Irish origin whose suspicion of the British and hatred of the State Department were legendary, he radioed Washington on May 11 to ask if there had been any change in the policy toward Indochina. When receiving a less than informative answer, he started addressing lengthy cables to Truman for "his eyes only." In one such letter he asked if he should trust reports from San Francisco indicating that the United States had "abandoned FDR's trusteeship policy, which is now only defended by China and the USSR." If U.S. policy was not opposed to imperialism in Asia, he pointed out that it was in conflict with the Roosevelt policy and asked why he had never received any written directive on Indochina.[61]

These messages came at a moment when there was a heated dispute between General Wedemeyer and British Admiral Lord Louis Mountbatten over which commander held responsibility for military operations in Indochina. Wedemeyer had taken Roosevelt's oral instructions seriously, doing his best to avoid supporting France. He reminded General Marshall of President Roosevelt's trusteeship plan and warned him of possible French and British political penetration into Indochina.[62] The pattern seems clear: Washington had abandoned the trusteeship plan, while Wedemeyer and Hurley continued to operate in the shadow of FDR.

The combined efforts of Hurley and Wedemeyer forced Washington to respond. Truman did not want to convey the impression that his policy was at odds with Roosevelt's; on the other hand, it was undesirable to have a conflict with France and Britain. Wedemeyer was therefore told on June 4 that "policy regarding operations into French Indo-China has been modified recently." There would henceforth be no objection to furnishing assistance to French military or naval forces, regardless of the theater of operations from which the assistance might be sent.[63] On the same day, President Truman sent Hurley a telegram that was less than clear: "I fully appreciate your . . . frank estimate of the world wide political intentions of those European Nations that are allied with us in this war. You may be assured that these matters are receiving full consideration in America's planning for the future."[64] Hurley was not satisfied. On June 6, he wrote to Acting Secretary of State Joseph Grew, complaining that he had not been informed of the recent change in U.S. policy; this was "embarrassing" to him, he wrote.[65]

Grew approached Truman and then composed a telegram that offers a textbook example of how to portray change as continuity. Grew first assured Hurley that the president fully appreciated the difficulties in which he and General Wedemeyer might be placed on account of the lack of specific directives. He then added:

> The President has asked me to say that there has been no basic change in the policy in respect to these two questions and that the present position is as follows: "The President assumes that you are familiar with the statement made by the Secretary of State on April 3, 1945, with the approval of President Roosevelt in which Mr. Stettinius declared that as a result of the Yalta discussions the 'trusteeship structure, it was felt, should be defined to permit the placing under it of such of the territories taken from the enemy in this war, as might be agreed upon at a later date, and also such other territories as might voluntarily be placed under trusteeship.' The position thus publicly announced has been confirmed by the conversations which are now taking place in San Francisco in regard to trusteeships."

Just as historians would do in the 1970s and 1980s, Grew took it for granted that Roosevelt had not imagined Indochina to be "taken from the enemy in this war." Throughout the discussions at San Francisco, Grew explained, the U.S. delegation had insisted upon the necessity of providing for a progressive measure of self-government for all dependent peoples looking toward their eventual independence or incorporation in some form of federation, according to circumstances and the ability of the peoples to assume these responsibilities. "Such decisions would preclude the establishment of a trusteeship in Indo-China except with the consent of the French Government," wrote Grew. He added, "The latter seems unlikely." The U.S. policy was formulated as follows: "it is the President's intention at some appropriate time to ask that the French Government give some positive indication of its intentions in regard to the establishment of civil liberties and increasing measures of self-government in Indo-China before formulating further declarations of policy in this respect."[66]

This telegram reflects a decision made by Truman to endorse the State Department's policy, although it conflicted with Roosevelt's intentions. Even if the telegram denied that any change had taken place, and even if the policy was described as resulting from a statement made with the late president's approval, the telegram indeed marked a break with Roosevelt's policy. This was understood in China. "It was obvious that the Truman administration had capitulated to de Gaulle's insistence that Indochina could be placed in trusteeship only with the consent of France," Archimedes L. Patti, an OSS officer who served in China and Vietnam, asserts in his memoir.[67] Ambassador Hurley "was not pleased with Grew's message, because it revealed what to him seemed a distinct change in U.S. policy . . . Hurley, uncharacteristically, after the June message, simply stopped protesting," writes Hurley's biographer, Russell D. Buhite.[68]

June 7, 1945, may thus stand as the key date marking the change in U.S. policy, but it is clear that the shift resulted from a long process driven by two main factors: the increasing importance of de Gaulle's France in international affairs and China's loss of significance in Allied strategy against Japan. As long as it was possible to imagine that Indochina would be conquered by U.S. and Chinese arms, Roosevelt had stuck to his policy for Indochina's liberation from both Japan and France. After the March 9 coup, it was more difficult to maintain an anti-French stand. Roosevelt considered changing his policy, but he did not do it. The change was partially implemented in April and May by a group of high officials and endorsed by President Truman during his conversation with Grew on June 7, 1945.

In a policy paper dated June 22, the State Department defined the new U.S. policy as follows: "The United States recognizes French sovereignty over Indochina. It is, however, the general policy of the United States to favor a policy which would allow colonial peoples an opportunity to prepare themselves for increased participation in their own government with eventual self-government as the goal."[69]

What's Interesting about FDR's Policy?

Roosevelt's Indochina policy has drawn much scholarly attention, although perhaps for the wrong reasons. The main reason has been the possibility of a "missed chance" or "lost opportunity." Proponents of this idea have argued that the Indochina wars could have been avoided if Roosevelt's policy had been implemented. Skeptics have compellingly objected that this outcome was impossible because of the Europe-first policy in Washington, because of China's weakness, and because of U.S. strategic priorities in the war against Japan. For strategic reasons it was unthinkable to divert resources to operations in Indochina, and the U.S. interest in stabilizing Western Europe made it imperative to avoid hurting French national pride.

There is another reason, however, for examining Roosevelt's policy. It may have had important consequences in Indochina. Roosevelt was the chief player in the Pacific War game. Once he realized that his wish for an Indochina invasion was impractical, he may consciously have sought to make the French and the Japanese believe that the invasion would come. If it had not been for Admiral Halsey's raid of the Indochinese coast on January 12, 1945, it is unlikely that Japan would have carried out the March 9 coup. And if the coup had not occurred, the French colonial regime would still have controlled Indochina at war's end. Since U.S. intelligence services followed the development of the Japanese coup plan through translations of radio intercepts, Roosevelt is also likely to have had advance knowledge of the coup. If he simply knew and did not act on the knowledge, then his policy did not shape Indochinese history. But if Roosevelt consciously deceived the Japanese into expecting an Indochina invasion, then his policy had consequences. No proof has been found that he sought to deceive Japan, but if he did, he would have advanced two aims at the same time—to distract Japanese attention from the real targets of U.S. strategic planning and to rid Indochina of French colonialism. The unintended effect, however, would then have been to play into the hands of a leader of great stature—Ho Chi Minh.[70]

In August and September 1945, the white-bearded Ho Chi Minh emerged as the winner of the Indochina game. All along he had expected Japan to be defeated, and he had consistently sought to tie his own movement to the United States and Nationalist China. In 1945 he was guilty of the same false assumptions as the Japanese. He expected an Allied invasion and prepared himself for assisting the invading forces. Instead he got a power vacuum and a sudden Japanese surrender. This provided him with an occasion more favorable for bloodless revolution than he could ever have imagined. He then proclaimed the republic that would later defeat both France and the United States.

FIVE

✦ ✦ ✦

Creating Defense Capacity in Vietnam, 1945–1947

DAVID G. MARR

GENERALLY THE FIRST thing a new nation tries to create is a national army. The army symbolizes as well as protects its distinctive identity. If the nation is born amid war and revolution, consolidation of armed force must take place while fighting—with the distinct prospect of more defeats than victories in the early stages. If the fight is for liberation from colonial rule, the nascent army is not likely to possess more than a handful of individuals with command experience.

While the Vietnamese revolution can be said to have begun immediately following Japan's violent termination of French colonial administration on March 9, 1945, the Japanese military had no interest in fostering a Vietnamese national army, although it did arm a few paramilitaries and encourage martial spirit among rapidly proliferating youth groups. With the sudden announcement five months later of Tokyo's surrender to the Allies, both paramilitaries and youth groups moved eagerly to seize the trappings of power, which included leftover French firearms, uniforms, and other military equipment. The Japanese mostly continued to protect disarmed French soldiers and civilians from Vietnamese assault, pending arrival of Allied forces.

Even though the small communist-led Liberation Army (Giai Phong Quan) that descended from the northern hills in late August 1945 had survived by employing guerrilla tactics, the Democratic Republic of Vietnam (DRV) established in Hanoi quickly showed that it intended to build a modern regular army capable of defending the entire territory of Vietnam, from the Sino-Vietnamese frontier to the Ca Mau peninsula. This was a matter of national honor. Moreover, the govern-

74

ment favored conventional structures, strategies, and tactics, whatever the continuing rhetoric about guerrilla warfare. This reflected the influence of those few cadres who possessed officer or noncommissioned officer (NCO) experience in the French or Chinese armies. Besides, it was much less difficult to teach new recruits basic conventional tactics than the subtleties of guerrilla struggle, which required initiative, flexibility, and guile. Battle reversals soon forced dispersed armed groups to teach themselves guerrilla tactics and to rely entirely on local sympathizers for provisioning, but this was not the first choice of the Vietnamese government or senior military leaders, even following the outbreak of full-scale hostilities in December 1946.

The tyranny of geography, poor communications, severe economic constraints, a paucity of specialized staff, and disruptive enemy counteractions meant that the DRV central government could never exercise the degree of command and control over subordinate institutions, including armed groups scattered around the country, that it wished. Hanoi's control increased rapidly in northern Vietnam, improved slowly in the center, and remained minimal in the south. Even in the north, the province remained the vital territorial level for recruiting, outfitting, and sustaining regular army regiments or battalions. The relationship between local administrative committees and local military commanders was often uneasy. A favorable rice harvest in May-June 1946 and subsequent tax collections meant that both Hanoi and provincial committees gained more leverage over armed groups and were able to expand the formal military system. Nevertheless, many local "militia" *(tu ve)* groups remained unpredictable, despite their enrollment in Viet Minh–affiliated national salvation associations.

The Indochinese Communist Party (ICP) was determined to control both the national army and militia groups, yet the degree of party mastery varied from considerable to nonexistent. This reflected the ICP's small membership base, its perceived need to distribute its cadres across every sector of society, and the government's desire to keep the party's profile low in the interests of mobilizing citizens from all walks of life. As events unfolded, some nonparty leaders of armed confrontations with the enemy demonstrated such prowess that they advanced to command of ever larger units. The government, if not the party, appreciated that good battlefield commanders did not necessarily make good politicians or vice versa. With everyone learning by doing, exciting opportunities opened in the army for committed youths of diverse origins.

Incoming Foreigners

When Ho Chi Minh declared the independence of Vietnam on September 2, 1945, he warned potential enemies that "the entire Vietnamese people are determined to mobilize all their physical and mental strength, to sacrifice their lives and property, in order to safeguard their freedom and independence."[1] Nonetheless, perhaps more than any other Vietnamese individual, Ho Chi Minh apprehended the raw power of the foreign forces descending on the fledgling DRV even as he spoke. Chinese soldiers were marching on Hanoi and Haiphong from the north. British units were approaching Saigon from the south. The French government had restated its intention to send troops from the metropole, and some twelve thousand French colonial soldiers under Japanese detention anticipated early release. French commandos were already operating in Laos and on the islands adjacent to Haiphong. Japanese forces in Indochina, totaling about seventy thousand, had to be taken into account as well.

At that moment, Ho Chi Minh and his lieutenants had no idea how many fellow citizens were armed and willing to defend the new nation. The Liberation Army unit that had just marched into Hanoi numbered about two hundred, out of a total of no more than 1,200 soldiers trained and tested during the previous nine months. Former Garde Indochinoise/Civil Guard (Bao An Binh) personnel had been given the choice of joining the Liberation Army or turning over their weapons and returning home; probably several thousand took the first option. A much larger number of young men had come into possession of firearms during the August Revolution and were declaring their readiness to fight and die for the fatherland (To Quoc). The government urged them to form militia *(tu ve)* units and report to the nearest Viet Minh branch or people's committee *(uy ban nhan dan)*. Meanwhile, hundreds of thousands of men and women of all ages wielded bamboo spears, machetes, or wooden guns to participate in military drills and armed demonstrations at countless venues around the country.

The government's immediate priority was to convince all these armed citizens not to provoke conflict with incoming Allied forces. Already Viet Minh groups had sniped at Chinese troops crossing the frontier. Other Viet Minh groups skirmished with Vietnam Nationalist Party (Viet Nam Quoc Dan Dang) and Vietnam Revolutionary League (Viet Nam Cach Menh Dong Minh Hoi) groups that accompanied Chinese forces. General Lu Han, the Chinese commander, decided to allow Ho Chi Minh's DRV provisional government to continue functioning so long as domestic order was maintained and rice provided to his troops. The Chinese government also rejected French requests to let colonial troops interned in Yunnan and Kwangsi since April recross the frontier.

The British, however, chose to take a company of French troops along with four companies of their own when flying into Saigon's Tan Son Nhut airport on September 12. The British commander, General Douglas Gracey, refused to deal with the DRV-affiliated committee that had taken power in late August. Instead, he declared martial law, then rearmed 1,400 French colonial soldiers to assist him in throwing Vietnamese out of administrative buildings, police stations, post offices, and government warehouses. French civilians as well as soldiers took this opportunity to run amok on the morning of September 23, cursing, beating up, detaining, and otherwise offending any native encountered. Vietnamese bands of disparate political tendencies struck back ruthlessly the night of the September 24, killing as many as forty French civilians, many of them women and children. Pending arrival of battle-hardened French regiments from the metropole, the British ordered Japanese infantry battalions to join British-Indian units in quelling Vietnamese opposition. Fires destroyed whole neighborhoods of Saigon, civilians fled the city, and most armed Vietnamese retreated to the adjacent countryside by late October. During the next three months, French gunboats coursed up and down the tributaries of the Mekong, armored columns dashed as far as Tay Ninh, Chau Doc, and Ca Mau, and Vietnamese resistance proved minimal. On February 5, 1946, the French commander, Jacques Philippe Leclerc, declared that "the pacification of Cochinchina is entirely achieved," a claim he would come to regret.[2]

Assistance from the Center and North

Hanoi received news accounts of the September 23 French assaults in Saigon that same morning. An urgent confidential message arrived too from the ICP's Southern Region Committee chaired by Tran Van Giau, requesting central instructions but also reporting that armed resistance had already been decided upon locally and was indeed underway.[3] This was a grave blow to the DRV's policy of avoiding conflict with

Allied forces. Whatever the French provocations, it must have vexed Ho Chi Minh and others to be presented with a policy *fait accompli*. The evening of September 23, Ho Chi Minh expressed frustration to Archimedes Patti, the American OSS representative in Hanoi, that relevant Vietnamese leaders in Saigon were either not receiving his instructions or disregarding them.[4] Yet to disavow southern actions was out of the question. The next day, top party and state bureaus telegraphed approval to counterparts on the outskirts of Saigon and told provincial committees throughout northern and central Vietnam to support their southern brethren.[5] Hoang Van Thai, Liberation Army chief of staff, traveled to at least six provinces during the next few days to start mobilizing contingents to be dispatched south.[6] Not until September 26 did Ho Chi Minh go on the radio to praise the "resolute patriotic spirit of southern countrymen" and to promise that the government and citizens everywhere would assist them in their "sacrifice and struggle to hold firm the independence of the country." As an implied rebuke for the murders of the night of September 24, Ho Chi Minh urged the people of the south to treat French prisoners mercifully *(khoan hong)*, so that the world at large and the French public in particular would understand that Vietnamese were "more civilized than the gang that goes around killing people and stealing countries."[7]

Word of French assaults in Saigon spread quickly among the people of northern and central Vietnam, sparking anger, fear, and urgent, animated discussion. For many, the euphoria of August was now replaced by grim awareness that war might be inevitable. The date September 23 became a metaphor for national danger. It galvanized public opinion and provided a focal point for action that transcended local revolutionary preoccupations or organizational affiliations. Without waiting for instructions from above, small bands of young men headed down the coast by train, district and provincial committees outfitted armed groups of thirty to two hundred men, and local people began to donate money, clothing, medicine, and food to support the anti-French resistance in the south. The first organized, reasonably well-armed, company-size unit arrived across the river from Saigon on September 25. It was from Quang Ngai, where violent revolutionary struggle had broken out months before any other province in central Vietnam, and mass mobilization was intense.[8] This Quang Ngai contingent, and perhaps several others arriving soon after, almost surely joined southern forces in their attempted blockade of Saigon, then retreated with them to the Mekong delta in late October. The first northern unit to head toward Saigon was Chi Doi 3, a unit of the Liberation Army that had been forged in the Viet Bac hills before the August Revolution.[9]

During November, a number of additional military units came down the coast as far as Khanh Hoa and Phu Yen provinces, in what was now popularly dubbed the Nam tien (Southern Advance) movement. This term had long been used by Vietnamese historians to characterize the migration of ethnic Kinh from the Red River delta to the Mekong delta over a period of seven hundred years in the process vanquishing the Cham and Khmer peoples. Nationalists of the early twentieth century, influenced by Social Darwinism, glorified the Nam tien as evidence of Vietnamese superiority compared with neighboring "races" *(chung toc)*. From late 1942, Viet Minh organizers along the Sino-Indochinese border had given the "Nam tien" label to certain armed groups and spoken of a "Nam tien strategy," sometimes referring to an advance on Hanoi, at other times dreaming of liberating the entire country to the Ca Mau peninsula.[10] In late 1945, Nam tien evoked heroic images of northern and central forces coming to the aid of their beleaguered countrymen in the south.

Most Nam tien groups possessed a mélange of French, Japanese, Chinese, and American rifles of different vintages, plus a sprinkling of carbines, shotguns, and muskets. Company commanders and platoon leaders sported pistols of all sorts. Finding ammunition for such a variety of firearms became a major problem, and much ammunition was too old or poorly stored to be reliable. Soldiers counted themselves lucky to be allotted twenty to twenty-five cartridges of any vintage. Grenades soon became valued weapons, and the Japanese grenade-launcher was highly prized. However, the detonators of locally produced grenades were notoriously unreliable and dangerous. Mines and explosives were in very short supply. Although soldiers carried machine guns of different sizes and origin, scarcity of ammunition limited their employment. The same restriction applied to the few available mortars and small artillery pieces.[11]

Commanders tried to arrange brief training courses for their men en route south and while waiting to be committed to battle. The most rudimentary skills came first: weapons disassembly and assembly; cleaning and firing; squad formations, movement, taking cover, and signaling; utilizing the terrain; entrenching; and bivouacking. However, because the instructors came from very different military traditions—

French, Japanese, Chinese, American—drills could be quite confusing to new recruits. Some commanders possessed French army small-unit training manuals for use when preparing lectures or making Vietnamese translations of specific lessons to give to platoon and squad leaders. The Chi Doi Vi Dan commander treasured a copy of *Binh Phep Ton Tu* (The Military Strategy of Sun-tzu), large passages of which he had memorized and used in classes. Maps were extremely scarce, and those who knew how to read maps were held in awe.[12]

Even before the August Revolution it was widely assumed that Vietnam's national army should have political officers, down to the platoon level if possible.[13] However, few Nam tien participants understood what a political officer was expected to do. There was persistent confusion over whether political officers had powers equal to military commanders or not, which the government did not clarify until mid-1946.[14] Individuals originating in Viet Minh units from the Viet Bac expected political officers to be ICP members and to report separately up the ICP hierarchy. While it seems that all party cells (Chi Bo) formed in the north had political officers assigned by the ICP, this was not the case with all units from the central coast.

From a strictly military point of view, it would have made more sense to withdraw Nam tien elements all the way from Bien Hoa to Khanh Hoa, destroying rail and road communications along the way, but trying to avoid engaging the Japanese. Even assuming a successful position defense, Vietnamese forces remained vulnerable to flank attack, isolation, and piecemeal destruction. However, the idea of surrendering such large chunks of the fatherland to the enemy without a fight went contrary to the entire spirit of nationwide struggle against the foreign invaders. In addition, the Nam Bo groups that had retreated together with Nam tien contingents would have been outraged, quite possibly accusing the DRV government of abandoning the south entirely. Another option might have been to break down into smaller elements, link up with provincial *tu ve*, and mount guerrilla operations. This happened for some groups, whether deliberately or by accident. Unfortunately, the region between Xuan Loc and Phan Rang was lightly settled, deficient in food, and way behind regions farther north in political proselytizing and mass mobilization. Equally important, the DRV government and most military leaders down the line appear to have been committed to conventional strategies and tactics, whatever the rhetoric about guerrilla warfare.

Nha Trang and Ban Me Thuot

Nha Trang, the largest town along the south-central coast of Vietnam, remained under Japanese control for at least three months following the Allied victory in mid-August, although a DRV-affiliated people's committee was allowed to function and self-defense groups trained enthusiastically. Several thousand wounded and ill Japanese personnel evacuated from Burma were cared for in Nha Trang, and at least five hundred French colonial soldiers and civilians remained under guard there as well. Vietnamese Nam tien groups heading down the coast from late September were under instructions to bypass Nha Trang itself. On October 20, two platoons of French marines landed in Nha Trang under Japanese protection. On British orders French colonial soldiers were released and rearmed by the Japanese. Six days later, two small French vessels tried to tie up at the Nha Trang pier but were driven away by Vietnamese fire. Tran Cong Khanh was made commander of Vietnamese forces on the Nha Trang front with the difficult job of unifying a variety of local and Nam tien groups. In early November, he welcomed the five hundred men of Chi Doi Thu Son, recruited from the provinces of Ha Nam, Nam Dinh, and Ninh Binh in the north. On November 19, a French battalion of 1,200 men landed under cover of gunfire from the cruiser *Triomphant* and strafing by French Spitfires. Nha Trang's Vietnamese population fled to the countryside, while squads of Vietnamese soldiers attempted to defend solidly constructed churches, villas, and administrative offices until they were reduced to rubble. Some Japanese units refused to take orders from the French, and several scores of men deserted to the Vietnamese side.[15]

A new front materialized on December 1 when a French armored column abruptly appeared in the central highland town of Ban Me Thuot, having moved swiftly from the Mekong delta up Route 14, encountering very few felled trees or obstacle ditches along the way. A platoon of Chi Doi Vi Dan, having arrived in Ban Me Thuot only the previous day from Khanh Hoa, was caught by surprise, ran out of ammunition, and was almost wiped out. A contest for Route 21 then developed, with Vietnamese units sniping at exposed French soldiers and using several machine guns plus a single 81-mm mortar until ammunition was expended. Resupply depended on several old buses and five elephants. Food ran short, as the area was sparsely populated and some minority people preferred French to Vietnamese rule.[16]

On January 25, a large French armored column swept along Route 21 all the way to Ninh Hoa, compelling cut-off Vietnamese units to march cross-country toward the northeast. The French capture of Ninh Hoa was one half of Operation Gaur, the other being an armored sweep through Dalat and Phan Rang, then up the coast to Nha Trang. This pincers offensive made the ten kilometers of trenches that Vietnamese units had dug just west of Nha Trang quite useless and indeed threatened to trap all of them in a French meat grinder. Many soldiers appear to have fled in panic. Some stragglers were killed by minority men and their heads turned in to the French for bounty. Others managed eventually to join local self-defense groups and fight in Khanh Hoa province until 1954.[17]

Between January 18 and February 5, General Vo Nguyen Giap traveled to central Vietnam to convey the determination of leaders in Hanoi, above all President Ho Chi Minh, to back armed resistance to the French invaders. In his role as chairman of the national Military Commision (Quan Uy Hoi), Giap also tried to evaluate the current military situation, appraise Vietnamese combat capacity, and canvass strategic options. The Nha Trang front was the first time Giap had seen fighting of any magnitude, complete with French naval gunfire, artillery, and air attacks. It was also the moment when French armored columns closed in from Ban Me Thuot and Phan Rang, and Giap received a cable from Ho Chi Minh to return to Hanoi. En route back to the capital, he detoured to An Khe, Pleiku, and Kontum in the central highlands—places he realized could be strategically important in the near future.[18] As it happened, the French chose to concentrate on the north from late February, leaving Vietnamese forces in the center precious time to regroup, tie in better with local organizations, and consider different tactics. The ambition to build larger-scale units was by no means abandoned.

Military Organizing in the North

In Hanoi from late August 1945, DRV leaders began to construct a national army, whatever the day-to-day preoccupations with the Chinese, American, British, French, or Japanese. Already the first important step had been taken in April, when ICP general secretary Truong Chinh brought the heads of Viet Bac armed contingents together with Central Committee members working in the Red River delta to assign responsibilities and devise a unified plan of action. All of Vietnam was divided into seven battle zones, of little practical consequence at the time, yet demonstrating strategic foresight and appreciation of the country's geographical peculiarities. In May, the two principal armed contingents, led by Vo Nguyen Giap and Chu Van Tan, were merged to form the Vietnam Liberation Army.[19] On August 25, as Viet Minh adherents celebrated the end of the old order, the Northern Region Revolutionary People's Committee ordered all armed groups to disband themselves and enroll in the Liberation Army. How they were to do this remained unspecified.

On August 28, Chu Van Tan was named minister of defense in the provisional government of the DRV, while Vo Nguyen Giap became minister of interior.[20] Giap was also de facto commander of the Liberation Army, although this was not announced. First priority was given on September 7 to establishing a General Staff Headquarters (Bo Tong Tham Muu), headed by Hoang Van Thai. Two days later, the army's Office of Communication and Liaison (Phong Thong Tin Lien Lac) was set up in the same building, headed by Hoang Dao Thuy, a respected teacher and Boy Scout organizer.[21]

Meanwhile, the fledgling Ministry of Defense blitzed other organizations with action messages.[22] On September 4, each northern province was instructed to send about ten men to a platoon leaders course, bringing along their own weapons, paper, pen, clothing, and twenty days' rations. All northern province revolutionary people's committees were told to send their "military commissioners" *(uy vien quan su)* to a Hanoi meeting on September 7. The Northern Minerals Bureau was asked what amounts of relevant chemicals it possessed for making gunpowder. A September 5 government decree forbade citizens from having contact with the French army, on pain of being put before a military court. Another decree assigned manufacturing of arms and ammunition to the former colonial Minerals and Industry Service and authorized it to requisition the necessary factories and materials. On September 13, a government circular to Liberation Army units (also published in the *Cong Bao*) prohibited them from frisking women while on patrol or initiating house searches. Any person detained was to be turned over quickly to the police for proper investigation. The same day, Ho Chi Minh signed a decree establishing military courts to try "all persons committing any act harmful to the independence of the Democratic Republic of Vietnam." A week later, all northern provinces

were ordered to provide within seven days a detailed report on the following: the number of soldiers in their jurisdiction, divided between
"assault militia" *(tu ve xung phong)* and former Civil Guard; the names of
unit commanders and political officers; numbers and types of weaponry;
quality of ammunition; method of food supply; and "how the problem
of uniforms is being dealt with." The Defense Ministry thus asserted its
authority to consolidate data on all armed groups and, by implication,
to control their subsequent activities.

From the beginning, the Ministry of Defense and other central offices also received a host of messages from below about specific military
matters that required attention.[23] On September 13, for example, Hung
Yen province sent eleven military questions to Hanoi, which were
mostly answered twenty-five days later by Nguyen Van Tran, a key member of the Northern Region Revolutionary People's Committee. Province
committees had to cover the expenses of Liberation Army units until
the Defense Ministry "unified arrangements for the whole country."
Design of uniforms and insignia for the entire army would be spelled
out by the ministry. Firearms permits were to be issued by province and
city-level people's committees upon written application and a letter of
introduction from the relevant national salvation association *(hoi cuu
quoc)*—a trenchant example of how government and Viet Minh operations overlapped, although this was not official policy. Women were not
yet to be recruited into the army (an answer that ignored women already serving). Soldiers could not take autos without paying for them.
Private vehicles were not permitted to fly the national flag. And printed
materials on military subjects were available for purchase (a list being
provided to Hung Yen). A question about how much soldiers should be
paid per month for "matches and tobacco" was left unanswered.[24]

While relying heavily on local people's committees to provision army
units, the government also launched public campaigns to convince citizens to increase overall food production, to donate money or goods to
patriotic funds *(quy)*, and to volunteer their time to a variety of defense
projects. In practice, the severe shortage of food in northern Vietnam
until the May-June 1946 rice harvest probably limited expansion of the
army more than the quantity of arms and ammunition. If local committees taxed farmers too heavily in the interest of increasing troop
numbers, they risked loss of popular support, not to mention more
starvation than actually occurred.

The Liberation Army was especially anxious to build communications capacity between units recognized as coming under its command. Telegraph and telephone messages continued to go via the civilian service. Radios became the object of enthusiastic army attention. ICP leaders turned over two long-range transmitters, while a variety of shorter-range sets and electric generators were acquired from civilian bureaus, and a number of radio operators from the former colonial army were located. By September 13, contact had been established with Radio Saigon; the Central Vietnam Revolutionary Military Committee in Quang Ngai; radio station VN3G in Hue; and the patrol boat *Crayssac,* captured from the French in Hon Gai a week earlier.[25]

After the flight of Vietnamese forces from Saigon city at the end of September, only one transmitter in the south managed to sustain contact with Hanoi, with the Quang Ngai station providing vital relay services. Operating from My Tho until forced to evacuate in late October, the transmitter ended up in the U Minh forest near the tip of the Ca Mau peninsula, far from most other surviving Viet Minh groups in the Mekong delta. Gradually a radio net was pieced together, using equipment purchased secretly in Saigon and two transmitters seized in a special attack on Tan Son Nhut airport. However, not until early March 1946 was the Southern Vietnam Command Headquarters (Bo Tu Lenh Nam Bo), much better located in Thu Dau Mot province north of Saigon, able to establish regular radio communication with General Staff Headquarters in Hanoi.[26]

Other specialized bureaus soon followed the Communications and Liaison Office in Hanoi. On September 15, 1945, an Arms Office (Phong Quan Gioi) was established within the Ministry of Defense, headed by Vu Anh and Nguyen Ngoc Xuan. For some months most receiving or purchasing of arms continued to take place at the army unit or province committee level. However, the Arms Office did succeed in purchasing from the Chinese two train car loads of weapons, which were promptly dispatched to the south. A Chinese ammunition dump of unspecified size was stolen as well. A team was dispatched to Dong Trieu plantation to seize one thousand sticks of dynamite, some black powder canisters, and detonators.[27] Numerous small factories and machine shops repaired firearms, made detonators for grenades and mines, and tried to fashion their own rifles, submachine guns, and antitank weapons. On October 25, the French-owned Star company in Hanoi was requisitioned and renamed the Vietnam Army Engineering Department (So Cong Binh Viet Nam), concentrating on arms repair and manufacturing of grenades. Workers at the requisitioned Mai Trung Tam factory managed to rebuild six French artillery pieces. Beyond Hanoi, the Arms Office played little role for many months. Instead, each group of artisans took its own initiative, then sought support from a local army unit, people's committee, Viet Minh branch, or party cell. A former French Army cartridge works in Tuyen Quang was revived and expanded. Fabrication of reliable gunpowder, TNT, and mercury detonators proved the biggest bottleneck. There were many horrible accidents.[28]

The Ministry of Defense aggressively sought out raw materials of military importance and by the end of 1945 could claim some success, at least in the north. The Fontaine distillery was "requested" to provide unspecified quantities of mercury, nitric acid, sulfur, and copper. Ten days later it was instructed to turn over 3.5 tons of copper ingots, 400 kilograms of aluminum, and 8 tons of cast iron.[29] Citizens volunteered information about discarded ammunition to local committees, which notified the Northern Region People's Committee, which told the Defense Ministry.

Establishing a national military school was another high government priority. Already during June-August 1945 in the Viet Bac hills, three short classes for platoon leaders and political officers graduated 234 students. Early in September, the new General Staff Headquarters organized the Vietnam Military-Political Academy (Truong Quan Chinh Viet Nam). Class 4 began a three-week course with an inordinate number of the 156 students turning out to be from Hanoi secondary schools. Some participants still possessed only wooden rifles. A mix of Viet Bac cadres and former Civil Guard officers and NCOs constituted the teaching staff. Besides the essential rifle familiarization, dry firing, parade drills, forced marches, and physical education, some hours of the curriculum were devoted to map reading, terrain assessment, small-unit movement, and guerrilla tactics. Political lectures treated the current situation in Indochina and the world at large, the liberation revolution, principles of leadership, and how to guide the thinking of subordinates. President Ho Chi Minh visited the academy, inspected the mess hall and lavatories, gave a short speech, and reviewed one class in drill formation. When the ranks presented arms by thrusting their bayonet-tipped rifles forward (a practice begun in the Viet Bac hills), President Ho advised the army to change to a non-threatening verticle rifle presentation, as soldiers would be drilling in front of the people, not the enemy.[30]

With the Chinese army units in the nearby Citadel complex paying close attention to DRV military efforts, it was decided to shift the academy to the Cité Universitaire and give it the more innocuous name of Vietnam Cadre Training School (Truong Huan Luyen Can Bo Viet Nam). Province-level Viet Minh committees from Hue northward nominated men for an expanded one-month course, with 525 being selected for the class that began training on October 15. The first ICP cell was formed among academy staff. Nonetheless, some university-trained students proceeded openly to criticize Viet Minh activities, provoking intense reeducation efforts from political instructors and the expulsion of a few recalcitrants. Henceforth prior screening and selection of students was made much more rigorous.

With the Ministry of Education about to reopen Hanoi University and academy staff eager to find space for live firing and tactical maneuvers, training was shifted to Son Tay, thirty-five kilometers west of Hanoi, a place of military significance for centuries. In early December the academy welcomed a new class, composed of 314 students from all three regions of the country. Each student received one former Civil Guard uniform, forage cap, and a pair of leather shoes, plus the use of one kapok mattress, mosquito net, and woolen blanket. The next class, which began its studies on February 15, 1946, with 327 students and a two months curriculum, had the luxury of three live rounds per student at the firing range, plus instruction in use of the machine gun, 60-mm mortar, compass, topographical map, and binoculars. During the class's last week, two units maneuvered against each other, practicing encampment, infiltration, ambush, attack, and defense. With graduation on April 16, a total of 1,500 command and political officers had gone through academy training since June the previous year.[31]

The Chinese Presence

From September 10, 1945, until at least early March 1946, the DRV government had to deal on a day-to-day basis with a profusion of Chinese army commanders and staff officers. Although it soon became evident that the overall commander, General Lu Han, was not going to allow the French to participate in occupation duties, the degree to which the Chinese would insert themselves into Vietnamese government affairs remained unclear until the end of 1945. At Ho Chi Minh's first meeting with Lu Han on September 16, attention focused on currency exchange rates, feeding the Chinese army, repairing roads, and maintaining order. Lu Han demanded to know the numbers, organization, and disposition of DRV armed elements. Ho Chi Minh reluctantly agreed to provide this information, even though at this point he himself possessed only fragmentary data. Following this meeting, Ho shifted most of the still small Hanoi armed contingent out of the city and decided to drop the emotive title of Liberation Army in favor of the lower-key name of National Guard (Ve Quoc Doan).[32] Ho undoubtedly appreciated that Lu Han could shove aside the DRV government in Hanoi any time he so wished but then would have to allocate a fair number of his own troops to try to quell opposition in the countryside.[33]

The Chinese price for not asserting martial law was unfettered exploitation of the northern Vietnamese economy and DRV acceptance of significant political roles for the Vietnam Nationalist Party and Vietnam Revolutionary League (Viet Nam Cach Menh Dong Minh Hoi). Top-level discussions on the latter issue proceeded correctly but slowly. Behind the scenes, the ICP was determined not to share leadership of the national army with cadres from those organizations, some of whom possessed considerable military experience in southern China. An armed standoff soon developed along the three main routes from Hanoi to China, with Nationalist Party and Revolutionary League units controlling the towns (Lao Kay, Yen Bai, Phu Tho, Viet Tri, Vinh Yen, Lang Son, Mong Cai), and DRV loyalists controlling most of the surrounding countryside. Chinese officers in the towns probably discouraged their Nationalist and Revolutionary League friends from launching attacks on nearby militia or National Guard positions, while DRV leaders explained to aggressive local adherents the dangers of Chinese retaliation and the larger strategic necessity to focus on the French threat.

The French Return to the North

In late October 1945, French army units that had fled to Yunnan in March-April made preparations to return to Indochina. The Chungking (Chongqing) government was amenable, but Chinese generals in Hanoi restated the danger of Franco-Vietnamese confrontations. In early November, the number of ethnic Vietnamese deserting from French units in Yunnan increased dramatically. Captain Nguyen Duy Vien took his fully armed company of *tirailleurs* across the frontier to Ha Giang town and a rousing welcome from Vietnam Nationalist Party adherents. In January 1946, about two thousand Rhadé, Lao, Thai, Dao, and Vietnamese who had remained loyal joined 1,400 French troops in marching to Lai Chau. The French were poised to attacked Son La when restrained by the March 6 Preliminary Convention. Following withdrawal of the last Chinese units from this area in May, the French tightened their control, resumed relations with local clan leaders, and talked of forming an autonomous "Thai Federation."[34] Fighting would ebb and flow through this region until final French defeat at Dien Bien Phu in 1954.

As it became apparent to DRV leaders that a Sino-French agreement was getting closer, fundamental strategic choices pressed down heavily. Only one thing was certain: the French were coming one way or another. To resist French reentry to northern Indochina before Chinese troops evacuated probably meant fighting them both at a time when Vietnamese armed forces were quite unprepared to fight either. To refuse to negotiate, and perhaps withdraw the DRV government from Hanoi as the French advanced, risked losing the initiative to the Nationalist Party or pro-French elements. To negotiate with the French endangered popular support for the DRV and carried the risk that the French would offer no concessions. The third option was given a major boost on January 20, 1946, by the resignation of Charles de Gaulle as head of the French government, followed by indications a few weeks later that General Leclerc wanted a Franco-Vietnamese agreement before his troops took up duties in northern Indochina.[35] Immediately following signing of the Sino-French agreement on February 28, Franco-Vietnamese discussions took center stage, only to falter over several vital issues. General Leclerc then told the Chinese he was bringing his twelve thousand troops into Haiphong harbor by March 6, with or without a Franco-Vietnamese agreement. Chinese officials in Hanoi proceeded to pressure both sides to reach a Preliminary Convention in the early hours of March 6, wherein the French recognized the Republic of Vietnam as a free state (*état libre*) within the Indochinese Federation and French Union, the Vietnamese government agreed to welcome fifteen thousand French troops to join with ten thousand troops to relieve departing Chinese forces, and France agreed to accept the results of a future popular referendum on the issue of unifying the three *ky* (regions).[36]

In the military annex to the March 6 Preliminary Convention, there was to be overall French command of the twenty-five thousand man

"relief forces" but with the ten thousand Vietnamese troop contribution commanded by Vietnamese officers "subject to the orders of the
military authorities of Vietnam." Unit movements, positioning, and
missions would be the object of subsequent combined staff meetings.
On March 18, General Leclerc led 1,200 troops and 220 vehicles into
Hanoi to the relief and delight of more than ten thousand French civilians who had gathered along Trang Tien Street to cheer and sing the
"Marseillaise." Colonial soldiers at the Citadel were rearmed, and
Leclerc stood on a balcony to declare Hanoi the "last step of Liberation
after Fezzan, Paris, Strasbourg and Berchtesgaden."[37] While an obvious
balm to French pride, especially for the civilians and unarmed soldiers
who had feared for their lives ever since the Japanese *coup de force* of
March 9, 1945, it is hard to imagine a ceremonial arrival in Hanoi more
likely to lacerate Vietnamese patriotic sensitivities. Only the pairing of
French and Vietnamese flags on arriving vehicles offered a muted
counterpoint.[38]

Rationalizing and Expanding the National Guard

During the summer of 1946, the Ministry of Defense and central Military
Commission worked hard to fashion the National Guard into a standing
army of credible proportions. Policy documents had been prepared earlier. In late March, President Ho Chi Minh had signed a decree outlin-
ing military structure, ranks, uniform, and insignias. The anticipated
structure bore a striking resemblance to the U.S. Army. In late May, Ho
Chi Minh issued regulations for a national armed forces (Quan Doi
Quoc Gia), which dealt with organization, recruitment, ranks, promotion, discipline, awards, offenses, punishments, and ceremonies.[39] Enlis-
tees had to be between eighteen and thirty, be declared fit by an army
doctor, and know how to read and write *quoc ngu,* the Romanized Vietnamese script. There was no mention of only males being accepted or of
the need for character clearance from either Viet Minh or administrative committee officials. However, province authorities were to compile
personal history files *(can cuoc ly lich quan doi)* on every soldier, as would
their units subsequently. The decree indicated minimum periods of time
in each rank, treated medical personnel as a special branch, and precluded political officers from outranking their commanders.

Military discipline, awards, offenses, and punishments were spelled
out meticulously in the May 22 decree. Orders from superiors had to

be obeyed without hesitation, criticism, or complaint, although provision was made for discussion and criticism at a later point, when everyone had equal rights to express their opinions. Political officers were to help commanders to consider options, but they were not to give orders or take military responsibility. Commanders had to agree with their political officer on "matters of a political nature."

Also during the summer of 1946, both the Defense Ministry and the Military Commission were able to flesh out their specialized branches. The ministry now contained bureaus for military production, arms manufacturing, politics, administration, training, engineering and transport, justice, supply, and medicine. The Military Commission included operations, general staff, politics, the Vietnam Relief Force Command, and the Vietnamese-French Central Military Liaison and Control Commission.[40] Communications between Hanoi and key locations had been substantially improved by the purchase of American radio equipment from withdrawing Chinese forces. A network of relay stations for military couriers was established, with particular attention to back routes in case the enemy controlled the roads.

Artillery remained the National Guard's most serious deficiency. In late June 1946, three old French 75-mm guns were consolidated into one artillery battery for the capital.[41] Doan Tue, formerly of the colonial artillery, received a letter from Hoang Van Thai to present himself for military service, where he was soon put to work translating a French artillery manual, coining Vietnamese terms along the way.[42] Also in June, urgent work began to design and produce a version of the American 2.5-inch bazooka, for use against armored vehicles, concrete bunkers, and river boats. It was the self-propelled shell with shaped change that posed the biggest challenge. Powder had to come from captured enemy artillery shells. In October, Ho Chi Minh brought back from Paris a German-trained scientist, Tran Dai Nghia, who joined the bazooka team at Giang Tien arsenal in Thai Nguyen to quickly produce fifty prototype projectiles and four tubes. When tested, the projectiles failed to penetrate. In March 1947, an improved model was used in battle for the first time.[43] However, the lack of heavy weapons would continue to restrict Vietnamese tactical options until 1950.

By August 1946, the Defense Ministry's arms-manufacturing bureau had convinced most local arsenals to abandon attempts to produce rifles and submachine guns in favor of upgrading their output of black powder, ammunition, detonators, grenades, mines, and mortars.[44] Plans were also afoot to shift some arms manufacturing away from the Red River delta to upland locations. Already the Giang Tien arsenal in Thai Nguyen employed about six hundred workers, including one hundred or more Japanese deserters.[45]

The Militia: Double-Edged Sword

In early September 1945, there were thousands of groups in Vietnam calling themselves militia *(tu ve)* or similar titles. These groups ranged from eager villagers drilling with spears, to excited youths who had acquired firearms when taking power at district or provincial levels, to previously existing clandestine organizations now armed and expecting to play key political roles in the cities. In Saigon many militia groups joined the four military "divisions" and then fell back on their own resources or disintegrated entirely under French attack. In the north and center, as we have seen, some militia groups headed southward to fight the French. Of those militia groups remaining behind, a few were accepted on a unit basis into the National Guard, although the General Staff's clear preference was to induct individuals and place them under separately selected platoon leaders and company commanders. At province and district levels, many militia groups liked to call themselves Liberation Army or National Guard units but were not recognized as such by the Defense Ministry or General Staff.

Militia groups in late 1945 not only prepared to fight foreign invaders but were intimately involved in local revolutionary upheavals and ongoing struggles for power. In most cases the central government expected province committees to be aware of this turmoil and take action where necessary. However, aggrieved parties had the right to petition the president or regional committees for redress, so a small portion of the conflicts or altercations involving militia groups show up in the files. During 1946, provincial authorities increasingly took responsibility for incorporating selected militia groups into province-supported battalions, which usually aspired to "regular army" *(quan chu luc)* recognition by Hanoi. This still left several thousand militia groups reporting to a wide variety of other organizations, whether local administrative committees, Viet Minh associations, the Vietnam Nationalist Party (until suppressed), or religious leaders (Catholics in the north and center, Hoa Hao and Cao Dai in the south). With the arrival of French forces in Hanoi and Haiphong in March, and especially their dispersal to other locations in April-June, the attitudes and behavior of militia groups took on new significance for the DRV government. If they sniped at French guards, abducted soldiers, or ambushed convoys, the government's strategy of "compromise in order to advance" could be jeopardized. Some such incidents did occur and were duly used by the French to question the DRV's capacity to maintain law and order.[46] However, DRV officials and military commanders managed to convince most militia groups that they could better restrict French actions by serving as guards, police auxiliaries, intelligence agents, porters, and builders of defense works.

Some local militia groups were more inclined to harass agents of higher Vietnamese authority than anyone else. This was especially true of tax collectors. By September 1946, the Northern Region Tax Department had forwarded enough complaints to the Northern Region Administrative Committee to compel the latter to issue a warning to all province committees. "Some local militia units have shown themselves lacking in a spirit of discipline, too enamored of personal interests," the message intoned. When tax officers showed up, the militia were to "maintain law and order, join in constructing the nation, and place the interests of the Fatherland above all else."[47] Another serious incident occurred in Nam Dinh in October, when armed tax agents intercepted four boats loading salt for illegal export, then moved to impound a row of salt-laden oxcarts on the shore as well. The agents were surrounded by members of the Bao Ve Quan (Guard Force) of the adjacent village, subjected to taunts and threats by a growing crowd, tied up, and eventually allowed to flee the area.[48] Yet this was at a time when the government was trying to collect and transport salt to upland warehouses on the prospect of full-scale hostilities with the French.

South-Central Vietnam

Following the collapse of the Nha Trang front at the end of January 1946, those Vietnamese combatants who had managed to evade French encirclement and retreat northward to Phu Yen were in bad need of encouragment and reorganization. By April, Nguyen Son declared establishment of three brigades *(dai doan),* each containing three or four regiments *(trung doan).* While the late March government decree on military structure had mentioned brigades, Nguyen Son was the only regional commander who tried to build them in 1946. We do not know the reasoning behind his decision, but it soon proved to be overly ambitious.

The Binh Dinh Twenty-third Brigade, with four thousand men but only 1,500 rifles, had its best units operating in the central highlands. On June 21, French forces struck northward from Ban Me Thuot, and within days took both Pleiku and Kontum. Over objections from some of his staff, Nguyen Son ordered a general withdrawal from the highlands to concentrate on defense of An Khe pass, a point of strategic significance since the eighteenth century. Subsequent fighting around An Khe was intense, with some Vietnamese units holding fixed positions to the death rather than retreat. Whatever Nguyen Son's experience in China, he had not taught his troops how to mount a mobile defense or to employ reserves in counterattack.[49]

After taking An Khe, the French found it impossible to advance the remaining seventy kilometers to Qui Nhon, due to thousands of Binh Khe district residents participating in wholesale destruction of the road and helping to build a series of trenches and redoubts in depth. Six months later, on December 21, French forces tried to resume their advance, backed up by 155-mm howitzers firing from An Khe. Although civilian casualties were heavy, Vietnamese forces had learned how to retreat tactically and then counterattack and had dispatched a unit behind An Khe to ambush supply trucks along Route 19.[50] Repeated French efforts to seize Qui Nhon did not bear fruit until March 1954, ironically just at the moment Vietnamese forces began to draw the noose around Dien Bien Phu far to the north.

The Thirty-first Brigade had two regiments in Quang Ngai to guard against possible French amphibious landings or parachute drops and two regiments in Quang Nam to watch the French "relief" contingent in Da Nang. Quang Ngai remained the revolutionary heartland for all of central Vietnam, dispatching units to the south, west, and north, training cadres, repairing firearms, manufacturing grenades and mines, and providing a headquaters for the Southern Resistance Committee. As many as two hundred Japanese deserters gravitated to Quang Ngai, where Nguyen Son put them to work as instructors, members of his staff, weapons technicians, engineers, mechanics, radio operators, and medics.[51]

Probably Nguyen Son's most lasting contribution to the anti-French resistance was his establishment in June 1946 of the Quang Ngai Ground Forces Secondary Academy (Truong Luc Quan Trung Hoc Quang

Ngai), which immediately enrolled four hundred students and continued to function long after his departure in November.[52] About half of the trainees had already fought somewhere to the south, while the other half were newly recruited high school students or young civil servants. Trainees were divided into four companies, each commanded by a Japanese instructor. The course was designed to produce qualified platoon and squad leaders after one year, with lots of lessons on map reading, reconnaissance, camouflage, use of terrain, communications-liaison, and night assaults.

Meanwhile, some Japanese instructors aimed to convince their Vietnamese students that spirit could overcome matter, that suicide units could defeat French armor, artillery, and aircraft.[53] This idea undoubtedly appealed to zealous young patriots in 1946. At the battle of An Khe, for example, some Vietnamese defenders fired on the advancing enemy to their penultimate cartridge, then directed the last bullet at themselves. Some wounded combatants unable to be evacuated used their last grenade to kill themselves and hopefully catch several unwary enemy soldiers as well.[54] Such actions were glorified by political officers and featured in newspaper accounts. More generally, Viet Minh propaganda asserted that willing, idealistic sacrifice for the just cause ultimately would vanquish the evil imperialists. On the other hand, academy students knew that Japan had lost its war, whatever the spiritual commitment. The Japanese mystification of warrior death did not have a Vietnamese counterpart. Some commanders asked for volunteers on what amounted to suicide missions, and many youths stepped forward. But if they could accomplish the job and still come back alive it was a cause for celebration.

Southern Vietnam

In early March 1946, when the best French combat units departed Saigon for Haiphong, a window of opportunity presented itself to leaders of anti-French armed groups in southern Vietnam who had undergone six months of demoralizing reversals. The last British troop units had departed in February, and Japanese units no longer were required to take part in military operations while waiting for Allied ships to take them home. Although the failure of Ho Chi Minh to gain French recognition of Cochinchina as an integral part of Vietnam in the March 6 Preliminary Convention angered many south-

erners, the French promise of a future referendum highlighted the
need to extend influence over as many people as possible in coming
months. However, the French still possessed thirty thousand soldiers
on the ground in Cochinchina and southern Annam. They also had
succeeded in recruiting thousands of Vietnamese "partisans" to accompany French units on patrol, share guard duties, and collect intelligence.[55]

By August 1946, French reports on the pacification of rural Cochinchina had become distinctly less optimistic compared to four months
prior, pointing to rebel bands that managed to reconstitute themselves
rapidly after each tactical setback and Viet Minh initiatives that para-
lyzed the French-installed administration. Rather than demanding absolute obedience, some Viet Minh leaders had adopted the more
flexible policy of obtaining the "semi-complicity of the population,"
probably a reference to the practice of allowing village notables to declare allegiance to France publicly while secretly assisting the anti-
French effort.[56]

The Modus Vivendi signed by Marius Moutet and Ho Chi Minh on
September 14 included a provision for a cease-fire in Cochinchina and
southern Annam to begin on October 30. Not surprisingly, both
French and anti-French forces sought to expand their areas of control
in the weeks leading up to the cease-fire. Whatever the outcome of
these maneuvers, however, the DRV government had decided to make
adherence to the cease-fire on October 30 a test of its capacity to control armed groups in the south and influence the southern population
at large. French and Vietnamese sources agree that shooting stopped
on cue at midnight, and the cease-fire held throughout Indochina for
several days. In some places it persisted for several weeks. Most French
observers were stunned by general Vietnamese adherence to the October 30 cease-fire and took this as disconcerting evidence of DRV government control or influence in the south. As if to punctuate this
pessimistic assessment, Nguyen Van Thinh, president of the French-
sponsored Autonomous Republic of Cochinchina, committed suicide
on November 10.[57] Early in December, the French secret police concluded that the "Viet Minh rebels" had benefited from the cease-fire,
being able to regroup their forces, to substitute their administration
for the separatist one in all areas not under direct French military protection, and to renew their calls for a popular referendum.[58] According
to another source, the Viet Minh controlled three-quarters of Cochin-

china.[59] Militarily speaking, this was a gross overstatement of DRV National Guard capacities in the south, especially given the continuing inclination of Binh Xuyen, Cao Dai, and Hoa Hao units to choose which orders they would obey from Nguyen Binh and which not. Either the local intelligence being received by General Nyo was faulty, or his superiors had reason to inflate the DRV threat in Cochinchina. The latter seems more likely, as Admiral Thierry d'Argenlieu, General Jean Valluy, and Léon Pignon now argued that France's future in Indochina could only be upheld by rapid escalation of pressure on the DRV government and armed forces in Tonkin.[60]

DRV Strategic Deliberations

During the summer of 1946, as the talks in France seemed to go nowhere, DRV leaders in Hanoi turned their minds increasingly to preparations for full-scale war. This shift of emphasis is obvious in a resolution passed on August 1 at the end of a two-day ICP Central Cadres Conference, which began by asserting grandly that the international balance of forces between the USSR and the imperialists had shifted substantially in favor of the former and that Indochina had became a very important geographical point of revolutionary confrontation. However, most of the conference resolution focused on Vietnam's perceived internal problems, including poor ethnic minority relations, parlous government finances, sluggish expansion of the national united front beyond the Viet Minh, petty leadership disputes (especially in central Vietnam), and lax discipline within the party. Toward the end of the resolution there was a long list of military deficiencies, perhaps simply noted down in the course of discussion. The armed forces were not unified, they lacked specialized units, commanders lacked experience, there was insufficient political work, no coherent military strategy existed, sabotage and demolition operations were deficient, efforts to mobilize minority peoples had been defeated (Trung Bo), main force units had been squandered (Saigon), the strategic initiative had been lost, there was too much faith in the 6 March Preliminary Convention and not enough preparation to take the offensive, and units had not been formed to seize weapons from the enemy.[61] Despite this litany of military weaknesses, there is no sense of pessimism in the resolution but instead an implicit conviction that each problem could be addressed and overcome. On the other hand, the resolution shows no awareness that preparations to take the offensive or to seize weapons from the enemy would in themselves speed up the clock ticking toward war.

From late August to early November, it appears that Vo Nguyen Giap and the new French commander for northern Indochina, General Louis Constant Morlière, shared an implicit understanding to prevent local clashes from escalating into war.[62] However, the failure of the September 14 Modus Vivendi to address most of the vital issues in dispute between the DRV and France meant that both sides stepped up military preparations. In mid-October, an ICP "All-country Military Conference" met outside Hanoi to grapple with continuing issues of command, cadre selection, logistics, political work, and day-to-day altercations with the French army. A conference resolution urged that the Ministry of Defense and Military Commission be merged to form the Defense Ministry–General Command, a proposal duly approved by the National Assembly several weeks later, with Vo Nguyen Giap put in charge. The Finance Ministry was pressed to simplify procedures for dispensing funds to Defense, to allow Defense to audit its own accounts, and to increase defense allocations in line with inflation.[63] The party clearly wanted the DRV government to be responsible for feeding regular National Guard forces, but the central administration already had great difficulty meeting the costs of weapons, ammunition, clothing, and shoes.

Between October 28 and November 9 the DRV National Assembly met in Hanoi to listen to formal reports, discuss and approve the draft constitution, and form a new government. On strategic questions Ho Chi Minh showed every intent of continuing peaceful negotiations with the French, while making it clear to the assembly that Vietnam's independence and territorial integrity would never be bargained away.[64] The Constitution gave the prospective "People's Assembly" (Nghi Vien Nhan Dan) the authority to declare war by a two-thirds vote of members present; if the assembly was unable to meet that power was delegated to its Standing Committee together with the government. The president was made commander in chief of the armed forces.[65] In Ho Chi Minh's new government, Vo Nguyen Giap was defense minister and Ta Quang Buu the defense secretary (Thu truong).[66] With the exception of Hoang Huu Nam, secretary of the Interior Ministry, none of the other twenty-one members of the new government had been involved in developing DRV defense capacity. Military matters were being left to the General Command–General Staff and to the Tong Bo Viet Minh when mobilizing the militia.

It is difficult to ascertain Ho Chi Minh's confidential position on strategic options following his return from France on October 20. He undoubtedly was watching the volatile French political scene closely and hoping the November 10 general election would produce a better climate for the negotiations scheduled for January 1947. On November 5, however, Ho prepared some tough notes that have come down to us with the title of "Urgent Work Now." The first section merely outlines the personnel required to carry out a variety of military, economic, political, and communications tasks, with particular attention to selecting good party members and young men and women who had demonstrated their potential in action. The second section deals entirely with "protracted resistance" *(truong ky khang chien)*—in a few paragraphs arguing why Vietnam would emerge victorious from what was certain to be a harsh, bitter conflict. Ho warns that the enemy would fight ferociously even when near defeat, aware that his entire imperialist inheritance was at stake. The enemy would send many troop reinforcements ("not more than one hundred thousand"), aircraft, and tanks, proceeding to ravage and terrorize, hoping to spread fear among the people until they surrendered.

> But we must understand: That's the extent of enemy power. We resolutely resist to get through that "blitzkrieg" *(chop nhoang)*, the enemy will run out of steam, and we will win. So, we must possess, and cause our people to possess, inner confidence and inner determination.

It did not matter if it became necessary to evacuate the cities, as the entire countryside would be held. Here Ho offered up Nam Bo as an example, where preparations admittedly had been inadequate, the terrain difficult, yet resistance had persisted for more than a year already. He concluded, "We have good terrain and more forces; we can certainly resist for some years *(may nam)*, until victory."[67] Ho Chi Minh was overly optimistic about controlling the entire countryside, and he chose to ignore the possibility that the French would recruit increasing numbers of Vietnamese to their ranks, yet his overall conceptualization proved valid.

Despite the threat of a French coup d'état that had hovered over the DRV state since March 1946, it was not until October that serious efforts began to establish bases away from Hanoi where central institutions could continue to function if required. This was a secret ICP operation, with Nguyen Luong Bang responsible for moving material (rice, salt, currency, machinery, raw materials) and Tran Dang Ninh for organizing personnel to prepare several "safe zones" *(an toan khu)*. Already the village of Van Phuc, adjacent to Ha Dong town, was providing a venue for leaders to meet free from direct French observation. Twenty-five kilometers to the southwest of Hanoi, a larger safe zone began to take shape in November, complete with communication links, storage facilities, accommodation huts, and defense works.[68] The second safe zone was located in Thai Nguyen–Tuyen Quang, from which the small Liberation Army had emerged in late August 1945. This zone had the advantage of preexisting Viet Minh networks, which the regional commander, Chu Van Tan, had continued to nurture following his brief stint as defense minister in Hanoi. However, the entire Viet Bac area was farthest away from the rest of the country, and the possibility of Chinese Nationalist attack from the rear had to be considered. Even so, once Thanh Hoa had been rejected and the Ha Dong–Son Tay safe zone came under increasing French pressure, a government move north to Thai Nguyen–Tuyen Quang was inevitable.[69]

On November 20, 1946, French security personnel took custody of a Chinese-owned junk unloading gasoline drums in Haiphong harbor; Vietnamese police attempted to reverse this action, shooting broke out, and mixed commission officers obtained a temporary cease-fire. Haiphong had been the scene of numerous such altercations earlier in the year, and each time a way had been found to defuse the situation. On November 23, the French launched a full-scale attack, including naval gunfire and artillery barrages. Although many civilians had fled Haiphong earlier, this massive shelling killed several thousand people, including hundreds of refugees in Kien An town to the south, which the French also bombarded from the sea.[70] Loss of Haiphong was a heavy blow to the DRV government and might have provoked a call for nationwide resistance to the French, but Ho Chi Minh was still intent on making contact with whatever government materialized in Paris following the November 10 elections (a process that did not produce a new French cabinet until December 12).

Vo Nguyen Giap states that Vietnam's armed forces totaled about eighty-two thousand men in early December 1946.[71] Unfortunately neither Giap nor any other available DRV/SRV source disaggregates this figure. The closest we have is a list of thirty-two regiments and eleven independent battalions for northern and central Vietnam, from which we might extrapolate a "regular army" of about forty thousand men (including unlisted specialized services).[72] It is interesting that French intelligence estimated the Vietnamese army to total forty thousand to forty-five thousand men as of October 1946, which they said was an increase of twelve thousand to seventeen thousand since the end of 1945.[73] No estimates are available for Nam Bo in late 1946, but it is unlikely that Nguyen Binh could count on more than five thousand troops obeying his orders without question. French forces throughout Tonkin, Annam, and Cochinchina totaled almost seventy-five thousand at the end of October, with more than half of them still located in the south.[74]

Hanoi Explodes

The fate of Hanoi, the DRV capital, had major political and psychological significance. As Vuong Thua Vu and Tran Do made the rounds of every neighborhood from late October, taking stock of available forces and considering tactical options, they understood that overt military preparations risked French protests and preemptive strikes, whereas refusing to act risked being taken by surprise and losing all chance of resistance.[75] The compromise was to begin working inside buildings and in back alleys, bashing holes in walls to facilitate covert movement, using the sewers to move under streets, constructing bunkers, and stockpiling supplies. From late November, defense preparations proceeded more openly, with trucks, oxcarts, and cyclos bringing sand and dirt into the city to fill sandbags and build fortifications and street obstacles. Noncombatants were encouraged to evacuate the city, and tens of thousands did so.[76]

Throughout early December 1946, senior Vietnamese and French officials maintained almost daily communication with each other in Hanoi.[77] From December 15, the French position hardened, and some Vietnamese militia groups became more belligerent, perhaps encouraged by opponents of further talks with the French. Local altercations over barricades, transport, mixed guard operations, and inspections multiplied. During the night of December 18–19, an expanded version of the Standing Committee of the ICP Central Committee met in Van Phuc village, chaired by Ho Chi Minh. The meeting resolved to launch an all-country anti-French resistance struggle, but no time or date was specified. Inside Hanoi, on the morning of December 19, militia "suicide squads" *(doi quyet tu)* were told that rockets would go off at 6:45 PM to signal the attack.[78]

That same morning, however, Hoang Minh Giam carried a short letter from Ho Chi Minh to French negotiator Jean Sainteny in Hanoi, urging immediate local talks to reduce the tense atmosphere, pending a response from Paris to Ho's diplomatic proposals of December 15.[79] Sainteny refused to meet Giam. When Ho received this news at 12:30, he is reported to have frowned, pondered the situation for a few moments, then stated simply, "Huh! Then [we] fight" *(Hu! Thi danh).*[80] Not until after 4 PM, however, did the General Staff cable all military regions from Da Nang northward to open fire as of 8 PM that evening.[81] A number of DRV government personnel in Hanoi failed to receive word of the impending attack, continuing routine functions in the Bac Bo Phu and allowing thousands of archival dossiers to fall into the hands of the enemy. The reasons for this command confusion on December 19 have never been explained by those Vietnamese leaders in a position to know. At the very least it demonstrated inability to coordinate what had become an incredibly intricate diplomatic/military *pas de deux.* Such disparate actions also probably reflected sharp differences of opinion within the DRV government, ICP, and Tong Bo Viet Minh. Whether anyone in the leadership disobeyed explicit orders is less likely, but there were increasing signs of ill-discipline and spontaneous violence initiated by militia groups.[82]

At 8:03 PM on December 19, the lights went out in downtown Hanoi, followed soon after by shots from a cannon positioned in the suburbs. The word had reached at least some units that these actions represented authentic signals for the attack. Workers at the Yen Phu power plant had managed to smuggle explosives past French guards and detonate them almost on time.[83] Aside from damaging a power station as well as the water plant, none of the other priority targets in Hanoi appear to have suffered. Most seriously, a 250-kilogram explosive charge failed to destroy the Doumer bridge, which connected the French in Hanoi to Haiphong. French defenses at Gia Lam airport and Shell oil tanks proved too strong for the Vietnamese units available. Some of the suicide volunteers wielding shaped charges on a wooden pole managed to destroy French armored vehicles—and quickly came to symbolize the Hanoi resistance in DRV propaganda.[84]

Unlike Haiphong, the French chose not to employ their artillery as a blanket weapon in Hanoi, probably because it would have jeopardized the lines of foreign diplomats and journalists. However, French aircraft dropped bombs on occasion, and some buildings were reduced to rubble by direct gunfire. From December 30, French troops attacked the suburbs, successfully flanking National Guard defenses.[85] Throughout January 1947, more than two thousand men and women continued to defend the Thirty-six Street complex downtown, relying on grenades, Molotov cocktails, and mines as well as machine gun and rifle fire. By early February, food rations had to be reduced to a bare minimum. On January 14, Vietnamese forces lost the Dong Xuan market after a bloody eight-hour battle at close quarters. Ammunition was now down to fifty rounds per firearm. Four days later, taking advantage of early morning fog, most remaining defenders sneaked across the Red River under the Doumer bridge, using twenty boats provided from the opposite side. Four days later they received a hero's welcome from ranking officials.[86] The second month of this Thirty-six Street defense was of little military significance, but the legend of the Capital Regiment continued to grow. In October 1954, as part of the Three hundred and eighth Division, the much strengthened Capital Regiment was given the honor of leading the triumphant (and peaceful) march back into Hanoi.

Collapsing and Rebuilding

From mid-February 1947, the French launched a series of attacks in Tonkin that shattered Vietnamese defenses and produced the same sort of panic that had occurred in Hue a couple of weeks earlier. Within days, the DRV "safe zone" in western Ha Tay and Son Tay was jeopardized.[87] This was the first time that Vo Nguyen Giap had witnessed a large-scale, modern military offensive. It was also his first personal experience of a "collapsing front" *(vo mat tran)*. As he stated bluntly:

> A collapsing front is entirely different from circumstances where our forces decide to retreat . . . Many units lose contact. Vacillation invades the thinking of cadres and soldiers. Some cadres run far, some soldiers suddenly desert. The people also become irresolute, believing the enemy is too strong. This phenomenon certainly will not cease if there is no standpoint, no method to cope with it in time.[88]

As Giap later admitted, however, the collapsing front "phenomenon" eventually stopped in northern Vietnam because National Guard forces "no longer deployed to block the advance of the enemy."[89]

On March 20, three National Guard battalions and one artillery company counterattacked Ha Dong town, catching the French by surprise and seizing several enemy positions. But they were not able to overwhelm enemy units taking cover in concrete colonial buildings, and they themselves were caught from the rear when French reinforcements arrived from nearby Hanoi.[90] Vo Nguyen Giap drew two lessons: Vietnamese forces lacked the capacity to do more than surprise the enemy, cause partial damage, and then withdraw expeditiously; and regiments were too large a unit currently to mount an effective attack.[91] During the 1947 rainy season, French attacks dropped off substantially, giving the National Guard and many militia groups time to regroup, reprovision, and retrain. Giap himself had time to reread Karl von Clausewitz and Mao Zedong. He increased his professional respect for French forces, admitting, "For the first time we saw clearly that the French army not only possessed very strong weaponry and equipment, but was expert in the military arts too."[92] Giap also convinced his peers that it would be a mistake to try to build National Guard brigades, as some still argued. On the contrary, regiments needed to be disaggregated, with one main force battalion and regimental headquarters staying together, while the other battalions dispersed their companies to specific localities. When an opportunity arose they could recombine, accomplish the mission, then disperse again.[93] Not until August 1949 was it feasible to establish the Three hundred and eighth Brigade (formally known as the Vanguard Army Brigade). Its commander was Vuong Thua Vu, who had been responsible for the Hanoi front in December 1946.[94] Soon Vietnamese units were being trained, reequipped and advised by the Chinese Red Army. The DRV finally had an ally.

SIX

◆ ◆ ◆

Forging the "Great Combination"

Britain and the Indochina Problem,
1945–1950

MARK ATWOOD LAWRENCE

IN 1945, BRITISH policymakers had little doubt what they needed to accomplish in Indochina. Britain, they believed, must work strenuously to guard French sovereignty and to provide the new French government with the military and economic strength to recover control. The challenge in realizing these goals was obvious. Decimated by years of war, Britain utterly lacked the political and material strength to restore the French position by itself. Clearly, London could achieve its objectives only with the support of the new Pacific hegemon that possessed seemingly boundless political clout and material wherewithal: the United States. Yet as the war against Japan drew to a close, Washington showed little but hostility for British aspirations. President Franklin Delano Roosevelt steadfastly opposed the recolonization of Indochina and advanced his trusteeship proposals. Even when American opposition waned following Roosevelt's death in April 1945, U.S. policymakers disappointed London by showing no interest in taking action to support a French recovery. Still wary of French designs, Washington embraced mere neutrality. Frustrated British officials, desperate to build Western unity behind French aims, begged and pressured their U.S. counterparts to change their minds.

By 1954, at the other end of the First Vietnam War, the situation had changed dramatically. As the climactic battle of Dien Bien Phu got under way, Americans were heavily engaged in Indochina, paying more than three-quarters of the costs of the war. American leaders spoke of Indochina with determination that would have delighted British counterparts a decade earlier. The failure of Western policy in the area, the

Eisenhower administration insisted, would mean "incalculable" set-backs for the free world, including possibly the loss of all Southeast Asia to communism. The British government, by contrast, now wanted little to do with the situation and resisted Washington's calls for West-ern unity. When President Dwight D. Eisenhower and Secretary of State John Foster Dulles asked London to support military interven-tion by a coalition of Western powers—the "United Action" plan—British policymakers dragged their feet. Foreign Minister Anthony Eden protested that Western activism on behalf of France would be a "great mistake," insisting that "none of us in London believe that inter-vention in Indochina can do anything." Even Prime Minister Winston Churchill, hardly one to shrink from unpromising military undertak-ings, wanted no part of the U.S. idea. "I have known many reverses myself," he asserted. "I have suffered Singapore, Hong-Kong, Tobruk; the French will have Dien Bien Phu." Eisenhower was outraged, com-plaining that London showed "woeful unawareness" of the risks the West was running by failing to join forces and to act boldly in Indo-china. But the damage was done. British opposition, in the words of historians George C. Herring and Richard H. Immerman, "struck a body blow at United Action."[1]

How can we account for this reversal of roles? Scholars have had little trouble explaining the shift in the American attitude. The com-munist victory in China and surging anticommunism at home, along with the perceived need for a robust and cooperative France at the heart of the anti-Soviet bloc of Western nations, led U.S. policymakers to set aside their doubts about French colonialism and to throw Amer-ican support behind the French war effort in 1950.[2] The British shift is more mysterious. As the Cold War intensified between 1947 and 1954, London lost interest in promoting a resolute Western coalition to fight communism in Indochina. Two possible explanations can be ruled out immediately. The shift did not result simply from personnel changes in London. Remarkably, two of the men who most strongly championed Western solidarity in 1945—Churchill and Foreign Secretary Anthony Eden—counseled caution a decade later when they held the same of-fices. Nor did the shift result merely from British anxiety over the possible use of nuclear weapons in 1954 if the United Action plan had gone ahead. To be sure, London's visceral opposition to nuclear op-tions as a way to rescue the besieged French garrison contributed to its hostility to American proposals. But nuclear anxiety was not the crux of the matter. London pushed not for nonnuclear forms of intervention but for a negotiated settlement of the war.

The mystery of British behavior merits scrutiny partly because of what we can learn about Britain's withdrawal from its long-standing global role during the Cold War. How and when did British leaders accept limits on their capacity for bold action in the Far East? Scholarly focus on the 1956 Suez Crisis and the later withdrawal from imperial strong points "east of Suez" has pulled attention from less prominent episodes in earlier periods that might offer insight into these central questions of British imperial history. An examination of British policy-making with regard to Indochina offers a useful window into London's rapidly changing appreciation of its weaknesses in the Far East and of its determination to draw on U.S. strength to manage the creation of a new postcolonial order and to preserve as much as possible of Britain's status as a great power. This study also builds on existing scholarship connected to British imperial decline by suggesting the complicated ways in which shifting calculations about Britain's own territories affected London's decisions with respect to colonial territories held by other powers.[3]

Additionally, British calculations in Southeast Asia deserve attention because of their connection to the history of U.S. intervention in Vietnam. A major development in the Vietnam conflict during the 1950s was, of course, the emergence of the United States as the principal non-Asian power in Indochina. This trend began with the Truman administration's decision in 1950 to grant military and economic aid to bolster the French war effort and culminated in 1963 with the coup against Ngo Dinh Diem, when Washington effectively took direct control. In part, this process reflected mounting American certainty of Indochina's importance to the West. But the process also reflected a gradual dropping away of other governments that had invested themselves in the Indochina controversy during the first Cold War years. By 1965, the Johnson administration found very few governments willing to fight alongside the United States.[4] Certainly, Britain was not among them. This skittishness had its roots in much earlier years. Examination of those roots illuminates some of the underlying problems that marred U.S. prospects of success during the American war.

This essay argues that British caution in Indochina, so evident by 1954, stemmed from a complicated set of calculations by the government of Clement Attlee in the crucial period from 1945 to 1950. These years rank among the most decisive in the history of Vietnam's twentieth-century wars. It was then that U.S. officials embraced the key assumptions that would guide Washington's policymaking over the next quarter century. These were also the years when Britain, the most likely Western partner (other than France) for the United States in its counterrevolutionary mission in Indochina, stepped into the background. It did so for two reasons. First, the Labour government calculated that it had much to lose by maintaining an assertive posture in Indochina. Not only did Indochina represent a drain on scarce British resources, but close association with the French war effort threatened to damage the government in the eyes of critical constituencies at home and abroad. Second, the government abandoned its leading role because it calculated that it could do so without significantly undermining the goal that London had pursued since World War II: the restoration of French rule. This confidence reflected growing British optimism by 1950 that the United States could be counted upon to pursue this objective at the forefront of a multinational "great combination" in Southeast Asia that served Britain's interests across the region without British leadership in every area.[5]

Wartime Calculations

During World War II, British policymakers supported the restoration of French colonialism in Indochina for three major reasons. First, they anticipated that an American challenge to French rule in Indochina would lead Washington to question colonial rule elsewhere in Southeast Asia. Most British officials had little regard for French colonialism, but they did not trust Americans to draw distinctions between the performances of the various colonial powers. "Any such attempt to abrogate French rule in Indo-China cannot fail to react on the position of other nations holding possessions in the Far East, e.g., the Dutch and ourselves," warned the British ambassador in Chungking.[6]

Second, British policymakers backed French rule because they believed that France was far more likely than any other potential source of authority in Indochina to reestablish political and economic stability. This was no small matter given British policymakers' conviction that Indochina would set the trend for the entire region. Anticipating the "domino theory" that would later play a central role in U.S. decision-making, London strategists envisioned the French territory as a crucial barrier between Chinese power to the north and the chain of resource-rich territories to the south and west, including British territories such as Malaya, Singapore, and Burma. It therefore seemed crucial to keep Indochina in reliable hands. "The potential threat to Australia, New Zealand, India, Burma, Malaya, and the East Indies Archipelago resulting from Indochina being in the hands of a weak or unfriendly power has been sufficiently demonstrated by the action of Japan in this war," asserted one Foreign Office study.[7]

Third, London supported French claims to Indochina out of conviction that everything must be done to restore France as a robust partner in European affairs. British policymakers were virtually unanimous in their view that a cooperative and reliable France would be essential to the stability of Western Europe in the postwar period. To deprive France of its territory in Southeast Asia risked torpedoing Anglo-French cooperation before it could even get started. "Any attempt to interfere with French sovereignty over Indo-China," asserted a 1944 briefing paper for Prime Minister Churchill, "would be passionately resented by France and would have incalculable results not only in the Far East but in Europe."[8] London's wartime confrontation with Vichy provided only the most recent evidence of the dangers Britain might face from an unfriendly France. Britain must never again "find a hostile power within 250 miles of London," insisted Foreign Office analyst Victor Cavendish-Bentinck.[9]

Motivated in all of these ways, the British military worked strenuously during the closing months of the Pacific War to back Gaullist efforts to assure that Indochina remained under French sovereignty following its liberation from Japan. At the end of 1944, the British Chiefs of Staff ignored U.S. objectives and welcomed French general Roger Blaizot and his fifty-member staff on a mission thinly disguised as a "personal visit" to the British-dominated South East Asia Command (SEAC) in Kandy, Ceylon.[10] Meanwhile, SEAC commander Lord Louis Mountbatten provided support for Free French operatives in Indochina throughout 1944 and encouraged cooperation between the British intelligence apparatus in the Far East and its Gaullist counterpart. In December 1944 alone, British forces carried out forty-six air operations and succeeded in establishing a radio network among resistance cells in Indochina, building up stores of military equipment for use in a possible future campaign against Japan, and occasionally transporting French agents into and out of the region.[11]

British officials recognized, however, that French needs over the long term greatly exceeded what Britain could offer. To restore French rule and—equally important to British planners—to repair the badly damaged Indochinese economy would plainly require impossible amounts of economic and military assistance. Five years of grueling war had taken an enormous toll on the British economy, leaving few resources for initiatives in peripheral locations on behalf of other governments. Between 1939 and 1945, Britain had lost about a quarter of its national wealth, run up a foreign debt of £3 billion, and become overwhelmingly dependent on the United States for war material of all sorts.[12] Such imbalances weakened London's influence around the world but held particular significance in the Far East, where the gap between Britain's commitments and resources was widest. Given Britain's own military preoccupations, British leaders repeatedly cautioned French counterparts that they could provide very little of what France needed most: military gear and ships to transport troops to Indochina. "The French must realise," insisted J. C. Sterndale Bennett, head of the Foreign Office's Southeast Asia office, "that, [despite] the best will in the world, equipment and transport difficulties are very great and that priorities must be arranged accordingly."[13]

Inescapably, British policymakers concluded that they could achieve their objectives in Indochina only by harnessing the vast military and economic power of the United States. In the near term, no other country could provide the military resources that Britain lacked in Southeast Asia. But American support seemed equally vital over the longer term. The cabinet agreed that Britain would be able to defend its Far Eastern possessions from new threats only if the United States participated in the construction of a new multilateral security system covering the entire region, including French Indochina. "France is unlikely, for some time at least, to be strong enough to defend Indo-China by herself, and it is therefore important to the future security of India, Burma, and Malaya and of the British Commonwealth and empire in the South Pacific that the United States should be directly involved in the event of an attack on Indo-China," asserted a 1944 postwar-planning memorandum endorsed by the cabinet.[14] Colonial Office policymakers similarly believed that only the United States could provide the economic and technical aid necessary to restore colonial economies badly damaged by the war. All in all, the cabinet agreed in 1944, it was "essential" that the United States participate actively in the postwar defense and economic rehabilitation of Southeast Asia. The governments of the three Pacific Dominions—Australia, New Zealand, and Canada—were even more adamant on the point. In their view, declining British capabilities left the United States as the sole possible guarantor of stability in the Far East.[15]

Accordingly, British diplomats struggled over the final months of the Pacific war to convince Americans to accept French and British plans for Indochina. To be sure, Churchill declined to press the matter with Roosevelt. The Foreign Office and the British Chiefs of Staff were not so accommodating, however, and peppered Washington with appeals to accept the restoration of French rule, especially after Japanese forces overthrew the French puppet administration on March 9, 1945. The coup strengthened the British case by provoking a modest resistance campaign by French troops in Tonkin. British officials could now insist that Washington throw its support behind French ambitions as a way not only to bolster political and economic stability in Southeast Asia but also to demonstrate support for an ally in the fight against a common enemy. Although French leaders were clearly alarmed by Japan's bid to erase the last vestiges of French sovereignty, Sterndale Bennett captured the cautiously upbeat mood in London when he pointed out that the coup "may in the long run work out in their best interests." The spectacle of French soldiers fighting and dying in a battle against Japan offered, Stendale Bennett insisted, "the best propaganda that the French could have in the United States" in their effort to win American support for French recovery of the territory.[16] British leaders watched intently for a change in Washington's attitude.

The Taint of French Colonialism, 1945

The months following the Japanese coup brought the British government little satisfaction. To be sure, as many scholars have observed, FDR showed uncertainty about the trusteeship scheme in the last weeks of his life.[17] More important, the new Truman administration abandoned the idea entirely during its first month in office and made clear to the French government that it would not block restoration of French rule. But all of this movement, while comprising a significant moment in the history of U.S. embroilment in Vietnam, fell short of what British officials desired: active American support of French aims and cooperation with nascent efforts to establish a new political and economic order in Southeast Asia. Instead, Washington embraced mere neutrality. The United States would not obstruct the restoration of French sovereignty, but neither would it give active backing. British leaders worried, too, that the revised U.S. attitude might prove fleeting. As the global situation developed, they feared Americans might rediscover their anticolonial enthusiasms.

Disappointed by the limited evolution in the U.S. position, British policymakers saw no choice but to go it alone, at least for the foreseeable future, to support the restoration of French rule. In the final weeks of the Pacific war, Mountbatten and the British Chiefs of Staff intensified their long-simmering diplomatic battle with U.S. general Albert Wedemeyer, the U.S. commander in Chungking, to define the boundaries of Allied military theaters in the Far East in a way that would permit British forces to carry out extensive operations in Indochina. Only by forcing that issue, Mountbatten recognized, could the British military give the kind of help that France required. Accordingly, the U.S. decision to cede the southern half of Indochina to postwar occupation by British forces—a minor agenda item at the Potsdam Conference in July 1945—represented a significant British victory. The decision fell short of hopes entertained by some officials that all of Indochina would fall to British jurisdiction, and it stemmed more from declining U.S. interest in the whole issue than any real shift in American attitudes about Indochina. Still, the division of Indochina provided London with an opportunity to reinstall a French military and administrative presence below the sixteenth parallel, a foothold that France could presumably exploit to recover the rest of the country from Chinese control.

As soon as Japan surrendered, British authorities moved quickly to make the most of their chance. At Mountbatten's insistence, London allocated scarce ships, including eight U.S.-flagged Liberty ships loaned by the United States, to transport French troops and military equipment to Indochina in the early fall. In Saigon, meanwhile, Major General Douglas Gracey, the commander of British occupation troops in southern Indochina, rearmed more than one thousand French soldiers who had been imprisoned since the Japanese coup in March. On September 24, British forces—mainly a division of Indian troops—went further by overturning the rudimentary administration that the Viet Minh had established in Saigon following Ho Chi Minh's declara-

tion of independence. Even as Gracey declared Britain's "strict impar-
tiality" in Vietnamese politics, he banned all demonstrations, processions,
public meetings, and unauthorized carrying of weapons. Looters and
saboteurs, he warned, would be "summarily shot."[18]

These actions achieved the desired result. Thanks to British support,
the new French administration and a reconstituted French military
gradually extended their control over most of southern Indochina during the autumn. But British activism also yielded an undesired, unexpected result: growing discomfort in London over the political
implications of siding so openly and forcefully with French colonialism. While Gracey moved ahead boldly in Saigon, the Labour Party's
left wing threatened to rebel against the government's complicity in
the French reconquest. The Labour cabinet that took power in July
1945 consisted mainly of men who championed the need to protect
Britain's global interests and promoted a cautious approach to colonial devolution. They were, as historian John Darwin has phrased it,
"remarkably unradical."[19] The party as a whole, however, encompassed
a wide range of views and paid at least lip service to the goals of development and self-determination in the colonial world. During World
War II, the party's study group on imperial questions, the Fabian Colonial Society, captured this reformist spirit in various publications focused on planning for the postwar period. "There lies immediately
ahead a period of great formative possibilities in colonial development, in which the British Government, under the stress of new economic circumstances, will probably be moving in the very direction
which we, as socialists, want, and in which it may prove possible to secure far-reaching progress," asserted one hopeful article in April 1945.
"Nevertheless," it cautioned, "there remain dangers from the opposing
interests of certain sectional groups, so that a policy of critical vigilance
will be just as necessary in the future as in the past."[20]

While many Labour politicians backed away from such rhetoric once
the Labour Party gained power in July 1945, a left-leaning bloc clung to
that vision and applied pressure on the cabinet to maintain a "socialist"
line on colonial matters. During October and November 1945, members of Parliament repeatedly put cabinet ministers on the defensive by
asking embarrassing questions about British activities in Indochina
and the Dutch East Indies, where British troops had also taken charge
of managing the transition to postwar administration.[21] In October,

fifty-eight of the 393 Labour members of Parliament signed a letter denouncing the role played by British forces in restoring French and
Dutch colonialism.[22] Opposition to the government's policy reached
the party's highest levels. "It is a matter of regret and bitter shame that
British and Indian troops should be sent to restore tyranny in the Pacific areas," the chairman of Labour's executive committee, Harold
Laski, complained on November 15. It was to be expected, he declared, that the "Tory-dominated coalition" of the wartime years would
engage in the suppression of "free peoples" in Asia; that the Labour
Party would preside over such actions was shameful.[23]

A second source of pressure added to the Attlee government's worries. As Gracey's forces reestablished French power in southern Indochina, nationalists elsewhere in Asia lashed out against British behavior.
Most worrying, Jawaharlal Nehru and other leading Indian nationalists
sharply criticized Britain's role in Indochina and, more specifically, its
use of Indian troops for colonial purposes. Nehru compared Britain's
occupation in Indochina to "the war of intervention which Fascist Italy
and Nazi Germany waged in Spain" and warned that Indians watched
"with growing anger, shame and helplessness that Indian troops should
thus be used for doing Britain's dirty work against our friends who are
fighting the same fight as we."[24]

Such complaints resounded loudly in Whitehall. As the Labour government accelerated plans to grant India's independence, it grew
more sensitive to the need to maintain harmony with key nationalists
who would likely come to power in a new Indian state. By October
1945, the relationship seemed to be in jeopardy. Indian opposition to
the British role in Indochina and the East Indies became so fierce that
the British commander in New Delhi refused to allow South East Asia
Command to use bases on the subcontinent as staging areas or transfer
points for French troops on their way to Indochina.[25] "Protest against
[the] use of Indian troops in French Indo China and Java has already
begun and may develop into considerable agitation," the viceroy reported from India at the end of September.[26] In Kandy, Mountbatten's
political adviser, M. Esler Dening, warned against any further actions
that might be interpreted abroad as suppression of legitimate nationalist aspirations. "I think we may find ourselves involved in a political
commitment which will not be in our interests and which may arouse
general criticism both in the Far East and in America," Dening wrote.[27]

British leaders reacted to the growing sense of danger in various ways. In London, the government stressed that its purpose in Indochina was merely to accept the surrender of Japanese troops. Addressing criticism from the Labour back benches, Foreign Secretary Ernest Bevin assured the House of Commons on October 24 that London had no interest in becoming "unnecessarily involved in the administration or in the political affairs of non-British territories."[28] In Kandy, Mountbatten urged French officials in Southeast Asia to help ease criticism by proclaiming a program of liberal reforms for Indochina, including a promise of eventual autonomy within the French empire.[29] Even Gracey, an archcolonialist who had spent his career in India, concluded at the end of September that announcement of a "firm but progressive policy defined in detail" was urgent if France wished "to avoid a running sore for many years."[30] To get Franco-Vietnamese reconciliation moving, Gracey's political adviser, Harry Brain, mediated a series of meetings between Viet Minh representatives and the French high commissioner for Cochinchina, Colonel Jean Cédile.[31] Those meetings accomplished little, but British officials worked hard to call public attention to their peacemaking efforts.[32]

Above all, British officials in both London and the Far East strove to limit British military activity in Indochina. As a first step, Mountbatten ordered Gracey to restrict his troops to the Saigon area and to rely as much as possible on French and even Japanese troops to maintain order. "Problems connected with the independence of Indo-China must be dealt with by the French, in the same way as the British had to deal with such problems in Burma and Malaya, and the Dutch in the Netherlands East Indies," Dening told General Jacques Philippe Leclerc, the newly appointed French commander in Indochina.[33] But the surer method of minimizing the political danger was to evacuate British troops from the country altogether. The Joint Planning Staff in London spelled out the logic:

In French Indo-China, as in other British and non-British territories in South and South East Asia, there are independence movements as to which precise information is at present lacking. It should not be our policy to take sides in this matter, either with the French against the [nationalist] movements or with the movements against the French. Preservation of an attitude of complete neutrality is the ideal but as long as British forces remain in Indo-China, it will be very difficult to sustain. Failure to sustain it on the other hand will involve us in very se-

rious international implications. It follows therefore that from the political point of view, the sooner British forces can be withdrawn from
Indo-China, the better.[34]

Immediately after toppling the Vietnamese administration of Saigon
on September 24, Mountbatten urged the Chiefs of Staff in London to
give "over-riding priority" to the shipment of French troops from
France. "Every day of delay in providing sufficient French troops to enable Leclerc to take over responsibility in [Indochina]," he wrote,
"magnifies the danger that British/Indian troops may become involved in large scale fighting on French territory."[35] The cabinet rejected the acceleration request because of the severe strain on British
shipping, but increasingly nervous SEAC officials in Kandy went ahead
anyway with planning for the withdrawal of Gracey's forces as soon as
adequate French forces were in place.[36]

The risks seemed to mount dangerously as French forces arrived in
Indochina at an agonizingly slow rate. Sterndale Bennett warned in
early 1946 that U.S. hostility toward the British performance in Saigon
might even imperil London's chances of winning the massive postwar
reconstruction loan then being negotiated in Washington. "[The
American] impression was that the position in Indo-China was getting
much worse and could cause some trouble [with winning congressional approval of the loan]," Sterndale Bennett wrote after talks at the
U.S. embassy in London.[37] Dangers in Asia also seemed to grow in ways
that threatened Britain's most essential postwar objectives. In New
Delhi, British officials predicted strong pressure to end all Indian involvement in British military activities if the controversial occupations
of Indochina and the East Indies were not ended quickly. The possibility of a sudden Indian refusal to participate in British imperial defense
presented the War Office with the nightmarish prospect that it might
lack the manpower to fulfill British obligations throughout the commonwealth and empire. "If we are unable to employ Indian troops outside India it will be necessary to reconsider our plans for deployment
not only in South East Asia Command but throughout the world," the
Joint Planning Staff warned.[38]

At last, in the first weeks of 1946, South East Asia Command judged
that French forces were sufficiently strong and began withdrawing
Gracey's division. South East Asia Command dissolved Gracey's headquarters in late January, and most of the Indian division departed

shortly thereafter, leaving only a small force to manage the upkeep of Japanese troops awaiting repatriation. British commanders carefully choreographed the withdrawal to dampen criticism of the role that they had played. The Chiefs of Staff urged "due publicity" for the removal of British troops in order to emphasize that Britain had fulfilled its role in Indochina—the disarmament and repatriation of Japanese troops—and was withdrawing without further ado. At a January 27 ceremony in Saigon marking his departure, Gracey declared his mission a "great success" but refused to accept decorations from the French military, a gesture aimed to impress upon international opinion that the British occupation had never been intended to serve French interests.[39]

The withdrawal heralded what would be, for the British, a much less stressful year in Indochina. British observers worried that French authorities were badly mismanaging the economic and political situation as they extended their grip in southern Indochina and then, following the March 1946 accord with China, the northern part as well. Alarm about the recovery of Indochinese rice production remained especially acute because of the risk that a shortfall in Indochinese exports would fuel turmoil in India, which relied heavily on rice from abroad. But the French government's frequent assurances of its liberal intentions in Indochina, coupled with the apparent willingness of Vietnamese nationalists to negotiate, encouraged optimism in London that the Indochina controversies of 1945 would be resolved through compromise and cautious devolution—precisely the sort of solution to colonial problems that London preferred. Britain seemed to have emerged from its Indochina occupation unscathed.

The Taint of French Colonialism, 1947

This improved situation unraveled in 1947 with the escalation of the Franco–Viet Minh War. Suddenly, British officials confronted grave new hazards in Indochina. The basic conundrum was familiar: On the one hand, British leaders wished to defend French interests in order to maximize stability in Southeast Asia and to show support for a key ally. On the other, they recognized the potency of anticolonial sentiment at home and abroad and were eager to avoid the taint that would inevitably come with an actively pro-French policy. The danger of alienating Asian nationalist opinion seemed especially grave. Hostility to French military action spread swiftly across East Asia as nationalists seized upon the war as a rallying point for anticolonial agitation. In Colombo, Ceylonese stevedores refused to service French ships.[40] Similar problems arose in Malaya and Singapore, where labor unions refused to refuel or handle goods on ships carrying war material or troops to Indochina.[41] Even in Japan, demonstrators protested French aggression outside the French embassy and demanded Vietnamese independence.[42]

Anti-French agitation was gravest of all in India and Burma, whose status as countries making the transition to independence conferred upon them a degree of moral authority in the region. In India, nationalist leaders Nehru and Sarat Chandra Bose, backed by assertive nationalist media, repeatedly expressed their sympathy for the Democratic Republic of Vietnam both publicly and in private conversations with Western diplomats. Meanwhile, radical nationalists in India, Burma, Malaya, and Ceylon urged the creation of volunteer forces to fight alongside the Viet Minh. French officials worried most, however, about a more realistic and immediate threat—Indian and Burmese reluctance to allow French ships and planes to pass through their territories. That resistance not only created propaganda problems but also raised alarm about the ability of the French military to maintain the lifeline of supplies and troops to Indochina. Increasingly anxious about a slowdown of troops and supplies reaching Vietnam, the French foreign ministry turned to the British government to apply pressure on Indian and Burmese leaders.

London responded cautiously, an indication of the serious dangers that British leaders saw looming in Asia. With Britain preparing to withdraw from India and Burma, policymakers viewed Southeast Asia as the new focus of British influence in Asia and as a crucial crossroads of trade and communication between Europe, Africa, and Australia. It was therefore crucial to avoid alienating Southeast Asian opinion through close association with France. "We must not appear to be ganging up with [the] Western Powers against Eastern peoples striving for independence," asserted Dening, now head of the Foreign Office's Southeast Asia division. "Rather should our aim be to contrive a general partnership between independent or about-to-be independent Eastern peoples and the Western Powers."[43] Following this logic, London declined to apply pressure on Asian governments to accommodate the French war effort. With backing from the British governor, Burmese leaders agreed to allow passage of no more than two French aircraft per day.[44] Similarly, the interim government in New Delhi agreed to allow only one transport plane per week to land in India or to fly through Indian air space. British authorities warned the French military that any attempt to exceed this limit might lead to refusal to allow any flights at all.[45]

New political pressures within the Labour Party heightened British caution. One Asia expert at the Foreign Office wrote in January 1947 that he dreaded the day when "awkward questions will be asked in Parliament" about the Attlee government's support for French colonialism.[46] That time arrived a month later when a Labour back-bencher objected to the government's plan to negotiate an alliance with France (the Treaty of Dunkirk) while the latter brazenly violated socialist principles on colonialism. Pinned in a delicate position, Ernest Bevin evasively replied that France was merely restoring order in Indochina in order to create "conditions in which her liberal program can find its realization." But the foreign secretary's discomfiture was plain. In a departure from earlier parliamentary statements about Indochina, Bevin made no mention of British support for France. Rather, he sought to distance Britain from the matter, asserting that Indochina was strictly "a matter for the French Government."[47]

All of this cautious behavior in no way meant that the British government had abandoned the view that French control in Indochina served Britain's interests in the Far East. A French military victory seemed the most likely way to establish economic and political stability throughout the region and to temper nationalist demands within Britain's Southeast Asian possessions. Accordingly, when British officials saw an opportunity to support the French military without risking political damage in Asia, they did so. London approved shipments of weapons for use by French troops as long as there was little chance of publicity. On one occasion, the British high commissioner in the Far East, Lord Killearn, rejected a plan to supply munitions from British stocks in Singapore. Such a move, he warned, could land Britain "in extremely deep waters" if it became known. Bevin's solution, approved by Attlee, was to send the munitions from Britain to metropolitan France, which could then reship the arms to the Far East on its own vessels.[48] The British government could, then, escape direct responsibility for its actions. When such a ruse was not possible, the British government erred on the side of caution. Despite French pressure to help enable planes and ships to pass through India and Burma, British authorities conceded to nationalist opinion in almost all cases, leaving the French to negotiate their own deals. The Royal Air Force worried about losing reciprocal rights for British planes and ships to stop in Indochina, but the much more serious threat of Asian outrage against Britain deterred London from helping France.[49]

Seeking the "Great Combination"

As early as 1944, the British government had foreseen that it could escape from its dilemmas in Indochina by attracting U.S. support for French policy. If the United States could be led to take charge of upholding the Western position in Indochina, in other words, Britain could shed both the material burden and the political risks connected to a policy of active support for France. In 1944 and much of 1945, London's eagerness for such a solution stemmed mainly from its acute awareness of Britain's material shortcomings in the Far East. With barely enough resources to secure British territories, officials understood the risks of taking on burdens in Indochina and the East Indies. The solution of securing a U.S. commitment in Indochina gained even more appeal following the Vietnamese revolution and the political complications that resulted from the British occupation below the sixteenth parallel.

By early 1946, London saw little prospect of bringing about a decisive shift in the American attitude. Discouraged, British officials aimed their efforts more at preventing a total withdrawal of U.S. interest from the Indochina problem than at encouraging an expanded American role. Around the end of 1945, for example, the British Chiefs of Staff struggled to prevent the United States from ending its nominal participation in South East Asia Command, a move that would have confirmed the impression of sole British responsibility for the status of Southeast Asian territories. As long as the United States remained formally a part of the SEAC command, British authorities could insist that their actions in Indochina served "Allied," rather than narrowly "British," interests.

The abrupt reintensification of the British government's dilemma following the outbreak of the Franco–Viet Minh War sharply increased London's determination to pull the United States into the region. In material terms, U.S. support for the French war effort would carry massive financial and logistical advantages for Britain. More important, linking the United States to the French cause would lessen the political risks by enabling the British government to withdraw to a secondary role in Indochina and by helping to recast the war as a struggle for democracy and stability rather than imperial conquest. The intensification of Cold War hostility during 1947 and 1948, combined with mounting international anxiety about the Viet Minh's communist orientation, created a clear opportunity to redefine the war in this way.

British officials were by no means convinced, it is important to note, that the Viet Minh amounted to a communist organization that fit neatly into the emerging Cold War paradigm. Since 1945, Foreign Office experts had expressed skepticism about French portrayals of the Viet Minh as a servant of international communism. British appraisals changed little over the following three years, even as Cold War tensions mounted in other parts of the world and Mao Zedong's communist forces gained momentum in China. In early 1948, the new commissioner general in Singapore, Malcolm MacDonald, noted that there was "still little sign" of Soviet activity in Southeast Asia and warned against misunderstanding the nature of communist activism in the region. "There is a tendency, perhaps more pronounced among our Dutch and French friends, to lump together under the term 'communists' all those—whether communists, nationalists or merely bad hats— who actively oppose colonial rule," insisted MacDonald. "If it is necessary to generalise on this point," he added, "it would be more accurate to say that if you suppress a nationalist severely enough you will find him tending toward Communism because it is the Communists who have consistently supported nationalist movements in dependent territories."[50] Again and again, British experts blamed the French for creating whatever communist menace existed in Indochina. "French opposition to legitimate nationalist aims," one Foreign Office study contended in November 1948, provided a "particularly favorable field for Communist penetration of the whole Nationalist movement."[51]

Despite such nuanced views, London appealed to Washington to take a more active role in Indochina as a way to combat the expansion of communism. Beginning in early 1947, British officials, hoping that Cold War tensions would heighten the appeal of international cooperation, dramatically stepped up their effort to build the United States into regional organizations designed to coordinate the policies of independent Asian states and Western governments. In March 1947, the Foreign Office asked the U.S. State Department to appoint an official with powers comparable to the British commissioner general for Far Eastern affairs in order to facilitate cooperation against the communist threat. The Truman administration rejected that idea but accepted another British proposal in October. The U.S. Joint Chiefs of Staff, acting mainly out of alarm about communist advances in China, agreed to hold talks with their British counterparts to consider harmonizing U.S. and British defense policies in the Far East.[52]

British diplomats redoubled their proposals for Western cooperation in 1948 as the situation in Indochina deteriorated and as London confronted problems of its own elsewhere in Southeast Asia. Commissioner General MacDonald declared a state of emergency in Malaya in June as communist rebels targeted major British economic assets in the colony. The urgency of the British response stemmed above all from the extraordinary importance of Malayan natural resources to the imperiled British economy. Amid persistent crisis fueled by dwindling dollar reserves, Malayan rubber and tin stood out as the most important dollar-earning commodities in the entire British empire. As historian Andrew J. Rotter has demonstrated, the Attlee government could tolerate no threat to resources critical to Britain's economic stability.[53]

This new crisis, along with other communist-tinged flare-ups elsewhere in Southeast Asia around the same time, heightened British alarm about a possible domino effect in Southeast Asia. A French defeat in Indochina would, in this view, create irresistible pressure on other parts of Southeast Asia already weakened by instability. "If the Viet Minh forces were to gain notable successes, this would have widespread repercussions in neighboring territories," asserted a Foreign Office overview of the situation. "Indo-China was the springboard for the Japanese attack against South East Asia, so it seems not impossible that it will become a springboard for the advance of Communism westwards across Asia."[54] The British ambassador in Bangkok was more direct. "The frontiers of Malaya," he declared, are on the Mekong."[55]

Consistently frustrated in their effort to hand the burden to the United States, British officials saw no alternative to new initiatives to support the French war effort. London increased transfers of military equipment and approved bilateral talks with French commanders about the defense of Southeast Asia. As in earlier years, however, British officials had little enthusiasm for such endeavors. Close association with French policy remained a cause of deep anxiety, partly because many British policymakers doubted that the new French scheme for building political stability in Vietnam—the Bao Dai solution—stood much chance of success. Even after the French government conferred new powers on Bao Dai in June 1948, British opinion remained deeply skeptical. The Bao Dai solution "appears more and more to be a puppet set-up," complained the British consul in Hanoi. "One cannot see how such a Government can possibly bring about any change in the atmosphere, except to harden the hearts of the Viet Minh."[56]

British anxiety also flowed from familiar sources. When a member of Parliament decried the war against the Viet Minh and lashed out at the government for reinstalling French colonialism in 1945, one Foreign Office aide conceded that there was "some truth" in the charge and cringed at the possibility of new controversy within the Labour ranks. It would be politically "difficult," wrote the official, to dodge pressure to criticize the brutality of the French war.[57] The other source of British anxiety—the animosity of Asian nationalists crucial to the prepetuation of British influence in Asia—also continued to weigh heavily. Nehru and other Indian leaders missed few opportunities to criticize the French war. It is important to point out that Nehru remained wary of Ho Chi Minh's communist loyalties and refused to provide material support. But he was adamant about the injustice of French policy and the cynicism underlying the Bao Dai policy.[58] Bao Dai was, in Nehru's view, a "nice boy" but, given the fundamental failure of French policy, "unable to succeed."[59]

British diplomats worked strenuously between 1948 and 1950 to convince independent Asian governments, especially those of India and Thailand, to change their attitudes toward French policy and to join a Western-led coalition. Endorsement by even one or two Asian nations would ease the dangers to Britain by giving far more credibility to claims that the Indochina war was a conflict between nationalism and communism, not between nationalism and colonialism. Backing from within Asia also promised to help bring about the ultimate solution to British problems in Southeast Asia: an alignment of Asian and Western powers united by an anticommunist agenda and backed by the material strength of the United States. "The U.S.A. is the focus of the whole, and without the U.S.A. the whole conception would break down," asserted one Foreign Office study.[60] Sir William Strang, the Foreign Office's permanent undersecretary, emphasized what he considered to be a natural division of labor within a new Far Eastern grouping. "We have a part to play in this area which can be played by no other power," he wrote. "It can best be played by a combination of British experience and United States resources."[61]

The problem, as always, lay in convincing Washington to accede to this arrangement. British officials had no doubt that American interests lay in preventing a Viet Minh victory in Indochina and thereby checking the spread of communism across the region. "Such a possibility could not be contemplated with equanimity by the other western powers or by the United States of America," insisted the Foreign Office in a 1948 cable to the British embassy in Washington calling for new efforts to make U.S. officials see sense.[62] Even a year later, however, British observers saw few signs that the Truman administration was moving toward engagement in the region. In February, the Washington embassy reported that the State Department seemed determined to focus on "perimeter problems"—Japan, Korea, Formosa, and Indonesia—and to "steer clear of commitments in the continental countries."[63] The U.S. attitude deeply frustrated British officials. One Foreign Office aide wondered when the Americans would "wake up to the fact that they, as well as ourselves, ought to do something about South East Asia."[64] The ambassador in Bangkok agreed that it was "high time" that the U.S. government "realized that our influence . . . throughout the Far East is beneficial to them and that they agree to work with, and not against, us."[65]

While applying steady pressure on Asian governments, British officials intensified their diplomatic campaign to change American attitudes toward Southeast Asia. In a grandiloquent April 1949 speech at the National Press Club in Washington, Foreign Secretary Bevin appealed for greater American support for Britain's role throughout the Far East. Pointing to a map of the world, Bevin instructed his audience to "see what Europe means." Moving his pointer from the United States across the Atlantic to the Middle East and then eastward across the Indian Ocean to Southeast Asia, the foreign secretary declared that he was tracing "the great road to millions of people who know a good deal of our language, who have been associated with us for a long time, [and] who are still very friendly people to whom Great Britain in the course of her career never did a greater thing . . . than to give India and Pakistan their freedom." Boasting of the spread of democracy across this swath of the world, Bevin urged that Europe and the United States move ahead hand in hand to promote further development. "The maintenance of Britain and Europe in this great combination," he added, "will mean an adhesion and a comradeship that will keep us free of totalitarianism, and will succeed in maintaining the greatest proportion of the population of the world based on liberty and freedom of the individual."[66] Bevin never mentioned Indochina, but there could be no question that an Anglo-American partnership in Southeast Asia meant throwing U.S. support behind French policy there.

Assuming a Secondary Role

Two months after Bevin's speech, the British government got its wish. On June 21, 1949, the U.S. government proclaimed the recent formation of Bao Dai's government and French promises of a new constitution for Vietnam to be "welcome developments" that would allow Vietnam to assume its "rightful place in the family of nations." Agreements between France and the Bao Dai regime, the statement added, would "form the basis for the progressive realization of the legitimate aspirations of the Vietnamese people." The declaration promised neither formal recognition of Bao Dai nor U.S. aid for the new Vietnamese state or the war against the Viet Minh. But in crucial ways, the statement signaled a breakthrough, one of the most significant turning points in the long flow of U.S. involvement in Vietnam after 1945. The result of mounting fears of communist expansion in Asia, the statement cleared the way for American economic and military aid that would come in 1950. For the British government, too, the U.S. declaration carried enormous significance but with precisely the opposite implication. While the United States, by lending political support to the French war effort, took a giant stride toward involvement in the Vietnam morass, London suddenly found the long-desired flexibility to move in the other direction.

Britain did not entirely disengage from the Indochina situation. There was, after all, a danger that total withdrawal would harm Britain's relations with France and squander London's right to a say in future developments. The partnership that British officials desired might give way to American domination. "It seems to me most important that we should not . . . give the impression of having lost interest in this country and that by giving some military and economic assistance, however small, we should gain the right to be represented on any organizations which may be set up here," the British consul in Saigon, Frank Gibbs, wrote in March 1950.[67] The War Office agreed to study a French request for new military aid and promised to "supply what we can."[68] On the whole, however, British officials displayed a much more cautious attitude once U.S. aid was forthcoming. When the French and U.S. governments squabbled in the spring of 1950 over the modalities of U.S. aid, for example, the British stood back from the fray. R. H. Scott, chief of the Foreign Office's Southeast Asian desk, insisted that Britain not overreact to signs of U.S. displeasure with France. "French policy has not been successful in Indo-China," he wrote. "If we want the United States to help clear up the mess we must accept the possibility of some friction."[69] With the United States active in Indochina, Scott recognized, the important battle had already been won.

The British government exercised its new flexibility at a meeting of foreign ministers in May 1950, just days after U.S. secretary of state Dean Acheson had formally offered his French counterpart U.S. aid for Indochina. While the U.S. and French governments wished to issue a trilateral declaration stating their common determination to promote development and resist aggression in Southeast Asia, Bevin refused to go along. A year or two earlier, the British government had been the principal champion of precisely this sort of trilateral action. With the United States now fully involved in Indochina, however, London was free to give highest priority to its anxieties about antagonizing Asian opinion. Any statement of Western solidarity, Bevin warned, would give the impression that Paris, London, and Washington were ganging up and failing to consult the Asian nations concerned. He would accept only a mild statement indicating that the three Western powers strongly supported efforts by the Asians themselves to fight communism. When French and U.S. officials clashed over wording of the statement, the entire effort collapsed.[70] Britain's retreat to the comfort of a secondary role in Indochina had begun.

As the Franco-American partnership deepened in the years that followed, Britain moved further into the background of the Western partnership and ultimately backed away from the "great combination" that it had helped to create. To be sure, Britain continued to sell considerable quantities of military gear to support the French war effort.[71] But London did so with increasing satisfaction that the United States was shouldering the main burden. The British consul in Saigon, H. A. Graves, happily reported in November 1952 that Washington was already bearing more than one-third of the costs of the war and that French complaints about shortages were groundless. "The equipment position,"

Graves wrote, "can only be described as satisfactory."[72] Even British equipment seemed to be abundant. "One might almost say that Sten guns in Tonking [Tonkin] are as common as umbrellas in Piccadilly," wrote the British military attaché in Saigon.[73]

Mounting British confidence expressed itself in the stiff financial terms that London sometimes required of France for British gear desired by the French military. In early 1953, for example, French authorities lashed out against London's policy of requiring an 80 percent down payment on equipment ordered from British sources.[74] More significantly, London's changed attitude found expression in the government's declining enthusiasm for the sort of multilateral military effort in Vietnam that had been eagerly solicited in earlier years. When Admiral Arthur Radford, the U.S. commander in chief in the Pacific, proposed in 1952 that the United States, Britain, France, Australia, and New Zealand hold five-power talks on defending against the Chinese threat to Southeast Asia, the British government showed little enthusiasm.[75]

Meanwhile, British leaders wanted the United States to maintain—and even increase—its support for the French war effort. While London had strong doubts about the conduct of the war, it hoped that the tide might yet turn and the Western position could be held. In July 1953, the cabinet agreed that Britain must do "anything [it] could to persuade the United States Government to give further assistance to the French in Indo-China." Holding off the communists in that territory, the ministers believed, was crucial to prevent "deterioration" of the British position in Malaya.[76] But various considerations militated against extensive British involvement alongside the French. Policymakers continued to fear a harmful drain on British resources, while many also worried that bold action in Indochina might provoke communist China to attack Hong Kong. Persistent worries that the Indian government would never welcome an assertive British role in Vietnam also suggested the necessity of maintaining a low profile.

The Dien Bien Phu crisis in the spring of 1954 produced the final step in the evolution of British policy. Now convinced that the Franco-American military partnership in Vietnam could not succeed at a reasonable cost, the British government concluded that the moment had come to cut Western losses and put U.S. resources to work in a different, hopefully more effective, way. The American fixation on defeating the Vietnamese revolution—so much desired in earlier years—now seemed excessive and even dangerous. It was time, British leaders insisted, to

negotiate an end to the war—and to French colonialism in Southeast
Asia. "We must decline to be drawn into the war in Indo-China or even
into promising moral support for measures of intervention of which the
full scope [is] not yet known," the cabinet agreed on May 3, 1954, as
Dien Bien Phu fell to the Viet Minh thousands of miles away. The Vietnamese victory, Prime Minister Churchill asserted, would surely "afford
great encouragement to Communists throughout the world." The best
that the West could now do, he and the other ministers agreed, was to
establish a new "system of collective defense" for the parts of Southeast
Asia and the western Pacific where Western interests could reasonably be defended.[77] Thus did the Southeast Asia Treaty Organization
(SEATO) emerge from the ashes of the failed Western attempt to prevent the defeat of France in Vietnam. From London's point of view, the
new alliance represented a second bid to draw upon U.S. resources to
hold a line of containment that would help protect British interests that
lay at one or two geographical removes.

Just four years earlier, British officials had been much pleased with
themselves for succeeding in their first bid—in their effort, that is, to
create the Anglo-French-U.S. partnership in Indochina that they had
sought for so long. In fact, it is important to note, British policymakers
deserve only minor credit for this result. While London helped shape
American perceptions of the Southeast Asia crisis and its geostrategic
implications, the Truman administration needed little guidance to
conclude in 1950 that Indochina faced a communist danger demanding a U.S. response. But the U.S. decision, no matter how it came
about, marked a significant victory for the British government. World
War II and its aftermath had made abundantly clear that London no
longer possessed the advantages of material abundance, political
consensus, or invulnerability to nationalist pressures in the Far East. A
Southeast Asian partnership with the United States offered the only
road ahead.

A similar process unfolded in the eastern Mediterranean around the
same time, culminating in the Truman Doctrine of 1947.[78] Just as in
Southeast Asia, Britain had played the dominant role in maintaining
the economic and political order in the Middle East. Other powers,
notably France, took part in—and benefited from—that system, but
Britain went unchallenged as the regional hegemon. The devastating
impact of World War II made clear that Britain would no longer be
able to play this role in either part of the world. Clearly, the United

States was the only Western power that could do so. British leaders flattered themselves that they could retain a high degree of influence over Washington's policymaking, but there could be no disguising the basic fact: the United States had assumed the British empire's traditional geostrategic functions. As in Greece and Turkey, the U.S. commitment to Vietnam represented the insertion of U.S. power where British will and power no longer sufficed. Whether American will and power were up to the task in Vietnam remained to be seen.

SEVEN

❖ ❖ ❖

French Imperial Reconstruction and the Development of the Indochina War, 1945–1950

MARTIN THOMAS

THIS CHAPTER CONNECTS the outbreak and development of the Indochina war in the years 1945–1950 to the reconfiguration of French party politics and colonial policy formulation in the early years of the Fourth Republic. It contends that the immediate postwar years witnessed the consolidation of an unprecedented imperialist consensus in French domestic politics. With the partial exception of the Parti communiste français (French Communist Party), none of France's major political parties even paid lip service to the gradual disengagement from colonial territories that was so much a feature of British imperial policy after 1945. The renewed French commitment to empire becomes more readily explicable when related to the reconstruction of French multiparty republican democracy after 1945. The domestic politics of the early Fourth Republic facilitated the prosecution of colonial war and impeded governmental consideration of imperial withdrawal. Whatever the successes of the early Fourth Republic in restoring France's place at the heart of postwar Europe, party rivalries were pivotal to the disastrous escalation of the Indochina war.

After the humiliation of defeat in 1940 and the breakdown of colonial rule in numerous overseas territories that followed it, the resurgent popular imperialism in postwar France seems remarkable. Historians have ascribed this new enthusiasm for empire to several causes. For D. Bruce Marshall and Andrew Shennan, the conjunction of a new constitutional system in metropolitan France, with the redesign of the overseas empire as the French Union, nurtured the comforting myth that a modernized French colonialism could survive in the postwar world.[1]

For Tony Smith, imperial possessions became integral to the republican discourse of renascent French power, commodities taken for granted as an essential component of national greatness. For Charles-Robert Ageron, the new imperialism in France traded on popular ignorance of conditions in the empire. Reassured that the empire had survived the vicissitudes of war, as the Fourth Republic took shape the voting public assumed that French colonialism would persist indefinitely. Once colonial violence escalated in 1947, enthusiasm for empire faded. And for James I. Lewis, the constitutional reconstruction of the postwar empire was the product of the unsatisfactory compromises made between specialist colonial officials and the new republican political elite in which center-right parties set narrow limits to colonial reform.[2]

It is easy, however, to construct a different image of postwar France. The establishment of a new republic was surely an opportune moment to rebuild the empire on a new basis. The array of political parties to emerge from the metropolitan resistance, plus the marginalization of the prewar French right after the Vichy years, lend weight to the assertion that the early years of the Fourth Republic were a missed opportunity for radical reform. As Martin Shipway has argued, one might have expected a more progressive "world view" among colonial officialdom a decade after the Popular Front's experiment in colonial reform during 1936 and 1937.[3] In fact, the unwillingness of the new republican establishment either to engage meaningfully with indigenous nationalism in the colonies or, at the very least, to restructure imperial control on less vertical lines was nowhere more apparent than in Indochina.

The discussion that follows revisits the colonial policies of the major governing parties in the immediate postwar years, focusing on those without significant imperial ties. It also links the prosecution of the Indochina war to the wider reconstruction of the French empire as the French Union, protectorates, and Associated States from 1946 to 1950. Finally, it analyzes the closed environment in which key policy decisions regarding Indochina were reached by successive French administrations in order to illustrate the widening gulf between metropolitan policymakers, the French public, and the Viet Minh leadership.

Colonial Consensus and War in Indochina

As Tony Smith argued some twenty-five years ago, the breadth of the French "colonial consensus" supportive of imperial commitments reflected two deeper truths. On the one hand, politicians on all sides of the Chamber of Deputies, media commentators, and Gaullist opponents of the new republic concurred that France's inability to meet the challenge of decolonization was a product of *"le système de la République"* itself. Failure stemmed from institutional inadequacy, not lack of political will. But, on the other hand, this blindness to the political and moral imperatives of colonial withdrawal was born of the successive recent humiliations to French national pride.[4] The stagnation of the Third Republic, the rapidity of defeat, the shame of occupation and collaboration, and the reliance on U.S. economic support induced an unquestioning faith in imperial possessions as one of the few remaining markers of French global power.[5] From 1944 to the escalation of the Cold War in 1947 this colonial consensus could be defined in negative terms, as an emotive refusal to contemplate imperial withdrawal. Between 1947 and 1950 French governments divided more sharply over colonial problems. But all insisted publicly that France would soldier on in Indochina, North Africa, and elsewhere. Only in 1950 did a dispassionate cost-benefit analysis begin of the economic and international price of colonial commitments.

There was certainly no failure of political will at the outbreak of the Indochina conflict. There was, however, a fatal breakdown of communication between Paris and Saigon. Léon Blum's all-Socialist transition government was ideologically and emotionally averse to war with the Viet Minh. But it was determined to reassert French imperial control in Tonkin. Blum was not informed of Ho Chi Minh's attempts to open a last-minute dialogue until December 26, a delay entirely consistent with the schemes of the Saigon High Commission hawks grouped around French commander General Jean Valluy to provoke the Viet Minh into hostilities in Hanoi.[6] A month earlier, on November 19, 1946, Léon Pignon, federal commissioner for political affairs within the Saigon administration, warned the government's Indochina committee (Comité interministériel de l'Indochine, or COMININDO) that decisive action against the Viet Minh was essential to break the "psychology of flight" that afflicted the French settler community in Cochinchina. Only by confronting the Viet Minh could France stem the decline made manifest by the Japanese coup in March 1945. Pignon's fear of creeping American economic imperialism added urgency to his plea.[7] His arguments were taken to heart politically, if not economically. Contrary to Foreign Ministry projections in 1946, French capital investment in

Indochina, historically dependent on state funding and a handful of large corporations, declined markedly in the late 1940s.[8] But the perceived political value of empire survived intact. The noncommunist political elite went to war ignorant about events on the ground but determined to retain the Indochina federation. Whatever their reservations, in December 1946 Blum's Socialist ministerial colleagues opted to fight. Seeing little prospect of renewed negotiations with Ho, when faced with the alternatives of capitulation or wider military operations Blum's cabinet chose the latter.

The French Indochina command was confident that the Viet Minh could be quickly beaten. This, and Blum's genuine belief that Ho's government had unleashed the fighting as well as a spate of atrocities against French civilians in Hanoi, led the Paris government to preclude any dialogue until the French army reestablished control. Ho made seven appeals for a cease-fire between December 21, 1946, and March 5, 1947. None were heeded.[9] Signs of colonial breakdown elsewhere—the Sétif uprising in Algeria in May 1945, West African railway strikes, and the Bamako Congress of black African nationalist groups in 1946, plus the Madagascar insurrection in April 1947—catalyzed French determination to defeat the Viet Minh insurgency.[10]

The immediate origins and subsequent escalation of the Indochina war unfolded against a backdrop of constitutional renovation and the renewal of party politics in postwar France. For the mass of French voters, revolutionary upheaval at the colonial periphery was obscured by their more urgent preoccupations at the metropolitan center. The connections between these events seem poorly understood. Historians acknowledge that French strategic policy was reformulated in the context of resurgent centrist politics in the early Fourth Republic. Superficially at least, the dominant centrism of the late Third Republic reemerged in new guise after 1946. But much remains to be said about the very different origins and outlook of the parties across this band of the political spectrum. One, the Mouvement républicain populaire (MRP), represented the political ascendancy of a republican social Catholicism long sought after, but hitherto unachieved, by Catholic liberals since the papal *ralliement* of the 1890s.[11] Another, the Radical Party, had dominated the parliaments of the late Third Republic. An establishment party *par excellence,* the Radicals' seemingly intractable grip on the levers of power was abruptly severed by France's defeat in 1940. A third, the Union démocratique et socialiste de la résistance

(UDSR), was a much smaller grouping, the latest in a long line of social democratic parties that, while nominally socialist, rejected the centralized discipline and Marxist rhetoric of the official Socialist Party.
Like other small parties to emerge after the war, the UDSR lacked a
core philosophy and defined itself in opposition to its larger rivals.[12]

There were other important differences between these new parties.
The MRP and the UDSR emerged from coalitions of wartime resistance movements in metropolitan France and French North Africa.
Each relied on provincial strongholds for support and found it difficult
to win a mass following in Paris, Lyon, or Marseille.[13] The Radicals, by
contrast, had to live down their inglorious association with the social
divisions and military shortcomings of prewar France. Few senior Radical politicians "had a good war." Several were interned in 1940. Others played junior roles in de Gaulle's Free French movement. And,
after the 1944 Liberation, the Radicals' rank-and-file membership was
eroded, both by the novel appeal of rival parties and by the seeming ir-
relevance of the old Radical Party calls to unity: anticlericalism and the
defense of *petit bourgeois* commerce. The party had to reinvent itself to
survive, a feat it only accomplished in the early 1950s under the modernizing leadership of Pierre Mendès France, an inspirational figure
who broke the mold of Radical Party centrism.[14]

In marked contrast to the Radical Party, the collective leadership of
the MRP lacked experience of colonial administration. Few senior
MRP figures had said or done much about the French empire before
being thrust into the heart of government in 1945. Yet the MRP incorporated a rigid colonialism into its vision of a reconstructed France
within two years of the party's formal establishment in November 1944.
And from 1946 to 1954 the MRP's iron grip on foreign and colonial
policy gave it unprecedented opportunity to regulate the pace and
complexion of imperial reform.[15] Where one might have expected the
Radicals and the Socialists to apply their greater expertise in colonial
affairs to the prosecution of the Indochina war, in fact it was the MRP
and their UDSR allies in the so-called Third Force coalition that dominated Far Eastern strategy. Several of this coalition's senior ministers,
renowned for their decisive and constructive approach to European
affairs—Georges Bidault, Robert Schuman, and René Pleven among
them—were far more intransigent in colonial affairs. A chasm separated the inventiveness and coherence of postwar French diplomacy in
Europe from the hard-line immobilism of imperial policy between
1945 and 1950.[16]

It seems then that much of the explanation for France's commitment to fight the Indochina war lies in the confluence of the postwar constellation of French party politics and a popular imperialist consensus. The new conservatism evident in French imperial policy traded on a "colonial myth" linking postwar recovery to the reconstruction of a highly centralized imperial system.[17] The inability of the governing elites that emerged in the immediate post-Liberation period to envisage a genuinely reformist imperialism had disastrous consequences in Southeast Asia. It was a center-left coalition, in which the Christian Democrat MRP played the leading role in colonial policy, which shied away from further negotiation with the Viet Minh in late 1946. It was a Socialist transition government that sanctioned the murderous bombardment of Haiphong in December of that year. And it was the "Third Force" coalitions dominated by the MRP, the Radical Party, and the Socialists that extended France's military involvement in Indochina in the years 1947 to 1950.

The Fourth Republic System and the War

Putting party rivalries to one side, in the first five years after the Liberation, colonial policymaking was shaped by three unresolved tensions inherent in the political system of the Fourth Republic. One was the conflict over the extent of executive powers within a reordered parliamentary system. France lacked a strong presidential figure at the apex of government for a decade after General de Gaulle's abrupt departure from office as interim head of government in January 1946.[18] This was positively desirable to the republican left. But to the center-right and the emerging Gaullist movement, hostile to the entire constitutional fabric of the new republic, postwar France was a rudderless ship of state drifting inexorably toward national and imperial decline.[19]

A second source of tension was the unprecedented postwar strength of the French communist movement, based on the Parti communiste français (PCF) and the communist-controlled trade union collective, the Confédération générale du travail (CGT). Debates over such diverse issues as reconstruction priorities, state nationalizations, food pricing, coal distribution, membership of the Western alliance, and, of course, the future of the empire were often overshadowed by the conflict between the PCF and its opponents, between communist and non-communist France.[20] The ideological struggle played out in France inevitably colored official and popular responses to a colonial war supposedly fought to defeat an unrepresentative Vietnamese communist insurgency.

A third conflict over long-term imperial planning conditioned policy on Indochina. Supporters of a centralized and assimilationist colonial policy, whose basic purpose was to remake overseas territories in the French cultural and political image, remained at odds with their opponents who insisted that empire could only survive in the postwar world as a looser federal structure in which authority was gradually devolved to local elites associated to France.[21] The persistence of fundamental disagreements over colonial reform was unremarkable. The assimilationist-associationist debate had continued since the 1870s. As the French Union took shape in 1945 and 1946, these old arguments were rehearsed anew over the issue of a federal or unitary French colonial system. In their support for rigid central control, the assimilationists became identifiable with an intransigent imperialism based on racial hierarchy and the innate superiority of French universalist values. By contrast, numerous associationists, seen in the interwar period as champions of colonial conservatism, reemerged after the war as enlightened federalist advocates of a uniquely French version of colonial "self-government." By 1947 the argument about the structure and operation of the French Union was confused. Federal in theory but unitary in practice, the new imperial system befuddled its most ardent advocates.[22] The MRP was typical in this respect. Proponents of European federalism, the MRP leadership actually undermined the federal principles of the original French Union project, lest the empire be weakened.[23] Party leader Georges Bidault, a precocious voice within successive coalition governments, sympathized with this ultraimperialism. As premier and foreign minister for much of the late 1940s he worked to keep the colonial bureaucracy intact, whatever the constitutional status conceded to individual territories in the French Union.[24]

The constitution of the Fourth Republic came into force on Christmas Eve 1946, less than a week after the Indochina conflict erupted in Hanoi. The new constitutional system looked set to repeat the problems of the Third Republic. The electoral law favored the proliferation of new political parties and local electoral pacts. These, in turn, ensured a system of coalition administration conducive to centrist government and policy compromise. Contrary to de Gaulle's wishes, the presidency was stripped of meaningful executive authority. Opponents of the regime and party activists frustrated by the unresponsiveness of parliamentarians criticized this style of government as elitist, self-seeking, and inert. The merry-go-round of potential ministers—or *ministrables*—vying for office precluded coherent imperial planning. Perhaps the feature of the new system to attract the most adverse comment was the assembly's capacity to undermine government policy, partly because of deputies' rights to force a vote of confidence and partly because coalitions rarely attracted a stable working majority and were therefore susceptible to recurrent ministerial crises. Between 1947 and 1951 the formation of a new Fourth Republic administration usually followed such a *crise*—typically initiated by a factional grouping within the Chamber of Deputies. Members of the National Assembly forced changes in government. Until the June 1951 general election, French voters did not.[25]

Yet French electors, at last including newly enfranchised women, were by no means idle in the new system. During 1946 the electorate went to the polls five times, culminating in the final round of the general election on November 10. One result of this constant cycle of campaigns and votes was that extraneous colonial issues were subsumed by argument about constitutional reform, coal supplies, and the future of Germany. The PCF was the principal beneficiary of this in the November elections. The center-left suffered most. Socialist (Section française de l'Internationale ouvrière, SFIO) support fell back sharply. SFIO capacity to hold the tripartite coalition in place diminished in consequence. And the UDSR struggled to create a securely funded national party organization capable of matching its main centrist rivals.[26] During 1946 the UDSR aligned with the Radicals in a loose interparty alliance, the Rassemblement des Gauches républicaines (RGR). The RGR block was united solely in opposition to the PCF and never developed other common policies. In practice, UDSR members were divided about links with other parties—the Radicals, the socialists, and the Gaullists in particular—making local electoral alliances with other parties difficult to sustain.[27] As for the MRP, its parliamentary strength declined only marginally, but the party lost its primacy in the Chamber of Deputies.

More importantly, the emergence of an unofficial Gaullist opposition, the Union Gaulliste, drove the MRP to court right-wing Catholics alarmed by the party's working arrangements with the socialists and communists. Unless the MRP made moves to conciliate its core voters, it faced a calamitous hemorrhage of support to its Gaullist rivals. That meant putting clear water between the MRP and the French left. By the end of 1946 then the MRP leadership had come to despise tripartism.[28] The party's drift to the right, presaged by its electoral cooperation with the one mainstream right-wing party to contest the elections, the Parti républicain de la liberté (PRL), continued apace in the coming year. In early 1947 the major dynamic in French government was the bitter acrimony between the MRP and PCF, supposedly partners in the cabinet. Ideological hostility between them was sharpened by more tactical considerations. By voting for the constitution, MRP fortunes became tied to the success of the new political system. Instead of being a reformist "movement" that broke the mold of left-right party politics, by 1947 the MRP epitomized the governing elite. Popular disenchantment with government policy or the complex parliamentary apparatus of the new republican state was sure to result in a loss of electoral support to the Gaullists.[29] During 1946 the MRP drew over 70 percent of its votes from the provinces. Its rank-and-file members were predominantly conservative, concentrated in western and northeastern France and in a more southerly arc from the Jura mountains in the east through the Massif Central to the Pyrénées Occidentales. Their support could not be relied on so long as the MRP worked alongside the communists.[30]

For its part, the PCF was determined to consolidate its primacy over the socialists. SFIO rhetoric became more vigorously anticommunist in response.[31] Effective in domestic politics, socialist defense of order was less convincing in colonial affairs. The SFIO was split between a rank and file mobilized by Secretary-General Guy Mollet and the party central committee *(comité directeur)* in opposition to colonial war, and those ministers who shared new premier Paul Ramadier's conviction that a military campaign in Indochina was unavoidable.[32] If the socialists could not agree among themselves, it was quite inconceivable that the tripartite coalition would formulate a common strategy towards the Viet Minh.[33] Problems over defense policy illustrated the policy paralysis characteristic of the tripartite coalition in early 1947. Ramadier appointed a communist, François Billoux, to the newly established post of minister of defense to bind the PCF to its coalition partners on strategic issues. But the prime minister also limited communist influence over defense policy by appointing three state secretaries responsible for the individual services. These junior ministers—one MRP, one independent, and one Radical—held greater responsibility for the day-to-day running of the armed forces. Far from ensuring interparty balance or coalition consensus, this reorganization stultified defense planning. The government's most contentious strategic problem—expansion of the war in Indochina—became a make-or-break issue for the coalition.[34]

Party Splits and the "Third Force"

The collapse of tripartism in May 1947 did not spell the end of inter- or intraparty disputes among the remaining parties in government. Socialist divisions were not ameliorated by Ramadier's decision to expel communist ministers from his cabinet in May. Angered by the expulsion of the Communists Socialist Party secretary, General Mollet spearheaded a rank-and-file campaign to end participation in government with the MRP. The SFIO Congress in Lyon in August witnessed acrimonious exchanges over Marshall aid and U.S. economic hegemony in Western Europe that resonated with the party infighting about the Indochina war.[35] Still coming to terms with France's attachment to a U.S.-led Western alliance in opposition to the Soviet Union, by late 1947 the Socialist Party was equally ambivalent about the French Union project.[36]

Throughout 1947 official preoccupation with a growing communist threat at home nourished colonial officials' anxieties about the diverse threats to imperial control as the Cold War intensified. Otherwise disparate events were connected into a single narrative of seditious activity.[37] The Ministry of Overseas France became convinced that North African, Malagasy, and Vietnamese nationalist groups planned a series of rebellions to overturn the colonial state. In this atmosphere of imperial paranoia, local administrations acquired greater latitude to suppress any dissent.[38] The appointment in May 1947 of General Alphonse Juin to head the French administration in Morocco typified the trend. Algerian-born and utterly committed to a French presence in North Africa, Juin's arrival was affirmation that the Paris government, now shorn of its communist ministers, was determined to safeguard the empire.[39] Defense of empire was increasingly justified with anticommunist rhetoric. When rebellion broke out in Madagascar on March 29, 1947, MRP and socialist ministers in Ramadier's administration identified a conspiracy by leaders of the Mouvement Démocratique de la Rénovation Malgache (MDRM), the island's leading nationalist party banned three months earlier. The MDRM's alleged communist sympathies

made it an irresistible target. Military retribution against the Madagas-
can population, administered in large part by expeditionary force units
en route to Indochina, was staggeringly brutal, a portent of the more
enduring colonial violence to come.[40]

The façade of imperial unity cracked on the few occasions that colonial problems occupied center stage in parliamentary debate. The November 1946 general election saw seventy colonial deputies enter the
Chamber of Deputies, in addition to fifty-four overseas representatives
in the upper house, the Council of the Republic. Although many of the
colonial deputies were reluctant to identify with metropolitan parties,
twenty-three were aligned with the PCF or the SFIO. These parliamentarians were reformist by inclination and at least nominally supportive
of the governing tripartite coalition. They were understandably eager
to influence imperial policymaking. The outbreak of the Indochina
conflict was the most urgent colonial issue before them. Parliamentary
dispute in early 1947 over the precise circumstances in which hostilities had broken out, the recall of Saigon high commissioner Thierry
d'Argenlieu, and the financing of the war concealed the more fundamental rift over communist participation in government.

The National Assembly debated Indochina policy over four days between March 14 and 18. The real issue at stake was not the conduct of
the war under new High Commissioner Emile Bolleart but the ideological direction of the Fourth Republic. On the floor of the Chamber
of Deputies François Billoux, France's first ever communist minister of
defense, famously refused to support the expeditionary force operations for which he, as minister, was theoretically responsible. The noted
socialist reformer Maurice Viollette, having advocated sweeping concessions, was even punched to the ground by enraged deputies from
the opposition benches. This incident, later expunged from the parliamentary record, reveals the actual tenor of the argument. The
Chamber of Deputies offered no way out of the impasse in Vietnam,
adding to public despondency about a remote conflict whose causes
and purpose seemed obscure.[41] The much-vaunted imperial system,
having promised so much in 1945 and 1946, was neither widely understood nor much liked. As the Indochina war intensified, so popular
support for imperial reconstruction diminished. An April 1947 opinion poll conducted soon after the assembly vote on additional military
credits for Indochina and the outbreak of the Madagascar rebellion revealed an equal split between those who expected the French Union to
survive and those who anticipated its collapse.[42]

Meanwhile the Viet Minh pushed southward from its power base in northern Tonkin during the 1947 campaigning season. Military communications were sabotaged, the agricultural economy was disrupted, and the tenuous French grip on the rural interior of Annam was exposed as village evacuations compounded a worsening Vietnamese refugee crisis.[43] Paul Ramadier's government brushed aside State Department advice that generous reform in Indochina was essential to offset these Viet Minh gains. Ministers were bolstered by advice from the French commander in chief in Vietnam, General Valluy, suggesting that Ho was banking on external intervention to restrain any French riposte. Over the coming months the Saigon High Commission also renewed its effort to persuade members of the Comité interministériel de l'Indochine (COMININDO) in Paris that American intervention was self-interested, driven not by anticolonialism but by the economic attractions of the Indochina market.[44]

Whatever the impact of these suggestions, the Americans were not easily appeased. The State Department was unimpressed by the worsening division among French officials in Saigon. High Commissioner Bolleart, his influential adviser Paul Mus, and General Valluy disagreed over the alternatives of cease-fire talks or a major military advance up the Red River delta in Tonkin.[45] In mid-September the U.S. ambassador to Paris, Jefferson Caffery, warned Foreign Ministry secretary-general Jean Chauvel that Washington was opposed to a major French offensive in Vietnam launched on the back of Marshall aid loan agreements.[46] Whether offered or withheld, Marshall aid was a formidable lever with which to influence the actions of colonial powers. The seismic consequences of U.S. disapproval of Dutch military action to restore control in Java in late July 1947 triggered waves of alarm throughout the French colonial administration. Initial American unease later turned into decisive economic pressure on the Dutch to withdraw, much as the French predicted. Stronger American support for France in Europe did not preclude U.S. support for greater United Nations involvement in colonial disputes. It was essential to limit unwanted interference from Washington in Indochina.[47]

Foreign Minister Bidault soon found a means to do so. He capitalized on American fears of social disorder in strike-ridden France to secure Washington's endorsement of talks with Bao Dai.[48] The resultant concession of greater autonomy for Vietnam under the auspices of the French Union amounted to little. The French retained control over foreign and military policy, customs, and trade. But the long-running cycle of talks with Bao Dai gave ministers room to maneuver with key allies. The planned French offensive in Tonkin, code-named Operation Léa, eventually began in October 1947 under General Raoul Salan. And Bidault's exchanges with Washington grew in confidence once the framework for the European Recovery Program was put in place. But the ministerial division and muddle characteristic of colonial policy persisted. Historian Hugues Tertrais has even suggested that French officials and military commanders in Indochina formulated the Bao Dai solution knowing that promotion of a monarchical nationalist alternative to the Viet Minh might foment civil war in Vietnam.[49]

Another round of governmental reshuffles in Paris caused renewed American pessimism. Socialist veteran Marius Moutet held the portfolio of minister for overseas France between January 1946 and October 21, 1947, when he was ousted in Ramadier's second ministerial reorganization. The prime minister himself then took the reins of the renamed Colonial Ministry. Moutet had a long pedigree as a colonial reformer.[50] However, his efforts to make the French Union a vehicle for colonial reform met greater success in black Africa than in Indochina. Moutet's inability to steer through reforms for Vietnam stemmed from three principal causes. First, he could not consolidate his personal influence within coalition ministries, despite close working relationships with Socialist premiers Félix Gouin, Léon Blum, and Paul Ramadier.[51] Moutet's temporary dissolution of the interministerial committee on Indochina reflected his sense of isolation among cabinet colleagues determined to prosecute a war against the Viet Minh. A second problem was that Moutet's limited influence in Paris was amplified in Saigon, where the administration often bypassed his instructions. By August 1946 Moutet was exasperated by High Commissioner d'Argenlieu's scheming to avoid renewed negotiations with the Viet Minh. D'Argenlieu's residual trust in the tripartite coalition dissipated once de Gaulle resigned in January. Distrust turned to antagonism with the signature of the accords between Ho and Jean Sainteny on March 6.[52] In late July Saigon officials kept Moutet in the dark over plans to convene a second conference at Dalat with those Vietnamese, Cambodian, and Laotian representatives willing to accept High Commission sovereignty in Indochina. These talks cut across the French government's very different scheme of negotiation with Viet Minh delegates in France. Once news of the second Dalat conference broke, the French press, aware of the hostility between Moutet and the new French premier, Georges Bidault, began speculating that d'Argenlieu refused to acknowledge the authority of the Ministry of Overseas France. In Moutet's words, the Saigon High Commission had "exploded a bomb" to destroy the chances of a peace accord with Ho. The senior MRP leaders grouped around Bidault accepted this. But the Socialists in government were dismayed. The contradictory objectives of the Dalat and Fontainebleau conferences exposed the confusion in Socialist policy and their loss of influence over colonial policy formulation to the MRP.[53]

Moutet's third difficulty was still more intractable. He was confounded by the SFIO's failure to define a coherent postwar colonial reformism. In Algeria, the socialists acquiesced in a reversion to an assimilationist administrative system that facilitated untrammeled settler dominion. By 1948 Governor-General Marcel-Edmond Naegelen aligned with the settler community to stifle nationalist pressure for political rights and a basic welfare provision for the Muslim majority. By contrast, socialist support for the reclassification of the Indochina territories as Associated States indicated a shift away from assimilationism.[54] But a shift toward what? Ultimately, Moutet rejected any severance of the imperial bond with France. Seen from a Viet Minh perspective, the French Union formula merely precluded independence.[55]

The collusion between senior MRP politicians and the Saigon administration is now well known.[56] The government was neither fully briefed about, nor in full control of, civil-military policy in Saigon. Party rivalries undermined ministerial collective responsibility, preventing cabinet discussion of colonial policy options, a pattern that would continue throughout the Indochina war. During 1946 the Ministry of Overseas France had, for example, repeatedly instructed Saigon to pursue a thorough purge of the national and regional administrations of the Indochinese federation to remove former Vichy sympathizers, outright collaborators, and corrupt officials. By the time a government investigatory mission arrived in November 1946 it was clear that little had been done to improve matters. D'Argenlieu left large numbers of erstwhile Vichyites in post, particularly within the regional magistrature. Corruption went unchecked. Junior officials enriched themselves through black-market trading, notably in Cambodia where the entire colonial administration was condemned as inept and self-serving.[57] Back in Paris, the socialists were still in disarray. The military operations sanctioned by Blum's administration in December were intended to coerce Viet Minh leaders back into talks, not to begin the reconquest of Tonkin. Ramadier's sterner resolve to pursue an offensive in 1947 provoked deeper division.[58]

With the rightward realignment behind the Third Force of Radicals, the MRP, and Socialists, by late 1947 France's governing parties seemed better equipped to fight the Cold War in Asia. On November 24 further ministerial changes saw Robert Schuman assume the premiership. For the next six months MRP politicians committed to the war— Georges Bidault, Paul-Henri Teitgen, and Paul Coste-Floret—occupied the Foreign Ministry, the Armed Forces Ministry, and the Ministry for Overseas France. But Schuman's Third Force administration lacked solid parliamentary backing. In late February 1948 the government majority in the Chamber of Deputies fell to just twenty-three out of a total of 618. The two largest parties in the coalition, the MRP and the Socialists, became reliant on a handful of right-wing independents. Desperate to restore government unity, Léon Blum proposed the amalgamation of all Third Force parties into a single movement. His plea fell on deaf ears. The fact was that the Third Force came together as a tactical alliance, not as a coalition with a common program. There was no agreement over colonial affairs. On April 23, 1948, the Ministry of Overseas France announced the replacement of its civil and military affairs divisions with new technical liaison services designed to improve policy coordination with other ministries. The reorganization was an admission of how little ministerial cooperation between Overseas France, the Quai d'Orsay, the Armed Forces, and colonial officials existed.[59] The fundamental disunity of the Third Force parties would dog Indochina policy for the next three years.

What held Schuman's administration together from November 1947 to July 1948 was the threat to existing parliamentary institutions posed by the communists and the Gaullist right. The communist menace receded after the government's defeat of the mass strike actions in October and November 1947 but remained a constant preoccupation in government. By contrast, Charles de Gaulle's Rassemblement du peuple français (RPF), less than a year old, garnered increasing popular support. Foreign policy success was crucial to buttress the government against mounting Gaullist criticism.[60] On December 18, 1947, Gaston Palewski, a key figure in the RPF executive committee, announced that the Gaullists rejected the drive toward Vietnamese national unification and would not be bound by any government commitments made with regard to it.[61] The RPF challenge added to MRP determination to ap-

pear strong over Indochina thus decreasing the likelihood of meaningful steps toward Vietnamese self-government within the Ha, Long
Bay accords eventually presented to the French National Assembly on
August 19, 1948.[62] The dismal prospects for a Vietnamese settlement
added to friction between the MRP and the socialists over the relative
merits of Bao Dai and his rival for power, General Nguyen Van Xuan,
head of government in Cochinchina.[63]

In late June 1948, a conference of State Department specialists met
in Bangkok to assess French prospects in Southeast Asia. They concluded that no progress had been made since the Indochina war began. The crux of the matter was that the French political elite did not
grasp the strength of Vietnamese nationalism. As matters stood, no
government could negotiate with the Viet Minh without handing "a re-
sounding victory" to the PCF.[64] As usual, party politics intruded to
block a solution. Socialist antagonism to Bao Dai as a reactionary puppet nourished the party's interest in renewed negotiations with the Viet
Minh. But MRP ministers, led by Minister for Overseas France Paul
Coste-Floret, blocked any such initiative throughout 1948. The appointment of Léon Pignon as successor to Bollaert in Saigon finally enabled Alain Savary, a socialist modernizer renowned for his opposition
to the war, to open talks with Viet Minh representatives in Cochinchina
in February 1949. Backed by Paul Alduy, SFIO leader in the French
Union Assembly, Savary worked for a cease-fire intermittently until
1954. Yet he never won full governmental support.[65]

During 1948 and 1949 more general trends in the global Cold War
allowed the governing coalition to paper over the cracks of interparty
disunity on Indochina. Fear of a resurgence of American anticolonialism declined.[66] Mao's advances in China made the Viet Minh more
credible as the vanguard of Southeast Asian communism. Previous arguments over the merits of an aggressive campaign of reconquest, and
a war fought to prop up an ineffective puppet regime, were drowned
out by the imperative of resistance to the communist challenge in Asia.
Conflict in Vietnam refracted the mounting tensions of the European
Cold War typified by the breakdown of the Council of Foreign Ministers, the Prague coup, and the Berlin blockade.

Coste-Floret was, however, reluctant to press for further reinforcement of the Far Eastern expeditionary force beyond the 108,600 troops
approved in the 1948 defense budget. To do so required consideration
of the use of French conscripts in Vietnam. It also meant confronting

U.S. refusal to endorse the use of Economic Cooperation Administration (ECA) funding to support operations against the Viet Minh. These were issues that all three governing parties preferred to ignore.[67] Nevertheless, the Indochina war brought the French government face to face with unpalatable choices. Henri Queuille's government, in office during 1948 and 1949, was anxious to accelerate France's trade recovery. In October 1949 the country registered its first balance-of-payments surplus since the end of World War II. The spiraling costs of war in Southeast Asia threatened to undermine this. Military manpower was equally problematic. Young servicemen were not sent off to die in Indochina, but large numbers of professional soldiers were. Colonial, North African, and Foreign Legion regiments bore much of the strain. But the losses of experienced French officers and noncommissioned officers (NCOs) amounted to a gradual disappearance of France's most seasoned combat troops.[68] The implication of both these dilemmas was that France could not afford the struggle, something that ministers were loath to admit.

Ministerial reluctance to risk political suicide by debating the human and financial costs of the Indochina war broke down acrimoniously in 1949. In January, Schuman confided to British foreign secretary Ernest Bevin that the nub of the problem in Indochina was to find viable leaders with whom to negotiate. In Schuman's eyes the Viet Minh remained inadmissible because Ho was "a creature of the Communists." Meanwhile, military operations had to proceed.[69] This difficulty was never surmounted. Instead, the sniping between the MRP and the socialists over the gamble on Bao Dai in Vietnam became public knowledge in the autumn as the two parties faced media scrutiny about the revelations of the so-called Generals' affair, a messy scandal originating with a leaked military report on the deteriorating prospects of expeditionary force success. What had been a thinly disguised rift between the two parties became a chasm once the Generals' affair hit French newsstands in September 1949.[70] The intrigue surrounding the leak to the Viet Minh of Chief of Staff General Georges Revers' pessimistic report on French military options obscured the fact that Revers was originally sent on a tour of inspection to Indochina to provide Paul Ramadier, then Socialist Defense Minister, with the evidence needed to overturn MRP policy in the Cabinet.[71] The Generals' affair added fuel to stinging parliamentary criticism of the final accords signed with Bao Dai on March 8, 1949. Gaullist deputies led by René Capitant and Edouard Frédéric-

Dupont condemned the absorption of Cochinchina, the epicenter of French economic and cultural influence in Indochina, into a unified Vietnam.[72] PCF deputies lambasted Vietnamese "national independence" as a colonialist sham. And most Socialist Party activists were inclined to agree, at least while Bao Dai remained the central figure in the projected Vietnamese national government. Ironically, this assessment was not dissimilar to that of the State Department's Office of Far Eastern Affairs, where distaste for French colonialism and its "running dog" Bao Dai ran deep.[73]

Decision-Making and Party Structures, 1948–1950

The combination of Socialist dissent, hostile parliamentary scrutiny, and public unease over worsening military losses drove MRP ministers toward more secretive and authoritarian decision-making. In April 1948 Coste-Floret restructured the interministerial committee on Indochina to oversee the implementation of the Bao Dai solution. The four-member committee was exclusively composed of MRP ministers—Coste-Floret, Schuman, Bidault, and Teitgen. The MRP grip on policymaking—to the exclusion of other coalition parties and even French president Vincent Auriol—became tighter still.[74] In the absence of a harmonious coalition partnership, effective civil-military liaison, or clear executive accountability, only sustained nongovernmental pressure might have forced a reassessment of the MRP's Indochina policy. Unfortunately, stronger popular pressure failed to materialize. Public interest in the "professional soldiers' war" in Southeast Asia was erratic. Remote, insoluble colonial problems taxed voter patience. In 1949 less than half of those asked by pollsters could offer even an approximate definition of the French Union.[75]

Nor did the MRP rank and file strongly oppose their party leaders before 1950. Departmental federations of the Socialist Party wielded influence over policy formulation through the SFIO executive and the party conference. But local MRP federations, including the largest from Brittany and Alsace, were a marginal presence in the MRP's policymaking structure.[76] The key policymaking forum was a thirteen-member bureau, attached to the MRP executive committee and dominated by the imperialist diehards.[77] The only specialist colonial group in the MRP's central structure was an *Equipe union Française* that never enjoyed much influence.[78]

Lack of sustained criticism from local federations left the MRP leadership free to pursue the war in Indochina. The disloyalty of MRP voters did not help matters. Between 1948 and 1950 the original concept of a mass Christian Democrat movement uniting republican and reformist Catholics began to collapse. From a high point of 230,000 members in 1947, MRP membership never exceeded 80,000 from 1950 on. The severity of this decline reflected voters' disenchantment with the Fourth Republic as well as with the MRP. Most former party members apparently opted for the Gaullist RPF, whose appeal rested not just on alternative policies but on also its unbending opposition to *le système*. What bears emphasis is that rank-and-file opponents of MRP policy were more likely to quit than to challenge party strategy through the MRP's internal machinery. It is hardly surprising then that the party's colonial policymakers were largely immune to spasmodic criticism from below.[79]

By 1950 the veneer of Third Force unity over Indochina had worn away. At the Council of Ministers on January 25, President Auriol, speaking as the guarantor of public safety, responded to a spate of work stoppages and other acts of sabotage designed to prevent the manufacture of arms or their transport to Indochina. Auriol stated that communist-directed industrial action constituted an attack on national sovereignty and an attempt to overthrow the policy of national defense determined by government and approved by parliament. Government plans were in hand to outlaw political strikes and dismiss the employees involved.[80]

The government's confrontational approach, so successful in defeating the PCF-CGT strategy in 1947, was doomed to fail in 1950. Communist opposition to the war, even its encouragement of worker sedition and soldier desertion, struck a chord with a nascent antiwar movement that spanned the liberal left. Opinion poll evidence indicated a worrying shift in metropolitan attitudes to the Indochina war.[81] A rising proportion of French voters were "turning off" the subject, ignoring media coverage of events in Vietnam. Still powerful in Vietnamese politics, the French settler population was just too small to have the emotional impact on French opinion of the far larger *colon* communities in North Africa. Yet among the major parties in France, only the PCF promised a clear antiwar line. Communist espousal of anticolonialism was a problem in itself as it made it harder for other anticommunist parties to follow suit. Socialists remained hopelessly caught between their rhetorical commitment to a negotiated solution, their reluctance to concede that this meant dialogue with the Viet Minh, and their endorsement of a continued French military presence. The MRP, still the party most deeply immersed in the running of the war, sanctioned wider military operations without a coherent long-term political plan to accompany them. During 1949 and early 1950 the UDSR's attitude to the war had been complicated by party leader René Pleven's tortuous efforts to rekindle wartime links with the Gaullists without entirely compromising the UDSR's role as an ally of the Radicals in the Rassemblement des Gauches républicaines. By the time Pleven took office as premier in July 1950, his party had moved squarely to the right. Pleven, however, relied on Socialist backing to keep him in office. So the old disputes over negotiation versus extended military action continued much as before.[82] Meanwhile, the Gaullist RPF, virulently opposed to the entire constitutional system, goaded all the governing parties for their ineptitude without offering a clear alternative.[83]

In parliamentary debate on Indochina policy and the preliminary inquisition into the Cao Bang "disaster" on October 19 and November 22, 1950, Radical Party leader Pierre Mendès France decried government inertia. He highlighted the futility of the Indochina conflict, focusing on its appalling human and material costs. Why expend so much blood and treasure in Indochina when it was insufficient to secure victory? Why prosecute a war that the majority of the French population professed neither to understand nor to want? Why compromise French power in Europe for the dubious benefits of maintaining a Far Eastern presence?[84] Always a politician willing to challenge received wisdom, Mendès France raised several taboo subjects. He advocated immediate negotiations with the Viet Minh over Vietnamese neutrality and warned that inaction would be fatal. Tragically, he failed to convince his fellow deputies.[85] Yet the decisive vote in support of the Pleven government's Indochina policy (337-187) on November 22 was deceptive. There was no real cross-party consensus over Indochina. The vote for Pleven was part acknowledgment of French reliance on U.S. material aid and part consequence of emotional ministerial appeals to national unity after the losses sustained at Cao Bang a month earlier.[86] In the coming year General Jean de Lattre's inspirational military leadership would also stem the tide of parliamentary and public criticism. But the basic causes of antiwar sentiment were unchanged.

Bao Dai was a poor choice, the Viet Minh better represented the popular will in Vietnam, and France could not afford an interminable campaign. Conflicts of interest between ministers struggling to hold
coalitions together and a Saigon administration determined to fight
on recurred until final defeat in 1954.[87]

Conclusion

Party politics in the early years of the Fourth Republic determined the
French approach to the Indochina war. The tripartite coalition and the
Third Force governments that succeeded it in 1947 limited the scope
for negotiation with the Viet Minh, discouraged close parliamentary
scrutiny of government actions, and relied on public disinterest to
prosecute the war unhindered. Party rivalries and shifting coalitions
were more often catalysts to changes in Indochina policy than reasoned debate or sustained engagement with the root problem of colonial oppression. The existence of powerful domestic challenges to the
republican order from the communist PCF and the Gaullist RPF only
made matters worse. The MRP exemplified the tendency among the
governing parties to subordinate colonial policy to the requirements of
the party's political survival. After the collapse of tripartism in 1947,
and the concurrent emergence of a strong electoral challenge from
the RPF, the MRP was divided between those members willing to govern alongside the Socialists and those reluctant to accept the break
with Gaullism. The MRP consolidated its power relative to the Socialists through its control over Indochina policy in the Third Force coalitions of 1947 to 1951. Other Third Force parties, the Radicals and the
UDSR especially, backed the MRP line over Indochina and so muffled
Socialist criticism of it. As with economic and financial policies, Socialist capacity to direct colonial affairs declined abruptly after 1947.
Rather than returning to opposition, however, the SFIO bridled at
extended military operations and the Bao Dai solution but failed to re-
pudiate either. Its culpability for the Indochina disaster was as complete as that of its more aggressive partners in government.

It seems then that the Fourth Republic system did indeed contribute
to the escalation of the Indochina conflict. Government by coalition
was not intrinsically at fault. Multiparty administration did not necessarily mean fudge and compromise as ministers struggled in vain to
conciliate potential dissidents within the National Assembly. The prob-

lem was rather more the nature of the opponents they faced. On the one hand, the communists incorporated their attacks on Indochina policy within a broader offensive against the governing elite. In doing so, the PCF made it harder still for the noncommunist left to advocate a cease-fire and talks with the Viet Minh. On the other hand, the Gaullists cynically manipulated the mounting evidence of failure in Vietnam to weaken the constitutional system they so despised. What had been a remarkable—and remarkably misguided—imperialist consensus in 1945, dissolved into bitter acrimony in 1947. The true victims of this process were not the squabbling politicians of metropolitan France but the people of Vietnam whose voices became inaudible in the din of interparty bickering.

EIGHT

Ho Chi Minh and the
Strategy of People's War

WILLIAM J. DUIKER

ON DECEMBER 19, 1946, military forces of the Democratic Republic of Vietnam (DRV) attacked French installations throughout the city of Hanoi. For the next three days, the two sides waged a bitter battle, as Vietnamese units (popularly known as the Viet Minh) gradually withdrew to prepared positions in the mountains skirting the Red River delta. The First Indochina War had begun.

On December 22, while the guns were still blazing in Hanoi, the Standing Committee of the Indochinese Communist Party (ICP) issued a statement to party members calling for a war of national resistance against the French colonial regime. The coming conflict, the ICP declared, would proceed in three stages. After a first phase of temporary withdrawal from the major cities, resistance forces would establish liberated zones in the countryside and begin to engage in periodic attacks on vulnerable enemy positions. In the final stage, Viet Minh units would launch a general offensive to defeat the French and unify the entire country under Vietnamese rule.[1]

To seasoned observers of international politics, the new Viet Minh strategy appeared to be a classical rendition of the doctrine of people's war as originally enunciated by the Chinese revolutionary Mao Zedong. In several articles written before World War II, Mao had outlined a strategy of protracted war that would escalate gradually to a final general offensive. It seemed clear that Vietnamese planners had decided to adopt the Chinese model in carrying out their own war effort.

As the years progressed, the Franco–Viet Minh conflict appeared to unfold according to the predicted scenario. After their retreat into the rugged terrain north of the Red River valley (known to Vietnamese as the Viet Bac, or "northern Vietnam"), Viet Minh forces gradually emerged from their mountain lair to confront the French in the lowlands. Then, in January 1951, under the command of the party's chief military strategist, General Vo Nguyen Giap, they mounted a general offensive aimed at seizing the entire Red River delta and occupying the capital city of Hanoi. When that assault was repulsed, the Viet Minh temporarily reverted to the second stage of guerrilla war. But in the spring of 1954, they returned to the offensive, launching a heavy attack on the French base at Dien Bien Phu, a small district capital in the mountainous northwestern corner of the country. The Viet Minh victory there in early May provided a backdrop for the peace conference that had just gotten underway at Geneva and became a major factor in bringing about an agreement to end the war.

In the years following the end of the Franco–Viet Minh conflict, the notion that the Maoist model had been an integral component of military doctrine in the DRV became accepted wisdom among analysts in the United States. Americans paid relatively little attention to the possibility that Vietnamese military planners had revised Chinese doctrine to fit their own circumstances, or that leading members of the ICP had played an active role in devising their own strategy of people's war. The only Vietnamese party leader to receive credit for formulating Viet Minh strategy was Vo Nguyen Giap, who in later years obligingly wrote a number of books and articles on the subject. Ho Chi Minh, president of the DRV and the founder of the ICP in the early 1930s, received even less attention. Although Ho has long been noted for his astute grasp of the techniques of diplomacy as well as his superb motivational skills, he is not generally considered an original thinker. Rather, he is seen as an opportunist whose intellectual talents were limited to formulating a pragmatic response to existing conditions.[2]

The purpose of this chapter is to examine the evolution of Vietnamese communist revolutionary strategy from its origins to the end of the war against the French. In particular, it will seek to demonstrate that although Ho Chi Minh was indeed a pragmatist who was willing to borrow from various sources to hammer out an effective strategy of national liberation, he played a more significant role in formulating the Vietnamese version of people's war than is usually assumed.

Roots

Biographers of Mao, in seeking the sources of his mature revolutionary beliefs, often point to his youthful experience as a formative factor in his intellectual development. Mao's father was a well-to-do but poorly educated farmer in central China who lacked all but the bare rudiments of a traditional Confucian education. Although educated at a normal school in the provincial capital of Changsha, the young Mao deeply resented the arrogance of urban intellectuals toward their rural compatriots and, after he became a member of the Chinese Communist Party, was quick to view the future of the Chinese revolution as taking place primarily in the countryside, rather than in the teeming coastal cities.

A comparison between Mao's upbringing and that of his contemporary, Ho Chi Minh, is instructive. Like Mao, Ho was born in a rural village deep in the countryside, and when he began in his early adolescence to attend school in the imperial capital of Hue, he was undoubtedly treated like a country bumpkin by many of his more cosmopolitan classmates. Like Mao, Ho chafed at the arrogance of Confucian mandarins, as well as of French colonial officials, and his first political act was to serve as an interpreter for peasants demonstrating against official corruption and high taxes in the spring of 1908.

Here, however, the similarities end. Ho Chi Minh's father was a scholar who instilled in his son a deep respect for the content of Confucian humanist teachings. Enrollment in a French-run school in Hue provided the young man with an admiration for the key tenets of Enlightenment thought. Unlike Mao, who always harbored a deep suspicion of the outside world, Ho Chi Minh was cosmopolitan in his interests and comfortable in dealing with Western leaders in the arena of international politics.[3]

In the summer of 1911, Ho Chi Minh left Indochina for the West with the goal of saving his country and learning more about European civilization. After several years of service as a mess boy at sea, he settled in France at the end of World War I and eventually became a founding member of the French Communist Party. What initially attracted him to communist ideology was not the Marxist vision of a classless utopia but the ideas of the Bolshevik leader V. I. Lenin, who had electrified radicals in Africa and Asia with his declaration that the new Soviet state must support nationalist uprisings throughout the colonial world as the first stage in provoking a worldwide socialist revolution against the capitalist order. Ho found Lenin's strategy of promoting alliances between communist parties and local nationalist groups highly relevant to the situation in French Indochina.[4]

Voice in the Wilderness

Inspired by Lenin's ideas, Ho rapidly emerged as the French Communist Party's chief spokesman for the colonial peoples. He soon found, however, that most party members had little interest in the "colonial question," which was generally considered to be a sidelight of the world revolution. In an article in the party journal *L'humanité*, he lamented that many militants in France "still think that a colony is nothing but a country with plenty of sand underfoot and of sun overhead, a few green coconut palms and colored folk, and that's all. And they take not the slightest interest in the matter."[5]

In the summer of 1923, he was invited to Moscow to study Marxism and work at Comintern headquarters, where he vocally criticized European communist parties for their inattention to the colonial problem and the revolutionary potential of the oppressed rural masses. As in Paris, however, his views were generally ignored, provoking him to lament to a friend that he was a "voice in the wilderness." Fortunately, the prevailing Leninist strategy for Asia was sufficiently flexible to fit his needs, so that on arriving in South China in late 1924, he immediately created a new organization based on a Leninist format. Known as the Revolutionary Youth League, it consisted of a broad alliance of workers, peasants, and the urban middle class designed to lead the struggle for national independence against the French. Cooperative efforts with other anticolonial parties were encouraged, although the league was careful to maintain its own independence of action. An inner core of committed revolutionaries formed the nucleus of a future communist party, which was expected eventually to carry out the second, or socialist stage of the Vietnamese revolution.[6]

The league had no immediate military component. In Ho's view, the peoples of Indochina were not sufficiently prepared to launch a revolutionary uprising to overthrow French colonial authority. But from his vantage point in Canton, Ho carefully observed the experience of the CCP in training its supporters in the techniques of guerrilla warfare, and in a short article that he authored later in the decade, Ho argued that a close alliance between workers and peasants was the proper road to revolution in colonial Indochina. By the late 1920s, Ho Chi Minh had thus laid down the foundations of a strategy of people's war to liberate his country from colonial rule.[7]

The mood was changing in Moscow, however, and in 1928 the Comintern suddenly shifted tactics and began to emphasize a more doctrinaire approach that focused on class struggle and urban-based revolution. Cooperative efforts with bourgeois nationalist or peasant parties were now discouraged in favor of efforts to organize the urban proletariat. When the ICP was formally established in 1930, its program obediently echoed the new line in Moscow. Younger members of the league who had been trained in Moscow openly criticized Ho Chi Minh for his now-outdated emphasis on national independence and peasant-proletarian alliance. A rural uprising that broke out in central Vietnam in the summer of 1930 appeared to confirm the views expressed by advocates of the new line: workers, farmers, and the urban bourgeoisie in other parts of the country did not rise in support of their compatriots in the central provinces but generally stood by as the French suppressed the uprising.[8]

During the next several years, Ho Chi Minh remained in eclipse. He arrived in Moscow in 1934 to find many of his old comrades in the grip of a reign of terror, as thousands of "old Bolsheviks" were tried and executed for allegedly treasonous activities. Ho apparently survived the purges only by virtue of continued support from influential supporters within the Comintern. But his prospects were about to improve. With the rise of Hitlerism in Europe and the triumph of militarism in Japan, Stalin changed tactics once again. At its Seventh Congress in 1935, the Comintern returned to the broad united front tactics that had been applied during the early 1920s. In 1938, a rehabilitated Ho Chi Minh returned to China, where he sought to restore contacts with leading elements of the ICP.

Inside Indochina, party leaders had been responding in their own way to the rapidly evolving events in the region. In early September 1939, French colonial authorities cracked down on the ICP's semilegal apparatus following the signing of the Nazi-Soviet Pact in late August. Two months later, the party's Central Committee issued a resolution calling for the formation of an alliance of progressive forces to launch a general uprising to overthrow the colonial regime. The tactics to be applied were not spelled out, although some party members, including the young activist Vo Nguyen Giap, had begun to give thought to the possible employment of guerrilla warfare. In the spring of 1940, Giap left for South China, where he met with Ho Chi Minh in April. For the first time in almost a decade, Ho was in direct touch with party leaders inside the country.

The Viet Minh Front

Having observed closely the dramatic rise of international tensions since his return to Asia, Ho was well aware of the potential significance of a Pacific war for the future of the Vietnamese revolutionary movement. When Japanese forces expanded into northern Indochina in the fall of 1940, he astutely realized the significance of the situation and made plans to return to Vietnam to launch preparations for a popular uprising at the close of what was rapidly becoming a global conflict. Lacking direct contact with Moscow or with CCP headquarters in North China, ICP leaders formulated their own approach for the coming struggle. The centerpiece of the strategy was the creation of a new four-class alliance (to be known as the League for the Independence of Vietnam, or Viet Minh Front) to seek the dual goals of independence and social reform.

In some respects, the new front resembled the broad alliance of anti-Japanese forces that the CCP had assembled in China. But there were some key differences. In the first place, Ho Chi Minh recognized that the Viet Minh alliance lacked the size and broad support sufficient to engage in widespread military operations against the dual adversary. As a result, he warned his colleagues that the first phase of preparations must concentrate on building up a political organization. In the meantime, small paramilitary units were created in the Viet Bac, where they would eventually be called upon to build a liberated base area and launch an attack on the delta at the end of the war. To help provide training materials for such military units, Ho translated into Vietnamese materials issued by the CCP for the use of its own guerrilla forces in China.[9]

Ho Chi Minh also viewed the international environment as crucial to his plans. In his judgment, because his country was still technically under colonial rule, one of the most important tasks for the party leadership was to seek external support for the Vietnamese struggle for national independence. That challenge was undoubtedly facilitated by the Japanese attack on Pearl Harbor on December 7, 1941, which brought the United States into the Pacific war. In the summer of 1942, Ho traveled secretly to China to seek support from Chiang Kai-shek's Nationalist government in Chungking (Chongqing). He also sought to establish contacts with U.S. military and intelligence representatives in South China. Although Ho viewed the United States as an imperialist nation that was fundamentally opposed to the spread of international communism, the promulgation of the Atlantic Charter the previous August had suggested that the Roosevelt administration might support the principle of self-determination for all colonial peoples at the end of the war.

To avoid alienating moderate elements at home and abroad, party leaders thus opted to reject the Maoist practice of placing the party openly at the head of the antifascist alliance. In Vietnam, the communist complexion of the Viet Minh Front was deliberately obscured, and primary emphasis was placed on the goal of national independence. A modest program to alleviate rural poverty was declared, but future plans to redistribute land holdings were postponed in order to avoid alienating the urban bourgeoisie and the patriotic scholar-gentry.

Ho's plans to establish a relationship with Allied governments were temporarily disrupted in August 1942, when he was arrested by local authorities suspicious of his political activities and held in prison for several months. After his release, however, he resumed his activities and was eventually able to patch together a shaky coalition—known as the Vietnam Revolutionary League, or Viet Nam Cach Menh Dong Minh Hoi—with noncommunist groups living in exile in South China. Recognizing that a key to success would rest in the ability of the new organization to present a moderate face to the outside world, he once again sought to disguise the role of the ICP in its formation, as well as his own background as an agent of the Comintern.[10]

In the winter of 1944–1945, Ho Chi Minh returned to northern Vietnam, where preparations for a general uprising at the close of the Pacific war were well under way. Some of his more militant colleagues, including the young Giap, urged a more aggressive approach in preparation for the final grasp for power, but Ho Chi Minh vetoed the proposal, arguing that a premature shift to military operations could provoke a response from Japanese occupation forces. "The phase of peaceful revolution has passed," he declared, "but the hour of the general insurrections has not yet sounded." As a consolation to his young colleague, Ho authorized Giap to form the first units of the future Vietnamese Liberation Army. To reflect the fact that their first duties would be primarily paramilitary in nature, they were to be called armed propaganda brigades.[11]

The August Revolution

By the spring of 1945, Viet Minh forces began to move southward from the border area in preparation for their planned general uprising. They now possessed some limited support from U.S. military representatives in South China, who had been assigned to train Viet Minh forces for their final assault against Japanese forces in Indochina. Still, the rapidity of the collapse of Imperial Japan in August operated to their disadvantage, since the movement in the southern part of the country was not yet well established and lacked direct communication with Viet Minh headquarters in the Viet Bac. As a result, when the war came to an end in mid-August, southern leaders had to share power with noncommunist rivals until Free French troops, arriving in October, consolidated power in Saigon and drove resistance elements into the countryside.

Nevertheless, the August Revolution, as it came to be known in revolutionary folklore, was a qualified success. Popular demonstrations, orchestrated by Viet Minh activists and supplemented where necessary by local militia units, resulted in a quick takeover of the northern and central parts of the country. A new provisional republic, with Ho Chi Minh as president presiding over a mixed cabinet composed of both ICP and noncommunist figures, was announced in early September. To allay suspicion of its motives, the ICP declared itself abolished in November, to be replaced by a Marxist studies group. The new government was faced with challenges on several fronts. Ho labored strenuously in the diplomatic arena, seeking to placate commanders of arriving Nationalist Chinese occupation forces and lobbying U.S. representatives for recognition of his new government, while seeking to negotiate a treaty with the French that would provide the DRV with at least some of the attributes of statehood. Militant Vietnamese nationalists and some party members opposed any concessions to Paris, but Ho argued that in view of Viet Minh military weakness, the DRV must be prepared to accept a compromise agreement calling for complete independence in five years.

Ho Chi Minh's focus on the diplomatic front reflected his view that the fate of the Vietnamese revolution, unlike that of its counterpart in China, depended in considerable measure on the shifting course of international politics. The immediate future of Indochina, he warned his colleagues, would depend on the state of relations among the victorious allies. If the Grand Alliance between the United States and the USSR held together, the former might decide to support Vietnamese independence against the French. But if tensions between Moscow and Washington increased, Washington would probably support the restoration of French authority in Indochina. If that happened, it would be necessary to exploit the contradictions among the Western allies to best advantage.[12]

Ho Chi Minh's analysis of the world situation was all too accurate. As U.S.-Soviet relations became strained during the months following the end of World War II, the White House became increasingly reluctant to challenge French actions in Indochina. Emboldened by U.S. support, the French adopted an intransigent attitude in negotiations with DRV representatives held in France during the summer of 1946. When an agreement proved elusive, Ho Chi Minh labored to delay a total breakdown in peace talks, but in November he finally authorized his senior military commanders to prepare for war.

People's War

With the outbreak of war in December 1946, party leaders, still operating in secret behind the veil of the Viet Minh Front, concluded that the strategy applied during the August Revolution, which had emphasized the role of political struggle leading to a general uprising, would no longer be appropriate. Once again, they turned to China for inspiration. On December 22, Viet Minh radio announced that the DRV would adopt a strategy of people's war. A few weeks later, the decision was reaffirmed with the publication of a treatise authored by ICP general secretary Truong Chinh and later translated into English as "The Resistance Will Win." The ideas presented in the book undoubtedly reflected the consensus view of the party leadership as a whole.[13]

The author elaborated on the earlier announcement that the coming conflict with the French would be waged as a protracted war based on Mao's famous three stages. In the first, or defensive (*phong ngu*), stage Viet Minh forces would retreat from heavily populated areas to defensive positions in the countryside. The second stage of equilibrium *(cam cu)*, which Chinh described as the key stage of the conflict, would be attained when French troops had reached their maximum strength and began to shift their attention to the task of pacifying the countryside and wiping out remaining Viet Minh units. This would be the moment when resistance forces would be called upon to intensify their activities and to wage guerrilla operations in enemy-controlled areas in order to expand the territory under their own control.

The final stage of general counteroffensive *(tong phan cong)* would consist of large-scale attacks on enemy forces involving both mobile and conventional forms of combat. The author cautioned that the transition from one stage to another could not be rigidly predicted and would depend upon a variety of factors, including the strength of the Viet Minh armed forces, the level of popular support for the insurgent movement, and the degree of demoralization of enemy troops.

Although there were a number of similarities between the ideas contained in the pamphlet and the Maoist doctrine of people's war, the Vietnamese approach differed from its Chinese counterpart in several respects. In the first place, Truong Chinh rejected Mao's analysis of the role of terrain in a revolutionary environment. Mao had argued that two factors unique to China permitted the successful application of people's war: first, its semicolonial status, which limited imperialist rule to the cities and left the rural areas substantially untouched by enemy control, and second, its vast territory, which allowed revolutionary forces to wage extensive guerrilla operations in areas far removed from the heartland of enemy authority.

Viet Minh leaders, of course, were confined to a much more limited physical environment and confronted an enemy armed with advanced weapons. Consequently, while Truong Chinh conceded that terrain was an important factor in protracted war, he asserted that popular support and a disciplined people's army led by the party could overcome the limitations of geography and colonial status. Even a country like Vietnam, he concluded, was not too small for the establishment of revolutionary base areas.[14]

Viet Minh strategists also departed from the Chinese model in their view of the preponderant importance of the world situation. Mao had devoted little attention to the role of international politics or to estimating its importance for events inside China. In Vietnam, where resistance forces were unlikely to achieve a decisive advantage on the entire battlefield, external factors would play a major role in promoting or hindering the revolutionary cause. The longer the war lasted, the more the Vietnamese revolutionary movement would earn the sympathy of democratic forces around the world, placing increased pressure on the French government to withdraw its troops. A shift in the world balance of power (presumably the growing political and military power of the Soviet Union or a victory by communist forces in China) might also further undermine the strength of the imperialist powers and redound to Viet Minh advantage.

Vietnamese strategists counted on psychological factors also to assist them in their efforts. Declining morale in the military ranks and increasing public resistance to the war on the home front would seriously weaken the French military effort. In bringing about such conditions, diplomacy might be used as a tactic, with what Truong Chinh described as "false negotiations" utilized to weaken the enemy's resolve while the revolutionary forces prepared for their final military assault.[15]

Withdrawal

By the time the December 22 directive had appeared, the first stage of withdrawal was already underway. Taking advantage of the enemy retreat, French forces seized the capital of Hanoi and occupied most of the lowland regions in northern and central Vietnam. They then reopened the major transportation routes down the coast to the south. Whenever possible, Viet Minh forces avoided combat in order to preserve their own small main force units, although there were some rearguard skirmishes in Hanoi and other urban areas undertaken by guerrillas or local paramilitary forces.

Beyond the cities, however, the Viet Minh remained in control of much of the countryside in northern Vietnam. In early April 1947, a central party cadre conference issued a resolution calling for an immediate shift to guerrilla operations in order to regain the initiative and establish a tactical advantage during the defensive phase. To achieve this end, a number of main-force regiments of the Vietnamese Liberation Army were broken down into small guerrilla units in order to harass French forces. Each village under Viet Minh control was instructed to establish a self-defense militia unit, while training programs on guerrilla warfare, taught by deserters from the French Foreign Legion and the Japanese army, were established in liberated areas. In the meantime, Ho Chi Minh launched a number of diplomatic initiatives to test the atmosphere in Paris and Washington. The response to his efforts was disappointing: the French had no interest in resuming negotiations, while the Truman administration was content for the moment to observe the hostilities from a distance.

For the Viet Minh it was a race against time to build up their strength before the French could break the back of the resistance. During the spring and summer, the French had limited their operations to consolidating control over highly populated areas in the Red River delta and along the central coast. But in the fall of 1947 they launched a major offensive in the mountains north of the delta in the hope of destroying the bulk of resistance forces and seizing the Viet Minh headquarters, now located in the jungles near the provincial capital of Tuyen Quang.

On the surface, the fall campaign was a success. French troops inflicted heavy casualties on Viet Minh units and then advanced northward to garrison frontier towns along the Chinese border. Additional clashes took place in the far northwest, where inexperienced Viet Minh units fighting for the first time in set positions absorbed heavy losses and were forced to flee into the mountains. Some troops abandoned their positions under pressure or refused to obey their commanders. Ho Chi Minh and his high command escaped capture, reportedly by less than an hour. French commander General Raoul Salan optimistically reported to Paris that enemy forces were now totally isolated and could be wiped out by simple police operations.[16]

Salan's analysis of the situation turned out to be far off the mark. Although the French offensive had disrupted enemy operations and forced the Viet Minh to change the location of their headquarters, Ho Chi Minh was still at large, and his movement still posed a potential threat to the security of French Indochina. In a tacit recognition that Salan had overstated the results of the fall campaign, French authorities decided to approach former emperor Bao Dai with a plan to form an autonomous government that could win support from moderates inside Vietnam. If the various noncommunist factions inside the country could be unified into a cohesive political force, there would be for the first time a viable alternative to the Viet Minh for the loyalty of the Vietnamese people. Although the public reaction to the French initiative was cautious, the willingness of many ardent nationalists to consider cooperating in a joint effort against the Viet Minh was evidence

that the latter were having some difficulty extending their urban political base beyond the radical fringe traditionally sympathetic to the revolution. Ho Chi Minh countered by broadening his own government,
replacing ICP members Vo Nguyen Giap and Pham Van Dong with
moderates.

The performance of the Viet Minh during the first year of the war
had thus been mixed. It had been able to survive the first French military onslaught but at the cost of severe losses of weapons, territory, and
personnel. On some occasions Viet Minh commanders had displayed a
lack of experience in applying the techniques of guerrilla warfare.
Truong Chinh cited the case of one officer who refused to allow his
troops to engage in combat on the grounds of preserving his forces. In
other instances officers reportedly lost control over their troops at the
height of battle, causing the soldiers to abandon the battlefield and
run away. On the political front, the movement was spreading its base
in the countryside but still suffered from a lack of commitment by
many poor peasants, especially in the south, where Viet Minh leaders
were struggling with limited success to broaden their base of operations in the marshy lowlands of the Mekong delta.[17]

Equilibrium

As it turned out, Viet Minh fortunes were about to improve. By the end
of 1947, recruitment in villages under Viet Minh control had begun to
rebound after losses from the French offensive, and the size of revolutionary armed forces was steadily on the rise. Although the French had
successfully occupied most of the Red River delta and dislodged the
Viet Minh from substantial parts of the Viet Bac, ICP party leaders
sensed that the enemy had reached his maximum strength and would
now turn his attention to pacification operations in place of ambitious
military operations. A meeting of the ICP Standing Committee in January 1948 formally decreed that the process of withdrawal was complete and announced the opening of the second stage of equilibrium.[18]

One of the key tenets of the second stage of people's war was that resistance forces must now attempt to seize the initiative on the battlefield. The main objective would no longer be simply to survive but to
wear down enemy forces and expand the territory under Viet Minh control, thus permitting an increase in recruitment and in the financial and
material resources available to the movement. In Indochina that meant

expanding operations into the central and southern parts of Vietnam as well as into neighboring Laos and Cambodia, forcing the enemy to divide its military forces and making them more vulnerable to attack. As Truong Chinh put it in an article written in 1947, "If the enemy attacks us from above, we will attack him from below. If he attacks us in the North, we will respond in Central or South Vietnam, or in Cambodia and Laos. If the enemy penetrates one of our territory bases, we will immediately strike hard at his belly and back . . . cut off his legs [and] destroy his roads." In preparation for the shift to the new stage, during the final months of 1947 a few mobile battalions were formed, and by early the following year the first battalion-sized attacks were launched upon enemy forces.[19]

The shift to a more aggressive approach quickly began to yield dividends. The size of revolutionary forces increased from fifty thousand at the beginning of the war to more than two hundred fifty thousand two years later. Viet Minh troop strength had reached near numerical parity with the French, although the Vietnamese were still inferior in firepower. The Viet Minh's political apparatus had also spread dramatically and now exercised control over 55 percent of all villages throughout the country, with a total of more than twelve million people.

The Communist Victory in China

Perhaps the most promising development at the end of the decade was the victory of communist forces in China. During the early years of the Franco–Viet Minh conflict, the DRV had only limited contacts with CCP headquarters in North China. Telegraph links were established in 1947, and a year later People's Liberation Army military units along the border began to cooperate with Viet Minh forces across the frontier. But in 1949 contacts increased dramatically with the imminence of the communist victory.

Since the creation of the DRV in September 1945, Ho Chi Minh had been reluctant to discuss the commitment of his government to the principles of Marxist ideology. In interviews with Western journalists, he had consistently stressed the determination of Vietnamese leaders to adopt a position of neutrality in international affairs. But the communist triumph in China presented the Viet Minh for the first time with the promise of support from a powerful ally. The elusive benefits of a policy of diplomatic neutrality now clashed with the growing promise of an outright military victory. In the fall of 1949, the DRV secretly sent two delegates to Beijing to feel out the leaders of the new People's Republic of China (PRC) on establishing diplomatic relations. The following January, an official delegation led by Ho Chi Minh visited Beijing to cement these ties and work out an agreement for military and economic assistance. From there Ho went on to Moscow, where Mao Zedong was engaged in negotiations with Josef Stalin on a new Sino-Soviet mutual security pact. The two communist leaders promised to support the Vietnamese struggle for national independence, although Stalin indicated that China should take primary responsibility for the project.[20]

Beijing agreed to grant diplomatic recognition to the DRV and to provide military assistance and advisers to assist the Viet Minh in their struggle against the French. That Chinese leaders viewed the conflict in Indochina through the prism of their own revolutionary experience seems clear. In a widely publicized speech in November 1949, PRC chairman Liu Shaoqi had declared that the peoples of Southeast Asia would eventually follow the Chinese model to overthrow oppressive colonial regimes and restore their own independence.[21]

During the next few months, Beijing established a Chinese military advisery group in northern Vietnam to provide guidance to Viet Minh planners in their struggle against the French. Training camps for Vietnamese cadres were constructed in South China, and a civilian advisery team was also established to assist the Vietnamese in remodeling their party and government along Chinese lines. Links between the two parties were now closer than they had been since the mid-1920s, when Ho Chi Minh had set up the headquarters of his Revolutionary Youth League in Canton.

The new relationship changed the character of the Indochina conflict in several respects. In the broadest sense, it led to a more open reliance by the DRV on the Chinese model of people's war. In the months following the establishment of full diplomatic relations, a spate of references appeared in the Vietnamese media on the significance of the Chinese experience for the Vietnamese revolution. Ho Chi Minh declared that Chinese aid had been a decisive factor in changing the Viet Minh approach to overthrowing the French. In an interview with the U.S. journalist Andrew Roth in August of 1949, Ho remarked that the Viet Minh movement had "changed its tactics" and was now following the Chinese model. Chinese training materials were translated into Vietnamese and distributed widely among the troops and political cadres, and study sessions were held to master the new doctrine.[22]

There was obviously an element of artificiality in the sudden outpouring of praise for the Chinese model, since the party had already declared its reliance on Mao Zedong's strategy of people's war at the beginning of the Franco–Viet Minh conflict in 1946. Still, the new relationship with Beijing resulted in several significant changes in Vietnamese revolutionary strategy. In the first place, the DRV openly moved into the socialist camp. Until now, the role of the Communist Party as the vanguard of the national liberation movement had been carefully concealed, and its commitment to violent revolution—a precondition insisted upon by Lenin at the formation of the Comintern in 1919—had been obscured by Ho Chi Minh's penchant for diplomatic maneuvering. Now, however, the famous "three treasures" *(san bao)* of Maoist doctrine—party, united front, and armed struggle—were adopted as the centerpiece of the Vietnamese revolution. At its Second National Congress, held in February 1951, the ICP (now renamed the Vietnamese Workers' Party, VWP) was formally reestablished. In his keynote speech to the congress, Truong Chinh declared that the VWP would play an open and leading role in the Vietnamese revolution, which was now clearly placed on a Marxist-Leninist path. Although the struggle against imperialism continued to hold priority over the antifeudal task, Chinh affirmed that once the imperialists had been defeated, a new government would be set up under clear party leadership that would "grow over" into a socialist revolution. Party leaders had thus tacitly abandoned the clear dividing line between the first and second stages of the revolution that had been introduced by Ho Chi Minh in the 1920s.[23]

When the results of the congress were made public, there was speculation in the world press that they represented a serious setback for Ho Chi Minh. After all, many of the changes adopted at the meeting—the new prominence of the communist party, the importance of class struggle, and the abandonment of gradualism—represented a departure from the views that he had espoused since the founding of the ICP in 1930. Whatever the truth of these assertions, Ho did not divulge his feelings on the matter and in his public remarks appeared to endorse the new strategy as appropriate to the current stage of the revolution.[24]

All for Victory

One reason why Ho Chi Minh may have given his blessing to the new strategy was that it permitted the VWP to reevaluate its strategic options in the war with the French. A dramatic increase in Chinese assistance would create conditions for a significant strengthening of Viet Minh forces and the launching of the third phase of people's war, the general offensive. In preparation for a possible escalation of the war, a national conference held in February 1950 called for a general mobilization of the population in liberated areas under the new slogan "All for the front, all for people's war, all for victory." Still, there were hints that some party members were skeptical whether conditions were ripe for an advance to the third stage. In a speech delivered to the Third National Conference, held in early 1950, Truong Chinh even implied he might be one of the doubters, cautioning that Chinese assistance did not guarantee success and adding that the Vietnamese people must still rely on their own efforts to bring about victory. The campaign, he pointed out, might even lead to direct intervention by Great Britain or the United States.[25]

The strongest case for a shift to the third stage was apparently made by General Vo Nguyen Giap. In a pamphlet published later in the year, Giap declared that conditions for launching the general offensive were present then. Although France continued to possess military superiority throughout Indochina, its will to resist was crumbling. At the same time, revolutionary forces possessed absolute moral superiority and strategic leadership. Finally, he pointed out, international factors were operating in favor of the movement. Resistance forces should thus advance cautiously but confidently toward a final military confrontation with the enemy, moving from limited attacks on smaller positions to large-unit attacks on major positions, ending with assaults on enemy cities. Because of the strategic importance of the Red River delta and its accessibility to the border area, Giap declared that the primary focus should be in the north rather than the south, where the French continued to hold the strategic advantage.[26]

Whether the final stage would be brief or protracted, Giap noted, would depend on the capabilities and leadership of the resistance forces and the rapidity of the disintegration of the enemy's will. In a gesture to the skeptics within the party leadership, he conceded that the results of the offensive could be affected by the unpredictability of the international situation, including the possibility of U.S. or British intervention. Also, the French might decide to consolidate their position in the south in case of a crumbling of their position in the north.

The General Offensive

As Viet Minh commanders prepared for transition to the third stage, their first priority was to seize control of the northern border region as a means of facilitating the movement of goods and personnel from China. While Viet Minh guerrilla units roamed the nearby mountains at will, the French continued to occupy a string of border posts from Lao Cai in the interior down to the coast. Despite the tortuous terrain, the French sent frequent military convoys up Route 4 as far as Cao Bang to maintain communications along the border.

In the early autumn of 1950, Vietnamese strategists, at the urging of their Chinese advisers, decided to test their new capabilities. Viet Minh units, now possessing substantially increased firepower, launched a series of aggressive attacks on enemy convoys and border posts. The campaign was stunningly successful, resulting in heavy French casualties and propelling them into a headlong flight to the coast, thus opening up the entire frontier to occupation by resistance forces. Chinese observers, however, noted a number of deficiencies in the Viet Minh performance, including a lack of troop discipline, inexperience on the battlefield, and a tendency by military commanders to ignore the needs of their troops and withhold bad news.[27]

The success of the fall offensive buoyed the optimism of Viet Minh leaders, some of whom now urged that plans be adopted for a larger offensive on the fringes of the Red River delta the following year. Skeptics feared that a general offensive would be premature, on the grounds that revolutionary forces still did not possess the capacity to engage in an open confrontation with the French. Supporters of the plan, however, argued that unless Viet Minh forces could expand their control over the delta, the shortage of rice in liberated areas could become desperate. Vo Nguyen Giap added that enemy morale was disintegrating and that revolutionary forces could move over to the third stage so long as they had a clear advantage over the enemy on a single battlefield, even though the French had a material superiority throughout the country as a whole.[28]

Ho Chi Minh, who had been pleasantly surprised at the results of the border offensive, expressed his own reservations about the new plan, reportedly advising one of his headstrong commanders that a major offensive, like a woman's pregnancy, must await its proper time. Chinese advisers were reportedly also ambivalent. Vo Nguyen Giap claimed that General Chen Geng, the chief Chinese adviser, had given his approval, but some civilian leaders in Beijing apparently expressed their reservations. In a letter to Ho Chi Minh in December 1950, Liu Shaoqi agreed with Ho's preference for a strategy of protracted war based on a policy of self-reliance, so long as it was rooted in careful preparations.[29]

In the end, party leaders adopted a compromise position put forward by Truong Chinh calling for a gradual transition to the third stage through a series of partial offensives on the margins of the Red River delta to test the level of French resistance. The Viet Minh offensive, which opened in January 1951 with an assault on the district town of Vinh Yen, provoked a vigorous response from French units, which made good use of newly arrived U.S. weaponry to drive Viet Minh forces back into the mountains with heavy losses. Later attacks elsewhere in the delta were also rebuffed, and by early spring the campaign had been abandoned. General Giap was forced to admit that it had been an error to confront the French directly on open terrain; he also conceded the shortcomings of the Viet Minh forces, which sometimes displayed a lack of aggressive spirit and tenacity. Ho Chi Minh, whose commitment to the general offensive had apparently been lukewarm at best, now alluded to the crucial importance of guerrilla operations and protracted war.[30]

Retrenchment

The failure of the 1951 general offensive, then, had a sobering effect on Vietnamese war planners. Viet Minh slogans no longer called for a general offensive and adopted the more limited objective of waging "an offensive during a strategic stage according to plan and to make the enemy lose." A key component of the new approach was to divide the enemy by extending the conflict into the mountainous northwest, as well as into neighboring Laos and Cambodia, and then to attack the enemy at selected points of vulnerability. Although Viet Minh leaders evinced little interest in resuming negotiations, it is clear that they were now counting on war weariness in France to force the French government to sue for peace.[31]

During the next two years, the benefits of the new strategy became apparent. The strength of Viet Minh forces continued to mount, while aid from China increased and public disapproval of *"la sale guerre"* (the dirty war) grew in France. To undercut support for the Viet Minh inside Indochina, the French had created a new autonomous government under Chief of State Bao Dai, but its dependence on Paris was obvious and earned it little public support. The only disquieting sign was the growing danger of direct U.S. military intervention. In 1950 U.S. president Harry S. Truman had responded to the creation of the Bao Dai government by providing France with military assistance to prosecute the war. In the spring of 1953, the new Eisenhower administration raised the ante by urging the French to adopt a more aggressive posture to seek total victory in Indochina.

Fighting and Talking

After the setback in the Red River delta in 1951, Viet Minh strategists had focused their attention on the mountainous northwest, where isolated French outposts lay vulnerable to attack by small resistance units. Successful operations in this area also opened up opportunities for an advance into northern Laos, thus creating a political problem for the French. But without major operations in the delta or along the coast, the probability of a dramatic advance on the battlefield was limited. As Viet Minh war planners gathered in the early fall of 1953 to discuss the following year's campaign, General Giap proposed a new campaign in the Red River delta to counter the French buildup there. Chinese advisers were more cautious, and with Ho Chi Minh's approval, planning began for additional operations in the northwest.

Now the Viet Minh strategy of protracted war finally began to pay dividends, as the French government began to express new interest in a negotiated settlement. It was a propitious moment for a diplomatic solution on the international scene as well, since both Moscow and Beijing, each for its own reasons, wanted an end to the war. Viet Minh leaders had some misgivings about engaging in peace talks, but Ho Chi Minh undoubtedly warned his more militant colleagues that without firm support from its allies—especially from China—a complete DRV victory was not feasible. In a November interview with the Swedish journal *Expressen,* he declared that the DRV government was always ready to search for a peaceful solution.

For the French, as well as for the Viet Minh, conditions on the battlefield would be a major factor in determining the shape of a final peace settlement. In the fall of 1953, the commander of French forces, General Henri Navarre, ordered the occupation of the district capital of Dien Bien Phu in the mountains near the Laotian border, as a means of disrupting enemy operations in the region. After lengthy discussions with their Chinese advisers, Viet Minh planners decided to attack the new French base in a bid to bring about a dramatic shift of the military balance of power on the eve of the peace conference, now scheduled to convene in Geneva in early May.

Viet Minh leaders were apparently convinced that an assault on Dien Bien Phu represented less of a gamble than the abortive 1951 general offensive, since resistance forces possessed a clear geographical advantage in the area. Located far from the enemy base of operations in the Red River delta, the French base would be difficult for the defenders to supply with equipment or reinforcements. Equally important, access to the Chinese border would facilitate shipment of Chinese weapons and other equipment to Viet Minh units operating in the area. Still, there would be an element of risk, since it would be the first time that the Viet Minh had decided to attack a target strongly defended by the enemy.[32]

The nature of the proposed attack apparently aroused some disagreement. General Wei Guoqing, the senior Chinese adviser, recommended a lightning assault based on the "human wave" tactics used successfully by Chinese forces in Korea. But after initial assaults on the base proved costly, Viet Minh leaders shifted in March to a more gradualist approach that called for seizing the enemy's outlying strong points one by one, while using artillery placed in the surrounding mountains to destroy the small airstrip and cut off the French source of supply. The base was finally seized by a massive Viet Minh assault on May 6, just as delegates were arriving in Geneva to seek an end to the conflict.

As Viet Minh leaders had hoped, the victory at Dien Bien Phu had a measurable impact on the negotiations at Geneva. Under increased public pressure to bring an end to the war, the French government agreed to accept a compromise settlement that called for the final departure of French military forces and the temporary division of the country into two separate regroupment zones. The Geneva agreement, which had been urged on the DRV by its chief allies, was not popular within the movement, where many felt that Viet Minh forces should have fought on to final victory. Ho Chi Minh, who had been persuaded to accept a compromise during a meeting with Chinese foreign minister Zhou Enlai in early July, attempted to calm fevered spirits by declaring at a party meeting held a few weeks later that "some comrades" were ignoring the fact that the Americans were behind the French. It was time, he said, for the Vietnamese people to bind up their wounds and begin building a new society in North Vietnam in preparation for reunification in the future.[33]

By the end of the war, then, the Viet Minh had replaced the Maoist three-stage scenario with a more nuanced approach that made greater use of political forms of struggle. They had learned that for small countries like Vietnam, an impregnable base area was less important than a reliable sanctuary beyond the frontier and that broad support from allies was essential when facing a powerful enemy whose base was outside the country. Finally, they had faced the painful reality that objective circumstances sometimes demanded that final victory be postponed indefinitely.

In the end, Viet Minh strategy had become an amalgam of the ideas of Mao Zedong and Ho Chi Minh with a dash of Lenin thrown in. Lenin had laid the political groundwork with his concept of a four-class alliance, while Maoism weighed in with the strategy of people's war. Ho Chi Minh adjusted Leninism in order to broaden the base of the movement and then contributed his own views on the importance of political struggle and diplomacy in promoting the revolutionary cause. What had been created then was not so much a new model of revolutionary war as a patchwork of ideas designed to meet the particular circumstances of the Vietnamese revolution. As an exercise in pragmatism, it was vintage Ho Chi Minh.[34]

Clearly, there was no classical Vietnamese model that could be adopted wholesale by revolutionary groups elsewhere in the world. In fact, the essence of the Vietnamese approach was to adapt elements from existing models to their own particular circumstances. Still, Viet Minh strategy offered useful lessons on how diplomacy and the techniques of psychological warfare could supplement revolutionary violence in countering the military advantages of a more powerful adversary.

The Legacy

How did DRV leaders apply the lessons of the Franco–Viet Minh War in their later conflict against the United States? When the VWP decided to return to the strategy of revolutionary war in January 1959, there was no immediate consensus on what specific approach to adopt in the south. Ho Chi Minh initially argued for a cautious policy emphasizing political struggle in order to avoid U.S. military intervention. But when Washington intervened to avoid a collapse of the Saigon regime, VWP leaders returned to the three-stage model, while recognizing that political struggle, diplomacy, and protracted war would be necessary to minimize the U.S. military advantage. Once again, the leading role of the party was disguised.

With the compromise peace agreement at Paris in 1973, U.S. combat troops withdrew from South Vietnam, and a peace process was put in place. When that failed, DRV war planners—no longer facing the threat of U.S. military intervention—returned to the original Maoist concept of a general offensive to complete their final takeover of the south two years later. Ironically, the final assault on Saigon was labeled the "Ho Chi Minh campaign" to honor their leader, who had died six years before.[35]

NINE

◆ ◆ ◆

The Declining Value of Indochina

France and the Economics of Empire,
1950–1955

LAURENT CESARI

THERE IS MUCH irony in French policy toward Indochina. The war that started in 1946 was more a colonial conflict than a confrontation between communism and anticommunism. In 1949, France granted the Associated States of Cambodia, Laos, and Vietnam no more independence than it had offered the Democratic Republic of Vietnam in 1946. The three states were brought under a protectorate regime that left diplomacy and defense in the hands of the French government. In its communications with other Western powers, however, the French Foreign Ministry began portraying the war as an East-West conflict as early as February 1947. At the end of 1949, it seemed that this policy had paid off. The United States now stood ready to provide material assistance to the French expeditionary force as part of its general strategy of containment of the People's Republic of China.

This success was a prelude to serious difficulties for France. The militarization and globalization of U.S. and Western containment policies left France badly overstretched. As the Western powers rearmed and sought to do the same with West Germany, French political leaders had to reevaluate to what extent possession of Indochina bolstered their claims to equal status with the United States and Britain as the third great power of the Western alliance. This reevaluation took place quickly. When Pierre Mendès France questioned the value of Indochina in October 1950 his colleagues in the National Assembly did not take him seriously. Yet his arguments had become widely accepted by December 1951, when he made a second speech on the topic. This chapter brings together data from scattered sources to show that Mendès France was right.

The argument will proceed in three parts. First, we shall see that Indochina became a marginal asset for France, both strategically and economically, as the war continued. Next, the chapter will explore the competing claims of war in Asia and of rearmament in Europe. Continuation of the war carried the risk that France might end up in a position inferior not only to the United Kingdom but also to West Germany. French leaders understood the situation and concluded in May 1953 that it demanded a "graceful exit" from Indochina. Last, the chapter will examine how the opposition of many members of the French National Assembly to the prospect of West German rearmament under the guise of the European Defense Community (EDC) created a situation that enabled the French government to extract American and Soviet acquiescence to such an exit.

Indochina as a Wasting Asset

What precisely were French interests in Indochina? Let us first consider economic interests. At first sight, Indochina in this respect deserved its reputation as the jewel of the French Empire. In 1940, 46 percent of all private assets invested in the French Empire were concentrated in Indochina. Yet this share had reached 55 percent in 1914. A slump in the rubber industry during the Depression of the 1930s, coupled with the rising risks of anticolonial uprising, had caused private capital to start leaving Indochina between the two world wars.[1] During the First Indochina War, private capital fled from the peninsula at a rapid pace (30 percent each year in 1947, 1948, and 1951, for instance). Most of these assets retreated to North and West Africa.[2] Between 1943 and 1954, the sum total of private assets in Indochina decreased by two-thirds (in real terms) and public assets by one-third.[3]

Wartime conditions increased production costs, while the traditional staples faced a contracted market after 1945. Synthetic rubber proved a convenient substitute for the original product for most purposes. Indochinese rice cost 10 percent more than Burmese and Siamese rice even between the two world wars, making it impossible to export except to metropolitan France. After 1945, France itself developed its own paddy fields in Camargue in southern France. Meanwhile, industrial development projects conceived by Vichy planners and then revived during the postwar period turned out to be idle dreams. In 1948, even the originator of the stillborn scheme to transform Indochina into the workshop of Southeast Asia admitted that its cost amounted to one-eleventh of the reconstruction plan for metropolitan France, whereas the productive capacity of Indochina was only one thirty-seventh of the mother country's productive capacity.[4] Thus, the role of Indochina as a supplier for metropolitan France was quite limited, even before 1945.

On the other hand, even during the war Indochina remained one of the most important buyers of products exported from metropolitan France, second only to Algeria. Its share in the value of exports from metropolitan France, which had sunk to 7 percent in 1939, recovered to 12 percent in 1953 and 10 percent in 1954.[5] These figures are all the more impressive in view of the fact that the three Associated States never agreed to sign any commercial treaty with France to ensure preferential status for metropolitan goods. But as long as the local currency, the piastre, remained overvalued (that is, until May 11, 1953), and as long as a French civil servant stood at the head of the Office Indochinois des Changes (Indochinese Currency Board, the administration in charge of delivering import licenses in Indochina), French goods enjoyed preferential treatment. The trick consisted in denying licenses to import from countries that did not belong to the *zone franc*, the French currency area. As a result, metropolitan goods accounted for 56.9 percent of the value of all Indochinese imports in 1947 and 78 percent in 1951 and 1953.[6] French shipping and airlines, as well as older, declining industries such as food processing and textiles, benefited greatly from this de facto monopoly. The decline of French exports to Indochina after the closure of the Office Indochinois des Changes on December 31, 1954, underlines how successful the previous policy had been. French goods accounted for 52.4 percent of the value of South Vietnam's imports in 1955 but dropped to 24.7 percent in 1956 and 19.4 percent in 1959.[7]

Nevertheless, French exports to Indochina did not come close to covering the cost of the war. From 1949 to 1954, the value of French exports to Indochina never accounted for more than half of war-related expenditures in the French budget.[8] While some economic sectors benefited from the war, military operations in Indochina were, on the whole, a serious drain. Although the United States shared the financial burden of the war with France from 1950 to 1954, it was only during the last phase of the conflict, when the United States underwrote the

Navarre Plan, that Indochina briefly paid dividends by channeling dollars into the French treasury. The United States covered 25.6 percent of war expenditures in 1952, 34.5 percent in 1953, and 66.7 percent in 1954—an average 41.9 percent for the three years.[9]

Rearmament in Europe was even costlier than war in Indochina. Through the end of 1950, the cost of operations in Indochina soared until they absorbed almost half of all French military spending. The French government responded not by reducing public investment in the civilian sector but by curtailing equipment of French forces outside Indochina. Both U.S. shipments of military goods to Indochina and NATO rearmament in Europe began in 1950. From then on, rearmament in Europe absorbed more of the French budget than operations in Indochina, but the war kept going. Military spending, as a percentage of France's gross national product, swelled accordingly from 1950 to 1953 and reached a level comparable to the figure for the United States. Meanwhile, public investment in the civil sector declined, while the French budget continued to show a deficit.[10]

Rearmament in Europe was costly not only because Indochina had taken precedence over Europe in French defense spending before 1950 but also because it was based on the enormously ambitious U.S. plan to create a "situation of strength," circling the Soviet bloc by building up conventional NATO forces. Since France had to carry on operations in Indochina at the same time, French representatives at the NATO Standing Group proposed in 1950 that the alliance adopt a strategy for the defense of Western Europe based on an atomic offensive by the U.S. Air Force. They hoped that such strikes would reduce both the length of military operations and the number—and, therefore, the cost—of ground divisions required. They pleaded in vain. NATO strategy remained based on the idea that the Western powers had to balance Soviet conventional forces. The situation changed in December 1954, when NATO adopted a new strategic plan. But even then, NATO planners concluded that a strategy emphasizing nuclear strength required numerous divisions to "bait" their Soviet counterparts. NATO strategy compounded the French government's problems, then, by making it certain that France was overextended during the Indochina war.

In this predicament French leaders faced a question: what mattered more—Europe or Indochina? The French Chiefs of Staff always maintained that the most important French interests were concentrated in

Europe. Under the Fourth Republic, French strategy remained focused on the European–Mediterranean–North African (and, to a lesser extent, French African) area often called "Eurafrique" ("Eurafrica"). In Europe, the French government wanted NATO to defend the continent as far to the east as possible. Rearmament in Europe was costly, but, on the positive side, it implied that the United States had laid to rest any temptation to adopt a "peripheral strategy" allowing Soviet divisions to probe deeply into Western Europe. The French government wanted NATO to defend Western Europe on the Elbe River, but, since West German forces were lacking, it was only in December 1954, when the alliance adopted its new strategic vision, that such a plan became possible. Before that time—that is, during the whole Indochina war—NATO planned for a quick retreat from the Elbe to the Rhine; the eastern border of France was, in fact, NATO's real line of defense against a Soviet invasion.

The strategic importance of North Africa was almost equal to that of Europe, according to most French military leaders, because had metropolitan France been invaded, North Africa would have provided a fallback position that, it was hoped, could later become a springboard for a counterattack, as during World War II. Compared to Africa, especially North Africa, Indochina was just too far away from metropolitan France. Even the navy, the service most concerned with colonial tasks, had been concentrating its operations in the Mediterranean since the interwar years. This priority was reinforced by the fact that, from the early 1950s, NATO funded the refurbishment of big naval bases in North Africa, such as Bizerte and Mers El-Kebir. While strategists agreed that Cam Ranh Bay (Tourane) had excellent potential as a naval base, it remained underdeveloped.

Therefore Africa, especially North Africa, was the really useful part of the French Empire. Opponents of the Indochina war such as Mendès France supported Eurafrican colonialism (eventually in the guise of an informal empire). Even the most overtly colonialist rationales for the Indochina war stressed not the value of Indochina itself but the danger of establishing a precedent there that would undermine French rule in North Africa. If France had relinquished control over the diplomacy and defense of the Associated States, the protectorates of Morocco and Tunisia would have asked for the same concession.

To turn now from defense planning to basic issues of foreign policy, the French government aimed at turning the NATO Standing Group into a three-nation directory of the United States, Britain, and France, with jurisdiction over the whole world. The French first advanced this idea in January 1949, even before the creation of NATO. Such a body would have given France equal status with Britain, allowed France to defend its interests worldwide, and provided France with insurance against U.S. and British flirtation with a "peripheral strategy" in Europe. By waging war in Indochina, France could plausibly plead that it remained a world power, thereby justifying its claim to membership in a worldwide directory. Foreign Minister Georges Bidault summed up the general feeling among French decision-makers in December 1953: "What is vital is the Atlantic Alliance and the Standing Group, where France is one of the Big Three, and it must strive to keep its rank there."[11]

The problem was that the Standing Group had no real power. The U.S. Joint Chiefs of Staff, who rated France merely as a regional power with responsibilities limited to Europe and North Africa, objected to the directory idea from the beginning. Secretary of State Dean Acheson overruled them, however, in order to pursue diplomatic objectives. He had conceived the Standing Group as a sop that would soften French misgivings about the economic reconstruction and eventual rearmament of West Germany, not as a body that would exercise real power. Accordingly, Washington insisted that the Standing Group cover only the same geographic area as the alliance itself and that its function be merely to coordinate strategic planning undertaken by other NATO bodies (under overwhelming American influence), rather than to supervise them, as the French government would have liked. In February 1953, in order to facilitate ratification of the EDC treaty by the French parliament, Bidault asked his British colleague Anthony Eden to agree to grant worldwide jurisdiction to the Standing Group, to add to NATO a Supreme Council as a political counterpart to the Standing Group, and to establish regular policy meetings among the Big Three about the Far East. Bidault got nothing. Eden and U.S. secretary of state John Foster Dulles agreed that French participation in the EDC meant that Paris enjoyed equal status with the other powers, not a position of privilege.

The position of Indochina in French strategic planning was not, then, important enough to back claims that France was a real great power, capable of defending its possessions in Asia as well as in Europe and in Africa. And in any case, Britain and the United States declined to grant such status to France.

The Indochina-EDC Nexus

Not only did Indochina not rank among vital French interests, but, from 1950 on, the war in Indochina and French rearmament in Europe worked at cross-purposes. In September 1950, the North Atlantic Council declared itself in favor of West German rearmament. In October, after the French defeat at Cao Bang, Pierre Mendès France warned that France must now choose between Europe and Indochina. The Pleven cabinet replied that American aid and the development of the armies of the Associated States would make this choice unnecessary. Such optimism was ill-founded. The French government was unable to prevent strategic overstretch, a fact widely acknowledged at the end of 1952.

What could the Associated States contribute to the war effort? Their financial contribution remained lower than expected. In 1949, each of them had been allowed to develop its own treasury department, and Vietnam had pledged to devote 40 percent of its public spending to defense. (Cambodia pledged 30 percent, while Laos spent nothing on defense.) On public finance, as on other issues, France did not hurry to grant the Associated States truly autonomous status. Vietnam, for instance, had no budget of its own before 1952. Accordingly, the Associated States let France and the United States do the military spending. The result was that the financial contribution of the Associated States to their defense amounted to only 1.4 percent of all costs in 1950, 4.4 percent in 1951, 5.9 percent in 1952, 6 percent in 1953, and 8.7 percent in 1954.[12]

Even more significant to French calculations about balancing commitments, the armies of the Associated States required a large number of French officers. These Frenchmen were necessary to put Indochinese armies on a par with French forces in technical capability and in officer-to-men ratio. It was imperative that they be trained according to French military norms so they could undertake joint operations with French forces. This was a political requirement as well, for without such interoperability on French terms, the notion of the French Union would have been meaningless. To accomplish these objectives, the French military assigned twice as many officers and noncommissioned officers (NCOs) as would have been required in a comparably sized metropolitan unit. The task of training Indochinese officers and NCOs according to French norms promised to take years. In the meantime, France would clearly have to provide the personnel to train and command the new forces, while also providing for its own expeditionary corps. Unsurprisingly, this situation created severe staffing problems in Europe since a heavy proportion of French officers were serving in Indochina. On December 31, 1952, this proportion amounted to 22 percent for the army, 13 percent for the navy, and 10 percent for the air force. For NCOs, the figures jumped to 35 percent for the army and 19 percent for the air force.[13]

Moreover, the National Assembly's unwillingness to contemplate sending conscripts to Indochina meant that only professional members of the armed forces served there, often for extended periods. Indochina simply dried up the pool of French regular soldiers; on December 31, 1952, 52 percent of army regulars served there. The proportion reached 42.5 percent for the air force.[14] Since few candidates were willing to spend long periods in Indochina, it became difficult for the armed services to recruit new regulars. This situation made staffing problems in Europe even more acute.

Since French forces were thinly spread across Europe, Indochina, and Africa, French commanders in Indochina had to wage war with fewer soldiers than they would have wished. At the same time, France was unable to meet its rearmament obligations under NATO agreements. At first sight, the French predicament in Europe was not critical. For one thing, fears of a Soviet invasion of Western Europe, kindled by the Korean War, abated after the Chinese and North Koreans agreed, with Soviet prompting, to open armistice talks at Kaesong on July 10, 1951. Moreover, the mammoth rearmament program undertaken by NATO during the second Truman administration was simply unfeasible. All European members of the alliance, not only France, were unable to reach their assigned goals, which the new Eisenhower administration hastened to reduce in April 1953. Still, given the prospect of West German rearmament, the undersized apparatus that France maintained in Europe was a cause of serious concern.

The Vietnamese chief of state, Bao Dai, and West German chancellor Konrad Adenauer put the French government in a difficult position by pursuing essentially the same policy. Under pressure from the Western powers, both sought to create an army from scratch, and both made the most of the resulting opportunity to extort "equal rights" with France. Both argued that such rights were necessary to win over the considerable number of skeptics who opposed such strenuous military exertions—namely, the fence-sitters in Indochina and the Social Democrats in West Germany.

Both Bao Dai and Adenauer had strong backing from Washington, and both pursued their aims assertively. Adenauer went as far as to claim for West Germany a seat in the NATO Standing Group. With the Truman administration advocating West German rearmament at any price, France could not long maintain its opposition to the creation of big German military units. At a meeting in Paris on January 20 and 21, 1952, the foreign ministers of Belgium, the Netherlands, Luxembourg, France, Italy, and West Germany decided that twelve West German divisions should be operational by 1954 as a part of a NATO target of forty-three divisions. Since the plan called for fourteen French divisions, it appeared that Paris had been able to preserve its edge over Bonn.

In fact, the situation was more complicated than it seemed. Since many French politicians were incensed by plans to rearm West Germany a mere five years after the end of World War II, Prime Minister René Pleven, prodded by Jean Monnet (then high commissioner for economic planning), decided in October 1950 to follow an indirect path by embedding German forces within a new supranational institution, the EDC. Strictly speaking, there would be no German army. West German rearmament would start only after the parliaments of the six participating continental states had ratified the EDC treaty. In this way, West German soldiers would wear only European uniforms, not German ones, which might have called to mind painful memories.

It was the EDC treaty itself that granted twelve divisions to West Germany. This clause made it certain that the French Assembly would never ratify the EDC as long as operations were underway in Indochina. Too many deputies simply found it unthinkable to allow West Germany to deploy twelve divisions at a time when France would not be able to reach that number in the European theater. From the beginning of 1953 to mid-1954, French forces in Europe consisted of five fully equipped divisions and seven reserve divisions.[15] Ratification of the EDC seemed to require, then, that the expeditionary corps in Indochina return to Europe. In fact, peace in Indochina (July 21, 1954) occurred before the EDC ratification debate in the French assembly (August 30, 1954). Before either of those events, though, NATO extended to West Germany almost cost-free security, requiring Bonn to pay only for the maintenance of Allied occupation troops on its soil.

This situation was detrimental to France. It gave West Germany time to strengthen its economy compared to that of France. Even if the EDC treaty had gone into effect as early as November 1, 1952, defense ex-

penditures would have amounted to only 25 percent of West German
public spending in 1952, against 36 percent in France. (The ratio of
public expenditures to the gross national product was similar in France
and in West Germany.) Low defense spending allowed West Germany
to stabilize its currency and balance its external trade by 1952—
accomplishments that French financial experts envied.[16] From a political point of view, by delaying the ratification of the EDC treaty and
West German rearmament, France disappointed its NATO partners
and raised the possibility that they would force West German rearmament upon France without any political safeguard other than Bonn's
membership in the Atlantic Alliance. Of course, France might veto the
admission of West Germany into NATO but only at the price of shat-
tering the alliance.

The risk of such an outcome was not high, however. In the short
term, French decision-makers worried more about the widening military gap between France and the two Anglo-Saxon powers. While
France waged a low-tech war in Indochina, Britain tested an atomic
bomb in October 1952. A study presented to Foreign Minister Bidault
in March 1953 showed that manpower expenditures in the French military budget vastly exceeded equipment expenditures, precisely the
opposite of the situation in Britain and the United States. France, the
study concluded, "belonged to the class of small continental European
powers which supply troops but are unable to equip them without foreign aid."[17]

The federalist aspects of the EDC heightened the contradictions in
which French policy was caught. On the one hand, the French government argued that its empire entitled it to equal status with Britain. On
the other hand, the EDC would grant West Germany equal rights within
a new organization that would set limits on the French government's
freedom of action toward its colonies. This contradiction stemmed
from factionalism within the Third Force governing coalition, and
especially inside the Mouvement républicain populaire (MRP). Members of the Christian Democrat MRP party maintained nearly uninter-
rupted control of the Foreign Ministry from September 1944 to June
1954 and of the Ministry of Overseas France (Ministry of Associated
States after July 1950) from November 1949 to June 1953. Jean Letourneau was minister for the Associated States from October 1949 to
June 1953. He belonged to the Bidault wing of the MRP, which accepted European federalism only as long as it was limited to definite

tasks and attached more importance to Big Three relations with Britain and the United States. By contrast, Robert Schuman, foreign minister from July 1948 to January 1953, set European federalism as his priority in order to control West Germany and to close the breach between the French and the Germans; he was also a less extreme colonialist than Bidault. Schuman took responsibility for the initiatives of Monnet, who, on his own authority and without any legal ground, had granted West Germany the principle of equal rights with France in April 1951 and then, in July, the right to maintain armed divisions.

Since the EDC treaty of May 27, 1952, had been negotiated by the Schuman wing of the MRP, it set limits to French liberty of action overseas. According to its Article 10, member states would be allowed to keep national forces for overseas use, but they could not use them without prior EDC authorization. Furthermore, a ceiling was imposed on the size of overseas forces to keep intact the strength of EDC divisions. Such provisions simply did not square with Article 62 of the French constitution, which stipulated that members of the French Union "pool all their resources to guarantee the defense of the whole Union" and entrusted the French government with "the coordination of these resources and the political direction necessary to prepare and carry out such defense."

Was American assistance in the Indochina war sufficient, as Pleven had hoped, to free France from the danger of imperial overstretch? Starting in the autumn of 1949, the French government repeatedly asked for American financial contributions (not simply military supplies) to support the Indochina war. For more than two years, these efforts came to naught, for the Truman administration refused to fund other states' public deficits. Things began to change during the NATO conference in Lisbon in February 1952. Prime Minister Edgar Faure agreed to raise overall French defense spending, as requested by NATO plans for the defense of Europe, but warned that France could not face its military commitments in Europe and Indochina at the same time and threatened to reduce expenditures in Indochina if the United States did not grant financial assistance to the war. He stressed that, failing such subsidies, Paris would need to negotiate an end to the conflict, for West Germany would dominate the EDC if France joined the body while still carrying the burden of the war. Schuman fully agreed.

The Truman administration relented and granted France $200 million worth of "off-shore procurements," explicitly for use in Indochina.

Under this new program, the United States paid in dollars to enable French arsenals to fulfill military production plans already laid out in the French budget. In effect, the arrangement meant that a fraction of the cost of the war was excluded from the French budget. French decision-makers deemed these procurements important because they used the savings to develop French arms exports. Since the EDC treaty allowed West Germany to maintain its own armament industry, it was essential that France become a strong exporter in this sector.[18] In Lisbon, the Indochina conflict became an export industry, a "dollars-earning machine" that worked for France.

In Lisbon, Faure also argued that, since the United States rated Indochina as a position of real strategic value for the whole Western bloc, all NATO countries should fund the war. Washington promised to give an answer in early 1953. The cabinet of Premier Antoine Pinay may have sought to pave the way for such financial requests when it insisted in December 1952 that the North Atlantic Council pass a motion of moral support for the Indochina war.

During the second half of 1952, the idea gained ground in Washington as well as in Paris that the United States should channel to the Indochina war as much of its military assistance to France as possible. The European desks at the State Department and the Mutual Security Agency speculated that the prospect of the French rolling back the Viet Minh might inspire Congress to appropriate more funds than the plight of France unable to meet its military commitments to NATO. Concentrating support on the war would also offer a way out of the EDC-Indochina contradiction. Total aid for French military procurements was estimated at $500 million for the fiscal year 1953–1954. Even if the United States fully equipped the expeditionary corps and the Associated States' armies, the needs for military equipment in Indochina would not be high enough to reach such a level. To spend the whole $500 million in Indochina, Washington would also have to cover pay for the Associated States' soldiers. Even then, the sum would be so great as to allow the Associated States to enlist more troops. In this way, the French Expeditionary Corps could be promptly withdrawn, and the French assembly would no longer have any excuse not to ratify the EDC treaty.

Meanwhile, in Paris, the Pinay cabinet had signed the EDC treaty but found no parliamentary majority to ratify it. This situation should have surprised no one, since the parliamentary elections of June 17, 1951, had returned 114 Gaullist members (none sat in the previous Chamber), whereas the MRP, which was the most pro-EDC party, had lost 50 percent of its voters. Pinay was careful not to share his doubts about ratification with the Americans. Instead, he took the line that concessions from Washington could mollify critics of the treaty. In this context, all the departments of his cabinet agreed that the concentration of American aid on Indochina would benefit France. It would allow France to get rid of the tight U.S. political control that was part and parcel of the procurement process. For instance, in October 1952, the United States had linked new procurements with an increase in French defense expenditures, causing a serious diplomatic incident. At the same time, orders for procurements could not be placed with firms that tolerated communist unions, whereas such unions were legal and had many members in France. Although anticommunist, French ministers and civil servants, like most of their Western European colleagues, resented such foreign meddling in internal affairs. Saving on Indochina would allow France to spend more on its armament industry. The Defense Ministry deemed U.S. deliveries to Europe insufficient and haphazard; it hoped that aid now specifically marked for Indochina would be given on a more regular basis. Most importantly, all departments hoped that raising the strength of Indochinese armies would prevent the United States from asking for an increase in the number of French soldiers serving in Indochina.

Thus, when France asked the United States to foot the bill for the expansion of the Associated States' armies, French ministers (with the notable exception of Letourneau) in no way planned for a decisive military victory over the DRV, whatever they might have said to the Americans in this regard. René Mayer, who was prime minister during the first half of 1953, admitted as much. "It seems clear," he wrote, "that among French businessmen and civil servants who know Indochina well, nobody believes anymore that it is possible to beat the Viet Minh militarily. Nevertheless, in order to induce the Americans to grant France sizeable direct aid, the idea has been propagated that extra efforts might yield decisive results."[19] In fact, Paris tried to get American aid to boost the overall French defense program and to strengthen French armament industries. Such considerations pertained to Europe, not to Indochina. While he asked for American money, Pinay felt no qualms about sending a secret mission to Rangoon to inquire about Viet Minh peace conditions. The French Chiefs of Staff had no objections. On November 19, 1952, they unanimously advised that "a choice now has to be made" between Europe and Indochina, "and the choice is obvious."[20]

A Graceful Exit?

The years 1953 to 1955 are so eventful that we must now turn to a chronological narrative to trace the interactions between Europe and Indochina during this period. We have seen that French retreat from Indochina had become an acknowledged necessity by the end of 1952. But it was quite another thing to put such an exit on the political agenda. This became possible thanks to a series of unpredictable events during the first half of 1953. Of course, French decision-makers wanted to minimize the political costs of such an exit. The very uncertainty that prevailed regarding ratification of the EDC treaty by the French assembly allowed them to win the "graceful exit" they were seeking at the Geneva Conference in 1954. But the rejection of the treaty by the French National Assembly less than six weeks after the Geneva agreements caused a crisis of such magnitude between France and the United States that Premier Mendès France decided to give the Americans a free hand, if not in all of Indochina, then at least in South Vietnam in order to mend his relations with the Eisenhower administration. The seeds of the next East-West confrontation over the peninsula, America's Vietnam War, were planted during these few months after the conference. All in all, then, the French retreat was not so graceful.

René Mayer and Joseph Laniel were the French premiers during the period that led to the Geneva meeting. Mayer believed that increased American funding of the Indochina war might ease the ratification of the EDC treaty. The Pinay cabinet had fallen because of the defection of the MRP, which disapproved of the premier's lukewarm efforts for ratification. Mayer vainly hoped to ratify the EDC with help from the Gaullists. For this purpose he appointed Bidault instead of Schuman at the Foreign Ministry and negotiated additional protocols to the treaty guaranteeing French freedom of action overseas. In spite of Italian and West German opposition, Mayer succeeded brilliantly. The six protocols of March 24, 1953, allowed France to withdraw troops from EDC divisions in case of "severe crises" overseas, with the judgment over their severity left to France alone. Moreover, the protocols gave French defense industries a monopoly over the equipment of French Union forces and extended the period during which voting rights inside the

EDC would be allotted according to a predetermined arrangement among member states, not according to their respective financial contributions to the organization. Thus, even if France had to face a protracted war in Indochina, leading it to pay a smaller sum than West Germany, the situation would have no political consequences.

Mayer was an outright colonialist but of the Eurafrican variety. He was a representative from Algeria and in his former capacity as treasury minister had been acquainted with the inflationary effects of the Indochina war. At the same time he negotiated the protocols, he approved the Alessandri–Bao Dai plan (later known as the Navarre Plan), which expanded Indochinese military manpower. But Mayer also told General Henri Navarre on May 7, 1953, that the object of the plan was only to provide France with a "graceful exit" from Indochina.[21] After some tactical victories, France would sign a compromise peace, its expeditionary corps would be brought back to Europe, and hopefully the EDC treaty would be ratified. With this perspective, Defense Minister Pleven pleaded in Washington in April 1953 for the simultaneous diplomatic settlement of the Korean and Indochinese conflicts.

Since the Gaullists were opposed to the EDC, Mayer's fall was inescapable. During his last days in power, the premier had to face a severe crisis between France and the Associated States. At the end of April and the beginning of May 1953, the daily *Le Monde* and the weekly *L'Observateur* revealed that certain French politicians had taken advantage of the overvaluation of the piastre to engage in illegal exchanges of currencies. On May 8, one day after the disclosures in *L'Observateur*, Mayer acted to end the scandal by devaluing the piastre from seventeen to ten francs, with immediate effect. He informed Letourneau and the Associated States of his decision but did not ask their advice. According to the agreements between France and the Associated States, however, the value of the piastre could not be changed before the latter had been officially consulted. On May 20, Bao Dai, one of the biggest speculators, publicly joined King Norodom Sihanouk of Cambodia to demand revision of the relationship between France and the Indochinese states. Paris was in a weak negotiating position since it now required the Associated States to increase their military manpower. But in France, Indochinese demands for increased independence swelled the ranks of supporters of a negotiated peace, leaving Laniel, Mayer's successor, with a double task. He now had to renegotiate the French Union and put an end to the war.

Bidault remained at the helm of the Foreign Ministry in the new

Laniel cabinet. He had many reservations about negotiating a peace, but he had to deal with political heavyweights such as Faure, the minister of the Treasury, and Paul Reynaud, senior minister for the Associated States, who were both favorable to the EDC and a quick end to the war. The ministers understood that U.S. funding of the Navarre Plan might cause France to lose its freedom of action in Indochina, even though Paris, and not the Associated States, remained the recipient of American money. Recognizing that risk, the junior minister for the Associated States, Marc Jacquet, a Gaullist, would have preferred that France decline the U.S. offer and fund the war by inflation. But in August 1953 Laniel decided in favor of Faure's anti-inflationary program—a victory for those ministers favorable to an exit from Indochina.

Reynaud was a vociferous supporter of the EDC, not out of kindness for Germany but because he was virulently opposed to communism and the Soviet Union. He also worshipped a balanced budget. He and Faure were willing to grant complete independence to the Indochinese states and leave them to their fates—with eventual American assistance if Washington so wished. France would then be able to concentrate on Europe, the theater that mattered most according to these ministers.

During autumn 1953, Reynaud bypassed Laniel and Jacquet and single-handedly renegotiated French relations with Laos and Cambodia. On October 22, he signed a draft agreement with Laos, which defined the French Union as "an association of peoples with equal rights" who agreed to "coordinate their policies within the framework of the High Council of the French Union." That was a far cry from Article 62 of the French Constitution, which left it to the French government to coordinate these policies. All other ministers protested, and the text was redrafted to specify "equal duties" alongside equal rights. The new text also called for the pooling of resources "to guarantee the defense of the whole Union." Nevertheless, even the new draft defined the French Union as "an association of independent and sovereign peoples." Even more important was the annex, which granted Laos a fully autonomous foreign policy and guaranteed mutual preferential trade relations between France and Laos, not because the two countries belonged to the French Union but on a bilateral basis. Thus, without any consultation with the French National Assembly, the new treaty redefined the French Union as a confederation between equal states on the pattern of the British Commonwealth. Cambodia and Vietnam got similar conditions during the first half of 1954.[22]

The Associated States conceived this "perfect independence," to use Laniel's words, as a reward for their extra military efforts. Conversely, Reynaud had met their demands because he believed withdrawal from Indochina was unavoidable anyway. After such concessions, it became impossible to justify war in Indochina out of fear of establishing a precedent that would endanger French domination over North Africa. Reynaud explained that the new treaties with the Indochinese states made it impossible to plan the inclusion of Morocco and Tunisia in the French Union. If the two protectorates joined the union, Reynaud asserted, "France would lose its domination over them, since obviously they would ask for the same independence that France, out of necessity, granted to the Associated States, for its own good as well as for theirs."[23] At the same time, Defense Minister Pleven planned a 1954 military budget that allotted 60 percent of all expenditures to the EDC. Thus, even though Bidault protested and Laniel had misgivings, the most determined supporters of the EDC in the cabinet paved the way for an exit from Indochina, well before the Geneva Conference.

Was this the end of the complex relationship between the Indochina war and the EDC? Not at all, since the United States feared that France might be tempted at Geneva to offer the Soviet Union a renunciation of the EDC in exchange for a graceful exit from Indochina. To avoid this possibility, the Eisenhower administration put pressure on France to have the National Assembly ratify the EDC treaty before the beginning of the conference. In return for U.S. funding of the Navarre Plan, Laniel promised in September 1953 that he would have the treaty promptly ratified. At the same time, however, U.S. secretary of state John Foster Dulles was convinced that if French opinion came to believe that the United States, after concluding an armistice in Korea, was forbidding France to do the same in Indochina, opponents of the EDC would benefit. To avoid that situation, he agreed on February 24, 1954, to put Indochina on the agenda of the Geneva meeting as long as the EDC had been ratified in the meantime. Bidault answered that he would do his best.

Bidault kept his word. During a cabinet meeting on April 15, he opposed Faure, who had advised to schedule the ratification vote after the Geneva Conference in order to take into account the possibility that the international situation might change in the meantime. The

Laniel cabinet fell before it was able to set a date for the ratification debate. Laniel and Bidault had hoped that the debate could take place in
the first days of April 1954, but the siege of Dien Bien Phu and rumors
about U.S. intervention in the war upset their plans. Dien Bien Phu
wounded French national pride, which made it impossible to debate a
supranational project at such a time. The Italian ambassador in Paris
aptly caught the mood: "Even the staunchest supporters of the EDC,"
he observed, "seem unable to dare, in view of developments in Indochina, to press in order to have the European Army issue dealt with in
present circumstances, for they seem to fear being charged with a lack
of understanding about France's serious situation, as well as about the
crisis the country is experiencing."[24]

Yet even without Dien Bien Phu, supporters of the EDC were probably a minority in the French assembly. The Socialist Party, which had
once supported the plan, suddenly demanded new conditions on
April 21, 1954. The next day, Gaullist members of the Laniel cabinet
published a communiqué opposing the premier's foreign policy. The
assembly's Foreign Affairs Committee declared itself against the EDC
on June 9, followed by the Defense Committee on June 18. No wonder,
then, that when he met with Mendès France for the transfer of power,
Laniel now told him that there was probably no majority in favor of ratification.

Soviet diplomats understood the situation and stood back from any
"global deal" in Geneva. It is well known that, during his negotiations
with Soviet foreign secretary Vyacheslav Molotov, Mendès France scrupu-
lously avoided linking Indochina and the EDC. It has been less often
noticed that Molotov did not insist on such a linkage. Yet his moderation was part of a subtle Soviet bargaining strategy. In March and April
1954, Soviet diplomats let the French Foreign Ministry and the French
embassy in Moscow know that the Soviet Union "did not link Indochina and other problems,"[25] but also that "French opponents of the
EDC . . . would deem peace in Indochina such an important signal of
international détente, that ratification of the EDC would look less important in this new context."[26] At the same time, Soviet diplomats in
London explained to British colleagues that Moscow agreed to partition Vietnam at the sixteenth parallel. In early summer 1954, after the
French assembly committees on foreign affairs and defense declared
themselves against the EDC, the Soviet Union feared less the ratification of the treaty than the entry of West Germany into NATO without

strings attached, which was the fallback position of the United States. To counter such a possibility, Moscow planned to call for a new international conference in the near future, where it would propose the neutralization of Germany.

Mendès France never displayed any conspicuous affection for the EDC, and he did not rule out the possibility of an East-West détente. But he was certainly unwilling to trade the latter for renunciation of West German rearmament. It is no wonder, then, that Soviet leaders, who had no praise high enough for Mendès France during the Geneva Conference, held him up to public obloquy when, at the end of 1954, he set himself the task of having the assembly ratify the entry of West Germany into the Western European Union and, for all practical purposes, NATO.

Even though the entry of West Germany into the Western alliance provided a substitute for the EDC, the Eisenhower administration resented the fact that Mendès France had not thrown his resignation onto the scale during the ratification debate of August 30, 1954. Whereas the Truman administration cared more about West German rearmament than about the European army as such, Eisenhower and Dulles attached much importance to the EDC itself. They conceived it as the best means to bring reconciliation between France and West Germany, which might become the nucleus of a West European federation so powerful that it would be able to provide for its own defense without the help of American troops (even though Eisenhower, to ease ratification of the EDC, disingenuously promised France in March 1954 that American divisions would remain in Europe). Mendès France knew that Washington was disappointed, and his policy toward Indochina after the Geneva Conference was explicitly designed to heal the breach between Paris and Washington. This gesture of sympathy did not cost him much, since he had been advising a "retreat to Africa" for years, even though he hoped that Paris would be able to remain influential in Cambodia and Laos, small countries proportionate to limited French means.

In fact, Mendès France, anxious not to appear soft in his dealings with communist countries, gave up any hope of maintaining independent policies toward the People's Republic of China and Vietnam as early as August 1954. In the wake of the Geneva Conference, Jean Sainteny had been nominated delegate general in Hanoi. According to the first draft of his instructions, he was to meet with Ho Chi Minh on his arrival. But they were rewritten between August 14 and August 23, and the new draft instructed him to avoid all political contacts, for fear that France be suspected of playing a double game between Saigon and the Democratic Republic of Vietnam. On August 28, to avoid trouble with the United States, Mendès France abandoned his plan to establish a permanent commercial mission in the People's Republic of China. For the same reason, he decided on September 6 not to contest the explicitly anticommunist and military terms in which Dulles wanted to couch the SEATO treaty. At the end of the same month, the minister for the Associated States, Guy La Chambre, who wished to plead with Washington in favor of new overtures to Hanoi, was reminded by Mendès France that "the Americans are the leaders of the coalition in South-East Asia."[27] La Chambre carried out his instructions faithfully. In the secret protocol he signed with U.S. undersecretary of state Walter Bedell Smith on September 29, the DRV was called a "Communist force aggressively opposed to ideals and interests of free peoples of Associated States, France and the United States," and France promised to "support M. Ngo Dinh Diem in establishment and maintenance of a strong, anti-Communist and nationalist government." The text also provided for direct U.S. assistance to the Associated States, including the military aid that France had banned during the war.[28]

Conclusion

After the Smith–La Chambre agreement, the Fourth Republic never fundamentally revised its policy of giving the United States a free hand in Indochina, especially in South Vietnam. This was logical, since Mendès France and his successor, Edgar Faure, had always deemed Indochina a remote position. Besides, both now had to deal with the Algerian war, and Faure needed American helicopters to wage it. During spring 1955, at Dulles's insistence, Faure shelved a French–North Vietnamese agreement about industrial joint ventures, which Sainteny had recently negotiated with the DRV, as well as Mendès France's pet project of opening an air route between Hanoi and Paris. Similarly, during the spring 1955 clash between South Vietnamese prime minister Diem and the sects in Saigon, Faure first tried to convince Dulles that keeping Diem in power played into the hands of the DRV. He relented on May 10, when he realized that the American secretary of state refused to budge. If one were to assign a symbolic date marking the definitive victory of supporters of Eurafrica over rivals with global ambitions for France, this one might well qualify. But even with the empire reduced to Africa, French armed forces would remain unable to fulfill their missions in Europe and overseas at the same time. Overextension was a long-term trend.

TEN

❖ ❖ ❖

"The Same Struggle for Liberty": Korea and Vietnam

MARILYN B. YOUNG

SOMETIMES AMERICANS SEEM to know themselves by what they are not. During the Cold War, the United States was not the Soviet Union. It was not a nation of conformists, despite David Riesman's cries and alarums about "other-direction." Nor was it militaristic, despite its defense budget, foreign bases, and foreign wars. Freedom of speech and association were secure, despite loyalty oaths, blacklists, and congressional committees investigating subversion. Above all, unlike its Soviet enemy (or some of its retrograde European allies), the United States was not and, by definition, could not be an imperialist nation. The contradictions between U.S. policy and its essential self-understanding, however sharp, have seldom cut to the bone, although every now and then there are problems.

The French insistence that their war in Indochina was the same as the war in Korea, for example, was potentially troubling. What could the reimposition of French colonialism in Indochina have to do with the struggle for democracy against communist aggression on the Korean peninsula? The connection, French officials repeatedly explained as they sought an increase in U.S. aid, was the common enemy, Soviet imperialism. With the conclusion of the Elysée Agreements in 1949, Indochina had been granted all the independence it could reasonably want. In the words of General Jean-Marie Gabriel de Lattre de Tassigny, the fight now was against "red colonialism," and in this, surely, Washington and Paris were united. Unless, as the French suspected, the United States wished to replace France in Southeast Asia altogether. For many in Washington, red colonialism could not effectively be

196

fought so long as the French variety of colonialization continued to co-operate in heightening the appeal of communism. Neither side could afford to push the other too hard: France must be kept in the war, and the United States must continue to finance the French war without taking it over. This essay is a brief examination of what has been, until recently, a persistent American dilemma: how to acquire, manage, or subcontract an empire without naming it, or better, in the name of the right of self-determination for all people. If, as the French argued, the U.S. war in Korea was indeed the same as the French war in Indochina, was it because the French had abandoned imperialism or because the United States had embraced it?

"One Front" or Two?

Jacques Soustelle, secretary general of the Gaullist Rassemblement du peuple français and former minister of colonies, posed the issue bluntly in a long essay with the title "Indo-China and Korea: One Front," published in *Foreign Affairs* in the fall of 1950. "The glow from the Korean battlefields," Soustelle wrote, "lights up the whole Asiatic front from Manchuria to Malaya." Communist success in China, the insurgencies in Malaya and Indochina, and North Korea's invasion of the South were all expressions of "the expansion of Soviet power toward the sea, pushing its satellites ahead, and exploiting against the West the nationalism, even xenophobia, of the Asiatic masses." After extolling the benevolent record of France in Indochina ("no one, even the Indo-Chinese themselves, could have done for Indo-China what France has done"), Soustelle explained the military situation this way: "The Viet-Minh forces . . . are inferior in number to the French and Viet-Nam troops, but they benefit by the tactical advantages of guerrilla warfare in a tropical country full of dense vegetation and marshes." Since U.S. troops were also tied down in Asia "for an unforeseeable length of time," it seemed obvious to Soustelle that "the entire strategy of the West in Asia must be conceived as a whole and that it would be foolish to consider Korea and Indo-China separately." The United States must declare its "common purposes" with France, he urged, "publicly before world opinion, above all in a way that the Asiatic people themselves will hear and understand them."[1]

Soustelle's urgent desire that Asian nationalists see the French war in Indochina as a Franco-American endeavor was exactly what worried

Washington. In addition to the issue of colonialism, the French seemed to be losing. Two U.S. survey missions were dispatched to Southeast Asia in June 1950 to assess the Indochina situation. The report of the first mission, led by Robert Allen Griffin, the former deputy chief of the economic aid mission to China, focused on the political problem, fearing "a repetition of the circumstances leading to the fall of China" if the French failed to satisfy Vietnamese demands for independence.[2] However, should the French throw themselves "passionately" into making Bao Dai's government work, China's fate might yet be avoided. The second mission, a joint State-Defense effort led by John F. Melby and Major General Graves B. Erskine, concluded that only the "proper application of sufficient military force, plus goading the French into a more offensive spirit can hold the lid on the Indochinese kettle" and then only for a limited period of time. In the long run, the French would have to commit themselves to ultimate independence ("with a specified period of five, ten, twenty, or thirty years").[3] Recollecting in tranquility half a century later, George Allen, an intelligence analyst for the army, noted that the function of any survey mission was to "propose a solution no matter how intractable the problem." Usually, he observed, "such study groups seem to listen selectively, to minimize negative factors, and to find reasons for doing *something*, rather than proposing that *nothing* be done."[4] In this case, the something the survey missions urged was that the French fight fiercely for the total independence of Indochina. Of course, as Allen observed, "France lacked the resources and the determination to wage war in the Far East merely for the sake of containing communism; if there was to be no French Union, there need be no war in Indochina."[5] The conclusion, though evident to Allen, proved elusive to both the Truman and Eisenhower administrations.

In the fall of 1950, General Douglas MacArthur, basking in the prospect of a quick and total victory in Korea, reflected on the French in Indochina. He found their situation "puzzling." The French had twice the forces at their command that MacArthur had had at the outbreak of hostilities in Korea and faced about half the number of enemy troops he had faced. "I cannot understand why they do not clean it up. They should be able to do so in four months." Was the French army any good at all, MacArthur wondered: "If the French won't fight we are up against it because the defense of Europe hinges on them . . . They have the flower of the French Army in Indo-China, and they are not fighting. If this is so, no matter what supplies we pour in they may be of no use." Admiral Arthur Radford ventured an explanation: "The French seem to have no popular backing from the local Indo-Chinese." But he did not dwell on this insight. Rather, he insisted: "We must stiffen the backbone of the French." President Truman was discouraged: "We have been working on the French in connection with Indo-China for years without success." Averell Harriman, in mild defense of French martial prowess, remembered hearing from officers who were there that the French had fought well in Italy. General Omar Bradley agreed but pointed out that those Frenchmen "were selected people who had escaped from France to continue the fight. We cannot judge the fighting of all French troops by them." This observation depressed Truman, who said it was "the most discouraging thing we face." Every effort had been made to persuade the French to do the decent thing, like the Dutch in Indonesia, but, asserted Truman, "the French have not been willing to listen." Should the French prime minister come to Washington, Truman swore, "he is going to hear some very plain talk. I am going to talk cold turkey to him. If you don't want him to hear that kind of talk, you had better keep him away from me."[6] Radford chimed in. He had seen some French ships in Hawaii and had the impression that "they were not anxious to go to Indo-China and were dragging their feet."[7]

In public sesssion, MacArthur praised the French commander in chief, General M. M. Carpentier, as a military man "enjoying the highest reputation." Later, when Truman, MacArthur, Harriman, and Dean Rusk, then assistant secretary for Far Eastern affairs, met to continue the discussion, Carpentier expressed his doubts. Asked his opinion of the essence of the problem in Indochina, MacArthur said the French needed to "get an aggressive General" and that such a man could "clean up the Viet-minh forces with French Union troops now available in Indochina."[8]

It was with considerable relief, therefore, that Washington greeted the news of the appointment of General de Lattre as both high commissioner and commander in chief of French Union forces in Indochina in December 1950. De Lattre, a heavily decorated, multiply wounded veteran of World War I and the colonial war in Morocco in 1925, had escaped a Vichy prison to join de Gaulle's Free French forces in 1943. From the moment his appointment was announced, de Lattre received excellent press coverage in the United States. A steady stream of upbeat articles reported a surge in French morale. Tillman

Durdin, a reliable weathervane of official U.S. opinion, reported from Saigon that although "[i]nformed persons realize that the situation basically remains critical . . . both French and Vietnamese, nevertheless, have been infused with a new spirit and energy." De Lattre had banished "defeatism" and with his "Napoleonic jaw and Roman nose has stirred widespread enthusiasm by a rare combination of showmanship, charm, energy and forcefulness." He "swept" from one end of Vietnam to the other, by plane and by car, delivering speeches in a "husky voice that ranges from a whisper to a fortissimo," making "heart-stirring points," talking to Vietnamese "of their independence, of the coming strength and greatness of their country, of France's determination to help in building a powerful Vietnam Army and of French sincerity in establishing the new Vietnamese state."

In effect, Durdin justified the French war to the American public by identifying it with the charismatic figure of de Lattre. His profile of the general in the Sunday *New York Times Magazine*, for example, credited de Lattre with having wrought a "miracle" and quoted his speeches with enthusiasm: "Within a week [de Lattre] had visited by air all the major cities of Indo-China and everywhere he declaimed: 'the days of looseness are over! We shall not yield another inch of territory.'" There were more details of de Lattre's physical appearance: his "quick smile," his war wounds, his "typically French" shoulder shrug, and the fact that, "like MacArthur," he preferred to be photographed with his hat on so as to conceal his thinning hair.[9]

In addition to his energy and his qualities as a tactician, de Lattre was the sort of Frenchman an American could admire. He wasn't much for reading, instead placing "prime emphasis on the human factor." Rather than deciding on the basis of reports or documents, he liked "to call in someone and talk things over."[10] According to a Reuters dispatch, de Lattre preferred orange juice to "choice French wines," served broiled chops and mashed potatoes for lunch, and although he came from a "long line of fighting men who served the French kings," his "tastes are strangely simple." His public demeanor verged on the "flamboyant," but he was democratic, as shown by a propensity to admonish anyone, from a sergeant major to a local priest, whose performance was not up to par. Nicknamed "D. D. T." after his initials, the general had expressed pleasure at the implication that his arrival had signaled the "cleaning up" of the dangerously deteriorating French position in Vietnam. Finally, his "spectacular 'strong man' characteristics" appealed to the "Asian temperament"; he had become a "rallying point for those bewildered by war and adversity."[11] In late August 1951, a feature article in the *New York Times Magazine* carried a picture of the general, staring in three-quarter profile into the distance, a cigarette between his lips, his expression determined. Once more, de Lattre's capacity to inspire his troops was described. He lectured the men that Vietnam was their opportunity to redeem French defeat in 1940. "In the army, and especially in the professional army," Michael James wrote, "[guilt over the defeat] has taken on the aspect of a psychosis. Every little victory against the Viet-minh is an answer to the world."[12] Neither James nor Durdin said much about the issue which most concerned Hanson Baldwin, the military correspondent for the *Times*. Baldwin acknowledged de Lattre's energy but doubted it was enough. "The French must yield more in substance, rather than merely in form, to the Vietnamese Government if the taint of 'colonialism' is to be avoided."[13]

Other close observers were less sanguine that an aggressive general would do the trick, but they had difficulty making their voices heard over the passionate advocacy of the U.S. embassy in Paris. Charlton Ogburn, public information officer in the Bureau of Far Eastern Affairs, complained of an American embassy official who dismissed all expressions of concern over the suppression of nationalist movements in Asia as products of an unnecessary preoccupation with the "patter of naked brown feet." Ogburn mused parenthetically that this patter should "by now have drummed its way into the hearing even of people in Paris." The United States was left with two "ghastly" choices: to let the communists take over Indochina or to "continue to pour treasure (and perhaps eventually lives) into a hopeless cause . . . and this at a cost of alienating vital segments of Asian public opinion." Ogburn argued that it was time to relieve "hostile Senators" of the illusion that Indochina was a clear case of communist aggression that must be met "in a hard-hitting, two-fisted manner." This might work "in the short run," but he feared it was "sowing the whirlwind" unless, Ogburn warned, "we intend when the time comes to commit American ground forces in Indochina and thus throw all Asia to the wolves along with the best chances the free world has."[14] John Ohly, deputy director of the Mutual Defense Assistance Program, was equally worried: ". . . we are certainly dangerously close to the point of being so deeply committed that we may find ourselves committed to direct intervention. These situations, unfortunately, have a way of snowballing."[15]

Ogburn's hostility to the embassy in Paris was more than matched by the hostility of French officials, including de Lattre, to Americans in Vietnam. "The French have been viewing United States economic aid activities . . . with suspicion and some disapproval," Durdin reported without further comment from Hanoi. "[They] appear to want United States aid, but without the Americans, the American label or any augmentation of American influence here."[16] To be sure, the U.S. minister in Saigon, Donald Heath, reported to the State Department, the French were grateful for American military aid. But economic aid was something else again, a wound to French *amour propre,* making them look, de Lattre complained, "like a poor cousin in Viet eyes." Deeply irritated, de Lattre banned any mention of American economic aid in the leading French language newspaper in Vietnam, lashed out in public against American missionaries, religious and secular, and refused to provide sufficient housing for the American military mission. "Yours is a rich country," de Lattre told Heath, "why don't you build houses. Or get rid of some of your ECA [Economic Cooperation Administration] men and your Amer[ican] missionaries, then we [could] house MAAG [American Military Advisory and Assistance Group]."[17] Disturbed by the ferocity of his attack, Heath wrote a long, three-part telegram to the State Department, expressing his conviction that tension over U.S. economic aid had become a serious obstacle overall to U.S. policy in Indochina.[18]

Much of Heath's concern drew upon a long private conversation he had had with the acting French diplomatic counselor in Saigon. French grievances focused, in particular, on the activities of STEM (Special Technical and Economic Mission), and Heath's telegram reported the complaints in detail. First, the counselor explained, France had never asked for economic aid but instead had been compelled to accept it in order to get the military aid it wanted.[19] Second, the publicity STEM projects received, along with U.S. efforts to negotiate direct, bilateral agreements with the Associated States, undermined the French Union. Americans seemed to think Indochina had been "discovered in 1950 and that history of civilization in Indochina began with arrival of US aid. If [a] water pump or tractor [is] delivered [to] Indochina, it becomes, in STEM publicity, [the] first water pump and first tractor that Indochina has ever had. If medical first aid station opened, it is inauguration of public health in IC." No attention was paid to what the French had been doing for generations and continued to do at "25 times the volume and with 1/25 the publicity."

Even worse than STEM self-aggrandizement, according to the French counselor, were the activities of the U.S. Information Exchange (USIE), whose popular English language classes reminded the French of nothing so much as the Russians, whose first step toward gaining influence was "to open Russian courses in blind belief that all that is good is in Russia." The French were particularly outraged by the fact that so many Vietnamese were learning English when so few of them "know French well and their time and effort might be better spent in acquiring really useful knowledge of French which will be much more important to them." Unless, the counselor observed suspiciously, "America expects Vietnam not to remain in French Union." USIE's translation projects were equally upsetting. The first book translated was a history of the United States: "This seems either absurd or offensive to most French who have found that even literate Viets know little of history of their own country and almost nothing of history of France . . . To expect them to read American history seems height of national egotism on part Americans."[20] Despite de Lattre's claim that the fight against "red colonialism" joined France and the United States, the Saigon legation reported dissatisfaction with USIE's translation of books that were either "violently pro-US or anti-USSR, issues which have little meaning for most Viets." And why, Heath was asked, were there five times as many Americans in Vietnam as all other foreigners combined? Clearly, America looked forward to the day when Indochina, absent the French, would become a "zone of US influence." Basic to this angry litany, Heath concluded, was the fear that American policy looked to the ultimate departure of Indochina from the French Union.[21] Heath was not entirely sympathetic to French strictures, but he was clear about the bottom line: "our most immediate concern in Indochina today is the mil[itary] def[ense] of its terr[itory] and that def[ense] today rests solely on the Fr[ench]." In "other less troubled parts of the world" it might be possible to dismiss what they said; not in Indochina. De Lattre, Heath thought, agreed with much of this criticism.[22]

"Our First Consideration is Real Estate"

Toward the end of June, Heath asked for a full-scale policy review. The directive under which he had operated since his arrival in 1950 required U.S. policy to "supplement but not to supplant" the French, on the assumption that French policy was "evolutionary and designed to perfect" the independence of the Indochinese states within the French Union. There was no alternative to the French: "Present-day Vietnam returned to peace by an international agency and given a coalition [government] as a result of some form of internationally-observed free election wld fall to the Commies no less surely, no less slowly, and perhaps rather more cheaply than did the East Eur states of the immed postwar period." All the French asked, in return for the lives and treasure spent in averting such a disaster, was loyal support from the United States. In the future, Heath intended to make it clear to all American personnel in Vietnam that "they must not listen or give encouragement to improper criticism of Fr[ench] sacrifices and intentions and that violation [of] this rule will be regarded as insubordination."

Heath was not insensible to the underlying causes of local American attitudes toward the French, and his summary of their views reads like an indictment of the French record. Some Americans, he observed, argued that "central facts IC problem are the rising tides of Asian nationalism and embittered hatred of Viet people for Fr[ance]; they maintain that enemy here is regarded as the Fr[ench] rather than [the Viet Minh] or Commies, that all sections of opinion unite on proposition [that] Fr[ance] must go and differ only as to means of their expulsion." Moreover, proposals for Vietnam's position in the French Union seemed to lack any provision for trade unions, independent political parties, or a parliament while retaining the French secret police, censorship, French domination of the economy, opium, a relaxed attitude toward corruption, and "the omnipresence of Fr[ench] officials, names and culture"—in other words, "the most sordid and restrictive colonialism." Some Americans in Vietnam urged total U.S. withdrawal from "this pestilence"; others wanted the United States to replace the French in the conviction that "all social ills will depart with the Fr[ench]." Only history would decide whether these negative impressions had any merit. But at that moment in time, Heath argued, they were irrelevant: there was no Third Force for Americans to adopt and support; there was no alternative to the French.[23]

In a strongly worded telegram from Paris, Ambassador David Bruce wholly endorsed Heath's effort to discipline American aid workers who sided with the Vietnamese. "Vietnamese [should] never be permitted to forget essential irreplaceable contribution French are making toward their independence and fate they wld meet if French were to withdraw. Nor must we ourselves forget ever present danger of having Viet-

namese play us off against the French."[24] Heath had been careful to ex-
empt Robert Blum,[25] who headed the ECA mission in Vietnam, from
any breach of protocol, and Blum was equally delicate in his response
to Heath's complaints, expressing his full agreement that U.S. policy
was to "supplement but not supplant" the French. That said, there
were real problems: "Basically the Fr[ench] are not very sympathetic
with our program and [would] much prefer to see our money used for
other purposes," wrote Blum. The consultation the French demanded
would not change this fundamental difficulty. Moreover, Blum acknowledged there was a deeper contradiction between the short-term
necessity of supporting the French and the long-term importance of
strengthening "local anti-Commie aspirations." Indeed, "in this part
of the world only [a] break with past offers a firm foundation for the
future."[26]

In Washington, the assistant director for non-European affairs in the
Office of International Security was more direct. The notion of instructing American personnel to avoid criticizing the French, Jonathan
Bingham maintained, "would seem to put United States personnel in
Indochina in the position of the 'Hear No Evil' monkey." It was hard to
believe Heath really meant what he said, for if his instructions were followed, "it would promptly get around Indochina that United States officials would 'not even listen' to Vietnamese complaints about the
French, no matter how well founded they might be." Heath's recommendations would gravely damage "our standing in Asia as a whole by
identifying us with colonialism." Moreover, Heath had said nothing in
his telegram about the importance of getting the French to move with
greater speed toward full independence for the Associated States. "It
should be possible to convince the French that such a course in the
long run offers them the only way to escape from the crushing military
burden they now carry in Indochina and at the same time avoid the
kind of an upheaval which could result in their losing Indochina altogether."[27]

De Lattre's unhappiness with the Americans intensified over the
course of the hot Saigon summer, as did the dissatisfaction of U.S. economic aid administrators in Saigon with both the French and their
American superiors. In a personal, "eyes only" telegram to the secretary of state in late July, Heath laid out his understanding of all the bottom lines: "Our primary objective in Indochina at the present time, our
first consideration, is real estate . . . We are interested above all else in

seeing to it that the strategic position, the rice, the rubber, and the tin of [Southeast Asia] shall be denied, as long as possible, to the Commie world." Anything that advanced that end should be encouraged; anything that detracted from it should be junked. The United States in Indochina was neither for nor against the French or the Vietnamese: "we have no permanently fixed ideological position in Franco-Vietnamese politics . . . For the immed[iate] future . . . Fr arms and Fr resources will have to do the job of def[ense] if it is to be done at all." It followed, therefore, that all efforts must be bent to support French policy, including the "nascent" French Union. The tension between officials in STEM and the French must be resolved in favor of the French. Indeed, with the possibility of an armistice in Korea it was likely that pressure would mount in France for "negotiated appeasement in Vietnam," leaving the United States in the position of urging the French not to "intervene less in IC but to continue their exertions beyond politically popular level."[28]

Livingston Merchant, deputy assistant secretary of state for Far Eastern affairs, summarized the controversy for Dean Rusk. Heath was convinced that the fundamental U.S. goal of keeping Indochina and thus all of Southeast Asia out of the hands of the communists could only be realized through single-minded support of France. Both military and economic aid should be channeled solely through France. The U.S. stake was concrete and material—tin, rubber, and rice—not in any sense ideological. The ECA, by contrast, wanted to give economic, though not military, aid directly to the Associated States in an effort to strengthen their independence. For Robert Blum and his associates, what the United States stood for mattered. It could not and should not stand for the continuation of French colonialism. Merchant thought Heath was probably right to suspect that the STEM staff allowed themselves to become allies of the Vietnamese against the French. "For one thing," he reasoned, "it is hard for me to believe that ECA or anyone else could persuade a doctor or an engineer, or a technical expert in almost any field to go to Indochina under present conditions unless he possessed a strong humanitarian motivation, which almost by definition would place his sympathies on the side of the native people and against their colonial ex-masters." The real question, he aked, was: "how best do we assure the preservation of Indochina from Communism?" If support for the French so alienated people that they joined the other side en masse, the country would be lost "just about as easily as a military victory over De Lattre by an invading Chinese Communist army."[29]

Still, Merchant warned, undermining the French could lead to their withdrawal and a similar rapid loss of Indochina. A proper assessment of the problem required a judgment as to the "sincerity of French intentions" and this boiled down to an analysis of de Lattre's intentions. Merchant noted that Heath clearly was enamored of de Lattre's "flamboyance, vigor and Napoleonic character," which had given heart to "French colonials and stoked the fear of Vietnamese who never believed French promises to begin with." But Merchant contended that the fundamental issues had to be solved in Washington, not in the field; de Lattre's forthcoming visit would be an opportunity to test the sincerity of his commitment to ultimate independence for the Associated States. The real hope lay in the creation of a national army, to which U.S. military aid should be channeled, while economic aid must be directed toward the strengthening of the "native regimes and not the French." At the same time, Merchant added, French sensibilities should be protected through consultation and an avoidance of excessive publicity.[30]

The U.S. legation in Saigon, meanwhile, was tireless in its promotion of de Lattre. In a long telegram to the State Department, the second-ranking official in the U.S. embassy, Edmond Gullion expressed his admiration for the general, who worked ceaselessly to "confront divided and listless Viets" hoping to "inspire and drive Viets out of their hesitancy in spite of themselves. He leads passionately this effort with wholly sincere faith, tremendous energy and unbounded will which has galvanized French Union forces and may yet transform political picture." Of course, Gullion hedged, when it came to Indochina, "imponderables" had often intervened to destroy the best laid plans. "The imponderables," Gullion explained, "constitute the spiritual order of battle of opposing forces in which the will and genius of De Lattre is arrayed against Stalinist dynamic. The critical imponderable is the extent to which De Lattre's spark can light the tardy flame of Viet's patriotism and fuel the ardor of the Fr[ench]."[31]

Americans had the opportunity to observe de Lattre directly in mid-September 1951. He arrived in the United States on board the *Ile de France,* holding his own, *Time* magazine reported, with fellow passengers like Humphrey Bogart and Lauren Bacall, themselves returning from the discomforts of filming *The African Queen* on location.[32] In re-

sponse to de Lattre's request, press photographers took his picture as
the ship sailed past the Statue of Liberty: "[De Lattre], impeccable
from kepi to pigskin gloves, turned his hawklike profile to the lenses
and pointed theatrically toward his country's copper gift to the U.S."
His sense of the moment was rewarded by a cover photo in *Time*, a full-
face portrait, lips pressed together in an expression both confident
and determined, against a background of flooded rice paddies in
which a military stockade flying the tricolor was reflected. "The war in
Indo-China," de Lattre told a press conference in New York, "is not a
colonial war, it is a war against Red colonialism; as in Korea, it is a
war against Communist dictatorship . . . We are fighting on a world
battlefield, for liberty and for peace . . ."[33] As *Time* approvingly summarized his views, Korea, Indochina, and Malaya were only "different
battles of the same war." De Lattre understood that Americans resisted
the comparison between the French in Indochina and the British in
Malaya, and he tried to address that resistance directly. France "is not
fighting in Indo-China with any idea of profit," he insisted. On the contrary, the war was costing the French billions a year. "We are there," he
went on, "because we have promised to protect the Associated States."
"A great many Americans do not know the truth about our position
in Indo-China," he acknowledged to a friendly reporter in New York.
Somewhat more mysteriously he promised to "bring them proof they
cannot deny. I shall also bring them proof that the war in Indo-china is
the same as the war in Korea."[34]

America Takes the Long View

To *Time* and *Life* he was a "formidable Frenchman," the "French
MacArthur," but "younger . . . and strictly non-fading."[35] An editorial
in *Life* embraced de Lattre's message whole: strategically, Indochina
was more important than Korea and "of all the new battlefronts where
American troops may soon be fighting . . . the likeliest;" de Lattre's
claim that French colonialism was a dead letter had become "increasingly true"; and, perhaps most important, he had banished neutralism
in Indochina—"those who are not with Ho are now against him." The
United States could further reduce those who supported Ho Chi Minh
by "giving their Asia-front hero the support he needs." If the war became a United Nations effort, it might well be that de Lattre would
command American troops, as Matthew Ridgway commanded Euro-

pean troops in Korea. "Why not? It's the same war. And he is another general who likes to win."[36]

The comparison between the wars in Korea and in Indochina preoccupied the editors of *Time* as well as de Lattre and his Washington colleagues. To win the support of the American public for increased levels of aid to the French in Indochina, it was necessary to demonstrate that the French, like the Americans in Korea, were resisting a war of aggression launched by communists against the legitimate government. Before making the case, the differences between Korea and Indochina had to be acknowledged. The situation in Indochina, *Time* explained to its readers, had begun as a "slow guerrilla nuisance" rather than the "dramatic shock of the Red attack in Korea . . ." To most of the world, including most Frenchmen, it was a "dubious cause" in a distant country of little interest. The arrival of de Lattre had changed everything. He had inspired the troops, cleaned the slackers out of saloons and brothels, shipped the incompetents home, and, unlike his predecessors, had "grasped at once the importance of a U.S. weapon ideal for jungle fighting: napalm." In a manner that would become familiar during the U.S. war in Vietnam, *Time* believed de Lattre's battlefield successes would persuade the public of the importance of Indochina, where "the battle lines of Asia and Europe merge." The possibility of victory had transformed a dubious cause into a worthy one.

Along with arguing the centrality of France's war to the overall struggle against communism, *Time* was anxious to restore the reputation of France to an American public that thought of the country in terms of "falling cabinets and rising black-marketeers," an "envious France," and a "timid" one. De Lattre's France, by contrast, was "a country so large that all the men of Western civilization have a home there." Above all, *Time* sought to sell the war in Indochina to the American public by merging it with the person of de Lattre himself. He was moody, impatient, touchy on issues of honor, intensely dramatic, a meticulous dresser, and a stickler for high sartorial standards in others (observing to a stenographer as he fired her: "You don't know how to dress, Miss, and your hair is dirty."). "Around him all women must be beautiful," a reporter who knew him told *Time*, "all men handsome and intelligent, all motorcars sleek and fast, all public appearances impressive." And yet, for all his force and drive, there was as well a humanizing sadness about the man, which the reporter attributed to the death of his son Bernard in combat in Vietnam: "Sometimes a sudden memory will wring from him an uncontrollable sob." At heart, de Lattre, like MacArthur, was "essentially an old-fashioned man who believes in the old-fashioned virtues," above all "duty—to France, duty to end all this killing, duty to end all this chaos in the world." Best of all, with sufficient help from the United States, de Lattre promised a quick victory in Indochina. The editors failed to comment that in this too he resembled General MacArthur in Korea.[37]

In public talks as in private conversations with officials, de Lattre insisted that the war France fought in Vietnam was not in any sense a colonial war or a war for profit. President Truman, according to the *New York Times,* believed him: "Truman Justifies War in Indo-China," the headline announced. The fight in Korea and the battle in Indochina were "the same fight for liberty."[38] In Washington, de Lattre opened his discussion at the State Department somewhat disingenuously: "since there was mutual agreement that colonialism was a dead issue, there was no reason to discuss the issue further." The real problems lay in the failure of the United States to deliver military supplies on time and in sufficient quantities. "Korea received practically everything," he complained, "Indochina what was left." Acheson and Truman agreed that Indochinese needs were indeed very important but would nevertheless be acted upon only after those in Korea had been fulfilled. De Lattre dropped the subject for the time being but returned to it, in different forms, throughout the meeting. He asked, he said, only for a simple yes or no: "did the U.S. admit that Indochina was the keystone in Southeast Asia? If the answer was No, nothing more could be accomplished, if Yes, the U.S. must provide the weapons to make resistance possible." He would continue to fight in Indochina because that was his duty, he said, "but it must be remembered that it was the American battlefield as well as the French."

Several days later, after a successful appearance on *Meet the Press,* de Lattre met with the Joint Chiefs of Staff and Secretary of Defense Robert Lovett. De Lattre appealed to them to understand that if he lost Indochina, then "Asia is lost." If northern Tonkin fell, so would Vietnam and with it all of Southeast Asia and India. There was worse to come: having ingested Southeast Asia and India and now lapping at the waters of the Suez Canal, the entire Muslim world might be engulfed. Then "the Moslems in North Africa would soon fall in line and Europe itself would be outflanked." This invocation of a future war of civilizations in addition to the struggle against communism already underway did not have its intended effect.[39] Lovett praised de Lattre for his presentation and agreed that his theater of operations was the same as that of the United States in Korea in one sense, but—and it was a crucial but—"the United States has a primary obligation in other theaters, whereas your primary obligation is in your own theater." De Lattre, in turn, suggested that unless the United States delivered the supplies it had promised, on time and in good order, there was not much point to his continuing. He could not tell his countrymen to proceed "without hope of victory." General J. Lawton Collins hastened to explain why some deliveries had been late, but de Lattre was not appeased. He hated to feel, as he sometimes did in the United States, that he was a "beggar." He said he would like to feel instead that "I am your man just as General Ridgway is your own man. Your spirit should lead you to send me these things without my asking." Lovett protested: "we all regard General de Lattre as a comrade in arms and will do everything possible for his theatre within our capabilities." The general shot back: "Do not say *my* theatre. It is not my theatre; it is *our* theatre."[40] The end result of de Lattre's trip was a speed up in military deliveries and an abiding sense of irritation caused by de Lattre's subsequent boasting that he had succeeded in changing U.S. policy.[41]

A few weeks after the visit, Dean Rusk, in a formal address before the Seattle World Affairs Council, felt obliged to clarify, once more, the nature of the struggle in Indochina. "Many Americans," Rusk conceded, "have been troubled in the past about the issue of colonialism in Indochina." But the issue was well on its way to solution despite the reasonable doubts felt by people in Indochina and other Asian countries. There was only one issue in Indochina, and that was whether its people would be allowed "to work out their future as they see fit or whether they will be subjected to a Communist reign of terror and be absorbed by force into the new colonialism of a Soviet Communist empire."[42] Nevertheless, some U.S. press reports continued to describe Vietnam as only semi-independent. The "average Vietnamese," one correspondent wrote, "still does not regard himself as independent. Much of the Communist appeal is based on the 'independence' issue and 'anti-colonial' propaganda." Despite communist "ruthlessness," the "young intellectuals with whom this correspondent talked . . . seemed to be more concerned about the presence of the French than about the threat of communism."[43]

Every now and then a report to the State Department suggested the full complexity of the situation in Vietnam. Robert Allen Griffin, for example, wrote to Acheson from a stopover in Singapore during a late November tour of Asia. What was going on in Vietnam was not just an anticolonial movement but rather a revolution. Moreover, the revolution would continue, along with communist popularity, for as long as the "independence" movement supported by the French consisted solely of "native mandarins who are succeeding foreign mandarins . . . The present type of govt in Vietnam is a relic of the past as much as Fr[ench] colonialism." The conflict went beyond nationalism and Francophobia, and it was one with which the United States was already familiar: "It is old Asian issue that destroyed the Kuomintang in China, Communist opportunity to exploit insecurity, and hunger and wretchedness of masses of people to whom their [government] has failed to make an effective appeal."[44] Heath responded from Saigon that, yes, Griffin was right about the "native mandarins," but unfortunately he knew of "no leaders with 'grassroots' support' who [would] join [a government] constituted on [the] basis [of] existing Franco-Vietnamese relations." Moreover, "if there were such persons, doubtful if Fr wld accept them or that they would be proof against against Asiatic neutralism or Viet Minh infiltration."[45]

In late December 1951, State and Defense Department officials met to discuss where things stood in Vietnam. General Hoyt Vandenberg raised the central question: was the United States prepared to see the French lose in Indochina? Lawton Collins disputed the idea that if Indochina fell, all of Southeast Asia would be lost. From a strictly military point of view, the British could hold Malaya even if the French withdrew from Indochina, and in terms of resources, Malaya and Indonesia were far more important than Indochina. Omar Bradley thought it would be impossible to "get our public to go along with the idea of our going into Indochina in a military way." But Paul Nitze wondered whether public reaction might not be worse if Indochina went communist.[46]

The possibility of Chinese intervention in Indochina, especially in the wake of a truce in Korea, loomed over all considerations of U.S. policy. The French and the British worried that this time the United States might take the opportunity to expand the war into China proper and insisted that even in the event of Chinese intervention, military action remain confined to Indochina itself. The Joint Chiefs of Staff, on the other hand, opposed any prior constraint. At a cabinet meeting in

March 1952, British prime minister Winston Churchill observed that "the Americans would like to extend the area of conflict beyond the actual point of aggression by bombing ports and communications, and possibly by mining rivers in China, and instituting a naval blockade of the China Coast." This would lead to total war or, of equal importance to Churchill, endanger Hong Kong and Malaya. Moreover, Churchill remarked, mixing the practical and the ethical, "It would be silly to waste bombs in the vague inchoate mass of China and wrong to kill thousands of people to no purpose."[47]

The gulf that divided the United States from the Europeans, including the British, was more fundamental than the choice of weapons or targets. What most frustrated the French was the resistance of American officials to the logic of the French situation. They were as eager to fight "red colonialism" as the Americans but insisted on the necessity of ongoing ties between Indochina and France. Why else were the French fighting? Why should the French public support the war? Indeed, successfully building the French Union would constitute the defeat of "red colonialism." De Lattre put it with the utmost clarity at a National Press Club luncheon during his visit to the United States: "The war declared by the Vietminh six years, ago," he told the assembled reporters, "did not have independence as its real objective, but rather the installation of communism. This war tried to eliminate all that was French in order to enslave Indo-China in the most terrible of dominations."[48] Washington understood this. At a National Security Council (NSC) meeting in late December 1953, Vice President Richard Nixon, fresh from a world tour, warned that if the French withdrew "the only capable leadership at the present time in Vietnam is Communist leadership."[49] "What people want," Nixon told the NSC, "we all know—independence and peace." Sadly, "we have got ourselves in the position of being 'against peace' and 'against independence'. . . Sometimes an anti-Communist line isn't the best line."[50] The United States might have to settle for half of Korea, but more was possible in Indochina if only the French would cooperate by offering, at the very least, independence within a reformed French Union.

The Americans, intent on defeating "red colonialism," were convinced that the only way to do so was by opposing colonialism of any color through the creation of a pliant, reliably anticommunist, independent Indochina under U.S. supervision. In 1953 and for the next two decades, this remained the American definition of Vietnamese independence. Of course nationalists would try to "eliminate all that was French" as part of their quest for full sovereignty. In contrast no genuine nationalist would ever wish to eliminate all that was American.

Decades later, in a discussion between American and Vietnamese policymakers and historians, Nicholas Katzenbach, who had worked on Vietnam in both the Kennedy and Johnson administrations, explained to the Vietnamese that "it should have been clear to everyone that the United States was opposed to colonialism after World War II, even if some of the policies of the United States tended to support the colonial powers in some parts of the world." Yet, he complained, his Vietnamese interlocutors seemed to think that the United States was "procolonial . . . even though everything that we did and said opposed colonialism in most parts of the world."[51] Colonel Herbert Schandler, who served two tours of duty in Vietnam, was more sympathetic to the Vietnamese point of view. Listening to a Vietnamese historian describe U.S. policy in 1950, Schandler, who now teaches at the U.S. National Defense University, said he could "sense how confusing it must have been, in 1950, for you to try to figure out why this country . . . had for some reason decided to become your enemy. But—and this seems to be something that was very hard for you in Vietnam to grasp, for obvious reasons—the United States was taking a *world* view of all these issues."[52] In this first decade of the twenty-first century, the notion that the worldview to which Schandler appealed was at the same time an imperial, even an imperialist, view is no longer shocking. These days, de Lattre would have had less difficulty reaching an understanding with Washington.

ELEVEN

◆ ◆ ◆

Assessing Dien Bien Phu

JOHN PRADOS

THE FIRST INDOCHINA WAR climaxed in 1954 at Dien Bien Phu, a mountain valley in northwest Tonkin, where a decisive battle determined the outcome of the conflict. Events of the first half of that year triggered major changes in many ways for France, for the United States, and for the Vietnams, North and South, that emerged from the fire of battle. Nevertheless the fight at Dien Bien Phu is much more often noted than analyzed. This is unfortunate because it has led to an incomplete understanding of the passage from the French war in Vietnam to the American one. The siege of Dien Bien Phu put the capstone on the fight of eight or nine years (depending upon what dating the historian puts upon its origin), which had consumed France and Vietnam.

This chapter will briefly outline the history of the siege of Dien Bien Phu in order to set the context for a larger discussion of its outcome and meaning. Assessments are possible at several levels. The more familiar are analyses of Dien Bien Phu in the context of the Geneva Conference and the French war. These issues will be covered here as well, but a principal object of this chapter will be to examine the effects of Dien Bien Phu on U.S. policy in Vietnam and Indochina, as well as the impact of the experience on American presidents, both incumbents and future chief executives, who would have the key roles in ultimate U.S. decisions about Vietnam policy.

The Background and the Battle

Following the visit to the United States by French general Jean de Lattre de Tassigny in 1951 and the acceleration of U.S. aid to the French in Indochina that then occurred, the war settled into an uneasy cadence. Viet Minh guerrilla forces made slow progress in the Red River delta of Tonkin, steadily establishing their presence in districts and villages throughout the area and increasing their hold on villages already favorable to Ho Chi Minh's side in the war. In Cochinchina in the South (Nam Bo to the Vietnamese), the Viet Minh were more or less held in check by a system of close territorial controls the French had imposed, and with the elimination of Nam Bo commander Nguyen Binh (possibly by the Viet Minh themselves), that stalemate was confirmed. In Annam, the center, from above Hue to north of Thanh Hoa there was no French presence at all.

Viet Minh regular forces made no effort to attack the Red River delta directly after the 1951 battles in which de Lattre had defeated them. The French created a fortified line at the edge of the delta and backed it up with mobile forces and a general reserve of parachute battalions to secure the area. Though no territory changed hands, the seriousness of the situation was suggested by the growing intensity of the fighting. Where in 1947 a French paratroop company (about two hundred men) could maneuver freely, by 1949 the force required for independent operations already stood at a battalion (eight hundred troops); in 1951 maneuvers required a mobile group (roughly 3,500); and by 1953 multiple mobile groups were necessary. The general reserve no longer committed paratroop battalions by themselves, except for specific limited purposes, and instead created its own airborne combat groups similar to the mobile groups. In terms of operations, in late 1951 the French Expeditionary Corps (CEFEO by its French language initials) launched an offensive to the west of the delta against Hoa Binh and was obliged to withdraw about three months afterward. That proved to be the last major French operation launched to regain territory outside the delta, with the CEFEO's subsequent efforts focused on sweeps within the delta, raids outside it, or reactions to Viet Minh movements. The Viet Minh, for their part, turned increasingly to assaults to the northwest of Tonkin, the mountainous area between the Red River delta and Laos, from where they could threaten another of the Associated States of French Indochina. Here the French fought a succession of battles from 1951 to 1953 in an attempt to blunt the Viet Minh advances.

Another measure of the growing intensity of the war was the degree of French reliance upon Vietnamese military personnel. In line with the experience of colonial Indochina, there was originally no Vietnamese national army at all, just Vietnamese citizens enlisted in the French colonial army. At the outset of the French war the military planners felt no more than twenty thousand Vietnamese troops were necessary, a number equivalent to that of Vietnamese in the French forces before World War II. As the war continued, French officials found it necessary to recruit auxiliary forces of Vietnamese and other ethnic or religious minorities. When it became necessary to concede a national stake to Vietnam, with the Pau agreement of September 1949, the French provided for a sixteen thousand person Vietnamese military. Within months that number had to be increased to thirty thousand, and during de Lattre's tenure, the demand to mobilize the Vietnamese— sharpened after 1950 when France passed a law prohibiting draftees from serving in Indochina—resulted in fresh plans for a military of one hundred thousand comprised equally of regulars and militia. In 1952 the State of Vietnam decreed general mobilization, and the French prepared plans to form a large number of light infantry battalions— plans taken in hand in the summer of 1953 by a new French commander in chief, General Henri Navarre. By December 31, 1953, there were 160,000 in the Vietnamese armed forces, including 112,000 regular troops and 47,000 auxiliary forces. There were also 70,000 Vietnamese directly serving in the CEFEO and another 20,000 guerrilla troops employed by French intelligence.[1] Despite these numbers the French military situation experienced little improvement.

With French military frustration, especially the frustration of the professional soldiers at risk in Indochina, came popular ennui. A poll taken in May 1953 revealed that 22 percent of the French populace paid no attention to news from Indochina and only 30 percent followed developments in the war. By February 1954, the figure for those who ignored Indochina had risen ten percentage points, and the number of people interested in Indochina developments—this on the eve of the battle of Dien Bien Phu—had declined to only 23 percent. As for policy, a May 1953 poll showed 15 percent of French men and women favored outright abandonment of Indochina, while 35 percent wanted negotiations with the Viet Minh and 15 percent advocated reinforcing the French army in the war. By February 1954, 18 percent favored withdrawal and 42 percent were for negotiations, while only 7 percent of the sample wanted to reinforce the French Expeditionary Corps. In both polls, the great number of those in France who expressed no opinion (29 percent in February 1954) was itself evidence of a lack of interest in the war in Indochina.[2]

The French government took notice of the war weariness of the metropole. When General Navarre took command in Indochina in the summer of 1953 he had orders to stabilize the situation, not in pursuit of military victory but as a gambit to create favorable conditions for negotiations. The Navarre plan included massive increases in the Vietnamese army, some French reinforcements, and active and offensive operations. He held some hope of actually defeating the Viet Minh in the 1955–1956 campaign season, which appealed to the United States, but these were not his instructions.[3]

The cabinet of Prime Minister Joseph Laniel did not believe it could pay for the Navarre Plan. Although the logic of American aid to the war effort in Indochina suggests that the burden on France was thereby reduced, and though other studies in this volume confirm that impression, the Laniel government at the time decided to approach Washington for additional aid to support the operations. After its own studies and extensive discussions at the National Security Council and elsewhere, President Dwight D. Eisenhower approved the additional aid in September 1953. American expectations of this additional effort were quite different from the French. At the key NSC meeting, which took place on September 9, Secretary of State John Foster Dulles predicted "it would probably take two or even three years to achieve a real decision" but that "a marked improvement . . . would be visible much sooner." Admiral Arthur Radford, chairman of the Joint Chiefs of Staff (JCS), told the same meeting that "this was the first time that the political climate had improved to a point where military success could actually be achieved."[4] In short, the United States nurtured actual hopes of military victory through the Navarre Plan.

General Navarre started off well enough, launching a series of raids into Viet Minh rear areas and strong sweeps around the Red River delta. The Viet Minh countered by sending one of their divisions (a force of seven thousand to ten thousand troops) through the mountains toward Laos. Navarre then sought to block this movement by means of a large-scale airborne landing at Dien Bien Phu—a valley close to the Laotian border—that took place on November 20. Subordinates understood that Dien Bien Phu would function as an air-land base after its capture, radiating strike forces out into the mountains, but the approach of large Viet Minh troop units quickly confined the French to their base. On December 6, Navarre issued a directive stating his intention to wage a pitched battle for the base, transforming Dien Bien Phu into an entrenched camp. The Viet Minh high command almost simultaneously made the decision to fight at Dien Bien Phu and set in motion a strong force of almost five full divisions. The attack forces took their time, made every possible preparation, and opened a siege of Dien Bien Phu on March 13, 1954.[5]

The fortified position at Dien Bien Phu had four major weaknesses. First, partly due to its origin as an offensive base, it was not as well prepared as it could have been. Second, significant portions of the entrenched camp were not integral to the main complex but separated from it, located on outlying hills. Third, the French artillery complement did not correspond to the size of the force at the camp and also was not completely dug in. Finally, and most important, the French were in a remote mountain valley and completely dependent upon aerial resupply and reinforcement. Moreover, located more than two hundred miles from the airfields of the Red River delta, the French were operating at extreme range, which further reduced the volume capacity of their air transport and increased the wear on the machines. Dien Bien Phu was defended by 10,800 French Union and Vietnamese troops, supplemented by soldiers from nearby ethnic minority groups, and about 4,300 reinforcements were subsequently parachuted into the entrenched camp during the fifty-five-day siege. Viet Minh assault forces plus their reinforcements numbered about fifty-five thousand.

The battle for Dien Bien Phu began in March 1954. In an initial phase the Viet Minh captured most of the outlying strongpoints of the entrenched camp. They then adopted traditional methods of siege warfare, whittling away at the French positions with constant assaults from trenches pushed close to the French lines. At the very outset of the siege the French lost the use of their airfields, and as their positions became further constricted, their ability to parachute troops and supplies into the remaining position steadily diminished. The Viet Minh did much to complete the isolation of the entrenched camp by placing strong antiaircraft forces, some of them manned by Chinese allies, all around the position. The entrenched camp at Dien Bien Phu was literally strangled despite anything General Navarre could do to support this forward position.

Within a week of the start of the siege, the United States was pulled into the deepening crisis when French armed forces chief of staff General Paul Ely visited Washington to ask for a variety of additional aid measures. Secretary of State Dulles and Admiral Radford of the JCS became involved in an initiative, dubbed Operation Vulture, to support the French by using an air strike by U.S. heavy bombers and carrier aircraft. President Eisenhower favored such an intervention but was unable to craft the combination of political and diplomatic support that would have enabled him to go forward. For a three-week period from the end of March 1954 through about mid-April, Washington was preoccupied with frantic maneuvers designed to create appropriate conditions for intervention. One key incident was a meeting between Dulles, Radford, and key congressional leaders, including minority leader Senator Lyndon B. Johnson, which took place at the State Department on April 3. From that point through at least June further schemes for intervention were discussed, including commitment of a Korea-size U.S. ground force or a Marine division and the loan of aircraft or even nuclear weapons to the French. As these discussions proceeded without a positive decision to intervene, Dien Bien Phu went down to defeat. The entrenched camp fell on May 7, 1954.[6]

In the meantime, a diplomatic initiative was also in progress. As noted, the Laniel government desired a diplomatic settlement. Viet Minh leader Ho Chi Minh, in a November 1953 interview published in Sweden, reciprocated by offering to engage in negotiations. That same week Le Dinh Than, Viet Minh representative to the World Peace Council, then meeting in Vienna, similarly declared, "To stop the war in Vietnam through peaceful negotiations is completely necessary and also possible."[7] A meeting in Berlin in January 1954 among the foreign ministers of the United States, Soviet Union, Great Britain, and France decided to convene a wider conference at Geneva on Far Eastern matters, primarily those related to Korea (where hostilities had ended in July 1953 but where political and military matters remained unresolved) and Indochina. That meeting opened late in April with Dien Bien Phu already in extremis. Thus decisions about U.S. intervention at Dien Bien Phu were taken not in a vacuum but in a situation where military action represented one track and a diplomatic resolution another for dealing with a complex problem.

An important factor in the British refusal to go along with the United States on intervention at Dien Bien Phu was London's interest in avoiding a more general war by brokering some agreement at Geneva. For France, already attracted to negotiations but pulled in the opposite direction by the need to repel the attack on Dien Bien Phu, the pressures were centrifugal; the French took both courses, requesting an American intervention but moving toward agreement at Geneva. The fall of Dien Bien Phu in early May weakened the French hand to the point that Foreign Minister Georges Bidault said he held only a "two of clubs and a three of diamonds." For the Chinese, as detailed in chapter 12 of this volume, a strong desire to emerge on the international diplomatic stage through a positive role at Geneva militated against increasing their level of activity in the French war. The Eisenhower administration's continuing efforts to craft a set of circumstances permitting an Indochina intervention, in the face of the clear diplomatic alternative, argues strongly for the interpretation that its basic stance in Indochina in 1954 was for victory at almost any cost.[8]

Did the French War Have to End?

As the Central Intelligence Agency (CIA) pointed out in its national intelligence estimate of April 30, 1954, "The fall of Dien Bien Phu would have far-reaching and adverse repercussions, but it would not signal the immediate collapse of the French Union political and military situation in Indochina." Agency analysts believed that disintegration "would be unlikely" (though they limited the term of their prediction to just two or three months) and pointed out that loss of the entrenched camp "would not in itself substantially alter the relative military capabilities of French Union and Viet Minh forces."[9] The French and Associated States forces remained powerful, with 605,000 troops, air forces, armored units, naval units, and all the appurtenances of modern warfare. The Viet Minh were estimated to have, at most, 291,000 soldiers, of whom only 185,000 were classified as regulars, and the largest and best concentration of these forces was at Dien Bien Phu, isolated in the mountains of northern Tonkin. Just to trek down from the mountains would require three or four weeks, and the monsoon season was about to begin. The same movement in the rainy season could easily take two or three months. The CIA therefore projected that the Viet Minh would not be able to regroup and prepare attacks against the Red River delta for that two- or three-month period. Agency information at the time showed that in the Red River delta the French and Vietnamese national forces numbered 192,000 compared with 76,000 Viet Minh, most of whom were regional forces or local guerrillas.

A key problem directly attributable to Dien Bien Phu was the evaporation of French general reserve forces. Eleven French, Vietnamese, and Laotian airborne battalions had made up the general reserve. Two of these had been at Dien Bien Phu at the start of the siege; four others and parts of a fifth had been parachuted in during the battle. Of the remainder, two battalions were Vietnamese and one Laotian—the latter, especially, not quite at the French standard. Only a single airborne battalion (and part of another) was available to back up French defenses. The United States staged an emergency airlift—another of Eisenhower's measures to sustain the French in Indochina—that brought two new paratroop battalions to Vietnam, but the units needed time to acclimatize and induct indigenous troop replacements.[10]

The CIA estimate did reflect the facts of the situation, but the agency had no way to make hard predictions regarding the psychological impact of the Dien Bien Phu debacle. The Vietnamese national army fighting with the French had substantial numbers of troops in its new light battalions, and these had had morale problems even before Dien Bien Phu. After the battle, desertion rates increased and the force became unstable at best. The portents for the Vietnamese were unclear. On the one hand, just a few months before (December 1953–January 1954) two of the Vietnamese paratroop battalions had put in a sterling performance defending the air-land base at Seno in the Laotian panhandle; on the other, the Vietnamese had one of their new full divisions now deployed in the central highlands of southern Vietnam, and that force would take part in the events a month hence (June 1954) in which French Mobile Group 100 was caught and destroyed in a series of ambushes. One public report suggested that Vietnamese outposts were falling at a rate of three or four a day, another that in a quiet southern province where there had not been a single engagement, the national army was losing two hundred rifles a month.[11] The Vietnamese Defense Ministry had only begun full operations in February and was experiencing teething pains.

There was also the immediate problem of the defense of the Red River delta. The CIA estimate made no effort to predict morale effects on the Viet Minh, as opposed to the French. Enthusiastic Viet Minh cadres pushed themselves to get out of the mountains and back to the delta. On May 8, the CIA director, Allen Dulles, told the NSC that a reappraisal of Viet Minh transport capacity indicated that with five hundred trucks the troops at Dien Bien Phu could be back around the delta in only two or three weeks.[12] And indeed, within six days of the fall of Dien Bien Phu, the French had indications that four of the Viet Minh divisions there had begun to move toward the delta. Before the end of May, some of the Viet Minh were beginning to emerge from the highlands. French intelligence, which had broken the Viet Minh codes, was well aware of these movements.[13] Hanoi was awash in a sense of impending doom. The U.S. Army attaché in Saigon reported at this time that the Viet Minh were advancing much more rapidly than anticipated and that "the French now anticipate that these divisions can be ready to attack the delta by June 15–20."[14] So public was the gloom that *Time* magazine was reporting in its May 31 issue that Viet Minh forces were passing a point just eighty miles away from Hanoi.[15]

During the last ten days of May, the French took to Washington their latest aid appeal—this time for a U.S. Marine division specifically to be committed to the Tonkin delta. In reply, Dulles cabled on May 21 that a Marine deployment was possible "within [the] context of [a] coherent and realistic overall plan for [the] conduct of collective military operations."[16] Admiral Radford, however, privately warned a French general, Paul Ely's deputy, on June 3 that there was no chance for this request to be granted.

General Ely himself was now in Indochina, having been sent to replace Navarre. He undertook Operation Auvergne, a withdrawal from exposed sectors in the delta and effort to reconstitute mobile forces and the general reserve. Simply keeping the highway open between Haiphong and Hanoi now required the concentration of four mobile groups and an armored subgroup, with another pair of mobile groups standing by at Hanoi—the equivalent of two full divisions. In early July the Tonkin theater command reported that in a delta offensive the Viet Minh would have a two-to-one advantage in numbers of battalions.[17]

Looming over all these military considerations was the basic political question: was France willing to carry on the war? To many observers, it seemed doubtful. At a Paris ceremony during the last days of the siege, Prime Minister Joseph Laniel had actually been manhandled by French antiwar protesters. The Laniel government, damaged both by the fall of Dien Bien Phu and the failure of its effort to secure ratification of a treaty on European defense, fell on June 12. It was succeeded by a cabinet under Pierre Mendès France, who explicitly committed himself to securing a negotiated settlement at Geneva.

A military solution of sorts was theoretically possible. As early as 1949 a French general, Georges Revers, then chief of army staff, had proposed a fresh strategy, de-emphasizing Tonkin, blocking the narrow neck of Indochina at the eighteenth or nineteenth parallel, and focusing forces in the south. Such an approach had not been acceptable in 1949, and the leak of the plan had heightened embarrassment about its contents.[18] In 1954 this strategy was the obvious alternative. However, no such maneuver could have been executed without giving up Tonkin, indeed without the Viet Minh storming into Hanoi and Haiphong. Having already lost at Dien Bien Phu, the French would not likely have survived a second disaster on the order of losing Tonkin.

Ultimately, the French public would have had to bear the burden of any continuation of the Indochina war. It was simply not willing to go on. Opinion polls taken when the Geneva agreements were reached in late July showed that 58 percent of respondents felt the provisions were the best obtainable under the circumstances, and another 8 percent believed the outcome had been excellent in view of the French position.[19]

Consequences for the State of Vietnam

Brief comment should be made on another level of analysis of these events, that of the Vietnamese Associated State that had fought on the French side, formally known as the State of Vietnam (SVN) but usually called the Bao Dai state. There are two key points to make here. One relates to the status and sovereignty of the Bao Dai government. The second pertains to the political situation in which Bao Dai found himself. In a sense Dien Bien Phu was both good news and bad news for the State of Vietnam.

Win or lose, the battle of Dien Bien Phu was a good thing for the Bao Dai government. Vietnamese nationalists who had sided with the French (as opposed to those nationalists who remained in the Viet Minh political front) had been struggling for years to achieve full independence. France had been torn between its colonialist past and its desire to mobilize Vietnamese nationalism to make progress in the Indochina war. The French had thus used the word "independence"

quite early—even in 1945–1946—but had continually hedged and surrounded the reality with qualifiers. In many respects the French Union
had been a fiction designed to enable Paris to grant independence to
Vietnam (and other states) while still retaining effective control. The
same was true of the notion of the Associated State introduced in 1949.
France spoke repeatedly of "perfecting" the independence of the Associated States, which meant giving the SVN and other former colonies
the governmental and administrative apparatus of nationhood. That
never seemed to happen. The government was created by the Elysée
Agreements of March 1949. The Pau Agreement of September, which
was supposed to flesh out the previously agreed principles, was mostly
sterile, as were the appeals to Vietnamese nationalists made by General
de Lattre in 1951. An essential reason for the slow development of the
Vietnamese national army was French suspicion that the Vietnamese
would turn against the metropole.

As the French turned to the United States for military and economic
aid for Indochina, France necessarily had to appeal to U.S. interests.
Paris resorted to the argument that a single global struggle against
communism was being fought in Indochina, like everywhere else—as
in Korea and as in Europe. Washington responded to this call, but the
other side of the coin was that if France was fighting an international
war in Indochina there was no reason to resist according full statehood
to the Bao Dai government. France's continued reluctance to do so reveals the inherent contradiction between neocolonial aims and internationalist aspirations.

Meanwhile, the increasing participation of the United States in the
French war put Washington in a position to pressure Paris to move forward on perfecting the independence of the Associated States. Two
elements of the Navarre Plan in 1953, the great expansion of the
Vietnamese national army with the light battalion program and the
need for special additional U.S. aid money, opened up the field for
American demands. The United States extracted a French pledge to
complete the political program as a condition for the extra aid. The
French accordingly exchanged their policy of delay and foot-dragging
for one of negotiation with the Associated States. These talks were in
progress as Dien Bien Phu fell. France and the State of Vietnam signed
treaties of independence and association on June 4. A French victory at
Dien Bien Phu would not have changed this evolution.

The actual French defeat, combined with an effort to continue the war, would have placed even more pressure on the French due to the need to prevent the demoralization of the Bao Dai government and to mobilize its resources to an even greater degree. In addition, the United States, as one of its conditions for intervention in Indochina (which would have come into play in this contingency), was demanding that France formally internationalize the war by inviting outside forces, creating a joint command, and promising not to leave the war. French compliance with these conditions would have solidified the freshly acquired status of the SVN.

Bad news lay in store for the Bao Dai government, however. Prince Buu Loc, then serving as prime minister, and other anticommunist nationalist figures such as Nguyen Van Tam, were considered compromised by their cooperation with the French, whose prestige was naturally heavily damaged in Vietnam by the disaster at Dien Bien Phu. The Buu Loc cabinet fell during the Geneva negotiations. To find an unsullied political figure Bao Dai reached out to Ngo Dinh Diem, then a Vietnamese expatriate in the United States. This was very likely an unavoidable consequence. To the degree that Diem already harbored intentions of creating a Vietnamese nationalist government without Bao Dai, which required overthrowing the state created in 1949, Dien Bien Phu had fateful consequences for Vietnamese politics.

Eisenhower and Vietnam

Dien Bien Phu led the Eisenhower administration to put in place almost all the elements that underlay the American war in Vietnam that raged in the 1960s and 1970s. In the heat of battle Eisenhower made statements echoed by later American leaders to justify the war. In the aftermath of the battle the United States took actions that structured the situation for those later leaders. In short, Dien Bien Phu provided the occasion when American policy was put on track in a way that made the later war nearly unavoidable for leaders who did not want to break with inherited U.S. policies in Vietnam.

There were five basic rationals used to justify United States conduct of a war in Southeast Asia in the 1960s. First was the notion of the "domino theory," the argument that if Vietnam turned communist all the nations of Southeast Asia would follow, and the line of communist encroachment would cross the Pacific and press directly on America. Second was the use of the device of a congressional resolution in place of a declaration of war to authorize the use of force. Third was the reliance upon a regional grouping of states as a framework for action. Fourth was the invocation of the "Munich analogy." Finally, at the level of direct action, was a commitment made directly to the noncommunist Vietnamese government. All of these elements were put into place at the time of Dien Bien Phu or in the months immediately following the lost battle.

The domino theory had been articulated privately in secret government papers, but before Dien Bien Phu it had never been relied upon in public to justify U.S. action in Vietnam. Most prominently, a State Department draft of the policy paper for Indochina from February 1952 argued, "It is possible . . . that . . . the loss of Indochina would in fact lead to loss to the Communist bloc of the entire Southeast Asian mainland, and eventually Indonesia as well." This was held to be even truer economically than militarily and, given U.S. objectives, called for actions up to "employment of U.S. forces in Indochina."[20]

After various deliberations, President Harry S. Truman approved a final paper to cover all Southeast Asia in June 1952. This document, NSC-124/2, put the matter even more starkly:

> The loss of any of the countries of Southeast Asia to communist control
> as a consequence of overt or covert Chinese aggression would have critical psychological, political and economic consequences. In the absence of effective and timely counteraction, the loss of any single
> country would probably lead to relatively swift submission to or alignment with communism by the remaining countries of this group. Furthermore, an alignment with communism of the rest of Southeast Asia
> and India, and in the longer term of the Middle East (with the probable
> exception of at least Pakistan and Turkey) would in all probability progressively follow. Such widespread alignment would endanger the stability and security of Europe.

The U.S. planners also felt that this "would render the U.S. position in the Pacific offshore island chain precarious and would seriously jeopardize fundamental U.S. security interests in the Far East."[21] If anything the final version of this policy envisioned even more extreme consequences of the fall of Indochina.

The Eisenhower administration reworked Truman's policy and came up with its own version of the paper, finalized just two months prior to the opening of the siege of Dien Bien Phu. This paper projected that "the loss of the struggle in Indochina, in addition to its impact in Southeast Asia and in South Asia, would therefore have the most serious repercussions on U.S. and free world interests in Europe and elsewhere." Again the consequences foreseen were quite dire, and the domino theory's validity, in terms of Southeast Asia, was virtually assumed.

At the height of the battle of Dien Bien Phu, during a press conference on April 7, 1954, President Eisenhower went public with the theory—and for the first time used the explicit image of dominos: "You have broader considerations that might follow what you would call the 'falling domino' principle. You have a row of dominos set up, you knock over the first one, and what will happen to the last one is the certainty that it will go over very quickly. So you could have the beginning of a disintegration that would have the most profound influences." Ike referred to the loss of Indochina, Thailand, the Malaysian peninsula, and Indonesia along with the loss of tin and tungsten from the region. Eventually, Eisenhower said, Japan, Formosa (Taiwan), and the Philippines, and even Australia and New Zealand, would be threatened.[22] This domino theory was used repeatedly, by Eisenhower and his successors, to make the case for the necessity of fighting in Vietnam.

The device of obtaining a congressional resolution authorizing the use of force to bypass the debate on and parliamentary requirements of a declaration of war was a second product of Dien Bien Phu. One can argue that Ike actually learned this from the controversy that ensued after Harry Truman failed to seek such authority when opening hostilities in Korea in 1950, but Dien Bien Phu marked the first actual attempt by the U.S. government to craft such a resolution. John Foster Dulles had it in his pocket when he met the congressional leaders on April 3. The text accused the People's Republic of China and "its agents in Indochina" of "armed attack against Vietnam" and authorized Eisenhower "to employ the Naval and Air Forces of the United States to assist the forces which are resisting aggression in Southeast Asia, to prevent the extension and expansion of that aggression, and to protect and defend the safety and security of the United States."[23] That the resolution was not ultimately presented for congressional approval does not change the fact that the practice originated at Dien Bien Phu.

In the crises off the China coast and in the U.S. intervention in Lebanon later in the 1950s, Eisenhower repeatedly sought exactly this kind of legislative authority, and American presidents have done the same ever since. It is notable that the Eisenhower draft explicitly stated that the resolution and authority granted by it would not be deemed to infringe upon Congress's right to declare war. Subsequent presidents have ceased to make that distinction.

A third product of the Dien Bien Phu crisis was the move to establish a regional alliance equivalent to NATO. In this case the desire to cloak the U.S. intervention as a multilateral enterprise, expressed as "united action" at the time, foundered on the relatively short time frame of the battle. The regional grouping actually materialized with the Manila Treaty of September 8, 1954, and was called the Southeast Asia Treaty Organization (SEATO). Created largely through talks among the U.S., British, Australian, and New Zealand governments during summer 1954, SEATO was a direct result of Dien Bien Phu. The alliance never had the force of NATO because its terms did not oblige states to go to war if other member states were attacked.[24] In addition, the states of Indochina were specifically prevented by the July 1954 Geneva agreements from joining regional alliances like SEATO and so were merely designated as protected states by the SEATO powers, a stipulation that further weakened the legal obligations of the powers in the case of war in Indochina. Nevertheless, the U.S. government in the 1960s would repeatedly invoke this product of Dien Bien Phu as establishing a juridical imperative for war in Indochina.

A lesson the Eisenhower administration took away from Dien Bien Phu as well was that frameworks for united action could not be created overnight. That led to efforts to establish other alliance structures in advance of specific occasions for action, notably the Central Treaty Organization (CENTO), with which the United States associated itself in July 1958. The drive to ring the Soviet Union with a network of regional alliances became so strong that analysts would identify the Eisenhower administration, and especially John Foster Dulles, with a tendency to "pactomania."

Another analytical term applied to international relations during the Cold War was the "Munich analogy." This was a reference to the 1938 conference in Munich that sanctioned Germany's takeover of portions of Czechoslovakia. Many U.S. policymakers after World War II believed that the appeasement of Hitler, chosen at the time in order to avoid war, had been a major error. During the Cold War the Munich analogy was employed to advocate strong action and to demonstrate the problems with appeasement. Dien Bien Phu brought with it the extension of the Munich analogy to Vietnam. Eisenhower first articulated the analogy in his effort to enlist the British for intervention at Dien Bien Phu. In a letter to British prime minister Sir Winston Churchill, transmitted by the State Department on April 4, 1954, Ike wrote: "If I may refer again to history, we failed to halt Hirohito, Mussolini, and Hitler by not acting in unity and in time. That marked the beginning of many years of stark tragedy and desperate peril."[25] Claims that a failure to fight in Vietnam would be appeasement, and similar invocations of Munich, would be a staple of justifications for the war in the 1960s.[26]

Consequences for Vietnam and the impact of Dien Bien Phu on Eisenhower come together in our final element, the Diem letter. On October 23, 1954, President Eisenhower sent Prime Minister Diem a letter in which he pledged U.S. aid to the struggling Saigon government. The pledge was conditional, however: "The Government of the United States expects that this aid will be met by performance of the part of the Government of Vietnam in undertaking needed reforms."[27] Diem did not in fact make the expected reforms and over the following months wavered constantly on promises made to American diplomats and Vietnamese politicians in this regard—so much so that in the spring of 1955 Eisenhower's personal representative in Vietnam, General J. Lawton Collins, concluded that Diem had to go. The Collins recommendation was accepted, then reversed.[28] U.S. aid was never halted. The question is, why did Eisenhower not enforce the condition he had imposed? This is more speculative than the preceding analysis, but it is worth linking Ike's letter and subsequent inaction to Dien Bien Phu as well.

Since as early as 1951, when Eisenhower had been only a general and the first field commander of NATO forces, he had pressed the French about their persistent colonial attitude toward Indochina and complained, to his friends and in his diary, regarding French inaction on the matter.[29] As already recounted, at the time of the Navarre Plan he had pressed the French to "perfect" the independence of the Associated States. He had then labored to bring about conditions considered necessary for the United States to save Dien Bien Phu, only to see the entrenched camp go down in defeat. In his memoirs Ike recounts that he had thought French strategy at Dien Bien Phu to be a mistake and had said as much to French officials. "Never had I been so sad to be so right," Eisenhower reflected. No doubt stemming from his frustration that the French would not provide assurances on internationalization and maintaining the war effort, Eisenhower also wrote that he often told Dulles that "France ought to recall General De Gaulle"[30] to lead France. The fall of Dien Bien Phu left Ike deeply depressed, and the emergence of a Saigon government under Ngo Dinh Diem presented him with conditions for which he had pressed for so long. In this context, the October 1954 letter must have represented Eisenhower's attempt to make good on the desire for action he had expressed at the time of Dien Bien Phu. In a sense, guilt over Dien Bien Phu led to an open-ended commitment once Diem had ignored U.S. conditions with impunity. Eisenhower's failure to enforce the conditions he had put on aid stems from the same reluctance to upset an ongoing endeavor that the United States had exhibited with the French.

The Eisenhower letter was invoked in turn by President Lyndon Baines Johnson in 1965 as part of his justification for expanding the American war with a massive commitment of ground troops. What then happened is also instructive: Ike gave the press interviews in 1965 in which he denied having made such promises in 1954. LBJ reacted quickly. He had his NSC staff assemble a thick folder of evidence and sent General Andrew Goodpaster, the assistant to the chairman of the Joint Chiefs of Staff but previously Ike's staff secretary, to Gettysburg, where Goodpaster presented the material. LBJ also called Eisenhower to talk about coordinating their comments on foreign policy. Ike subsequently retracted his claim that no commitments had been made in 1954.[31]

Waiting in the Wings

All the Americans who would serve as president during the U.S. war in Vietnam were already on the political scene at the time of Dien Bien Phu. Two of them—Lyndon Johnson and Richard Nixon—would actually have important (if cameo) roles in the Eisenhower administration's effort to put together an intervention project. Gerald R. Ford was a member of the House of Representatives. John F. Kennedy was the junior senator from Massachusetts. Nixon was Ike's vice president. Johnson, the senior senator from Texas, was the minority leader in the U.S. Senate. All of them witnessed the crisis and learned from it. This section will comment rather extensively on Johnson and briefly on Kennedy and Nixon. Ford, who came to the White House only after the major American role had ended, will not be considered.

Senator Kennedy had been interested in Indochina from the early stages of his congressional career. He believed that only committed Vietnamese would continue to fight the fanatic Vietnamese of Ho Chi Minh. As a member of the U.S. House of Representatives (JFK was elected to the Senate in 1952), Kennedy had visited Indochina in 1951 to see for himself, as one of those Americans who responded to General de Lattre's calls to conceive of Indochina as another front in the Cold War. But in Saigon Kennedy had bristled at the shallow views of embassy officers who saw no problems in the French war effort. He grated so much on de Lattre that the latter complained to U.S. authorities. JFK returned to say, "In Indochina we have allied ourselves to the desperate effort of a French regime to hang onto the remnants of empire."

This was virtually the same as what Eisenhower had written in his diary. But Kennedy's view was different in a key respect. As he saw it, "The task is to build strong native non-Communist sentiment . . . and rely on that as a spearhead of defense rather than upon the legions of General de Lattre. To do this apart from and in defiance of innately nationalistic aims spells foredoomed failure." On the television news show *Meet the Press*, Kennedy said, "Without the support of the native population there is no hope of success in any of the countries of Southeast Asia."[32] As a senator, Kennedy forged links with Vietnamese politician Ngo Dinh Diem.

At the time of Dien Bien Phu, JFK told interviewers that it would take many months of hard work to organize united action, that U.S. intervention was unlikely, and that "the lack of popular support for the war among the people of the Associated States of Indochina and, consequently, the lack of a crusading and reliable native army with an effective officer corps prevents the wholehearted nationalistic drive against the Communists which is essential for military success."[33] Eisenhower came to share many of those views, resulting in his administration backing Diem's rise to power. But the perceived need to turn aside challenges to Diem's authority led Ike to ignore the South Vietnamese leader's authoritarianism and refusal to enact reforms.

Having started with a good appreciation of realities, Kennedy backed himself into the same place Eisenhower was headed. JFK's commitment to Diem, at a time when the two could only theorize about what needed to be done in Vietnam, survived Diem's control of the Saigon government and his total failure to enact reform. As president, Kennedy behaved as if dynamism in American action plus a rhetorical flourish or two could substitute for a popular and effective Saigon government. Kennedy moved the nation toward Vietnam involvement, not away from it. His eventual turn against Diem in 1963 only accelerated that trend.

As for Johnson, much has been made of LBJ saving America from intervention at Dien Bien Phu. Popularized by journalist Chalmers Roberts in a widely noted article, "The Day We Didn't Go to War,"[34] this story centers upon the consultation that Secretary Dulles and Admiral Radford had with congressional leaders, including Senator Johnson, on April 3, 1954. It has been repeated uncritically by most historians dealing with Dien Bien Phu ever since. Naturally the journalistic scoop relied upon leaks, from Representative John W. McCormack (according to Roberts), but also quite likely from LBJ himself, and the resulting article portrayed Johnson very favorably in the midst of the election campaign of 1954, which LBJ ended up winning handily. A more thorough investigation, however, reveals quite a different story.[35]

At the time of the State Department meeting with Dulles, Senator Johnson's last direct contact with Indochina had been at the White House, where President Eisenhower had held a legislative meeting for congressional leaders on January 5, 1954. Conversation pertained entirely to routine matters, and Dien Bien Phu had not yet been assaulted. Johnson saw Eisenhower again at a White House dinner for Speaker Sam Rayburn on February 16. The senator worked hard to fashion bipartisan politics in the Senate as a strategy to gain some role in policy, and the sessions with Eisenhower were one fruit of that approach.[36] Secretary Dulles's sounding was something different, a briefing the administration could avoid only at its peril. Proceeding with intervention without consulting Congress in any way would have invited major political, even constitutional controversy. Dulles began by saying that Eisenhower had asked him to convene the leaders and added that the administration needed a congressional resolution on the use of force in Indochina. Admiral Radford then gave a briefing on the military situation at Dien Bien Phu. Both emphasized the seriousness of the situation and alluded to the domino theory, and Radford spoke of using bombers to strike the Viet Minh around the entrenched camp. The ensuing discussion went over many issues and was by no means one-sided. Some favored giving Eisenhower what he wanted.

The key question was Johnson's. The minority leader asked what had been done to recruit allies for this intervention, and Dulles had to admit that none had been lined up. Chalmers Roberts and those who follow his account portray this question as a deal breaker, a wrench thrown by LBJ to derail the project, but an entirely different interpretation is possible. For one thing, it had been just four days since Dulles himself had given a speech in New York coining the phrase "united action," and it was perfectly logical to ask what had been done about this. Secretary Dulles's own record of this meeting concludes that "if satisfactory commitments can be obtained [from allies], the consensus was that a Congressional resolution could be passed."[37]

At the April 3 meeting Johnson could simply have been asking how the administration was planning to line up bipartisan support for Indochina intervention. This point is reinforced by the fact that immediately after the session with Dulles, Senator Johnson proceeded to take soundings among his Democratic colleagues about their positions on intervention.

Johnson wrote no memoir covering this period, did not keep a diary, and gave no oral histories or other interviews that bear on the subject. The most authoritative sources on Johnson's position on Indochina are thus the newsletters LBJ himself sent out every two weeks to his Texas constituents. These were typically written by senior aide George Reedy and other assistants and occasionally by Johnson himself, and they usually reflected his thinking. Senator Johnson's newsletters for this period consistently and repeatedly make the case for U.S. intervention in Indochina.

The April 3 imeeting with Dulles is reflected in Johnson's newsletter on April 15. There LBJ explicitly mentioned the State Department briefing, argued that in Indochina "we are at the crossroads," and spoke of the need to make "hard decisions—the kind that will tax all our determination and willpower." Johnson asserted that the fall of Indochina "would be disastrous to all our plans in Asia" and, echoing President Eisenhower's news conference of April 7, brought in the domino theory by raising the specter of "the loss of all Southeast Asia and probably all of Asia. Ultimately we might be driven out of the Pacific itself!"[38]

As for the supposed deal breaker, the matter of allies for united action, Senator Johnson said in the same issue of his newsletter, "Shall we continue without clear assurances that others will join us? Or shall we withdraw altogether and fall back upon the concept of Fortress America?" The choice among these stark alternatives was clear: Johnson was for intervention, without allies if necessary. LBJ simply noted that the answers to the questions of Indochina "must be based upon the full knowledge and consent of the American people."

The last point was a clear reference to public opinion. At the time of Dien Bien Phu there was little enthusiasm for intervention in Indochina. In Senator Johnson's constituent mail seventy persons expressed opinions on intervention (including one letter with many signatures). Sixty-three of LBJ's voters opposed entering the war.[39]

Regardless of those opinions, Johnson continued to advocate an activist course, a further indication that this was his true policy position. Secretary Dulles held another briefing for the congressional leadership on April 20, following initial visits he had made to London and Paris. In his April 24 newsletter Senator Johnson declared that a Viet Minh victory "would be a heavy blow to freedom" that would leave communism "in a commanding position *to take over the entire continent of Asia*" (Johnson's italics). Again, *"Indochina is a rich prize"* (his italics), and "it is impossible to exaggerate the seriousness of the situation." Johnson's office put out the identical text as a press release a few days later.

Not until May 1, with Dien Bien Phu on its last legs, did a Johnson newsletter say that he shared the prayers of those Americans who hoped the crisis "will not end in another war to be fought by our young men." Even after the fall of the entrenched camp, the Johnson newsletter of May 15, in terming the loss of Dien Bien Phu a major setback, quoted LBJ's floor speech to the Senate on this occasion: "We are ready to meet the President and the Administration *more* than half way. As responsible men, *we are ready at any time to cooperate in the preservation of our country*" (LBJ's italics). Like some other American leaders, Lyndon Johnson seems to have changed his position on intervention, and his first view is not the one historians usually attribute to him.

Johnson had perhaps the best opportunity to learn from Dien Bien Phu, but the lessons he carried away were not those of "The Day We Didn't Go to War." Rather LBJ learned to manage the politics of commitment, not to question rationales for action. The American intervention in Vietnam in 1964–1965 shows careful political fine tuning. During his 1964 presidential campaign, LBJ promised not to send "American boys" to fight "Asian wars." But the Johnson administration resolutely turned aside French and other diplomatic efforts to neutralize Vietnam along the lines of the Geneva agreements on Laos of 1962.[40] There was an administration program for involvement. It included a congressional resolution. The action plan provided for covert activity to provoke an overt response that could then be countered by applications of American naval and air forces. And when he sent in the ground troops, President Johnson insisted on "many flags," that is, contingents of allied forces that would endow the U.S. effort with a multinational character. Johnson's intervention was Dien Bien Phu's Operation Vulture done right, though it proved no more successful than some feared a 1954 action would have been.

Richard Nixon also stood in the wings during the crisis although he, like Johnson, had a big role to play later. As vice president of the United States, Nixon sat on the National Security Council and gave advice at every stage. He also participated in certain private meetings, including one that focused on whether to inform allies that the United States was contemplating the use of nuclear weapons if it intervened. And Nixon gave a speech on April 16 following which he answered questions in a fashion interpreted to be testing the waters for reactions to an intervention with ground forces. Vice President Nixon's private advice was for intervention. Having pressed for action, Nixon would be disappointed in the events of 1954. As he wrote later of the parts played by the key figures, "Dulles and I both believed that if the Communists pushed too far we would have to do whatever was necessary to stop them. Eisenhower fully agreed, although I think that Dulles and I were probably prepared to stand up at an earlier point than he was."[41]

The French, once they decided they wanted out, went for a quick settlement. Foreign Minister Georges Bidault presented an outline proposal for an agreement at Geneva as early as May 8, just hours after the fall of Dien Bien Phu, with French wounded still on the battlefield. The main components proposed—a general cease-fire, regrouping zones for the armed forces, and international supervision—were the essential framework of the eventual Geneva agreements. Nixon favored U.S. rejection of the accords and believed that permitting the French defeat had enabled the erstwhile ally to run away from the war. As president, Nixon would not do that. He pressed constantly for more aggressive maneuvers during his time in the White House.

In his 1968 campaign Nixon hinted at a secret plan to end the Vietnam War. In a campaign speech at Denver on September 25, candidate Nixon had the audacity to declare: "I am proud of the fact that I served in an administration that ended one war [Korea] and kept the nation out of other wars for eight years."[42] No one aware of Nixon's real role at Dien Bien Phu, or indeed in other Eisenhower crises, called him on this claim, and the "secret plan" turned out to be a formula for escalation, an attempt to coerce the Vietnamese enemy into agreement through a bombing campaign, in a concept somewhat similar to Operation Vulture at Dien Bien Phu. In office Nixon extended America's Vietnam war for an additional seven years, long enough to provide a decent interval between Washington's decision (under Johnson, it should be noted) to reverse course in Vietnam and the final fall of the Saigon government. To attain that objective required a series of escalations like the one contemplated at Dien Bien Phu. Nixon did not learn from Dien Bien Phu, or perhaps he took away the wrong lessons.

Conclusion

Dien Bien Phu can be assessed on a number of levels. At the strictly military level it proved to be the last, decisive battle of the French war in Vietnam. The French were still powerful after losing Dien Bien Phu, but they lacked mobile and reserve forces and would have found it extremely difficult to regroup before losing the Red River delta. At the same time declining public support for the Indochina war could hardly have survived the additional shock of the loss of the Hanoi-Haiphong complex. That the French emerged from the Geneva negotiations as well as they did is a product of diplomacy, in particular the Viet Minh relationship with the People's Republic of China, and is beyond the scope of this chapter.

At the level of the Vietnamese state, consequences flowed more from the general status of the war than the specific situation at Dien Bien Phu. Win or lose, the Vietnamese state allied to France was bound to attain full independence at this point due to forces both endemic and extraneous to the situation. American and international pressures from the outside and the necessities of mobilizing Vietnamese nationalists in the conflict obliged the French to take the full set of measures they had resisted since the inception of the State of Vietnam.

Dien Bien Phu did have specific political results for both Vietnamese states, however. For the State of Vietnam, the defeat revealed French strategy as bankrupt, and Paris's loss of prestige sapped the credibility of the Bao Dai government. With old-line politicians tarred by their French associations, Emperor Bao Dai was forced to turn to the man who would overthrow him, Ngo Dinh Diem. Thus Dien Bien Phu pushed the State of Vietnam over the precipice at the very instant it achieved the long sought goal of independence. For the Democratic Republic of Vietnam and the Viet Minh, Dien Bien Phu served to fully consolidate the Vietnamese revolution, bringing a surge in morale and energy that would have assisted mightily in overwhelming the French Expeditionary Corps had the war continued.

For the United States, military intervention at Dien Bien Phu was successfully avoided. The American war in Vietnam was thereby delayed for a decade. At the same time, Washington received an opportunity it did not take: to promote the peaceful reunification of Vietnam. With that means to ending conflict left unexplored, the die was cast, and the heat of Dien Bien Phu forged all five of the major elements that would eventually lead to the American war. To the degree that fighting in Vietnam would later become a drain on U.S. national security, Dien Bien Phu ultimately had a highly deleterious effect on the United States.

As the first major foreign crisis of the Eisenhower administration, Dien Bien Phu also had significant short-term impacts on the president in power. The administration subsequently engaged in efforts to prepare in advance for crises by creating regional alliances and securing congressional resolutions. Eisenhower's administration also came away from the crisis with the impression that threatening the use of force, "brinkmanship" in the idiom of that day, was a valuable tool in international relations. For the remainder of the administration the tactic of pushing to the brink of conflict would be relied upon, with multiple instances of threatened use of nuclear weapons, and crises became an essential feature of Eisenhower's tenure. At least three times off the China coast, once in the Middle East, and twice over Berlin the Eisenhower administration engaged in brinkmanship crises. To the extent that Dien Bien Phu seemed to teach that these tactics were feasible, that crisis increased the danger inherent in U.S. international security policy through the remainder of the 1950s.

Waiting in the wings were the key leaders who would guide America into its own Vietnam war not very long after Dien Bien Phu. These men learned lessons from Dien Bien Phu that, combined with the elements justifying war that were forged in the crisis, made the American war close to inevitable. John F. Kennedy developed the notion that dynamism in U.S. action plus rhetorical nods toward indigenous nationalisms could substitute for a southern Vietnamese political evolution that had ground to a halt. Lyndon B. Johnson learned to manage the politics of commitment. Richard M. Nixon found at Dien Bien Phu confirmation of his impression that aggressive maneuvers were the best ones in foreign policy. The ideas these men carried from Dien Bien Phu had much to do with the later events of America's most disastrous war.

TWELVE

China and the Indochina Settlement
at the Geneva Conference of 1954

CHEN JIAN

IN LATE 1953 and early 1954, the First Indochina War reached a criti-cal juncture. With Dien Bien Phu under siege by the Viet Minh forces, it became increasingly evident that the balance of power on the battle-field was changing in favor of the communist side. Against this back-ground, policymakers in Washington repeatedly warned that further escalation of the communist offensive in Indochina could result in di-rect American military intervention. In the meantime, Beijing's lead-ers, while enhancing China's military and other material support to the Viet Minh, demonstrated strong interest in a settlement to the In-dochina conflict through international negotiations. It was within this context that the process leading to the Geneva Conference of 1954 and the settlement of the Indochina issue unfolded.

As is well known, the 1954 Geneva Conference was held at the height of the Cold War confrontation between the two contending blocs, and the diplomatic negotiations at the conference were thus extremely dif-ficult. The conference dealt with two main issues: Korea and Indo-china. Those participating in the conference reached no agreement on Korea, but they—although without U.S. commitment—worked out a settlement on Indochina. As revealed by newly available Chinese sources, Beijing's leaders, Zhou Enlai in particular, played a crucial role in shaping the settlement. Indeed, on the eve of the conference, Beijing conducted a series of meetings with Viet Minh and Soviet lead-ers to form a communist negotiation strategy. After the conference failed to reach any agreement on Korea, Zhou endeavored to adjust and coordinate the strategies carried out by Beijing, Moscow, and the

Viet Minh, while at the same time developing working relationships with the delegations from Britain, France, Laos, and Cambodia. When the conference reached a critical juncture on the Indochina issue in mid-June 1954 after its failure to reach any agreement on Korea, the Chinese, with Moscow's backing, applied great pressure on their Vietnamese comrades. At an important meeting between Zhou and Ho Chi Minh in early July, the Chinese and Vietnamese reached a consensus that a peaceful settlement had to be reached at Geneva to avoid America's direct military intervention in Vietnam. Consequently, largely due to Zhou's efforts, the Geneva Conference was able to work out a settlement on Indochina.

What were China's changing negotiation strategies during the Geneva Conference? What motives underlay Beijing's positive attitude toward reaching a diplomatic settlement on Indochina? How did Beijing coordinate its negotiation strategies with Moscow and the Viet Minh? And, on a more personal level, what role did individual politicians, and Zhou in particular, play in bringing about the Indochina settlement? This chapter, drawing on Chinese sources that have become available in recent years,[1] will try to reconstruct the shifting Chinese approach at the Geneva Conference, to explore the complicated relationships among the communist actors, and to reveal the considerations underlying their decisions to pursue peace in Indochina.

Preparing for the Conference

In retrospect, the years 1953 and 1954 represented a crucial turning point in postwar international relations. In July 1953, the Korean War ended with the two sides reaching an armistice agreement. In the meantime, in the wake of the June 17, 1953, popular uprising in East Berlin, the question of a divided Germany had become highlighted in international politics. Against this backdrop, for the purpose of emphasizing to the world that the Soviet Union, now under a new post-Stalin leadership, was willing to solve international disputes through diplomacy, Moscow proposed on September 29 a five-power foreign ministers' meeting that would also include representatives from China to examine "measures to relax international tensions." On October 8, Zhou announced that Beijing fully supported Moscow's proposal. From January 25 to February 18, 1954, the foreign ministers from the Soviet Union, the United States, Britain, and France met in Berlin. The meeting's participants did not reach any agreement on the German question and Austrian and European security, but they agreed to convene a conference in Geneva to discuss issues related to "reaching a peaceful settlement of the Korea question" and "restoring peace in Indochina." While the United States, the USSR, Britain, France, and China would attend discussions on both Korea and Indochina, the sessions on Korea would also be attended by countries that had participated in the Korean War, and the sessions on Indochina would be attended by "other interested states."[2]

Beijing's leaders viewed the result of the Berlin conference as a big "international victory." Although the Berlin communiqué included a caveat stating that "neither the invitation to, nor the holding of" the conference at Geneva "shall be deemed to imply diplomatic recognition in any case where it has not already been accorded,"[3] the simple fact that the People's Republic of China (PRC), after being excluded from the international community since its establishment five years before, would now attend an important conference of world leaders in the de facto capacity as one of the "five powers" sent an unmistakable message that the "new China" had emerged as a major power on the international scene.

In late February and early March, Zhou made time in his extremely busy schedule to read "a large amount of documents, telegrams, materials and intelligence reports, as well as all the exchanges between the U.S. and the Soviet governments."[4] In the meantime, he convened a series of meetings with his associates at the Foreign Ministry to discuss how to prepare for the conference. At a meeting on February 27, Zhou gave a long speech that reflected some of his basic thoughts at the moment. He pointed out that the Geneva Conference would play "an important role" in relaxing international tensions, so China must actively participate in it in order to promote "new China's international reputation." Zhou also indicated that the conference probably would not achieve a major breakthrough on Korea due to America's negative attitude. However, he thought that the prospects on Indochina seemed different. "While France seems interested in reaching a peaceful solution to the Indochina issue," observed the Chinese premier, "the U.S. is not. Therefore, it seems that France is reluctant to let the U.S. put its nose into Vietnam." Zhou thus asked his associates to contemplate whether China should adopt "a general policy line of showing the carrot to France while using the stick to deal with the U.S." He particularly mentioned that Chinese propaganda about the Geneva Conference ought to "concentrate its criticism on the U.S., and should leave France with some hope."[5]

Under Zhou's direction, the Chinese Foreign Ministry worked out a "Preliminary Paper on the Assessment of and Preparation for the Geneva Conference" in late February. The document contended that the PRC "must actively participate in the Geneva conference" and "must make it a success" in order to break up America's "blockade, embargo and rearmament policies" against China. The document further argued that such an aim was not only necessary but also feasible. "The opinions of the U.S., Britain and France are far from identical on Korea and many other international issues; indeed, the contradictions among them sometimes are very big, and they are facing many internal difficulties too." All of this, argued the Chinese analysts, had created space for the PRC to "strengthen its diplomatic and international activities," allowing Beijing to "strive for reaching some agreements [on Korea], even if only temporary [in nature] and limited [in scope]." It was on the Indochina issue, emphasized the document, that "we must try our best to make sure that the conference will not end without any result; even under the circumstance that no agreement can be reached, we still should not allow the negotiations for restoring peace in Indochina to be undermined completely, and should create a situation characterized by 'negotiating while fighting,' thus increasing the difficulties inside France and the contradictions between France and America." On March 2, the CCP Central Secretariat approved this document "in principle."[6] The next day Beijing formally announced that its delegation would attend the conference in Geneva.

Beijing's attitude toward the Geneva Conference reflected several of its leadership's basic considerations. First of all, with the end of the Korean War, Beijing's leaders sensed the need to devote more of China's resources to domestic issues. In 1953 and 1954, they were contemplating the introduction of the first five-year plan, as well as a shift of China's resources to the "liberation" of Nationalist-controlled Taiwan.[7] After five years of sharp confrontation with the West, many leaders in Beijing perceived that for the purpose of promoting socialist transformation and reconstruction at home, China needed a more stable international environment. They saw the Geneva Conference as a good opportunity to demonstrate a reconciliatory and positive approach and a commitment to peaceful coexistence.[8] Mao Zedong also endorsed this approach.[9]

Second, the Chinese Communist Party (CCP) leadership saw China's presence at the Geneva Conference as a valuable opportunity to boost its international reputation. This was particularly important for Mao and the CCP not only for international reasons but also because of subtle domestic considerations. Since the birth of the People's Republic, the phrase "we the Chinese people have stood up"—the announcement that Mao made at the PRC's formation—had played a central role in legitimizing the revolutionary programs Mao tried to carry out in China. In 1954, when Mao and his comrades were eager to "construct the foundation of a socialist society" in China, they understood that they would be in a strong position to push the party's mass mobilization plan at home if they could demonstrate to ordinary Chinese— possessors of a "victim mentality"[10] that made them eager for an assertive international policy—that China had returned to the ranks of the great powers. Thus, China's performance at the Geneva Conference became a crucial test case that would have a profound impact upon Mao's continuous revolution and China's domestic development.

Third, Beijing's positive attitude toward diplomatic activities in Geneva was related to a deep concern over possible direct American intervention in Indochina. China had been deeply involved in the First Indochina War.[11] With insights gained from their Korean War experience, Beijing's leaders were worried that if a peaceful settlement could not be worked out for Indochina, American military intervention there would follow. They approached this problem with a "worst case assumption": they would try everything possible, including pursuing a compromise at Geneva, to prevent American intervention; only if the Americans directly entered the war in Indochina would they consider sending troops to stop American forces from approaching China's borders, as well as to maintain the momentum of the Vietnamese revolution.

In mid-March, Zhou sent a telegram to Ho Chi Minh and the Vietnamese Workers' Party (VWP) Central Committee, contending that "the current international situation and the military conditions in Vietnam are favorable for the Democratic Republic of Vietnam (DRV) to put more emphasis on carrying out a diplomatic struggle." No matter what result the Geneva Conference would achieve, "we should actively participate in it." Zhou also raised the possibility of reaching a ceasefire in Indochina by temporarily dividing Vietnam into two parts, arguing that "if a ceasefire is to be achieved, it is better that a relatively fixed demarcation line be established so that [the Viet Minh] can control a unified area." Zhou particularly mentioned that the sixteenth parallel could be "one of our options."[12]

From late March to early April 1954, Ho and Pham Van Dong, the DRV's deputy prime minister and foreign minister, visited Beijing and, together with Zhou, Moscow. In their discussions the Chinese leaders stressed China's experience gained from the negotiations to end the Korean War, emphasizing that it was necessary to maintain "realistic expectations" for the Geneva Conference. According to Chinese sources, the Vietnamese leaders agreed.[13]

Beijing's positive attitude toward the Geneva Conference was also consistent with the intentions of the leaders in Moscow, who, after Stalin's death, also needed to focus on domestic issues and to avoid a confrontation with the West in Asia.[14] During the first three weeks of April, Zhou visited Moscow twice to discuss the Chinese-Soviet strategy at Geneva. The two sides agreed to cooperate at the forthcoming conference. Soviet foreign minister V. M. Molotov stressed that it was possible for the Geneva Conference to solve one or two problems, but the imperialist countries would certainly stand up for their interests. Therefore, insisted Molotov, the communist camp should adopt a realistic strategy compatible with this situation. Zhou made it clear that the Chinese would try their best to listen to the opinions of the Soviets. These discussions resulted in a consensus: even with the attempts of the United States to sabotage the conference, if the communist side acted realistically, a peaceful solution on Indochina could still be found.[15]

The First Phase

The Geneva Conference began on April 26, 1954, and concentrated at first on Korea. As predicted by the Chinese, it quickly turned out that it was extremely difficult for the contending sides to reach an agreement. Indeed, they were unable to find compromises on even the meeting's agenda. Consequently, the discussions on Korea became deadlocked.

This development was not beyond the expectations of the Chinese. In a telegram to Beijing on April 28, Zhou pointed out that "the discussions on Korea have already entered a deadlock—this is because the U.S. does not intend to solve the question, France is not in a convenient position to discuss this issue, and Britain has made it clear that it does not want to cast its opinion on this issue either." Under the circumstances, Zhou believed that more attention should be paid to Indochina. He mentioned that Georges Bidault, French foreign minister and head of the French delegation, was "eager to discuss the Indochina question" and had already approached Molotov and expressed the desire to meet with the Chinese. Zhou predicted that discussion of Indochina could begin ahead of schedule.[16]

Two days after he dispatched his telegram to Beijing, Zhou through Molotov's arrangement, met with British foreign minister Anthony Eden at a luncheon at Molotov's villa. Although the conversation was generally "informal," Zhou and Eden touched on a series of important issues. The Chinese premier, in a diplomatic way, complained to Eden that while the PRC never refused to recognize the United Kingdom, Britain failed to recognize the PRC at the United Nations. When Eden inquired about whether the Chinese would be willing to play a role in persuading the Viet Minh to release wounded prisoners, Zhou immediately responded that this would not be a problem at all if the concerned parties met directly. He also used this opportunity to imply that it was the Americans who intended to block direct exchanges of opinions between the "concerned parties."[17] For Zhou, the meeting with Eden was important not only in that this was the first time that he had a face-to-face meeting with the leader of a major Western power but also in that it confirmed his earlier speculation that the British, like the French, were more concerned about Indochina than Korea.

The Geneva Conference opened discussion of Indochina on May 8, the day after Viet Minh troops finally seized Dien Bien Phu. Despite the fact that the Vietnamese communists seemed to agree during preconference consultations with Beijing and Moscow to divide Vietnam temporarily into two zones, victory at Dien Bien Phu made them believe that they were in a position to squeeze more concessions from their adversaries. Pham Van Dong, head of the DRV delegation, announced that in order to settle the Indochina problem, the Viet Minh would ask for control over most of Vietnam through an on-the-spot truce, to be followed by a national plebiscite that they knew that they would win. Pham also indicated that the DRV delegation, while denying the presence of Viet Minh troops in Laos, would pursue a settlement of the Laos and Cambodia problems as part of a general settlement for Indochina.[18]

Testing Options for Compromises

Zhou and the Chinese delegation (like the Soviets) originally sup-ported the Viet Minh's stand on pursuing an overall settlement in Viet-nam, Laos, and Cambodia. But the Chinese premier was more eager than Pham Van Dong to create an atmosphere favorable for the dis-cussions to continue. On the same day that the conference's delibera-tion of Indochina began, Zhou met with Dong and urged him to issue a statement to the effect that the Viet Minh would release seriously wounded enemy captives at Dien Bien Phu.[19] After Dong made the statement on May 10, Zhou sent a telegram to Wei Guoqing, chief Chi-nese military adviser at the Viet Minh headquarters, instructing him to monitor the Viet Minh's management of the evacuation of wounded captives and report to him at any time.[20]

Beginning on May 17, the discussion on Indochina was conducted in a series of restricted sessions. Following Zhou's and Molotov's instruc-tions, Andrei Gromyko, representing the Soviet Union, and Wang Jiaxiang, representing China, had previously met with Dong on the evening of May 15 to coordinate the aims and strategies of the com-munist side. They decided to oppose treating Laos and Cambodia as separate issues in the peace settlement, to insist upon linking a politi-cal solution with a cease-fire, and to insist that the United States should not be allowed to transport more weapons and ammunition to In-dochina once France ended military operations there.[21]

Zhou worked hard to pursue a political settlement that would reflect the above principles. In addition to arguing for these conditions at the restricted sessions, Zhou had three more meetings with Eden on May 14, 20, and 27, at which he explained the logic underlying the condi-tions set by the communist side, while showing flexibility to some of Eden's suggestions.[22] In a series of telegrams to the CCP leadership in late May, Zhou reported that "some progress has been achieved in the discussion of the Indochina issue at Geneva" and that "reaching a ceasefire [there] now appears possible."[23]

However, Zhou also worried that the conference's discussion on Indochina might hit a stalemate. On May 29, Zhou, Molotov, and Dong met to discuss how a cease-fire should be pursued.[24] The next day Zhou dispatched a long telegram to Beijing, summarizing what he saw as the main problem with the communist negotiation strategy—a lack of proper understanding of the complexity of the Indochina question and, in particular, the differences between Vietnam, Laos, and Cambodia. Acknowledging that "the national and state boundaries between the three associate countries in Indochina are quite distinctive," Zhou pointed out that "the royal governments in Cambodia and Laos remain regarded as legitimate governments by the overwhelming majority of their people." Therefore, he argued, "we must strictly regard them as three different countries." Zhou further contended that on the ceasefire question the two sides would "now enter discussions of substance, which involves three key issues, namely, dividing zones, ceasefire supervision and international guarantee." He recognized that "on all three issues, there exist huge differences between the two sides." Therefore, Zhou reported, both he and the Soviets believed that the communist side would "need to develop a more clearly defined solution that will better fit the current situation, and otherwise we will be unable to express our opinions in the negotiations, and will fall into a passive position." Zhou thus concluded that "we should persistently take the initiative to pursue peace."[25]

It is interesting to note that Zhou made clear in the telegram that the Chinese and Soviets agreed on the "need to develop a more clearly defined solution that will better fit the current situation." In actuality, what Zhou meant was that the Viet Minh would have to change its unyielding attitude toward settling the Indochina issue. After the CCP leadership approved Zhou's proposal,[26] he quickly acted to create a "more clearly defined solution." He first worked with the Soviets to redefine the communist strategy on dividing Vietnam into two zones. In several telegrams to the CCP Central Committee (he asked them to be conveyed to the VWP too), Zhou highlighted the benefit of this approach. He argued that an on-the-spot cease-fire "is not favorable to us," as this would not guarantee that the Viet Minh would control Vietnam's entire northern part and would make the cease-fire extremely difficult to manage. Instead Zhou strongly favored "dividing [Vietnam] into two big zones in the north and the south." He also emphasized that in making concrete plans for the division, "we should not set our bottom line for this solution of 'big adjustments' too high; instead, we should leave enough leeway."[27] Later, Zhou clarified that "leaving enough leeway" meant that when the question of whether the dividing line should be set at the sixteenth parallel or the eighteenth parallel was raised, "we should not give an immediate answer, and should allow ourselves an opportunity to study the issue more carefully and then to give our response."[28]

Breaking the Stalemate

On June 15, the conference had its last plenary session on Korea, which concluded with no result. The failure of the Geneva Conference's Korean part placed great pressure on the conference's discussion of Indochina by showing that the entire conference could end without achieving anything. Indeed, according to one Chinese source, Jean-Paul Boncour, a member of the French delegation who was eager to avoid the conference's total failure, approached the Chinese delegation on the evening of June 14, informing the Chinese that the United States intended to sabotage the entire conference and then to place the blame on China. Reportedly, Boncour advised the Chinese that "now only you are in a position to save the conference from a total collapse."[29]

While the Geneva Conference was at this crossroad, a major political change occurred in France: the French parliament, reflecting the public's impatience with the immobility at Geneva, ousted Prime Minister Laniel on June 12 and, five days later, replaced him with Pierre Mendès France, who, as a longtime leading critic of the war in Indochina, promised that he would lead the negotiation to a successful conclusion by July 20 or would resign. It was against this backdrop that Zhou and the Chinese leadership saw an opportunity to push forward the negotiations on Indochina.

On June 15, after the collapse of the Korea negotiations at Geneva, the Chinese, Soviet, and Vietnamese delegations held an important meeting to discuss how to evaluate the situation and coordinate strategy among them. Zhou pointed out straightforwardly that the Viet Minh's refusal to admit the existence of its forces in Laos and Cambodia had made it difficult for the negotiations to move forward. He warned that this rigid attitude would render the discussions on Indochina fruitless and that the Vietnamese communists themselves would lose a golden opportunity to achieve a peaceful solution of the Vietnam question. Zhou proposed that the communist camp adopt a new line in favor of withdrawal of all foreign forces from Laos and Cambodia, including the "volunteers" dispatched by the Viet Minh, so that "our concessions on Cambodia and Laos will result in [the other side's] concessions on the question of dividing the zones between the two sides in Vietnam." Molotov, who had already had several private discussions with Zhou, strongly supported Zhou's proposal. Pham Van Dong, under heavy pressure from the Chinese and the Soviets, finally consented to this new strategy.[30]

The three leaders then discussed how to carry out the new strategy. They decided that Zhou would ask to meet with the delegates from France and Britain the next morning to reveal the new approach, so that they would not take a confrontational attitude at the next afternoon's meeting. The three leaders further decided upon a division of labor for presenting the new strategy at that meeting: Zhou would offer a proposal on military issues, Dong would present a proposal on political settlement, and Molotov would introduce a proposal concerning the composition of a supervisory committee made up of neutral countries.[31]

On June 16, at 12:30 PM Zhou met with Eden to communicate to the British the changing communist attitude toward Laos and Cambodia. Zhou first pointed out that China was particularly upset with the conference's failure to make any progress in settling the Korea issue. He then turned to the Indochina issue, stating to Eden that Beijing was willing to recognize the royal governments of Laos and Cambodia on condition that the United States did not maintain military bases in these two countries. Zhou further emphasized that "China hopes to see Laos and Cambodia become India-type countries in Southeast Asia, and is willing to live peacefully with them." The most important part of the conversation came when Zhou admitted that Vietnamese "volunteers" had been sent to Laos and Cambodia and that "some have left and some may still be there." Zhou told Eden that "if they are still there, our opinion is that, as with all other foreign forces, they should evacuate [from these two countries]."[32]

The same afternoon, at 3:30, the fourteenth restricted session on Indochina was convened at Geneva. As prearranged by the communist delegations, Zhou spoke at the meeting, pointing out that "he had stated on several occasions that conditions are not the same in each of the three countries of Indochina; there are differences between all three although they cannot be disassociated in a clear-cut manner." He put forward six proposals concerning a cease-fire in Indochina, including one calling for the withdrawal of all foreign forces from Laos and Cambodia.[33] Zhou did not specify that the Viet Minh troops should also withdraw from these two countries. However, now that he regarded Laos and Cambodia as distinct from Vietnam and had admitted that

Vietnamese "volunteers" had been sent to these two countries, it was evident that Viet Minh troops would be included in the "foreign forces" that should leave Laos and Cambodia.

On the same day that Mendès France became French prime minister, June 17, Zhou met with Bidault, the first such meeting between Chinese and French leaders at the Geneva Conference. Zhou reiterated what he had told Eden the day before: Beijing hoped to see Laos and Cambodia maintain peace and neutrality and was willing to recognize the royal governments in these two countries. In addition, Zhou emphasized that China had no objection to Laos and Cambodia remaining in the French Union if "the two countries themselves so choose." Zhou also stressed that the principle that "all foreign forces should withdraw" should apply to both French and Viet Minh troops.[34]

Zhou's efforts, together with an eagerness on the part of the French and the British not to allow the negotiations on Indochina to fail, helped the conference reach an agreement on June 19 on the format of the military talks that would lead to "the cessation of hostilities" in Laos and Cambodia."[35] Then, in order for various countries to prepare for further discussions, the foreign ministers' meeting on Indochina adjourned for the next three weeks.

For Zhou, this break offered an opportunity to further coordinate communist strategies for managing what was supposed to be the last, yet most crucial, stage of the Geneva Conference. Top on Zhou's agenda was how to persuade the Vietnamese communists of the necessity of making adequate concessions in the final settlement, a point that he summarized in a long telegram to the CCP leadership on June 19. Citing his experience at the conference, Zhou contended that in order to get the best possible deal on Vietnam, the communist side would have to make proper concessions, especially in Cambodia and Laos. He pointed out that the Viet Minh leadership did not quite understand this issue and asserted that the VWP Central Committee's proposal for a comprehensive settlement had failed "to hit the point." If this situation was allowed to continue, warned Zhou, "the negotiation cannot go on, and this . . . will not serve our long-range interests." Zhou further emphasized:

At present, the proposal from our side should emphasize Vietnam and should be prepared to make due concessions in Cambodia and Laos . . . If we take the initiative to make concessions in Cambodia and Laos, we will be able to ask for more gains in Vietnam as compensations to us.

Our position in Vietnam being relatively strong in various aspects, we will not only be able to keep our gains there, but also will be capable of gradually consolidating and expanding our influence . . . The situation we are facing now is that if the concrete military solutions we are to introduce are reasonable, we will be able to strive for cutting a quick deal with France, thus reaching an overall settlement. This will allow us to push the new government in France to resist America's interference, and will also allow us to delay [The Western powers'] rearmament in Europe. This is beneficial to both the East and the West, and this is the key question that we must make clear [to the Vietnamese] . . . The emphasis of our strategy at this stage should be to encourage the [peace] initiatives by the French, to keep the French from listening to the Americans completely, to make the British support stopping the war, and to quickly reach an armistice agreement [with them] as long as the conditions seem reasonable.[36]

Considering the complexity of the issues involved here, Zhou found it difficult to "reach consensus" with the Vietnamese comrades "merely through telegraphic exchanges." He therefore proposed to use the conference break to travel to Guangxi, a Chinese province neighboring Vietnam, to meet with the VWP leaders.[37] On June 20, Zhou reported to Beijing that he had agreed with Molotov and Dong to meet Viet Minh leaders—and Ho Chi Minh and Vo Nguyen Giap in particular— to "discuss the issues related to the negotiations [in the next stage] and the zonal division, so that a consensus will be worked out, and the negotiations at Geneva will make further progress." The CCP leadership approved Zhou's plans the same day.[38]

Zhou now turned his main attention to Mendès France, hoping to ascertain the new French prime minister's attitude toward reaching a settlement on Indochina. In his telegram to the CCP leadership on June 19, Zhou devoted a long paragraph to analyzing Mendès France and his policy tendencies. He pointed out that "although Mendès France favored stopping the war in Indochina, he is not a genuine leftist politician, and his purpose is to use the slogan of peace to form a majority among various bourgeois parties. As he has to satisfy the requests from various groups, his [attitude] is by no means stable." However, Zhou emphasized that Mendès France "is different from Bidault in the sense that he has made it clear that his cabinet will survive only under the condition that the war stops in Indochina." Therefore, as Zhou viewed it, the prospect for reaching a settlement on Indochina had never been so promising. Considering that the French, after the Dien Bien Phu defeat, might not want to negotiate directly with the Viet Minh, Zhou contended that it was important that "we should take the initiative to pull the French to us, so that a settlement can be reached."[39]

Zhou wasted no time in taking "the initiative to pull the French." On June 23, he met with Mendès France in the French embassy at Berne, Switzerland. The Chinese premier began by telling Mendès France that he "had lived in France" and had "good feelings toward the French people." He hoped to see "France's international reputation become higher." He then inquired about the new French government's conditions for reaching a settlement on Indochina. Zhou emphasized that the PRC definitely wanted peace in Indochina and that Beijing was opposed to U.S. intervention as well as its plans to internationalize the war. At Mendès France's request, Zhou also agreed to help persuade the Viet Minh to speed up the negotiations.[40]

In the meantime, Zhou squeezed time out of his busy schedule to meet with Tep Phan, head of the Cambodian delegation, and Phoui Sananikone, head of the Laotian delegation, on June 20 and 21. The Chinese premier paid close attention to these meetings, promising that the PRC would respect Cambodia's and Lao's sovereignty and independence in the hope that they would become a "new type of country like India, Indonesia and Burma—where there exist no foreign military bases—in the region." He also encouraged them to establish a direct relationship with the Viet Minh.[41] Leaving Geneva on the evening of June 23, Zhou was convinced that a peace settlement on Indochina was more than possible if he could persuade his Vietnamese comrades to accept it.

Rebuilding Chinese–Soviet–Viet Minh Consensus

During the last week of June, Zhou Enlai traveled to India and Burma for a series of meetings with Indian prime minister Jawaharlal Nehru and Burmese prime minister U Nu. In the joint Sino-Indian and Sino-Burmese statements that Zhou, together with Nehru and U Nu, introduced the "five principles of peaceful coexistence," also known as *Pancha shila*.[42] For Zhou, this initiative was closely related to his diplomatic activities at Geneva. The People's Republic would now be in a position to announce to the world that the "new China" was a rational

actor in international affairs and that its challenge to the existing international order was aimed at a better "new world."

In accordance with Zhou's plans, the Chinese and Vietnamese leaders met in Liuzhou, a city close to the Chinese-Vietnamese border,
from July 3 to 5. Attending the meeting on the Vietnamese side were
Ho Chi Minh, Vo Nguyen Giap, and Huan Van Hoan, and on the Chinese side were Zhou Enlai, Wei Guoqing, Luo Guibo, Xie Fang, Chen
Manyuan, and Qiao Guohua.[43]

The meeting began on the morning of July 3 with Zhou asking about
the actual balance of force between the two sides on the battlefield.
General Giap then gave a report concentrating on the military situa-
tion. He stated that the enemy had suffered a huge setback at Dien
Bien Phu but was far from defeated. After Dien Bien Phu, according to
Giap, the French had sent new reinforcements to Indochina, giving
France 470,000 troops, including 190,000 French soldiers, 240,000 Bao
Dai regime soldiers, about 20,000 Laotians, and 15,000 Cambodians.
By comparison, the total strength of the Viet Minh was around 310,000,
of whom 295,000 were Vietnamese soldiers, 18,000 (including 14,000
Vietnamese volunteers) were part of the Laotian resistance force, and
3,000 (including about one thousand Vietnamese volunteers) were
part of the Cambodian resistance force. As for the Vietnamese economy, Giap acknowledged that the Viet Minh's position was weak because big cities such as Hanoi, Saigon, Hue, and Da Nang were still in
the enemy's hands. Giap concluded that fundamental changes in the
balance of force on the battlefield were yet to occur. Wei Guoqing, the
chief Chinese military adviser to the Viet Minh, confirmed Giap's opinion. Zhou then raised another key question: "If the U.S. does not interfere, and under the condition that France will dispatch more troops,
how long will it take for us to seize the whole of Indochina?" Giap
replied that if the United States did not intervene, in a best-case scenario, it probably would take another two to three years before the Viet
Minh would win final victory; yet it was more than possible that the war
would last for another three to five years.[44]

Beginning on the evening of July 3, Zhou gave a lengthy presentation about the military situation in Indochina and, in light of the remaining dangers, how the communists should negotiate at Geneva. He
first emphasized that the Indochina war had already been internationalized and that "this is a key feature of the current situation." Zhou
added, "In terms of the scope and degree of internationalization, the
Indochina issue even has surpassed the Korea issue. In Korea, [where]

the enemy side of sixteen countries acted under the name of the United Nations, and China dispatched volunteers, it was only one step away for the war to become a world war." "However," continued Zhou, since both the USSR and the United States "wanted to localize the war [in Korea]," the war finally stopped. By comparison, stressed Zhou, "the war in Indochina not only has involved the three [Indochina] countries, but also has influenced all of Southeast Asia, and has influenced Europe and the whole world as well." Zhou reasoned that the Indochina war would logically "have [an] impact on Burma, Thailand, Malaya, Indonesia, Pakistan, India, as well as on Australia, New Zealand, Ceylon, and the Philippines," and it would have a big impact on Paris since "France has colonies in Asia and Africa." Consequently even London would feel a major effect, he said, as "Britain has close connections with Pakistan, India, Ceylon, Malaya, Hong Kong, Australia and New Zealand, and is extremely sensitive to any change in Indochina, and will not simply let it happen without doing anything."[45]

At this point, Zhou turned to the danger of American intervention in Indochina. He contended that since the imperialist countries had been worried about the expanding influence of the Chinese revolution, they absolutely would not allow the Vietnamese revolutionaries to win a great victory. Therefore, Zhou stressed, "if we ask too much [at Geneva] and if peace is not achieved, it is certain that the U.S. will intervene, providing Cambodia, Laos and Bao Dai with weapons and ammunition, helping them train military personnel, and establishing military bases there." Considering all of this, Zhou argued that "we must isolate the U.S. and break up its plans, otherwise we will fall into the trap prepared by the U.S. imperialists . . . Consequently, even in a military sense we will not be able to seize [parts of] Vietnam."[46]

In order to bolster his argument, Zhou further cited "the example of Korea" as supporting evidence: "The key to the Korea issue lay in U.S. intervention. It was completely beyond our expectation that the [American] reinforcement would arrive so quickly . . . If there had not been U.S. intervention, the Korean People's Army would have been able to drive Syngman Rhee's [troops] into the ocean." Because of American intervention, "we only achieved a draw at the end of the war, and were unable to win a victory." Zhou thus contended that the primary task facing the Viet Minh was to prevent the situation in Korea from being repeated in Indochina.

In concluding his presentation, Zhou raised "seven crucial questions" and answered them one by one. First, "does there exist a contra-

diction between [peacefully settling] the Indochina issue and fulfilling
the internationalist mission of the international communist movement?" Zhou argued that there "exists no such contradiction," otherwise it would not be true internationalism. Second, "is it better to seize
all of Vietnam peacefully or by means of war?" Zhou believed that
"from every perspective, it is now clear that it is impossible to seize all
of Vietnam merely by military means." Therefore, the peaceful way was
the only feasible way. Third, "can Laos and Cambodia be united [with
us] peacefully, or can they be united [with us] by means of war?" Zhou
said that it was apparent that, again, this had to be done by peaceful
means. In questions four to seven, Zhou asked: "Will we be able to separate France and the U.S. peacefully or by means of war? Will we be
able to separate Britain and the U.S. peacefully or by means of war?
Will we be able to divide the Bao Dai clique peacefully or by means of
war? Will we be able to pursue cooperation with [other] Southeast
Asian countries peacefully or by means of war?" Zhou replied to each
of these questions by emphasizing that only by adopting "a peaceful
way" could the communist side achieve its aims. Thus Zhou concluded
that "we are now facing only one main task, and that is to achieve
peace. If the war were to become internationalized, that would not be
favorable to us, and we would lose space for maneuvering as our rear
and flanks would be exposed to [the enemy's] threats." Therefore,
stressed Zhou once again, "the central issue is how to prevent America's intervention" and "how to achieve a peaceful settlement."[47]

At the meetings of July 4 and 5, Zhou outlined a desirable settlement
based on four basic conditions: (1) achieving simultaneous cease-fire
in all three countries of Indochina; (2) adopting the sixteenth parallel
as the demarcation line between the two sides (and if that did not
work, then considering adopting Route 9, which was close to the seventeenth parallel, as the demarcation line); (3) forbidding transportation of weapons and ammunition into Indochina after the settlement;
and (4) removing all military bases from the three countries. Zhou explained that Cambodia and Laos were different from Vietnam and that,
on condition that they did not join any military alliance or allow foreign military bases, these two countries should be permitted to pursue
their own paths of development, thus becoming "India-style Southeast Asian countries." Predicting that these views would encounter resistance among the Vietnamese cadres, Zhou emphasized that among
all the tasks to be completed, "the central task concerns the cadres, and

the top cadres—namely members of the Politburo—in particular. It must be made clear among [VWP] Politburo members why it is necessary to achieve a ceasefire."[46]

According to Chinese records, Zhou's presentation seemed to have left a deep impression on the Vietnamese leaders, especially on Ho. At last, Ho agreed to adjust the Viet Minh's aims and strategies in accordance with Zhou's advice and made the following statement:

> Now Vietnam is standing at the crossroads, either heading to peace, or heading to war. The main direction [of our strategy] should be the pursuit of peace, and we should also be prepared for [continuously] fighting a war. The complication of our work is that we have to prepare for both possibilities in our strategy. For the ordinary people, and even for our cadres, this issue will appear extremely complicated. Our slogan in the past has been "to carry the resistance through to the end," and why do we now want to pursue peace? Our cadres will ask "which is correct?" I agree that the primary issue is to persuade our cadres. There are many difficulties in this regard. But [to solve this problem] will first of all depend on the efforts by us, the Vietnamese comrades. In addition, we will also depend on the help of the Chinese comrades . . . What the [Vietnamese] Workers' Party Central Committee will need to do is to persuade high-ranking cadres . . . We do not have much time left. Our problem is that we do not have enough cadres, but the work facing us is enormous.[48]

Consequently, at the conclusion of the meeting the Chinese and the Vietnamese leaders reached a consensus on the strategies for the next phase of the Geneva Conference: On the Vietnam problem, they would favor dividing the country temporarily along the sixteenth parallel, but since Route Colonial 9 (the only line of transport linking Laos to the sea) was located north of the sixteenth parallel, they would be willing to accept some adjustment to this solution. On the Laos problem, they would try to establish Xam Neua and Phong Sali, two provinces adjacent to China, as the concentration zone for pro-communist Laotian forces. On Cambodia, they would allow a political settlement that would probably lead to a noncommunist government there.[49]

When Ho returned to Vietnam, the VWP Central Committee issued instructions in the "July 5th Document," which reflected the agreements between Ho and Zhou. In mid-July at the VWP Central Committee's sixth meeting, Ho endorsed the new strategy of solving the

Indochina problem through a cease-fire based on temporarily dividing Vietnam. Ho criticized the "leftist tendency" within the party that he said ignored the danger of American intervention and paid no attention to the importance of diplomacy.[50] All of this, especially Ho's stress on the American danger, clearly reflected Zhou's influence.

On the afternoon of July 6, Zhou returned to Beijing. The same evening, Mao Zedong chaired a meeting of the CCP Central Secretariat, attended by Zhou, Liu Shaoqi, Zhu De, Chen Yun, and Deng Xiaoping. The CCP leaders, after hearing Zhou's briefing on the Sino-Vietnamese meeting, decided that a CCP Politburo meeting would be convened to discuss Indochina.[51]

The meeting, held on July 7, was attended by about one hundred top party cadres. Zhou reported that the Chinese delegation at Geneva had adopted "a policy line to pursue cooperation with France, Britain, Southeast Asian countries and the three countries in Indochina—that is, to unite with all the international forces that can be united and to isolate the United States—so that America's plans for expanding its world hegemony will be undermined."[52] The central part of this policy, he emphasized, lay in achieving a peaceful settlement of the Indochina issue. Zhou believed that, judging from the progress that had been achieved at Geneva, the settlement could be reached. Mao supported Zhou's report, pointing out that "for the purpose of uniting with the majority and isolating the few [the United States], we should make concessions when such concessions are necessary, and should adhere to our own stand when such adherence is possible."[53]

On the morning of July 9, Zhou flew from Beijing to Moscow. The next day, he met with Georgi M. Malenkov, Kliment Y. Voroshilov, and Lazar M. Kaganovich. Zhou briefed the Soviet leaders on his recent visits to India and Burma as well as on the meetings between the Chinese and Vietnamese leaders and discussed with them the strategies that the communist side should adopt during the next stage in Geneva. In a telegram to Mao and the CCP leadership, Zhou summarized the opinions of the Soviet leaders:

At present, what should be introduced [by our side] are fair and reasonable conditions that the French government is in a position to accept, so that the agreement on restoring peace in Indochina will be quickly achieved. In order to reach a quick armistice, our conditions should be concise and clear, which will help avoid U.S. interference and sabotage, thus allowing the agreement to be more easily reached. If our conditions are complicated and loaded with trivial details, the discussion will be prolonged and side issues and new problems will crop up unexpectedly, which will delay the negotiations and cause the loss of opportunities, thus being favorable to America's sabotage effort. The bourgeois class in France is weak-willed, and it is impossible for them to accept conditions that go beyond their capacity. Therefore, if our conditions are complicated and loaded with trivial details, the Americans will take advantage. If the right timing is missed, the pro-American and pro-war factions in France will rise again, and the Mendès France cabinet will inevitably collapse. This is unfavorable to the settlement of the Indochina issue.[54]

Zhou Enlai pointed out that the Soviet leadership's appraisal of the situation was "compatible with the opinions we have discussed in Liuzhou and in Beijing." He further emphasized that the central question was how to "strive for quickly achieving an agreement." He mentioned that he would meet Molotov and, in particular, Dong immediately after returning to Geneva to ensure that the new strategies would be carried out.[55]

The Final Phase

Zhou flew from Moscow to Geneva on the afternoon of July 12 and met with Molotov at 7 PM. After Zhou's briefing on the Liuzhou conference, Molotov inquired in particular about Zhou's opinion on whether it was feasible to set the demarcation line at the sixteenth parallel. Zhou informed Molotov that he and Ho had agreed that they would strive for a sixteenth-parallel solution, but, if necessary, would also accept the seventeenth parallel as the provisional demarcation line.[56]

At this moment, Zhou found that Dong, apparently still reluctant to accept the new negotiation strategy, demonstrated no enthusiasm in carrying out the VWP's July 5th Document. So he arranged a meeting with Dong late on the evening of July 12. After explaining to Dong that the July 5th Document was based on the consensus reached by the Chinese, Soviet, and Vietnamese parties, Zhou again emphasized the danger involved in direct American intervention in Indochina. He argued that since the beginning of the Indochina war, the United States had never been a bystander. With France suffering from a series of defeats, "at a certain juncture, the U.S. may suddenly escalate its intervention and create a most serious situation [for us]." Zhou, as in Liuzhou, again used America's intervention in Korea as an example to support his argument. He mentioned that after the outbreak of the Korean War, when the Korean People's Army was marching toward Pusan, "Comrade Mao Zedong had raised the issue of America's escalating military intervention to Comrades Kim Il Sung and Choi Yong Kun, and asked them to treat it seriously." However, the North Koreans ignored these warnings, and "shortly after that, America's intervention escalated, pushing [the North Koreans] down to the Yalu River . . . Later with China dispatching more than one million volunteers, they were driven back to the 38th parallel and a stalemate then emerged." By contrast, emphasized Zhou, "our forces in Vietnam have not yet reached a situation similar to the one before Pusan." Zhou quoted Ho in advising Dong that "America's non-intervention policy is only a temporary phenomenon, and this will only be maintained until the coming November, when the U.S. Congress holds elections. If a ceasefire is not achieved by then, the situation will change dramatically." Therefore, Zhou contended that the communist side "must actively, positively and quickly carry out negotiations to pursue a settlement, and must make the negotiation simplified . . . so that Mendès France will not step down . . . [At present], the main issue is how to set up the demarcation line in Vietnam, and we may consider proposing the 16th parallel as the line . . . Time is short, and any delay will lead to unfavorable consequences." By the end of the conversation, Zhou promised, "with the final withdrawal of the French, all of Vietnam will be yours." Dong finally yielded to Zhou's logic, if not to his pressure.[57]

With a consensus on the communist side, Zhou was in a better position to concentrate on negotiating with the French. Learning that Mendès France and Eden would hold talks with U.S. secretary of state John Foster Dulles in Paris, Zhou decided he would meet them first to convey that the communists were willing to make concessions. At 10:30 AM on July 13, Zhou met with Mendès France. When Zhou found that the demarcation line had become the central concern, he made it clear that while the communists would prefer a line at the sixteenth parallel, they were willing to make compromises. Indeed, during the talks, Zhou promised to Mendès France that "if France is willing to take a step forward, Vietnam will be willing to take an even larger step to meet the concessions made by France."[58] At 11:45 AM the same day,

Zhou met with Eden. He told the British foreign secretary that the Chinese and Vietnamese leaders had reached a consensus on pursuing a peaceful settlement in Indochina and that the Viet Minh were willing to make necessary compromises. He reiterated that "if France is willing to make further concessions on the question of zone division, the Vietnamese will also be willing to make more concessions to meet the concessions made by the French."[59]

Zhou continually played a decisive role in the final stage of the Geneva Conference. When Mendès France insisted that he would resign before setting the dividing line further south than the seventeenth parallel, Zhou, with Molotov's support, made the decision to change the Communist demand from the sixteenth to the seventeenth parallel and persuaded the Vietnamese to accept this adjustment.[60] As a result, the Geneva Conference reached a settlement on Indochina in the early morning hours of July 21.[61]

Conclusion

Beijing was a main patron, as well as a beneficiary, of the Geneva Agreement of 1954. As discussed in this chapter, China's policy at the conference was shaped by its strategic needs at that time, which included a desire to focus on domestic problems after the end of the Korean War (i.e., promoting the "socialist revolution and reconstruction" at home and dealing with the Taiwan issue), determination to take precautions against possible American military intervention in Indochina, and the desire to forge a new international image compatible with Beijing's new claims to support peaceful coexistence. Zhou Enlai was the central figure in China's diplomatic activities at the conference, and he left Geneva on July 23 with nearly everything he could have hoped for before he came: the creation of a communist-ruled North Vietnam would serve as a buffer zone between communist China and the capitalist world in Southeast Asia (in this respect, the difference between the sixteenth and the seventeenth parallels did not really matter to Beijing); the opening of new dialogues between China and such Western powers as France and Britain would help break the PRC's isolation; and, much more important, the crucial role played by China at the conference implied that for the first time in modern history China had been accepted by the international society—friends and foes alike—as a real world power. With this status, Mao and his fellow Chinese leaders could convincingly tell the Chinese people, as well as the rest of the world: "we the Chinese people have stood up." Confident of its new global stature, the communist regime was able to enhance its authority and legitimacy in the minds of the Chinese people, providing fresh momentum to Mao's "continuous revolution" aimed at transforming China's state, society, and international outlook.

Yet Beijing's handling of the Indochina issue at Geneva in 1954 also sowed a seed of potential discord between the Chinese and their Vietnamese comrades. As is well known, only two years after the signing of the Geneva Accord on Indochina, when the United States and the Ngo Dinh Diem regime in Saigon broke the agreement on the national plebiscite in Vietnam, the road to the Second Indochina War was paved, and the conflict would last until the mid-1970s. When the Vietnamese communists contemplated the path leading to the war, they became increasingly convinced that they had committed a terrible mistake because of the pressure from Beijing and reached a very bad deal at Geneva in 1954. Not surprisingly—though ironically—a unified communist Vietnam and China would enter the Third Indochina War as adversaries only four years after the end of the second war. In retrospect, the origins of the confrontation between the two communist actors can be traced back to their relationship at the Geneva Conference of 1954.

THIRTEEN

* * *

After Geneva

The French Presence in Vietnam, 1954–1963

KATHRYN C. STATLER

BY MID-JULY 1954 the weary Geneva Conference participants saw the light at the end of the tunnel. On July 21, French and Viet Minh representatives signed the Geneva Accords, bringing the First Indochina War to a close, temporarily dividing North and South Vietnam at the seventeenth parallel, and calling for elections in 1956 to reunify the country. For France, eight years of "dirty war" had finally ended. French leaders took the conference provisions seriously, and, at the time, it appeared that Paris would play a major role in implementing them. The international situation evolved quickly after the conference, however, as the Ngo Dinh Diem government and the Eisenhower administration supplanted the French presence in Vietnam: an outcome that none of the signatories to the Geneva Accords had anticipated.

The First Indochina War compelled the French, Americans, and Vietnamese to confront the forces of decolonization and Cold War. On the one hand, North-South tensions drove the war as the Vietnamese struggled to break free of the French imperialist yoke to establish an independent nation and as the Americans reluctantly supported a colonial ally. On the other hand, the East-West conflict played out on the battlefield during the eight-year conflict as the United States and Britain supported the French war effort and as the Soviet Union and People's Republic of China furnished Viet Minh forces with military aid. A final force must also be considered—West-West relations. Escalating Franco-American disagreements over the conduct of the First Indochina War eventually led to a breakdown in Western unity, propelling Paris and Washington to pursue separate policies before, during, and after the Geneva Conference. This interplay of decolonization, Cold War concerns, and West-West discord became most apparent at the Geneva Conference but did not end there. Although the escalating Cold War and the weakening French Empire caused U.S. officials to sneer at the French colonial effort and "civilizing mission," they too eventually attempted to create an artificial edifice in Vietnam. The Eisenhower administration insisted on replacing the French and supporting South Vietnamese prime minister Diem because Washington saw no anticommunist and anticolonial alternative. Ultimately, the transition from French to U.S. control in Vietnam represented a transition between two different types of imperialism—the old-fashioned French variety and a new American neocolonial, or informal, one.

Although U.S. actions in South Vietnam cannot be compared to the first phase of French colonialism in the late nineteenth century, when the French engaged in a bloody conquest of Indochina, a number of similarities exist between the second phase of French colonialism and post-Geneva nation-building by the United States. While French colonialism and American neocolonialism differed markedly in some respects—the American version was more indirect, informal, and incomplete—both versions rested on similar perceptions of Indochina as a place to be constructed. Paris planned to export its belief in the universal value of its civilization, as did Washington. The French called their economic, moral, and cultural policies in Indochina *mise en valeur*, or "development," while the Americans preferred the term "modernization." In the aftermath of Geneva, the United States tried to project the idea that it was pursuing a moral mission based on generosity, benevolence, and protection, just as the French had prior to Geneva. And both the French and the Americans employed subtle tools of empire, including cultural and language institutions, exhibits, propaganda, military and economic assistance, and political pressure, in order to spread their values.[1]

In the Franco-American competition for influence in South Vietnam after Geneva, Paris rapidly lost ground to Washington. Because of France's apparent withdrawal from North and South Vietnam, scholars have tended to downplay the French role in Vietnamese affairs in the period between the First and Second Indochina Wars, dedicating perhaps a sentence or two either to blame the French for their refusal to "endorse the United States's Diem experiment" and "share Franco-American responsibility for the security of non-communist Southeast

Asia," or to criticize the Americans for "displacing France as the major external power."[2] In fact, the situation was far more fluid than either of these positions allows. Franco-American tensions shaped developments in Vietnam in subtle, unexpected ways. For example, Franco-American difficulties in arriving at a coordinated strategy toward Diem reduced the French political presence. In addition, South Vietnamese and American determination to replace France at every level—whether political, military, economic, or cultural—increased Franco–South Vietnamese conflict and led France to disengage from its responsibility to the Geneva Accords. Despite these setbacks, the French struggle to maintain some influence in their former colony led to a continued French presence via education, cultural exchanges, aid programs, commercial trade, and language courses.

Indeed, by the early 1960s France had staged a considerable comeback. Paris's support of South Vietnam's bid to enter the United Nations in 1957 caused Diem to view the continued French presence in Vietnam as a counterweight to the sometimes heavy-handed U.S. role. Franco–South Vietnamese relations thus improved while the American–South Vietnamese relationship became increasingly strained. To the astonishment of most observers at the time, the French presence endured in Indochina as French officials worked behind the scenes to help reform the Diem government and maintain French cultural institutions. Indeed, events appeared to have come almost full circle ten years after the Geneva Conference, except France and the United States had switched roles. Now French officials warned their American counterparts about the risks of increasing involvement in Vietnam and unofficially advised leading South Vietnamese figures rather than vice versa. The vestiges of the First Indochina War and its immediate aftermath would haunt the French, Vietnamese, and Americans for years to come.

Diem and the French Presence

The French government's primary goal after Geneva was to avoid a resurgence of war. Emperor Bao Dai's appointment of Ngo Dinh Diem as prime minister presented an immediate problem to this plan given Diem's antipathy toward France and his unwillingness to uphold the Geneva Accords. Compounding the problem was the Franco-American relationship in Vietnam. Although France and the United States had agreed to a policy of "joint action" in South Vietnam, U.S. determination to keep Diem in power eventually led to a decline in French political control.

While the French saw Diem as a risky experiment at best, not all French officials opposed Diem, as Eisenhower administration officials tended to assume. In fact, there was considerable internal debate in Paris and Saigon.[3] Many French officials publicly acknowledged Diem's flaws: "his ineffectiveness, his inability to match Ho Chi Minh's leadership qualities, personality, and mystique, his lack of support in the South, his dearth of political finesse, and the challenges he faced from various politico-religious sects, parts of the army, and some Catholics," as one historian has phrased it.[4] Yet the alternatives—reestablishing Bao Dai, staging a coup d'état, or creating a more pliable South Vietnamese government—were equally worrisome. Immediately after Geneva, the French still considered themselves masters of the game in Saigon, but the French high commissioner, General Paul Ely, recognized the importance of securing U.S. cooperation in supporting a South Vietnamese government. To avoid American accusations of unilateral abandonment of South Vietnam and to maintain a voice in the decision-making process, French officials in Vietnam and at the French Foreign Ministry, or Quai d'Orsay, advocated integrating French and U.S. policies as closely as possible.[5]

A coordinated policy appeared elusive. During a series of high-level talks in September, French and American officials agreed to support the Diem government in an attempt at joint action, yet only two months later, French prime minister Pierre Mendès France accused the United States of "replacing" France in South Vietnam and "refusing to consider alternatives to Diem."[6] When Edgar Faure, Mendès France's successor, assumed control in early 1955, he assured U.S. officials that it was the policy of the French government "to work 100 percent with the U.S." in Indochina and that the "closest Franco-American cooperation [in Indochina was] not only important to Indochina states but essential to the Free World." According to Faure, the French government would "not play a double game in Vietnam," following one policy in the South and another in the North.[7] Despite these claims, the United States and France continued to disagree about Diem's chances for success.

Diem faced his biggest challenge to date in March 1955 as the Cao Dai, Hoa Hao, and Binh Xuyen sects united to overthrow his government and as French officials in Paris decided the moment had come to replace Diem.[8] As the crisis deepened, the Faure government repeatedly urged the Eisenhower administration to set up meetings between France and the United States to resolve the crisis through Diem's removal. In mid-April, a list of questions from the State Department asking for specific alternatives to Diem indicated to the French that the Americans were at last thinking about replacing him. In response, French officials produced a detailed plan. The Foreign Ministry argued that the French and Americans must agree on a successor to Diem and that "regime change" should be carried out as soon as possible.[9]

It appeared that the moment for joint action had arrived. French officials believed they had convinced Eisenhower and Secretary of State John Foster Dulles "to sacrifice Diem in exchange for close Franco-American cooperation."[10] On April 27, Washington sent instructions to the American embassies in Paris and Saigon to initiate a change in government. Yet, on that very same day, fighting broke out between forces loyal to Diem and the three sects, and Dulles blocked the instructions to replace Diem. For the next few days it was not clear which side would win, and French and U.S. officials continued to meet to discuss options.[11] But by May 2, when Eisenhower's special representative, General J. Lawton Collins, returned to Saigon, Diem had reestablished control of Saigon. The French felt betrayed by the Americans after having received what they considered guarantees to replace Diem. Paris had devoted substantial time to formulating a plan for a new government, coordinated with Ely and the sects, and worked with the United States in a number of Franco-American meetings. Ely complained that the French had insisted that the Vietnamese should determine their own government but that "it was along the Potomac that Diem's fate had been decided and where future South Vietnamese governments would be decided."[12]

The sect crisis was critical to the diminishment of French political influence in Vietnam. The consolidation of Diem's regime in 1955 gradually shifted the balance of power between the Western allies in Vietnam, with the United States supplanting France. This process culminated in Paris in May 1955 in a series of talks among American, French, and British representatives in which U.S. officials underscored the fact that they were taking charge in Vietnam. Ely left the country at the end of May, claiming that "a common policy between France and the United States was now impossible."[13] The spring 1955 sect crisis thus destroyed

Franco-American attempts to create a coordinated policy. France had grudgingly supported Diem to avoid breaking the unity of action among the Western powers. In the end, France lost not only Franco-American cooperation in Indochina, but also its influence over Vietnamese political affairs.[14]

The 1956 Elections and the French Military Presence

The specter of the 1956 elections posed the next challenge to French influence in Vietnam. By mid-July 1954, the participants at the Geneva Conference had reached agreement on most major issues except for the difficult problem of national elections to reunify the country. The Viet Minh refused to end hostilities until all parties settled on a specific date. As a result, the French and Viet Minh agreed in both the cease-fire agreement and the final declaration to hold the elections in July 1956, under the supervision of an international commission.[15] Despite the vague wording of the two documents, the French took the elections seriously, fearing that a failure to hold them would violate the spirit of Geneva. More importantly, Paris worried that if the elections did not take place, North Vietnam would have a pretext to renew the war.[16] At the same time, French officials wanted to avoid promoting the elections too forcefully for fear of creating a diplomatic rift with the United States.[17]

Most scholars attribute the failure of the 1956 elections to U.S. determination to avoid them, which coincided with Diem's refusal to consider holding the vote.[18] The situation, however, was more complex. Despite American and South Vietnamese intransigence, the French would probably have insisted on the elections, but Washington and Saigon's determination to end the French military presence in South Vietnam caused Paris to reconsider its position. The American assumption of the training of the Vietnamese National Army on January 1, 1955, the South Vietnamese call for the dissolution of the French High Command and withdrawal of the French Expeditionary Corps by April 1956, American–South Vietnamese interference with the French Military Training School, and the end of the French role in the Franco-American Training Relations Instruction Mission led the French government to reevaluate the nature and extent of their responsibilities to the Geneva Accords and hence the 1956 elections.[19]

The French military presence created a major obstacle to smooth

Franco-Vietnamese relations after Geneva. According to South Vietnamese officials, "Franco-Vietnamese relations would improve" and the elections issue "could be resolved" once the French High Command and its forces had withdrawn.[20] The Diem government also insisted on taking over command of the French-controlled military training school. In addition, the number of Vietnamese to be trained in France declined rapidly from 1955 to 1956, while Vietnamese to be trained in the United States quickly grew.[21] The French were also forced to reduce their presence in the Training Relations Instruction Mission (TRIM), which had been a joint Franco-American attempt to train and organize the Vietnamese army. French forces were placed under U.S. command, and General Samuel T. Williams, who oversaw the American Military Advisory and Assistance Group (MAAG), notified the remaining French officers in TRIM that, due to the dissolution of the French High Command, they would cease their functions as of April 28, 1956. U.S. interference also caused the French to consider withdrawing their air and naval missions in Vietnam. Although Washington did not want the two missions to leave since limits on the size of the American force in Vietnam prohibited the United States from replacing them, Dulles conceded that "it might be the lesser of two evils just to get the French out."[22]

In the end, Washington offered Paris one final deal. If the French agreed to use one thousand French officers to recover U.S. equipment still in Vietnam, in a so-called Temporary Equipment Recovery Mission (TERM), then the Americans would intervene with Diem to support a continued French military mission. It appeared that the Americans were attempting a quid pro quo—French help with American priorities in exchange for the continuation of a French military presence in Vietnam.[23] According to the French ambassador to South Vietnam, Henri Hoppenot, if the French endorsed TERM, France would continue to be held responsible for the application of the Geneva Accords, South Vietnam would think France supported its policies unconditionally, and Paris would encounter problems with Hanoi.[24] Hoppenot concluded that "France would find itself in the worst possible situation because it would be responsible for the application of the accords, in particular the non-augmentation of military personnel, and, at the same time, would be associated with the United States and South Vietnam in violation of this accord."[25] The Foreign Ministry agreed with Hoppenot's argument and declined to support TERM, claiming that "since Diem insisted that the French withdraw the FEC [French Expeditionary Corps] from South Vietnam before he would begin consultations on the 1956 elections, Paris no longer had any responsibility to enforce Geneva."[26] Subsequently, in a May 14, 1956, note to the co-presidents of the Geneva Conference, Anthony Eden and Vyacheslav Molotov, the French government stated that it had "relinquished all responsibility" for the Geneva agreements.[27]

In summer 1956, Hoppenot sent French foreign minister Christian Pineau a long and detailed letter on Franco–U.S.–South Vietnamese problems in South Vietnam. Pineau concluded that the "non-elections were key" to Diem's survival as South Vietnam became even more determined to maintain its independence vis-à-vis France. Regarding the Americans, Pineau noted that although Dulles and the State Department had repeatedly assured France of their willingness to establish Franco-U.S. cooperation in Vietnam, "the facts showed otherwise." French officials recognized that the Vietnamese and the Americans no longer needed French aid and that France inspired "neither hatred nor envy."[28] Diem's refusal to work with France, the withdrawal of French forces, the dissolution of the French High Command, the diminishment of the French military school, and the loss of standing in TRIM led France to disengage from its responsibilities to the Geneva Accords and hence the 1956 elections. As a result, the elections did not take place and Washington continued to consolidate its presence in South Vietnam.

Holding On: The French Economic and Cultural Presence

By the end of 1956, France had lost political and military control in South Vietnam to Diem and the Americans. Two lines of defense remained—the economic and cultural fronts. The Foreign Ministry thus urged French representatives in South Vietnam "to try to build up economic and cultural domains" and reestablish a "climate of confidence between France and Vietnam and develop collaboration between the two countries."[29] Through aid programs, commerce, educational institutions, foreign exchanges with the Vietnamese, and French language classes, Paris sought to preserve economic and cultural influence in Vietnam.

The French handed over a number of economic powers to the South Vietnamese during negotiations in late 1954. The Diem government took control of its financial, customs, and monetary policies as of January 1, 1955, the same date that the United States began direct aid to South Vietnam, bypassing the French.[30] According to French statistics, exports to Indochina had steadily declined since 1954. In 1953 France had supplied 80 billion francs in exports to Indochina. A year later, the total was 63 billion, while the figure sank to 50 billion in 1955 and around 20 billion in 1956.[31] The United States contributed to France's reduced financial role in various ways. By November 1955 the United States had replaced France as the top exporter to South Vietnam. In January 1956 the piastre was officially pegged to the dollar. French exports diminished by more than half, and twenty thousand French bureaucrats headed back to the metropole. The preferential tariff for French companies ended on March 1, 1956, and French products were unable to compete in the race for imports financed by the U.S. aid program.[32] France did not simply disappear from the economic scene— French enterprises continued to command a considerable share of Vietnamese industrial and business activity, and a substantial amount of capital remained in Vietnam—but the French economic presence continued to decline.[33]

The French staked their last hope for control on the cultural front.[34] At first, French attempts to retain cultural influence did not look any more promising than efforts to maintain political, military, and economic control. In December 1954, the French and Vietnamese reached a number of cultural agreements, which formed the basis of French plans to preserve influence in South Vietnam.[35] In a second series of meetings, this time between the French and the Americans, French officials tried to "sell" the French presence to their American counterparts. During the December 1954 meetings, Ely, Collins, and their subordinates defined Franco-U.S. policy on a number of issues, including public order, information and propaganda, education, and training of administrative personnel. Ely urged that the French and Americans work together to ensure that South Vietnam did not slip into isolation and neutralism, or worse, drift down the communist path. Ely, clearly playing to American myopia on the subject of communism, indicated that the French wanted to keep Vietnam turned toward the West and urged American officials to remember that French was "*the* language in Vietnam, that all the books were written in French, and that Vietnamese teachers, priests, and many parents all spoke French."[36] During the meetings, Collins affirmed that Washington respected French cultural influence and did not seek to replace France in Vietnam.

Despite Collins's claims, Franco-Vietnamese and Franco-U.S. accords agreeing to uphold a number of French cultural and educational institutions were routinely ignored. Much to French annoyance, the U.S.-led National Institute of Administration replaced the French School of National Administration in 1956, thus violating the 1954 accords and imperiling France's cultural presence. According to the ever-raucous Hoppenot, France should "fight against the regression of spoken French, improve the training of technical personnel, engineers, doctors, and professors, provide more French grants to Vietnamese, and increase Franco-Vietnamese contacts."[37] Evident in Hoppenot's remarks was concern that the French language was losing ground to English as France withdrew, leaving the Vietnamese with fewer opportunities to speak French. According to the director of the French cultural mission, Jean-Pierre Dannaud, the French language was dying out not because of a "nationalist, anti-communist, anti-colonialist, clerical, americanophile spirit," but because of "Vietnamese timidity and loss of speaking French habitually." The answer, Dannaud suggested, was to "organize more discussions, movie nights, and sports events to recapture the French language."[38]

Although French officials in Saigon desperately tried to prolong their country's cultural mission, from 1954 through 1956 France saw a steady decline in the number of French books, journals, and newspapers imported by Vietnam. By 1956 these imports had been cut in half. Subsequently, French books and journals disappeared from the shop windows in Saigon, while France also lost control of the last French newspaper in Vietnam, *Le Journal d'Extrême Orient*.[39] As English broadcasts became commonplace, France was also forced to sell its radio station, Radio France Asie, to South Vietnam in February 1956, and the French news service, Agence France-Presse, began to lose its edge as Anglo-Saxon agencies challenged its hegemony.[40] Dannaud's belief that if France simply continued to "export professors and import peanuts, then South Vietnam would remain in the French orbit" did not seem to be bearing fruit.[41] In the cultural field, too, the United States began to overshadow France.

The New Franco–South Vietnamese Relationship

The French presence in South Vietnam reached an all-time low by 1956, but Diem's foreign policy successes and improved internal security, along with major French concessions, eventually resulted in more amiable Franco-Vietnamese diplomatic relations. In June 1956, the arrival of Hoppenot's replacement, Jean Payart, suggested that France had phased out the old high command structure and was ready to manage its affairs through a normal embassy.[42] A French parliamentary mission to Vietnam, led by Frederic Dupont, was favorably received, and following the mission a Franco-Vietnamese friendship society began. According to the departing Hoppenot, Diem "no longer needed a scapegoat for South Vietnamese problems" and could thus afford to be more cordial to the French, as demonstrated by his warm reception of the of the Dupont mission.[43] A smoother Franco–South Vietnamese relationship had finally materialized.

Although Franco-Vietnamese relations had improved, many French officials continued to resent the increasing U.S. presence. In mid-August, Hoppenot sent a remarkable document to the Foreign Ministry, detailing how the United States had "evicted" France from Indochina. Since 1945, he asserted, the United States had gradually supplanted the French, "first through economic aid, followed by military control, and finally through a preponderant political influence in all councils and organizations of the Vietnamese government." According to Hoppenot, even though the State Department promised collaboration, "the policy of replacing the French was pursued by those in Saigon who had little responsibility to the Embassy." These groups did not hesitate to use anti-French propaganda to eliminate the French. The Pentagon, CIA, and technical-assistance groups were not content to replace the French at the posts circumstances forced them to abandon but "tried to eliminate them from all areas." Hoppenot asserted that U.S. ambassador G. Frederick Reinhardt had made little effort to work with the French and that they had been only indirectly informed of U.S. actions, "never consulted or forewarned" even when American actions affected the French directly. Hoppenot believed that it was "the combination of American anti-colonialism and anti-communism" that had led to France's displacement: France had seen NATO allies act as if the French presence in Vietnam "belonged to a closed era" and that "any surviving remnants would not be tolerated except where the United States did not seek to replace France."[44]

The Quai d'Orsay was well aware of U.S. hostility toward colonialism. In an attempt to appease both the Americans and South Vietnamese, Paris appointed Jean Payart as ambassador. Payart's appointment marked an important transition for the French, Americans, and Vietnamese, as the new French representative was untainted by colonial associations. In a meeting with the new ambassador, Diem recognized that there were "valuable aspects" to the French mission in Vietnam. Diem, according to Payart, understood that "American aid always came with a price" and wanted to avoid American control of his country after he had "worked so hard to end French colonialism." Diem had thus begun to view France as "a counterweight to excessive American influence."[45]

Ultimately, a breakthrough occurred in Franco–South Vietnamese relations, not through economic or cultural influence but because of a single French political decision. In early 1957 a major controversy broke out over South Vietnam's attempt to join the United Nations. North Vietnamese foreign minister Pham Van Dong sent a note to the General Assembly and to the Security Council demanding that they reject South Vietnam's proposal.[46] The French chose to support South Vietnam's claim. Enthusiastic French support for South Vietnam's entry into the United Nations went a long way toward improving Franco–South Vietnamese relations. Diem stated that "France had chosen between North and South Vietnam for the first time since the Geneva Conference."[47] Although South Vietnam's demand for UN membership was ultimately rejected, Franco–South Vietnamese relations continued to improve.

The New Franco–North Vietnamese Relationship

As France struggled to redefine its relationship in South Vietnam after Geneva, it also attempted to maintain a separate presence in North Vietnam. French officials insisted in Washington and Saigon that preserving such a presence would keep communications open between Hanoi and the West and would allow France to monitor North Vietnamese activities, but Washington periodically accused France of conspiring with North Vietnam.[48] Continued relations with the Democratic Republic of Vietnam (DRV), and attempts to create a dialogue with China and Russia, made France's international position appear too pro-communist in Washington's eyes. Hoppenot concluded that in Asia, after "paying the price of a hot war," France had become "one of the victims of the Cold War."[49] French documentation makes it fairly clear that the French were not in fact trying to make a deal with the

DRV. The French wanted to maintain an economic and cultural presence in North Vietnam but were not planning to double-cross the
United States in order to do so. Instead, Paris hoped to exploit the new
communist policy of "peaceful coexistence" to the benefit of French
interests in North Vietnam.[50]

Such hopes faltered in the face of North Vietnamese animosity. The
Mendès France–Pham Van Dong agreements of July 21, 1954, which
guaranteed the exercise of private rights of French nationals and the
continuation of French cultural establishments, faced enormous
obstacles. Jean Sainteny, who had been appointed French delegate
general to the DRV in August 1954, was charged with the almost impossible task of securing safeguards for French businesses and institutions.[51] His job was made even more difficult by North Vietnamese
discriminatory practices and other forms of interference that led to the
loss of a great number of French commercial and industrial enterprises throughout 1955.

North Vietnamese hostility stemmed in part from French indications
that the North would not be officially represented in Paris. In summer
1955, Sainteny had prepared a letter agreeing that Ho Chi Minh could
appoint a personal delegate to Paris, but Edgar Faure never signed the
document, fearing South Vietnamese and American reactions to the
arrival of a Viet Minh representative in France. Faure allowed only a
commercial attaché instead, and Paris reminded the DRV that the
French delegation in Hanoi and North Vietnamese commercial representation in Paris did not imply normal diplomatic relations.[52] North
Vietnamese officials retaliated by refusing entry visas for French citizens, sparking strikes among domestics, and attempting to bribe or coerce French military personnel for spying purposes. In addition, Hanoi
refused to consider a replacement for the former French minister in
Hanoi, Jean-Baptiste George Picot, until the diplomatic recognition issue was settled.[53]

Controversy surrounding the 1956 elections also increased tensions
between Paris and Hanoi. In late 1954, Sainteny recognized the importance of the elections to the North Vietnamese, noting that "it is indeed undeniable that any policy tending to confirm the partition of
Vietnam by opposing free elections carries within it the seeds of a new
conflict."[54] Ho Chi Minh and his advisers made every effort to see that
the elections took place. The North Vietnamese repeatedly attempted
to ensure that the Geneva co-chairmen, as well as the International

Control Commission, China, and France, pressured Washington and Saigon to cooperate.[55] In adopting a diplomatic strategy, the North Vietnamese focused primarily on France. The DRV welcomed Sainteny's arrival in Hanoi and stated its willingness to preserve cultural contacts with the French. Many of these moves undoubtedly were made with an eye toward the elections because Hanoi assumed France would maintain control in the South.

Perhaps the most significant mistake Hanoi made with respect to the elections was its miscalculation in assuming that France would maintain control of South Vietnam until at least 1956. North Vietnamese officials, along with most of the international community, had counted on Diem's inability to maintain control and continued French command of decision-making in South Vietnam. The North Vietnamese could not have known how quickly the French would yield to Diem and the Americans. According to French reports, the Viet Minh grossly underestimated the Diem regime, believing it would "fall like a ripe fruit either during the general elections or from internal subversion." When, against all odds, Diem managed to maintain power and refused to discuss the elections, the Viet Minh realized that their chances of reunifying the country through political means were quickly diminishing. As a result, Hanoi accused the French of "shirking their obligations" and the Americans and Diem of "sabotaging the Geneva Accords."[56]

The French government had tried to preserve its influence in North Vietnam without imperiling more significant interests in South Vietnam or aggravating the United States, but such a policy appeared untenable. With France's lack of interest in installing an official mission in Hanoi or an official DRV mission in Paris and its unwillingness to pressure the South Vietnamese to begin consultations for elections, Franco–North Vietnamese relations quickly soured.[57] According to the French minister to North Vietnam, Albert Chambon, by 1960 reunification of the country had become the North's biggest goal. Paris feared that the day of reckoning between North and South Vietnam was fast approaching.[58]

The French Resurgence

Despite diminishing French presence in North Vietnam, by 1960 Franco–South Vietnamese relations had undergone a dramatic improvement from their dismal state four years earlier. France was once again making its voice heard as it continued its cultural and economic presence while reestablishing a political one. French enterprises in South Vietnam maintained their positions, and French exports to Vietnam began to increase.[59] Of the fifteen thousand French remaining in South Vietnam, three hundred teachers still taught and five hundred French firms continued in the plantation, industry, commerce, and banking sectors.[60] Relations between Paris and Saigon received an additional boost when Christian Pineau arrived in early March 1958, marking the first time a French foreign minister had set foot in South Vietnam. His visit raised Vietnamese opinion of the French and cemented the choice France had made in favor of Saigon and against Hanoi. France thus began to lay the foundation for renewed political influence. In part, French success stemmed from the increasing amity toward France and hostility toward the United States displayed by Diem's brother and chief political adviser—Ngo Dinh Nhu. Although Paris applauded improved Franco-Vietnamese relations, French officials in Saigon cautioned the Foreign Ministry that "France should not try too quickly to regain a larger political role." Instead, the French government should let things take their own course while "trying to work quietly" for more French influence.[61]

The South Vietnamese, along with most of France, heralded General Charles de Gaulle's return to power in 1958. De Gaulle had emphasized the importance of South Vietnam as a noncommunist nation in a number of speeches. The Vietnamese were also drawn to de Gaulle's idea of France as a "Third Force" in Europe that maintained its liberty of action vis-à-vis the United States and the communist bloc. After a long talk with Diem in March 1959, the French ambassador to South Vietnam, Roger Lalouette, notified the Foreign Ministry that Diem felt French policy had "turned around" and that, "just as De Gaulle advocated a third force between capitalism and communism in Europe, Diem hoped to create his own third force in Asia."[62]

Cultural issues remained a concern for Paris. Most Vietnamese wanted to learn English, since primarily American tourists and businessmen visited Vietnam, and Diem refused to let students study in France since they often failed to return to South Vietnam after their studies. But Lalouette asserted that the French language and culture could still persevere. The Americans, he pointed out, did not have the professors to replace French ones, while the Vietnamese desire to keep universities strong worked in France's favor.[63] Throughout 1959, Franco-

Vietnamese relations steadily improved as U.S.–South Vietnamese ties deteriorated. This was not a coincidence, according to Lalouette; the Vietnamese were feeling an "overpowering American presence."[64]

Three French organizations continued to provide technical and cultural assistance in 1959—the French cultural mission, the mission of technical and economic assistance, and a group of professors at the University of Saigon. According to French officials at the university, the cultural mission was flourishing—two French-run high schools in Saigon, another at Dalat, colleges at Nha Trang and Da Nang (Tourane), and an overflowing of students in the primary schools in Saigon due in part to "Franco-Vietnamese affinity and superior French teaching."[65] Moreover, after a three-year suspension of the program, Vietnamese students were finally allowed in 1960 to return to France to study.

The strongest French asset remained the cultural one. The Vietnamese intellectual and ruling class was steeped in French culture, and Paris was "Mecca" not only for the sophisticated and rich but also for all aspiring toward a higher education. Most educated Vietnamese spoke French well and could quote Racine or Verlaine. French influence in Vietnamese education was pervasive. Paris continued to designate a significant amount of its total overseas expenditures for cultural purposes in Vietnam. An event at the end of 1960 symbolized the significant progress the French had made in maintaining a foothold in Vietnamese affairs. In December 1960, the French produced a successful exposition in Saigon on French books and journals, which demonstrated to the French that they had not lost their cultural influence in Vietnam. The triumph of the Exposition of the French Book was a shining moment for the French presence in Vietnam.[66] It appeared France's cultural role would continue.

At the same time that French cultural initiatives became more popular, so too did the insurgency in the South. French officials thus considered taking new political initiatives. According to the French chargé d'affaires in Saigon, Fourier Ruelle, "rebel activity had been increasing since September 1959, Diem was completely isolated, and the creation of commandos and increases in MAAG personnel did not resolve the problem." The Saigon embassy believed a complete overhaul of South Vietnamese military policy was necessary, contending that "the agrovilles were useless and the population was increasingly restless." Ruelle argued that the time had come "to examine the situation with France's allies," but France should have a policy regarding Vietnam before confronting the policies of others. "Close cooperation with the British and Americans, a serious examination of the situation, and permanent contacts with London and Washington appeared to be the best way of discreetly attaining France's goals." Ruelle concluded that France should adopt a more pro-Diem stance and that France needed to do more to maintain South Vietnamese stability.[67] In response to Ruelle's letter, the chargé d'affaires of the Asian department at the French Foreign Ministry, Etienne Manac'h, agreed that France should become more involved, attempting to craft an overall policy for Vietnam that the Americans had failed to provide.[68]

France's status in South Vietnam continued to rise with the Franco-Vietnamese Accords of March 24, 1960, which transferred the last piece of French public property to the Vietnamese government and allowed Paris and Saigon to move forward with economic exchanges. The political relationship between the two countries had also become more stable. France had once again become an important player in South Vietnamese affairs.[69] According to Lalouette, what the United States had not yet accepted was that a "rebirth of amity" toward France existed among the Vietnamese and that "increasing Franco-Vietnamese collaboration was paired with increasing anti-Americanism."[70] French observers in Saigon watched helplessly as the South Vietnamese and Americans failed to resolve divisive political, economic, and social problems in the South.

French officials in Saigon had become staunch advocates of reform in South Vietnam. In May 1960, Lalouette suggested to U.S. ambassador Elbridge Durbrow a tripartite meeting to discuss South Vietnamese domestic difficulties.[71] Wary of moving too fast, Paris forbade Lalouette to take the initiative for holding a three-power consultation on the means to remedy the situation in Vietnam since the French position "could be misunderstood or interpreted as a return to colonialism."[72] Another attempt at political reform came when R. P. Lebret, director of a French research institute, sent a letter filled with suggestions on government reform to Ngo Dinh Nhu. Lebret had been invited by the National Bank of Vietnam to examine Vietnamese problems, and French officials in Saigon hoped that Lebret's study would constitute the "psychological shock" needed to revitalize the regime.[73]

Before the reforms mentioned in Lebret's study could be discussed, a military coup attempt broke out in Saigon on November 10. In a meeting with Lalouette following that event, Nhu stated that the French had

been "totally correct in their actions" during the coup but that he believed that American agents had supported the rebels. Therefore, Nhu
wanted "to work more closely with the French since he could not trust
the Americans."[74] French officials in Saigon thus once again became
political advisers to a South Vietnamese government.

Conclusion

At first glance, the evidence seems overwhelming that France had lost
all political, military, economic, and cultural influence in both South
and North Vietnam in the two years following the Geneva Conference.
Difficulties in coordinating Franco-U.S. policy, Diem's determination
to pursue his goals free of French influence, South Vietnamese and
U.S. insistence on French withdrawal, French disengagement from the
1956 elections, an ever-smaller economic and cultural mission in South
Vietnam, and increasing Franco–North Vietnamese tensions all indicated an end to the French presence. But France's apparent withdrawal from Vietnam turned out to be incomplete and temporary.
Although Hanoi continued to blame France for failing to implement
the 1956 elections, Saigon grew more receptive to French diplomats as
well as French economic and cultural establishments. French support
of South Vietnam's bid to enter the United Nations in 1957 went a long
way toward easing remaining tensions between Saigon and Paris. In the
late 1950s, the French continued to make political progress with the
Diem government and cultural progress with the Vietnamese people.

By the early 1960s, then, France had made a miraculous comeback
in South Vietnam. In many ways, the French had come to be more respected by the South Vietnamese than the Americans. The French did
not overtly challenge the Americans in Vietnam, but they worked quietly to reform the Diem government, to maintain their economic and
cultural influence, and even to rebuild a moderate political presence
as Vietnamese disenchantment with the Americans grew. French President Charles de Gaulle warned Washington as early as 1961 against
deepening U.S. involvement in Vietnamese affairs. He subsequently
began to call for the neutralization of Vietnam, whereby the United
States would withdraw and the Vietnamese themselves would settle
their conflict without external influence. De Gaulle advocated a return
to a Geneva-type conference or bilateral deal between Hanoi and
Saigon to determine how neutralization would be implemented.[75] As a

result, until Diem and Nhu's assassination in 1963, French officials played at least a partial role in encouraging the Diem government's willingness to reopen discussions with the DRV.[76]

In the end, the North-South and East-West struggles that had driven the First Indochina War reappeared. This dynamic was complicated by West-West competition for influence as Paris sought to keep Vietnam French while Washington insisted on making it American. As a new era unfolded in the early 1960s, the *présence française* endured in Vietnam despite the ever-growing *présence americaine.*

FOURTEEN

◆ ◆ ◆

Chronicle of a War Foretold

The United States and Vietnam, 1945–1954

ANDREW J. ROTTER

CONTRARY TO MUCH popular thinking, hindsight is not always 20/20; if it were, there would be no need for historians, and that would be catastrophic. But hindsight is surely clearer than foresight. In Gabriel García Márquez's novella *Chronicle of a Death Foretold*, an unidentified character slides a warning letter under the door to Santiago Nasar, who was involved in an unfortunate rumor concerning the virginity of a young woman about to be married. The letter, which reported to Santiago the "precise details of the plot" to kill him, remained unobserved on the floor when Santiago left home that day.

We all know that the future occasionally offers up clues, indications of what may come. Like Santiago Nasar, we are inclined to miss these indications, or find them unintelligible, or lose them in the welter of other possibilities for what might happen or in the busyness of our everyday lives. Santiago Nasar was on his way to see the bishop, whose boat was bearing him up the river early one February morning, and in his excitement stepped over the envelope lying on the front hall floor. Macbeth and Julius Caesar missed their cues. So did Americans, prior to Pearl Harbor, the North Korean attack on the South, and the attacks of September 11, fail to see what was coming. There was too much noise in the channel (to use a now-common phrase), and they could not hear the audible warning signals.

So, too, with U.S. involvement in the Vietnam War. While it is hard to specify precisely the moment of American entry into that war, many point to President Lyndon B. Johnson's decisions in late 1964 and early 1965 as the critical steps toward military intervention. On December 30,

1964, Johnson wrote to Maxwell Taylor, the U.S. ambassador in Saigon: "We are facing war in South Vietnam. I have never felt that this war will be won from the air, and it seems to me that what is much more needed and would be much more effective is a larger and stronger use of Rangers and Special Forces and Marines . . . I myself am ready to substantially increase the number of Americans fighting in Vietnam."[1] His doubts about air power notwithstanding, Johnson six weeks later authorized a program of sustained bombing attacks on North Vietnam. In early March, he sent in combat troops, the first so designated. Some 3,500 of them came ashore at Da Nang. They would be followed by many thousands more.

And so, apparently, it began: the troop escalations and the B-52 bombings, more napalm and defoliants and "harassment and interdiction" artillery fire aimed seemingly at random at the Vietnamese countryside, the battle of Ia Drang and the siege of Khe Sanh, the Tet Offensive in 1968, and the Eastertide Offensive in 1972. The My Lai killings, the executions at Hue, the abuse of prisoners in Hanoi and Saigon, the chronic instability of the South Vietnamese government, the expansion of the war into Laos and Cambodia, and of course the massive antiwar demonstrations in the United States and elsewhere— these are how most Americans remember the Vietnam War, defined as the period from Johnson's fateful decisions of 1964 and 1965 to the uneasy signing of the Paris Peace Accords in January 1973. By its end, it cost over fifty-eight thousand American and between two and three million Vietnamese lives.

Questions concerning the causes and main features of the war tend to focus on this eight-year period. Why did President Johnson commit the United States to war? Why did he and other leading policymakers believe that American interests or values were at stake in such a far off place, and what were those interests and values? Did Johnson and the others assume an easy victory, and if so, why? What was the role in the war of ideologies, including nationalism, communism, and liberal capitalism? Why was it so difficult to fight this war, so hard to find the enemy or halt his progress, so hard to strategize properly, and, perhaps above all, so hard to get the South Vietnamese to fight for the Saigon government? From whence came dissent against the war? And why did it take so long to end the conflict?

These are good questions. And all of them, posed either as questions, problems to be solved, or simply features of the U.S. struggle in

Southeast Asia, were legible more than a decade before Lyndon Johnson's critical decisions of 1965. The future sent a message to the past, just as some anonymous person tried to warn Santiago Nasar that danger lurked outside his door. The Vietnam War was an agony foretold. Between 1945 and 1954, it would have been possible—the conditional needs to be stressed—to locate at least eight themes that would characterize the war after 1965, all of them already discernible in U.S. policy toward Vietnam and Southeast Asia generally.

The first of these themes was American cultural ignorance and racial condescension. Both were clearly present and mutually sustaining after 1965. Robert McNamara, secretary of defense from 1961 to early 1968, embraced the Vietnam War with a sense of purpose and confidence that belied his ignorance of Southeast Asia (and that he later regretted). "I had never visited Indochina," he admitted in his 1995 memoir, "nor did I understand or appreciate its history, language, culture, or values." The same, he pointed out, was true for virtually everyone else responsible for making Vietnam policy for presidents Kennedy and Johnson.[2] Those who might have known something about Vietnam had been purged from the State Department as security risks during the heyday of the Red Scare. Policymakers were ignorant, for example, of centuries-long Vietnamese resistance to Chinese imperialism, of possible affinities between Vietnamese Confucianism and socialism, and of the importance the Vietnamese attached to polite behavior, even by their social or political superiors. Even less did the U.S. military understand the Vietnamese, and even less than that did it show them respect. Of the American soldiers, the novelist Tim O'Brien wrote:

> They did not know the names of most villages. They did not know which villages were critical. They did not know strategies. They did not know the terms of the war, its architecture, the rules of fair play. When they took prisoners, which was rare, they did not know the questions to ask, whether to release a suspect or beat on him. They did not know how to feel. Whether, when seeing a dead Vietnamese, to be happy or sad or relieved . . . They did not know good from evil.[3]

Some of them knew enough to show their hatred or contempt for the Vietnamese, referring to them as "gooks," engaging in rape, and collecting noses or ears from their corpses.

American ignorance of the Vietnamese and racial contempt for them existed long before U.S. Marines appeared at Da Nang. Navy lieutenant John White sailed on the brig *Franklin* to Vietnam in 1819, part of an expedition seeking U.S. trade with the country. White carried out his duties with considerable distaste. He thought the Vietnamese a filthy people, whose "dirty habits," he wrote, "engender vast swarms of vermin and render their bodies highly offensive to more than one sense." They also drank to excess, showed no respect for personal space, and displayed a wantonness that White found alternately amusing and distressing. In Saigon, "the populace would crowd round us, almost suffocate us with the fetor of their bodies, and feel every article of our dress with their dirty paws, chattering like so many baboons."[4] Little understanding had been gained a century later, as Mark Bradley has noted; early twentieth century American travelers, journalists, and academics characterized the Vietnamese as lazy, primitive ("Annamites at best are never clean," wrote Virginia Thompson), prevaricating, and altogether inferior to westerners.[5]

By 1945, some of the harshest descriptors of the Vietnamese were less fashionable and thus less commonly used. But American ignorance and racism, if the second was now more often veiled, both persisted and predicted the continuation of anti-Vietnamese feeling into the 1960s and 1970s. U.S. functionaries, in their ignorance, had difficulty spelling the name of Vietnam's leading figure, variably rendering it "Hoo Chi Minh," "Mr. Hoe," "Ho Chi Mink," "Ho Chi Mina," and "Ho Tchih Ming." (Ho obligingly signed several letters to American acquaintances "Hoo.")[6] Reporting from Saigon in July 1947, Charles S. Reed contended that "few of the Annamites are particularly industrious" and denigrated their "honesty, loyalty, and veracity."[7] Respectable people generally avoided coarse characterizations of the Vietnamese in sharply racial terms, including claims that they were primitive and dirty. Instead, American policymakers used the vocabulary of maturity to locate the Vietnamese along a spectrum of development: the Vietnamese, they said, lagged behind the West economically and politically because they were not fully grown up. The stature of the Vietnamese, and the relative absence of facial and body hair on the men—both much commented on by Americans who encountered them—made them look younger than they were. "The Annamese are attractive and even lovable," allowed William C. Bullitt, the former U.S. ambassador to the Soviet Union and France, but they were "essentially childish."[8] To Donald Heath, ambassador to Vietnam (rather, the French "Associated States") in 1953, the Vietnamese were practitioners of "emotional,

irresponsible nationalism" (words as suggestive of effeminacy as immaturity) and imbued with an extraordinary "degree of naiveté and childlike belief" that others would protect them.[9] Dwight Eisenhower's
secretary of state John Foster Dulles thought the Vietnamese had re-
gressed beyond childhood, insisting in May 1954 that if the Associated
States were given their independence by the French "it would be like
putting a baby in a cage of hungry lions."[10]

Here, of course, was the reason why these characterizations had political import: if the Vietnamese were lazy or immature, they were not
ready to govern themselves. Back in 1924, the U.S. consul in Vietnam
observed that "Indochina is one of the quietest portions of Asia. The
Annamites as a race are very lazy and not prone to be ambitious."
Three years later, his successor begged off sending monthly political
reports to the State Department because "there were almost no political developments to report"—this less than three years before the Yen
Bay rebellion shook the French colony.[11] Given the intensity of the
Vietnamese independence movement that declared itself to the world
on September 2, 1945, it would thereafter be difficult to claim that the
Vietnamese were lazy. Instead, the French and Americans judged the
Vietnamese leadership impulsive, impatient, and (again) insufficiently
mature to run their own country. The State Department's Policy Information Committee put it this way in late August 1950:

> The new Asian nations are like youths who have reached man's estate
> and are now on their own. Like youths, they have to make their mis-
> takes and suffer the consequences if they are to acquire inner equilib-
> rium and stability. In normal times, this process could be allowed to
> work itself out with some assurance that all would be well in the end.
> The situation is given a radically different complexion, however, when
> a single false step will deliver the novitiate into the clutches of an armed
> thug.[12]

The thug, of course, was world communism. A year and a half later,
as the French struggled to prevent a series of battlefield setbacks from
becoming a full scale military disaster, Secretary of State Dean Acheson
told the Senate Foreign Relations Committee that the French had
done all they could to liberate their subjects. "The Vietnamese," he said,
"have got all the liberty and opportunity that they can possibly handle
or want." A people so politically callow could not possibly cope with
more.[13]

Try as the French and Americans might to suppress at least their public utterances averring their racial superiority to the Vietnamese, old habits died hard, or sometimes not at all. Occasionally the condescension implied by the ascription of immaturity to the Vietnamese was replaced by an open racism that the Vietnamese deeply resented. Ho Chi Minh once said: "To the colonialists, the life of an Asian or an African is not worth a penny," and there is no reason to think that the French gave him cause to change his mind.[14] Or, for that matter, the Americans. Why can't we figure out what's going on in the minds of ordinary Vietnamese? someone asked the U.S. consul in Saigon, George Abbott, in 1948. "In the first place," Abbott replied, "we just couldn't do it because of our white skin. A white man would be very conspicuous in Indo-China. In order to [be] an effective intelligence officer, he would have to have a little brown blood. Then, we wouldn't be able to trust him."[15]

At least one American understood the effect on the Vietnamese of the growing U.S. presence in their country between 1945 and 1954. R. Allen Griffin, a newspaper publisher who had previously served with the Economic Cooperation Administration in China, was dispatched by Acheson to Southeast Asia in early 1950 with instructions to figure out whether and how U.S. economic aid to the region might be constructive. The focus of the Griffin mission was Vietnam, "the strategic key to Southeast Asia," as an official in Japan told the group. Griffin did his survey and made his recommendations, and that summer, following his return, he described his impressions of the peoples of Southeast Asia to an audience at San Francisco State College. They don't all like us, he admitted. We are rich, sometimes "ostentatious in our spending," and infrequently "exhibit the virtue of humility." We do not care to understand their history; "we are ignorant of their literature and traditions and often fail in the social niceties. And sometimes our kindness appears somewhat condescending." Southeast Asians were familiar with racial discrimination in the United States, in part because "many of their students who have come to this country have been victims of slights and humiliations due to our rude and ignorant color-consciousness."[16] Just what Griffin thought might be done about these problems he did not make clear. That they persisted into the wartime period after 1965 is evidence that most other Americans ignored or discounted them.

The second theme of the post-1965 period of the war that had prece-

dent in the years 1945 to 1954 was the American conviction that Vietnam was a Cold War crucible, a front in the conflict between the Soviet
Union and after 1949 the People's Republic of China on the one hand
and the United States and its allies on the other. Thus, it was not just
Vietnam or Indochina that seemed to be at risk but a significant piece
of territory in a conflict that was all encompassing and constant-sum; a
victory for communism would be a defeat for what Americans called
"the free world." President John F. Kennedy, who refrained from sending combat troops to Vietnam but nevertheless put the United States
on the path to doing so by significantly increasing the number of military advisers there, linked the U.S. commitment to South Vietnam to
its obligations elsewhere, for in the Cold War with the Soviet Union, he
said, "I don't know where the non-essential areas are."[17] Neither did
Lyndon Johnson and his advisers. As Johnson moved toward choosing
war in the fall of 1964, Maxwell Taylor warned from Saigon that "if we
leave Vietnam with our tail between our legs, the consequences of this
defeat in the rest of Asia, Africa, and Latin America would be disastrous."[18] Johnson had a nightmare that an American bomb would hit a
Soviet ship at anchor in North Vietnam's Haiphong harbor, killing a
high-ranking Russian officer. He worried even more about the Chinese, who were, like the Soviets, helping the North Vietnamese with
abundant economic and military assistance. A U.S. invasion of North
Vietnam, recalling as it would the American–United Nations–South
Korean crossing of the thirty-eighth parallel in Korea in 1950, gave the
president dreadful flashbacks; when someone expressed skepticism
that the Chinese would send troops to fight Americans in a neighboring state, Johnson replied: "That's what MacArthur thought."[19] And, as
the Taylor quotation above indicates, the Johnson administration
never abandoned its fear that other Southeast Asian nations, and third
world nations everywhere, would tumble like dominoes should South
Vietnam fall to communism. Though to some extent the domino theory had lost traction by the mid-1960s, Secretary of State Dean Rusk
still cleaved to it years after the war had ended, and Johnson told Doris
Kearns that he "knew that if the aggression succeeded in South Vietnam, then the aggressors would simply keep going until all of Southeast Asia fell into their hands, slowly or quickly."[20]

All of these assumptions concerning the Cold War significance of
Vietnam and Southeast Asia had come fully into Washington's view between 1945 and 1954. The efforts by the French to resume colonial sta-

tus in Indochina following the Japanese surrender in 1945 forged a link between remote Southeast Asia and the vital European front in the anticommunist struggle. If, as the Truman administration soon came to believe, the Soviet Union looked to extend itself into what George Kennan called "every nook and cranny available to it in the basin of world power," and if France, whatever its faults, was to be the most important continental bastion against the expansion of communism, it followed that the United States should do nothing to threaten or weaken the French government's effort to restore France's standing in Indochina. The French did their best to persuade the Americans that the battle for Vietnam was a Cold War contest with implications that stretched well beyond its borders. When U.S. ambassador to France Jefferson Caffery questioned Charles de Gaulle's plans for Indochina in March 1945, de Gaulle snapped:

> What are you driving at? Do you want us to become . . . one of the federated states under the Russian aegis? The Russians are advancing apace . . . When Germany falls they will be upon us. If the public here comes to realize that you are against us in Indochina there will be terrific disappointment and nobody knows to what that will lead. We do not want to become Communist; we do not want to fall into the Russian orbit; but I hope that you do not push us into it.[21]

The French continued to play the communist card for the nine years that followed, and the Americans were sure it was a trump. To some extent de Gaulle and his successors believed what they were saying. The Red Army might cross the Rhine. More likely, Josef Stalin could exert influence in France through the popular French Communist Party, which was supported by much of France's labor movement. French communism would benefit enormously from France's political instability, caused in part by the nation's ongoing economic difficulties. These, in turn, could be in good part attributed to the loss of French resources to the war in Vietnam, which had begun in earnest in December 1946. U.S. assistance in the form of Marshall Plan aid began flowing to the French in mid-1948, but expenditures in Vietnam constituted what the NATO supreme commander Eisenhower called in 1951 "a draining sore in their side."[22] Still, the Indochina war and resources to fight it were increasingly, in the Americans' view, essential to the battle against world communism, headquartered in Moscow. The French subscribed to the "ten pin theory," meaning that if one of their colonies fell free of French control, others would soon fall too. Vietnam was the head pin in the metaphor.[23] Its imagery was compatible with that of the domino theory, which the French used readily in their conversations with the Americans. Few used it better than the much-admired General Jean de Lattre de Tassigny, who told an American colleague: "Tonkin [northern Vietnam] is the key to Southeast Asia, if Southeast Asia is lost, India will burn like a match and there will be no barrier to the advance of Communism before Suez and Africa. If the Moslem world were thus engulfed, the Moslems in North Africa would soon fall in line and Europe itself would be outflanked."[24]

Fully convinced that France was vulnerable to communism, that Ho Chi Minh was an agent of world communism, and that the loss of Vietnam to communism would put in jeopardy nations neighboring Vietnam and those nations' neighbors, U.S. policymakers between 1945 and 1954 recognized Vietnam as a critical front in the Cold War. Dean Rusk, who presided over the war as secretary of state during the 1960s formed his convictions about the domino theory and Soviet involvement in Indochina as assistant secretary of state in the 1940s and 1950s; in 1951, he insisted at a congressional hearing that Vietnam's communists were "strongly directed from Moscow and could be counted upon . . . to tie Indochina into the world communist program."[25] (In fact, the Soviets were hoping to stay clear of involvement in the Vietnam conflict. When Ho came to Moscow in early 1950 seeking help Stalin gave him the cold shoulder, remarking dismissively at one point: "Oh, you orientals. You have such rich imaginations."[26]) In October 1949, the CIA warned that a communist victory in Indochina, "in conjunction with pressures from Communist China, would almost certainly greatly strengthen an existing tendency in Thailand, Burma, and Malaya to seek accommodation with Communist China." Two months later, the National Security Council (NSC) put it slightly differently but reached the same conclusion: "The political offensive of the Kremlin or its protégés . . . tends to gather additional momentum as each new success increases the vulnerability of the next target." It was "now clear that southeast Asia [was] the target of a coordinated offensive directed by the Kremlin."[27] This thinking carried over into the Eisenhower administration. Advocating U.S. military intervention in Vietnam on behalf of the French in late January 1954, Admiral Arthur Radford claimed that if Tonkin fell to Ho's Viet Minh, all of Southeast Asia would go.[28] Though he did not agree with Radford, President Eisenhower nevertheless insisted: "Indochina was the first in a row of dominoes. If it fell its neighbors would shortly thereafter fall with it, and where did the process end?" The president made it clear that he, at least, did not wish to find out.[29] Thus, from 1945 to 1954, U.S. policymakers believed that Vietnam meant more than itself: it was a Cold War flash point that pitted against each other two dramatically different ideologies. The world was watching to see which would win, and human freedom and dignity hung in the balance. The Soviets and Chinese, through their agent Ho Chi Minh, were hoping to extend totalitarian communism to Indochina, Southeast Asia, and beyond. The Americans, despite the foibles of their allies, were trying to stop them. The men of Lyndon Johnson's administration would understand the conflict in precisely the same way in 1965.

This takes us to a third theme readily discernible in both the earlier and later periods of U.S. involvement, and that is the surprising centrality of Southeast Asia in American strategic and economic calculations. "Veetnam, Veetnam, that's all I hear them say!" Lyndon Johnson once erupted concerning his critics, and so it must have seemed. Johnson termed Vietnam "that bitch of a war," stealing time and money from the "woman I really love," the collection of domestic welfare and social justice programs he called the Great Society.[30] The war seemed to draw everything into its vortex, and it came to obsess Johnson. During the siege of U.S. Marines at Khe Sanh in 1967 and 1968, Johnson had a scale model of the battlefield built and placed in the White House War Room. In the dark days of the Tet Offensive he went largely without sleep; he left the White House mostly to pray with his "little monks."[31] The Vietnam War distorted U.S. relations with the Soviets and the European allies and forced into the shadows policy initiatives to be taken elsewhere in Asia, in Latin America, and in Africa. In the end, the war wrecked Lyndon Johnson's presidency. All that from what the president called a "piss ant" country and what had once seemed a brushfire of a war.

While it is perhaps unsurprising to discover that the first two themes—derogatory American representations of the Vietnamese and the American perception that the First Indochina War was a Cold War conflict—were common to the periods 1945–1954 and 1965–1973, it is striking to find that between the end of World War II and the Geneva Conference of 1954, Southeast Asia, and especially Indochina, moved from the distant periphery of American concerns to their very center. Indeed, by 1950 the Truman administration had concluded that Southeast Asia was a fulcrum on which rested the recovery of developed, noncommunist nations. As William S. Borden, Michael Schaller, and others have demonstrated, holding the line against communism in Vietnam was felt vital to the preservation of a liberal capitalist "great crescent" in East Asia and thus to the economic recovery of a prostrate Japan. In the immediate aftermath of World War II, U.S. officials responsible for the occupation of Japan, all but masters of the island nation's fate, planned to democratize and reform Japanese institutions on a scale comparable to that of the New Deal. But as the Japanese economy languished and communism won out in China, U.S. authorities, most prominently General Douglas MacArthur—a virtual proconsul in Tokyo—reversed course, abandoning the extreme makeover of reform for the practical course of economic recovery. That meant Japan would need to trade, importing food and natural resources in exchange for its manufactures. Japan had for many years traded on this basis with China, but after 1949 the Americans no longer believed that Sino-Japanese trade had much of a future. The solution seemed to be to establish trade links between Japan and the nearby nations of Southeast Asia, whose economies were complementary to the Japanese. Thailand and Burma were rich in rice. Indochina held some iron ore, British Malaya rubber and tin, and Indonesia, newly independent in 1949, was a source of oil. There were whispers in Washington about the return to East Asia of Japan's star-crossed "Co-Prosperity Sphere," and the Southeast Asians, who were not consulted about American plans, were dubious of them at best. But U.S. policymakers believed Japanese economic recovery was an urgent matter by 1950, and a Southeast Asia secure against communist encroachment and open to trade with Japan was an essential element in their design.[32]

No ally was more important to Washington than Great Britain. Through World War II the United States had sustained Britain with military aid under the Lend Lease program, and after the war was over the Americans provided the British with a hefty loan (albeit with terms) and then an enormous outlay of Marshall Plan aid. The British were grateful and the assistance helped. But when, in mid-1949, recession bruised the American economy, the British went into a tailspin: with the nation hemorrhaging dollars at an alarming rate, the Labour government called a halt to sterling-dollar convertibility. Yet dollars remained critical to the British, who produced little that Americans wanted to buy and thus had little hope of balancing their transatlantic trade account. The Marshall Plan was proving insufficient to Great Britain's economic needs; the notorious "dollar gap" between the allies yawned wider.

First the British, then belatedly the Americans, recognized that a partial solution to London's dollar deficit might be found in Southeast Asia, specifically the British colony Malaya. Before World War II, the United States had paid cash for large quantities of Malayan rubber and smelted tin, both of which were vital to U.S. industry. The British then sold Malaya a variety of foodstuffs and light manufactured goods, for which they received payment in dollars. When the Japanese occupied Malaya in 1942, cutting the supply of rubber and tin to the United States, the Americans had developed synthetic rubber (not an exact substitute for tree-source latex, but close) and built the nation's first tin smelter, meaning that they could now import raw tin (especially from Bolivia) and refine it themselves. Thus, when the war ended and British Malaya was once more able to provide rubber and tin for the U.S. market, the Malayans found their goods rebuffed by the Americans, who no longer needed them. As it became clear by 1949, however, that showering Britain with Marshall Plan dollars would not permanently solve British economic problems, the Americans allowed themselves to be persuaded that restarting the prewar trade triangle made good long-term sense. The choice was "trade, not aid," as a U.S. treasury official put it. And so, despite the relative disutility of Malayan rubber and tin to the U.S. economy, the Americans decided in late 1949 to increase their purchases of both products. It was the economically rational way to put dollars into British hands, and at least the goods could be stockpiled.[33]

But if Southeast Asia was to provide trade partners for Japan and Great Britain, the region would have to be secured against apparent communist encroachment. Given the domino theory, victory by the French in their war against the Viet Minh was, claimed U.S. policymakers, critical to the preservation of a noncommunist Southeast Asia and thus demanded American support. As the French were fond of saying, they were fighting in Indochina on behalf of the free world. In December 1949, David K. E. Bruce, the U.S. ambassador in France, insisted that the United States must take certain "practical measures" to stop "Communist expansionism at the Tonkinese border." "If that is not done," Bruce cautioned, "Burma and Siam [Thailand] will fall like overripe apples and the British . . . will be forced to reconsider the tenability of their position in Malaya." The practical measures Bruce had in mind were "courageously and speedily" to support French exertions in Vietnam.[34]

The problem was that the French were doing badly in the war and as a result undermining political stability and economic recovery at home, even while Vietnam remained convulsed. Seeking an alternative to Ho Chi Minh, the French had persuaded the former Vietnamese emperor (and Japanese instrument) Bao Dai to leave the fleshpots of the French Riviera and return to his country as head of the Associated State of Vietnam "within the French Union." The Americans were unenthusiastic about Bao Dai—Charles Reed, head of the State Department's Division of Southeast Asian Affairs, called him "a French-inspired and French-dominated political zero"—and vexed by the ineptitude of the French military campaign against the Viet Minh.[35] Moreover, the French were squandering in Indochina money and lives that would be, in the Americans' view, far better spent (if expenditure was to be their fate) in Western Europe. Southeast Asia became central to U.S. policy by 1949 precisely because its disposition was intimately connected to that of vital Western Europe. By the spring of 1949, U.S. officials had privately concluded that West Germany would have to be rearmed and its army integrated with a larger Western European force, if the security of Western Europe was to be preserved. That was the purpose of signing the North Atlantic Treaty in the spring of 1949. The French, though key signatories of the treaty, were at first conspicuously distant from its military apparatus. The reason was noted by the State Department: "Some 130,000 troops of the French Union are pinned down in Indochina. The sooner part of these troops are released (as a result of military victory) for service in Europe the better the national interests of both the United States and France will be served."[36] "When we reached the problem of increasing the security of Western Europe," George Marshall reflected, "I found all of the French troops of any quality were all out in Indochina . . . and the one place they were not was in Western Europe."[37]

For these reasons, the Truman administration extended diplomatic recognition to the Bao Dai government. Then, some six weeks prior to the outbreak of war in Korea, it granted his Associated State a small amount of economic aid and gave the French fighting on his behalf some military equipment. These decisions were made with some hesitation. But Vietnam and Southeast Asia were too important to be ignored. As John Foster Dulles told two congressional committees in early 1953, the situation in Indochina was "more dangerous" than any other in the world

> because the loss of Indochina would probably have even more serious repercussions upon the Indian-Asian population than even the loss of South Korea and, also, because what is going on in Indochina has very serious repercussions in Europe and upon the mood of France, and the willingness of the French to move in partnership with Germany toward the creation of unity and security in Europe so we can have a western Europe which is of vital importance, if that area is to be made secure.[38]

So it was that Dulles and Eisenhower would increase the level of U.S. assistance to the French in Indochina. So it was that, by the end of 1954, the United States would replace France as backer of an anticommunist government in Vietnam. U.S. policy had resolved in favor of greater involvement in Vietnam.

Dulles's comparison of Indochina to Korea circa 1953 suggests a fourth theme apparent in both the First and Second Indochina Wars: the ease with which Americans transferred what they understood as the lessons of one Asian conflict to another. In the early 1960s, the analogy preferred by U.S. Vietnam policymakers was to the British response to the Malayan "emergency" between 1948 and 1956. The Malayan situation, the Americans reasoned, was in important ways similar to the one they faced in Vietnam during the early 1960s: the enemies were communist guerrillas assisted by the Chinese; Vietnam and Malaya were close together and looked somewhat the same physically; and, above all, a Western power bore the brunt of the battle against the guerrillas—and in the Malayan case had won. Roger Hilsman, assistant secretary of state in the Kennedy administration, endorsed the creation of protected "strategic hamlets" in South Vietnam—specially built villages into which peasants were herded to keep them from aiding, or being harassed by, the Viet Cong—because the "technique was used successfully in Malaya against the Communist movement there."[39] The architect of British strategy in Malaya, Robert Thompson, was brought in to advise the Americans and South Vietnamese president Ngo Dinh Diem on how to fight the guerrillas. "We had found nothing new in Vietnam except in scale or intensity," Thompson would write. "It was to us a matter only of adapting strategy, tactics, and methods to a slightly different environment."[40]

By late 1964, Thompson had backed away from that optimistic comparison.[41] American officials to some extent had moved on too. Johnson and his advisers increasingly adopted the Korean analogy to shape their decisions to escalate the war in early 1965. Bombing and ground troops in Korea had stopped a communist offensive fifteen years earlier and thus saved a noncommunist southern state from annihilation. They found little reason to imagine that things would be different in Vietnam.[42]

Neither Malaya nor Korea seemed helpful analogies to Vietnam decision-makers between 1945 and 1954. The former conflict looked promising but was not yet resolved at the time of the Geneva Conference, while the latter was at best a raw and recent memory. The analogue chosen by policymakers instead was the Philippines. Like Malaya, the Philippines looked physically familiar to officials who worked on Vietnam. The Philippines had a colonial past: first the Spaniards, then the Americans, had ruled over a Southeast Asian people they deemed unready for self-government. But the Filipinos had learned something about democracy from their American tutors, and in 1946 the United States made good on its earlier promise to grant the Philippines independence. Not all Filipinos accepted American terms, rejecting even the government the Americans had left in place. The Huks, a collection of impoverished peasants, Democratic Socialists, and Maoists, went into rebellion in the late 1940s. The Philippine president, Elpidio Quirino—described by the American journalist Stanley Karnow as "a limp, indecisive figure"—tried to negotiate with the Huk leader, Luis Taruc, but the talks went nowhere and the Huk rebellion intensified. Quirino, complacent and corrupt, seemed powerless to stop it. Of him, Taruc said: "We couldn't have had a better recruiter."[43]

As the islands slid toward chaos, the Americans, by 1949 intent on securing the great crescent against the advance of communism in East Asia, grew alarmed that Quirino and the Huks would inadvertently conspire to destroy what years of American tutelage had made. Quirino made Secretary of State Acheson think of Chiang Kai-shek. The key was to find a stronger figure, pro-American but also willing to implement reforms that would win him popular support among Filipinos who might otherwise go over to the Huks. So emerged Ramon Magsaysay, a Filipino legislator who had visited Washington in early 1950 and there impressed the CIA agent Edward G. Lansdale. Magsaysay thereafter became "America's proxy." Washington promised to increase its military aid to the Philippines government if Quirino appointed Magsaysay as defense secretary, to which Quirino agreed. Lansdale came to the Philippines and helped fashion Magsaysay into a Huk-fighting populist—incorruptible, abstemious, and happiest when greeting farmers in rural villages. Lansdale also provided Magsaysay with an arsenal of counterinsurgency tricks, including fake broadcasts of "Huk 'voices' from tombs, a sign to the superstitious of their malevolence," as Karnow puts it. The insurgency ended, and in 1953 Magsaysay won election to the presidency over Quirino.[44]

While Magsaysay's presidency proved disappointing (and brief—he was killed in a plane crash in 1957), the Americans believed him a model statesman who had brought peace and justice to a troubled Southeast Asian nation. Lansdale they anointed a miracle worker whose talents were presumably portable. The next job was South Vietnam in 1954. The French were by then reeling and on their way out, having suffered a devastating military defeat at Dien Bien Phu. Bao Dai, left in place south of the seventeenth parallel by the terms of the Geneva Agreements that July, appointed, at American insistence, Ngo Dinh Diem as his prime minister. At a meeting at the Pentagon in early 1954, Dulles told Lansdale "that it had been decided that I was to go to Vietnam to help the Vietnamese much as I had helped the Filipinos."[45] Diem was to be South Vietnam's Ramon Magsaysay; Lansdale would teach him what that meant.

Lansdale was less sanguine about the task than Dulles and more alive to the differences between the Philippines and South Vietnam. For U.S. policymakers, however, there was always an analogy to be made. Lansdale had enabled Magsaysay to defeat a radical guerrilla movement in the Philippines, a place with a recent colonial past, with jungles and rice paddies, with intrigue and official corruption and only a fledgling's knowledge of democracy. There was every reason to think he could help Diem defeat his enemies in Vietnam.

As much as they understood the struggle in Vietnam as a Cold War contest, U.S. policymakers also believed that they were battling Vietnamese nationalism, albeit a force that had been commandeered by international communism—the fifth continuity between the first and second Vietnam wars. Lyndon Johnson talked often of taking the war to the north, its presumed source; without northern support and supply, the insurgency in the south would wither, he thought. At the same time, Johnson recognized that most Vietnamese aspired to unite their

nation and pull free of foreign control. Meeting the material needs of
the South Vietnamese people would go a long way toward weaning
them from the communists and refashioning a nationalism that was
compatible with American wishes for Vietnam. "Damnit," he declared,
"we need to exhibit more compassion for these Vietnamese plain
people . . . We've got to see that the South Vietnamese government
wins the battle . . . of crops and hearts and caring."[46] This view implied
that nationalism was a free-floating entity that could be detached
from the malignant parasite of communism and neatly reattached to
American-style liberal capitalism, or its South Vietnamese variant.
Johnson acknowledged its importance.

So did the foreign policymakers in the Truman and early Eisenhower administrations. They were frustrated with French intransigence because they knew it only made converts for the Vietnamese
nationalist cause and that this meant, overwhelmingly, converts for Ho
Chi Minh. Like their successors in the 1960s, statesmen and politicians
regarded communism as a parasite on nationalism but one very difficult to discourage. As Acheson put it tersely in May 1949: "Question
whether Ho as much nationalist as Commie is irrelevant. All Stalinists
in colonial areas are nationalists."[47] As their successors would be, they
were impressed with the power of nationalism. In 1953, Senator Everett
Dirksen, a Republican from Illinois, wondered aloud about the strength
of the Viet Minh: "What makes them so tough? What is the force that
makes them resist? It is an ideological force. It is the nationalism which
they preach." Given that, Dirksen suggested, it was pointless to send
millions of dollars in military equipment to the French-backed Bao Dai
regime; nationalism was stronger than guns, and Ho Chi Minh was nationalism's champion.[48] (Both Dulles and Eisenhower conceded Ho's
popularity.)[49] And, like their successors, the Vietnam decision-makers
between 1945 and 1954 believed that the best way for Bao Dai to challenge Ho Chi Minh, to vie for the loyalty of the Vietnamese people, was
to implement reforms that would convince them of his concern for
their safety and welfare.

Long before the Americans encouraged Diem to create "strategic
hamlets" as a way of isolating the population from the Viet Cong, the
French started a "pacification" program of their own in the countryside, with American approval and financial support. Like the Americans of the early 1960s, the French viewed with approval British efforts
to win popularity in Malaya through the creation of "New Villages,"

model communities designed to help the peasantry pursue a liveli-
hood under government protection. In the early 1950s, the French
and the Bao Dai government established *agrovilles* along these same
lines. *Agrovilles* were meant to serve as models of village life and to attract both the admiration of the peasantry and U.S. dollars. Bao Dai
never had much interest in the *agrovilles*—even the French thought he
should spend more time cultivating his rural citizenry—but Diem
thought them intriguing, if only as a better way to fight his adversaries,
and it was his interest that provided the link between the pacification
plans of the French and those of the Americans, between the First
Indochina War and the Second.[50]

There is a footnote to be added with regard to the relationship of nationalism to communism. It concerns the role played by Ho Chi Minh
during and just after World War II. Just as the Americans regarded nationalism as an inevitable, potentially positive, but highly volatile force
in Indochina and elsewhere, so did Ho Chi Minh seem to think that
the American commitment to justice and liberty, well chronicled in the
American past and revealed in American policy toward the Philippines, could work to the benefit of his revolution, so long as it over-
matched the equally determined American commitment to the success
of world capitalism. Americans who met Ho Chi Minh in the mid-
1940s, most of them agents of the Office of Strategic Services, often
wondered at the relative strength of his nationalism and his communism. Ho, in turn, tried to figure out how the Americans would balance
their traditional anticolonialism with their concern for France's postwar economic stability. Each side thought the other misunderstood
its intentions—one more misunderstanding that persisted in U.S.-
Vietnam relations after 1965.[51]

Harry Truman and Dwight Eisenhower did not send U.S. troops into
battle in Vietnam while Lyndon Johnson did, and this constitutes a critical difference in U.S. policy between the French war and the later period. But common to U.S. policy in both periods (and herewith a sixth
theme) was a desire to avoid, as much as possible, exposing American
soldiers to harm, by seeking others—the French and Vietnamese from
1945 to 1954, the South Vietnamese after 1965—to fight the war themselves. One of Lyndon Johnson's greatest agonies was his inability to
get the South Vietnamese to fight the Viet Cong and the North Vietnamese on their own behalf. When he first sent U.S. combat troops to
South Vietnam in 1965, he nevertheless, and perhaps perversely, "hoped

to keep the involvement of 'his boys' to a minimum," according to Doris Kearns.[52] Every added escalation thereafter was undertaken as a way of protecting those soldiers already in Vietnam from enemy attack. This was necessary, the president and his generals believed, because the South Vietnamese army—the Army of the Republic of Vietnam, or ARVN—was unable or unwilling to take responsibility for the nation's safety. "I wish the southern members of the clan would display the fighting qualities of their northern brethren," said one U.S. general wistfully in 1966.[53] Still, by late 1967, given the rising human and political costs of U.S. involvement, the administration had decided to try to cap U.S. force levels and hand the greater burden of fighting to the ARVN; here was the earliest expression of the policy that would be called "Vietnamization" after 1969.

U.S. policymakers between 1945 and 1954 were eager to maintain what might be called the "Francofication" of the war, and to encourage at the same time an early version of Vietnamization. Though gradually drawn into supporting the French and their Vietnamese allies with economic and military aid and moral support, and though willing to send U.S. agents and advisers to help oversee the administration of this aid, both Truman and Eisenhower refused to send U.S. combat troops. The best policy, they thought, would be an effective effort by the French. There should be reforms to attract the *attentistes,* or "fence sitters," including a gradual loosening of political control over the Associated States. The French must abandon their "childlike faith" in air power and take the war to the enemy on the ground and on all types of terrain.[54] And the French should build a Vietnamese army—"the prompt creation of an effective National Army is our best *if not our only hope* in Indochina," wrote the State Department's Livingston Merchant in 1951—which they must train and alongside which they then must fight.[55] A joint State-Defense report put this quaintly in late 1950: "Much of the stigma of colonialism can be removed if, where necessary, yellow men will be killed by yellow men rather than by white men alone."[56]

The best example of the U.S. unwillingness to commit its soldiers to war in Vietnam during this period, and the best example of its continued determination to promote the Francofication of the war, was Eisenhower's reluctance to intervene to save the French garrison at Dien Bien Phu in 1954. The French, surrounded and rapidly losing their perimeter to the advancing Viet Minh forces, urgently requested

U.S. military help. Eisenhower held a number of high-level discussions about what to do. He consulted congressional leaders, sent Dulles to cajole the British into helping the United States (through "united action") preserve Vietnam from communism, and even mulled over the possibility of using U.S. aircraft to attack the Viet Minh; "of course," said the president, if this were done "we'd have to deny it forever."[57] Eisenhower seemed to be looking for an opportunity to intervene.

But most recent historians of the American response to the Dien Bien Phu crisis have concluded that Eisenhower did not believe that U.S. military intervention was a good idea. Ike hated to say no to the French, and he was alive to the consequences should a French defeat lead to their decision to withdraw from Vietnam completely. Yet he was "convinced that no military victory is possible in that type of theater," that Vietnam, while strategically vital to the preservation of a noncommunist Southeast Asia, was tactically indefensible by U.S. troops. He therefore placed in the path of U.S. military intervention a series of conditions—congressional consent, British agreement on "united action," and a French promise to set a timetable for the achievement of independence by Vietnam—each one of which he knew was unlikely to be met. As Melanie Billings-Yun has written, Eisenhower "invited a public rejection of military action."[58] Of course, even after the French surrendered at Dien Bien Phu in May, conceded Vietnam above the seventeenth parallel to the Viet Minh at Geneva that summer, and then withdrew from the country altogether in 1955, Eisenhower refrained from sending U.S. forces. He hoped that the actions he did take, including increased economic and military support for the Saigon government, the informal attachment of South Vietnam to the newly formed Southeast Asia Treaty Organization (SEATO), and the CIA "black psy-war" orchestrated by Edward Lansdale, would be sufficient to stop the advance of communism in Southeast Asia. He continued to believe that military intervention would not be effective: if undertaken, he wrote a friend, it would "lay [us] open to the charge of imperialism and colonialism or—at the very least—objectionable paternalism."[59] Let Frenchmen kill the Viet Minh—or, if the Frenchmen failed, let Asians kill other Asians.[60]

Yet another theme of the Vietnam War prefigured in the period 1945 to 1954 was the extent to which U.S. presidents and their advisers believed American credibility was at stake in Vietnam and thus the certainty of humiliation should the United States fail to achieve its objectives there. For Lyndon Johnson, the prospect of personal and national humiliation offered powerful reasons to stay the course in Vietnam. Johnson thought his reputation, as a politician and a man, was on the line. To lose Vietnam to communism would ruin him politically, as surely, he felt, as the "loss" of China and bloody stalemate in Korea had wrecked Truman's presidency. Losing Vietnam would figuratively emasculate him: he would be the only U.S. president ever to have lost a war, and to an enemy whom Johnson scorned as sneaky, treacherous, and otherwise effeminate. In July 1965, as Johnson was making critical decisions to escalate the war rapidly (and without saying much about it publicly), he was confronted by his undersecretary of state, George W. Ball, who argued that the United States should withdraw from Vietnam rather than ratchet up the stakes by sending in more troops. In objecting to the president's plans, Ball quickly realized that Johnson's "main concern was to avoid undermining our credibility." Johnson returned to the issue several times during this conversation: "Wouldn't we lose all credibility by breaking the word of three presidents?" "No," Ball replied. Johnson asked again: "Aren't you basically troubled by what the world would say about our pulling out?" "No," said Ball once more. McGeorge Bundy took up the case; "the world, the country, and the Vietnamese people," he said, "would have alarming reactions if we got out." Even after Johnson began talks with the other side in 1968, the U.S. negotiating position was constrained by his, then Richard Nixon's, perception that American credibility would be shaken if the nation was seen as making too many concessions.[61]

The United States had not by 1954 committed itself nearly so heavily to the struggle. Still, in ways direct and indirect, U.S. decision-makers from the end of World War II to the Geneva Conference made reference to the stakes for American credibility in Vietnam. In late 1951, Korea and Indochina were on the agenda for a meeting between representatives from State, Defense, and the Joint Chiefs of Staff. Several speakers were glum about the fates of both places, prompting Paul Nitze, director of the State Department's policy planning staff, to warn, "If we get an armistice in Korea and then quietly swallow the loss of Indochina, the adverse public relations consequences would be tremendous. We should consider very carefully what is involved." (This in turn elicited a suggestion from General Omar Bradley, chairman of the Joint Chiefs, that perhaps "we could use the 'larger sanction' [i.e., the atomic bomb] in the Indochina situation as well as in Korea.")[62] Members of the Senate would express similar concerns. Meeting in the midst of the Dien Bien Phu debacle in April 1954, a group of senators discussed the wisdom of intervention. Walter F. George, a Georgia Democrat with clout among his colleagues on foreign policy matters, suggested that "if we don't go in we will lose face," whereupon Robert Kerr, an Oklahoma Democrat, "slammed that big fist of his down on the table saying, 'I'm not worried about losing my face; I'm worried about losing my ass'"—credibility of a different sort.[63] Mike Mansfield, the Democrat from Montana who would later become a sharp critic of U.S. intervention, had a different view in July 1954. Geneva, he claimed, "was a mistake; and the result is a failure of American policy. It is a profoundly humiliating result."[64] Mansfield had only to check the body language of the French and their allies following the signing of the accords to find confirmation for his views.[65]

Dean Acheson's influence spanned the Cold War, from his presence at its creation in the 1940s to his service as one of Lyndon Johnson's "wise men" during the darkest years in Vietnam. Prestige mattered a great deal to Acheson, who defined it as "the shadow cast by power." Prestige was indivisible in the superheated environment of the Cold War. In 1954, Acheson was no longer secretary of state, but he continued to think and talk about American power and prestige, and at a time when the problems of Vietnam were front-page news Acheson held forth with a group of former colleagues: "Our difficulty [about colonialism], I think we see so clearly now in connection with Indochina. That if this thing goes to pieces, does the whole thing go to pieces? Everything? Maybe it does. One reason perhaps it does is that there isn't anything to fall back on."[66] American prestige, and thus the credibility of the United States, would unravel if torn anywhere in the world.

There is one last recurrent theme in U.S. policy toward Vietnam during both periods, and it is in many ways the most striking of the eight themes discussed here. It is that, despite the generally upward trajectory of U.S. involvement in the conflict, there were at all times high level opponents of military intervention in Vietnam. This hardly needs demonstrating for the period after 1965. George Ball questioned escalation of the war in 1965, as noted above, and his criticisms were echoed then and especially later by General Matthew Ridgway, James Thomson, and Clark Clifford. Defense Secretary McNamara apparently suppressed growing doubts about the course of the war for several years, until the

fall of 1967, when he conveyed his concerns to the president. Many senators and members of Congress had by that time joined the chorus of
dissent. In the wake of the Tet Offensive in early 1968, McGeorge Bundy
and even Acheson decided that enough was enough; as Acheson put it,
"we must begin to take steps to disengage."[67]

It is perhaps less well known that many influential officials during
the period of 1945 to 1954 strongly opposed U.S. military intervention
in Indochina, and for many of the same reasons that their successors
did so after 1965. Matthew Ridgway was a doubter from the beginning,
arguing in May 1954 that the Vietnamese landscape was favorable to
guerrillas and that the U.S. would thus have to pay a tremendous price
to win.[68] Others in the military were similarly skeptical, agreeing with
General J. Lawton Collins that "if we go into Indochina with American
forces we will be there for the long pull. Militarily and politically we
would be in up to our necks." Vice Admiral Arthur C. Davis wrote, mem-
orably, on the fallacy of "partial involvement": "one cannot go over
Niagara Falls in a barrel only slightly."[69] Members of Congress, then as
later, warned against overcommitment. Representative Frederic Cou-
dert, a New York Republican, suggested in 1951 that the French war in
Indochina had more to do with Vietnamese nationalism than international communism; Republican Senator Barry Goldwater of Arizona
invoked the U.S. Declaration of Independence to explain Vietnamese
aspirations and to disparage the efforts of the French; and Senator
Theodore Green, a Democrat from Rhode Island, dismissed French
justifications for war as the usual shameful and self-defeating recourse
to the "white man's burden" argument.[70]

There were doubters in the State Department too, particularly those
with experience of East Asia or some bureaucratic responsibility for the
area. In 1946 and 1947, Abbot Low Moffat, chief of the Department's
Division of Southeast Asian Affairs, lamented his Europeanist colleagues' "fixation on the theory of monolithic, aggressive communism."[71] Livingston Merchant hoped to prevent U.S. aid flowing to the
Associated States at least until the French had agreed to promise them
independence at some future date. Officers in the State Department's
Division of Southeast Asian Affairs, including Moffat's successor
W. Walton Butterworth, Charles Reed, Kenneth P. Landon, and Charlton Ogburn Jr., tried without success to keep the United States from
unqualified support of the Bao Dai experiment. In early 1951, having
lost the battle but still hoping to keep in check U.S. aid for the Associ-

ated States, Ogburn let fly: "Can we not start being the judge of other peoples and stop being the one who is judged? Can we not be a little harder to get, and let the favor of the United States be what other peoples aspire to? Darn it, they are the ones who are threatened with a fate worse than death—not we."[72]

The highest-level dissenter during the 1950s was, of course, President Eisenhower. It is tempting to speculate on what might have been had Eisenhower been president instead during the 1960s, when the level of insurgency and North-to-South troop infiltration rose and the stability of the South Vietnamese government declined. When Johnson sought advice from Eisenhower in February 1965, the aging general told him that he might need to send troops to Vietnam and that nuclear weapons could not be ruled out.[73] Perhaps he had forgotten what he said eleven years before, or perhaps he no longer considered it relevant: "There was just no sense," he told the National Security Council then, "in even talking about United States forces replacing the French in Indochina. If we did so, the Vietnamese could be expected to transfer their hatred of the French to us. I can not tell you . . . how bitterly opposed I am to such a course of action. This war in Indochina would absorb our troops by divisions!"[74]

Despite his vehemence, or maybe shrewdly in search of confirmation of his views, Eisenhower allowed others, including members of Congress, to have their say. He studiously failed to attend a pivotal meeting between administration officials and leading lawmakers on April 3, 1954, though he had an important role in scripting it. What emerged was a formidable reluctance on the legislators' part to countenance sending U.S. forces to bail out the French at Dien Bien Phu. After the meeting, one of the senators who had attended returned to the Capitol and met with four colleagues, who were eager to debrief him. One of the four, Albert Gore of Tennessee, recalled what he had heard: "Eventually, the reaction of the congressional representatives was solicited, and, according to [the] Senator's description, he outlined his opposition and told us that he pounded the President's desk in the Oval Office to emphasize his opposition."[75] Someone got it wrong; the meeting was not held in the Oval Office. But there is no reason to doubt that strenuous opposition to intervention was registered that day by Senator Lyndon B. Johnson of Texas.

Mansfield, Acheson, Eisenhower, and especially Johnson—they should have seen it coming. The envelope was on the floor in front of them; they, and others, had even participated in the writing of the note inside. Santiago Nasar was too focused on other things to spot his warning, and to some extent that was true of U.S. foreign policymakers in the 1960s. More than that, policymakers missed the foretelling of the war because, deep down, they were arrogant enough to think that warnings didn't matter, that they could handle it, come what may. García Márquez lets readers know that Santiago Nasar was arrogant in his behavior toward the servant girl Divina Flor, whose wrist he grabbed on his fateful morning, and to whom he said, "The time has come for you to be tamed."[76] Santiago Nasar was dead within the hour. His certainty in his own strength and authority had made him vulnerable. So too with the United States, which had failed to heed the warnings sent forth from an earlier and more innocent time.

Notes

Contributors

Index

Notes

Abbreviations

AOM	Dépôt des archives d'outre-mer, Aix-en-Provence, France
CCS	Combined Chiefs of Staff
DDEL	Dwight D. Eisenhower Library, Abilene, Kansas
DDF	*Documents diplomatiques français*
DDRS	Declassified Documents Reference Service
FMA	Foreign Ministry Archive of the People's Republic of China
FO	Foreign Office
FRUS	*Foreign Relations of the United States*
HSTL	Harry S. Truman Library, Independence, Missouri
JCS	Joint Chiefs of Staff
MAE	Ministère des affaires étrangères, Paris
Memcon	Memorandum of conversation
NARA	National Archives and Records Administration, Washington, D.C.
PTNT	Phong trao nam tien (Southern Advance movement)
PRO	Public Record Office, Kew, Great Britain
RG	Record Group
SHAT	Service historique de l'armée de terre, Vincennes, France
WO	War Office

1. Introduction

1. "Dienbienphu," *New York Times*, May 6, 1954.
2. For various perspectives on the battle of Dien Bien Phu, see Bernard Fall, *Hell in a Very Small Place: The Siege of Dien Bien Phu* (New York: J. B. Lippincott, 1967); Jules Roy, *The Battle of Dienbienphu* (New York: Carroll and Graf, 1984),

Martin Windrow, *The Last Valley: Dien Bien Phu and the French Defeat in Vietnam* (New York: Da Capo Press, 2004); Pierre Rocolle, *Pourquoi Dien Bien Phu?* (Paris: L'Histoire Flammarion, 1968); Marcel Bigeard, *Pour une parcelle de gloire* (Paris: Plon, 1975); Vo Nguyen Giap, *Dien Bien Phu*, 5th ed. (Hanoi, 1994); Howard R. Simpson, *Dien Bien Phu: The Epic Battle America Forgot* (Washington: Brassey's, 1994); Douglas Porch, *The French Foreign Legion: A Complete History of the Legendary Fighting Force* (New York: HarperCollins, 1991); Lawrence S. Kaplan et al., *Dien Bien Phu and the Crisis of Franco-American Relations* (Wilmington: Scholarly Resources, 1997); John Prados, *The Sky Would Fall: Operation Vulture: The U.S. Bombing Mission in Indochina, 1954* (New York: Dial Press, 1986).

3. The literature on the war is large, though much of it is dated. See, for example, Yves Gras, *Histoire de la guerre d'Indochine* (Paris: Plon, 1992); Alain Ruscio, *La guerre française d'Indochine* (Paris: Complexe, 1992); Jacques de Folin, *Indochine, 1940–55: La fin d'une rêve* (Paris: Perrin, 1993); Philippe Devillers, *L'Histoire du Viet-Nam de 1940 à 1952* (Paris: Le Seuil, 1952); Jacques Dalloz, *The War in Indochina, 1945–1954*, trans. J. Bacon (New York: Rowman and Littlefield, 1990); Ellen J. Hammer, *The Struggle for Indochina* (Stanford: Stanford University Press, 1954); Bernard Fall, *Street without Joy* (Harrisburg, Penn.: Stackpole, 1961); Lloyd C. Gardner, *Approaching Vietnam: From World War II through Dienbienphu* (New York: Norton, 1988). On the war as experienced in one southern province (My Tho), see David W. P. Elliott, *The Vietnamese War: Revolution and Social Change in the Mekong Delta, 1930–1975* (Armonk, N.Y.: M. E. Sharpe, 2003), 115–162.

4. For a helpful overview of these issues, see Robert J. McMahon, "The Study of American Foreign Relations: National History or International History?" in Michael J. Hogan and Thomas G. Paterson, eds., *Explaining the History of American Foreign Relations* (Cambridge: Cambridge University Press, 1991), 12. For an appeal for new international histories of the Vietnam wars, see Fredrik Logevall, "Bringing in the 'Other Side': New Scholarship on the Vietnam Wars," *Journal of Cold War Studies* 3, no. 3 (November 2001): 77–93.

5. For a remarkable example, see Piero Gleijeses, *Conflicting Missions: Havana, Washington, and Africa, 1959–1976* (Chapel Hill: University of North Carolina Press, 2002).

6. Examples include Matthew Connelly, *A Diplomatic Revolution: Algeria's Fight for Independence and the Origins of the Post–Cold War Era* (New York: Oxford University Press, 2002) and Jeremi Suri, *Power and Protest: Global Revolution and the Rise of Détente* (Cambridge, Mass.: Harvard University Press, 2003).

7. Ralph B. Smith, *An International History of the Vietnam War*, 3 vols. (New York: St. Martin's Press, 1984–1990); Lloyd C. Gardner, *Approaching Vietnam*; Christopher Thorne, *Allies of a Kind: The United States, Britain, and the War against Japan, 1941–1945* (Oxford: Oxford University Press, 1978); Robert J. McMahon, *Colonialism and Cold War: The United States and the Struggle for Indonesian Independence* (Ithaca, N.Y.: Cornell University Press, 1981); Walter LaFeber, "Roosevelt, Churchill, and Indochina, 1942–1945," *American Historical Review* 80 (December 1975): 1277–1295.

8. For example, Robert K. Brigham, *Guerrilla Diplomacy: The NLF's Foreign Relations and the Viet Nam War* (Ithaca, N.Y.: Cornell University Press, 1999); William J. Duiker, *The Communist Road to Power in Vietnam*, 2nd ed. (Boulder: Westview, 1986); William J. Duiker, *Ho Chi Minh: A Life* (New York: Hyperion,

2002); Mark Bradley, *Imagining Vietnam and America: The Making of Postcolonial Vietnam, 1919–1950* (Chapel Hill: University of North Carolina Press, 2000).

9. Ilya V. Gaiduk, *Confronting Vietnam: Soviet Policy toward the Indochina Conflict, 1954–1963* (Stanford: Stanford University Press, 2003); Gaiduk, *The Soviet Union and the Vietnam War* (Chicago: Ivan R. Dee, 1996); Chen Jian, *Mao's China and the Cold War* (Chapel Hill: University of North Carolina Press, 2001); Qiang Zhai, *China and the Vietnam Wars, 1950–1975* (Chapel Hill: University of North Carolina Press, 2000). These same authors have contributed key essays in two collections that, like the present volume, have attempted in recent years to explore the Vietnam problem from a variety of national viewpoints. See Peter Lowe, ed., *The Vietnam War* (London: Macmillan, 1998) and Andreas Daum et al., eds., *America, the Vietnam War, and the World: Comparative and International Perspectives* (Cambridge: Cambridge University Press, 2003).

10. For example, Peter Busch, *All the Way with JFK? Britain, the U.S., and the Vietnam War* (Oxford: Oxford University Press, 2003); Peter Edwards, *Crises and Commitments: The Politics and Diplomacy of Australia's Involvement in Southeast Asian Conflicts, 1948–1965* (Sydney: Allen & Unwin, 1992); Mark Atwood Lawrence, *Assuming the Burden: Europe and the American Commitment to War in Vietnam* (Berkeley: University of California Press, 2005); and Fredrik Logevall, *Choosing War: The Lost Chance for Peace and the Escalation of War in Vietnam* (Berkeley: University of California Press, 1999).

11. Daniel Hémery and Pierre Brocheaux, *Indochine: La colonisation ambigue* (Paris: La Decouverte, 2004); Duiker, *The Communist Road to Power in Vietnam;* David G. Marr, *Vietnam 1945: The Quest for Power* (Berkeley: University of California Press, 1995). On the critical events of 1945, see also Stein Tønnesson, *The Vietnamese Revolution of 1945: Roosevelt, Ho Chi Minh, and de Gaulle in a World at War* (London: SAGE, 1991).

12. Lawrence, *Assuming the Burden,* chap. 3; Hammer, *Struggle,* 107–115.

13. Stein Tønnesson, *1946: Déclenchement de la guerre d'Indochine* (Paris: Harmattan, 1987); Martin Shipway, *The Road to War: France and Vietnam, 1944–1947* (Providence, R.I.: Berghahn Books, 1996); Philippe Devillers, *Paris, Saigon, Hanoi: Les Archives de la guerre 1944–1947* (Paris: Gallimard/Julliard, 1988); idem, *L'Histoire,* 289–310; Duiker, *Ho Chi Minh,* 353–383.

14. Gras, *Histoire,* 159–186.

15. Lawrence, *Assuming the Burden,* chap. 5; Joseph Buttinger, *Vietnam: A Dragon Embattled,* vol. 1 (New York: Frederick A. Praeger, 1967), 667–734.

16. Chen Jian, *Mao's China and the Cold War,* 118–144. See also Zhai, *China and the Vietnam Wars.*

17. Lawrence, *Assuming the Burden,* chap. 6; Ronald Spector, *United States Army in Vietnam: Advice and Support: The Early Years, 1941–1960* (Washington, D.C.: Center of Military History, U.S. Army, 1983), 97–121.

18. Michel Bodin, *Soldats d'Indochine, 1945–1954* (Paris: Harmattan, 1997).

19. Bernard Fall, *The Two Viet Nams* (New York: Praeger, 1964), 122–125; Henri Navarre, *Agonie de l'Indochine* (Paris: Plon, 1956), 62–88, 103–110.

20. See note 2 above.

21. Quoted in Robert D. Schulzinger, *A Time for War: The United States and Vietnam, 1941–1975* (New York: Oxford University Press, 1997), 66–67.

22. Spector, *Advice and Support,* 191–214; David L. Anderson, *Trapped by Success: The Eisenhower Administration and Vietnam, 1953–1961* (New York: Columbia University Press, 1991); Melanie Billings-Yun, *Decision against War: The Eisen-*

hower Administration and Dien Bien Phu (New York: Columbia University Press, 1988).

23. Chen, *Mao's China*, 138–144; Gaiduk, *Confronting Vietnam*, 28–53; James Cable, *The Geneva Conference of 1954 on Indochina* (New York: St. Martin's Press, 1986); Richard Immerman, "The United States and the Geneva Conference of 1954: A New Look," *Diplomatic History* 14, no. 1 (1990). See also Chen Jian's essay in the present volume.

2. Making Sense of the French War: The Postcolonial Moment and the First Vietnam War, 1945–1954

1. *Sondages* 16.4 (1954): 10.

2. Secretary of State to Paris embassy, Feb. 3, 1947, in U.S. Department of State, *Foreign Relations of the United States 1947, Vol. 6: The Far East* (Washington, D.C.: U.S. Government Printing Office, 1972), 67–68.

3. Nguyen Dinh Thi, "Nhan duong" (Recognizing the way), Dec. 31, 1947, reprinted in Vien Van Hoc, *Cach mang, khuang chien va doi song van hoc, 1945–1954:* Tap 1 (Revolution, resistance, and the literary life, 1945–1954: vol. 1) (Hanoi: Nha Xuat Ban Tac Pham Moi, 1985), 9, 18; translation in Kim N. B. Ninh, *A World Transformed: The Politics of Culture in Revolutionary Vietnam, 1945–1965* (Ann Arbor, Mich.: University of Michigan Press, 2002), 69, 70.

4. George C. Herring, *America's Longest War: The United States and Vietnam, 1950–1975,* 4th ed. (New York: McGraw Hill, 2002), xiii. See also George McT. Kahin, *Intervention: How America Became Involved in Vietnam* (New York: Knopf, 1986), and Marilyn B. Young, *The Vietnam Wars, 1945–1990* (New York: Harper, 1991).

5. The most important work focusing on the economic and postwar liberal order building dimensions of the Truman administration's decisions is Lloyd C. Gardner, *Approaching Vietnam: From World War II through Dienbienphu* (New York: Norton, 1988). See also Michael Schaller, *The American Occupation of Japan: The Origins of the Cold War in Asia* (New York: Oxford University Press, 1985), and William S. Borden, *The Pacific Alliance: United States Foreign Policy and Japanese Trade Recovery, 1947–1955* (Madison: University of Wisconsin Press, 1984). On domestic politics, see Robert Blum, *Drawing the Line: The Origins of the American Containment Policy in East Asia* (New York: Norton, 1982).

6. See, for instance, R. E. M. Irving, *The First Indochina War* (London: Croon Helm, 1975); Alain Ruscio, *La guerre française d'Indochine* (Paris: Complexes, 1992); Bernard B. Fall, *The Viet Minh Regime: Government and Administration in the Democratic Republic of Vietnam* (New York: Institute of Pacific Relations, 1956); and Ton That Thien, *The Foreign Politics of the Communist Party of Vietnam: A Study in Communist Tactics* (New York: Crane Russak, 1989).

7. Mark Atwood Lawrence, *Assuming the Burden: Europe and the American Commitment to War in Vietnam* (Berkeley: University of California Press, 2005). See also his "Transnational Coalition-Building and the Making of the Cold War in Indochina, 1947–1949," *Diplomatic History* 26 (Summer 2002): 453–480, and his essay on British policy in this volume.

8. See Stein Tønnesson, *The Vietnamese Revolution of 1945: Roosevelt, Ho Chi Minh and De Gaulle in a World at War* (London: Sage, 1991), and his *1946, Dé-*

clenchement de la guerre d'Indochine: les vêpres tonkinoises du 19 décembre (Paris: Harmattan, 1987).

9. Mark Philip Bradley, *Imagining Vietnam and America: The Making of Postcolonial Vietnam, 1919–1950* (Chapel Hill, N.C.: University of North Carolina Press, 2000).

10. Gary R. Hess, *The United States' Emergence as a Southeast Asian Power, 1940–1950* (New York: Columbia University Press, 1987).

11. French scholarship on the war has tended to operate in a largely national register, though more recently there has been some attention to the Vietnamese dimensions of the conflict. Among the most important works are: Philippe Devillers, *Histoire du Viet Nam de 1940 à 1952* (Paris: Seuil, 1952); Devillers, *Paris-Saigon-Hanoi: Les archives de la guerre, 1944–1947* (Paris: Gallimard, 1988); Michel Bodin, *La France et ses soldats: Indochine, 1945–1954* (Paris: Harmattan, 1996); Jacques Dolloz, *La guerre d'Indochine, 1945–1954* (Paris: Seuil, 1987); Georges Fleury, *La guerre en Indochine, 1945–1954* (Paris: Plon, 1994); and Ruscio, *La guerre française*. For an invaluable and comprehensive overview of French-language scholarship on the war, see Alain Ruscio, *La guerre "française" d'Indochine (1945–1954): les sources de la connaissance* (Paris: Indes Savantes, 2002).

12. Andrew Rotter, *The Path to Vietnam: The Origins of the American Commitment to Southeast Asia* (Ithaca, N.Y.: Cornell University Press, 1989). See also Ritchie Ovendale, "Britain, the United States and the Cold War in South-East Asia," *International Affairs 58* (summer 1982): 447–464.

13. Fred Logevall's forthcoming study of the French war promises to address this imbalance in important ways.

14. "National Intelligence Estimate, Indochina: Current Situation and Probable Developments," December 29, 1950 in *Foreign Relations of the United States (FRUS), 1950*, vol. 6: *East Asia and the Pacific* (Washington, D.C.: U.S. Government Printing Office, 1976): 868–869.

15. Heath (Saigon) to U.S. Secretary of State, November 27, 1950, *FRUS, 1950*, 6:939.

16. If the often fractious nature of American, French, and British relations over Vietnam after 1950 have yet to receive authoritative treatment grounded in archival sources, Kathryn Statler's essay in chapter 13 of this volume; Hugues Tertrais's *La piastre et le fusil: Le coût de la guerre d'Indochine, 1945–1954* (Paris: Comité pour l'histoire économique et financière de la France, 2002); Annie Roulet's *Un aspect des rapports franco-vietnamiens: la formation de l'armée vietnamienne, 1948–1954* (Université de Strasbourg III, 1988); and the essays collected in *Dien Bien Phu and the Crisis of Franco-American Relations, 1954–1955*, ed. Lawrence Kaplan et al. (Wilmington, Del.: Scholarly Resources Books, 1990), suggest the persistent problems that divided the Western alliance on Vietnam.

17. Qiang Zhai, *China and the Vietnam Wars, 1950–1975* (Chapel Hill: University of North Carolina Press, 2000), chaps. 1–3; and Chen Jian, "China and the First Indo-China War, 1950–1954," *China Quarterly* 133 (March 1993): 85–110.

18. Ministry of Foreign Affairs, Socialist Republic of Vietnam, *The Truth About Vietnam-China Relations over the Last Thirty Years* (Hanoi: Vietnamese Ministry of Foreign Affairs, 1979). See also Edwin E. Moise, *Land Reform in China and Vietnam: Consolidating the Revolution at the Village Level* (Chapel Hill: University

of North Carolina Press, 1983); Bui Tin, *Following Ho Chi Minh: Memoirs of a North Vietnamese Colonel* (Honolulu: University of Hawaii Press, 1995), 23–34, 44–56; and Georges Boudarel, "Comment Giap a failli perdre la bataille Dien Bien Phu," *Nouvel Observateur,* April 8, 1983, 97.

19. Zhai, *China and the Vietnam Wars,* 64.

20. Ilya Gaiduk, *Confronting Vietnam: Soviet Policy toward the Indochina Conflict, 1954–1963* (Stanford, Calif.: Stanford University Press, 2003), and Mari Olsen, *Solidarity and National Revolution: The Soviet Union and the Vietnamese Communists, 1954–1960* (Oslo: Institutt for forsvarsstudier, 1997).

21. Ilya Gaiduk, *The Soviet Union and the Vietnam War* (Chicago: Ivan R. Dee, 1996), 71.

22. Gaiduk, *Confronting Vietnam, 3.*

23. Sophie Quinn-Judge, *Ho Chi Minh: The Missing Years* (Berkeley: University of California Press, 2002).

24. Quinn-Judge, *Ho Chi Minh,* 206, 219, and 200–233 passim.

25. Gaiduk, *Confronting Vietnam,* 11.

26. Zhai, *China and the Vietnam Wars,* chaps. 1 and 2.

27. Gaiduk, *Confronting Vietnam,* 211.

28. See, for instance, Keith Taylor, "Surface Orientations in Vietnam: Beyond Histories of Nation and Region," *Journal of Asian Studies 57* (November 1998): 949–978.

29. Greg Lockhart, *Nation in Arms: The Origins of the People's Army of Vietnam* (Sydney: Allen and Unwin, 1989); Christopher Goscha, *Thailand and the Southeast Asian Networks of the Vietnamese Revolution, 1885–1954* (London: Curzon, 1999); and Bradley, chap. 5 of this volume.

30. *Cuoc Khang Chien Than Thanh cua Nhan Dan Viet Nam* (The Sacred Resistance War of the Vietnamese People), vol. 2 (Hanoi: Nha Xuat Ban Su That, 1958), 40–41, cited in Lockhart, *Nation in Arms,* 185.

31. Bradley, *Imagining Vietnam and America,* 148–149.

32. Lockhart, *Nation in Arms,* 188–221. See also Andrew Vickerman, *The Fate of the Peasantry: Premature "Transition to Socialism" in the Democratic Republic of Vietnam* (New Haven: Yale University Center for Southeast Asian Studies, 1986), 49–72, and Hy Van Luong, *Revolution in the Village: Tradition and Transformation in North Vietnam, 1925–1988* (Honolulu: University of Hawaii Press, 1992), 147–158.

33. Goscha, *Thailand and the Southeast Asian Networks;* Bradley, *Imagining Vietnam and America,* 151–158.

34. Goscha, *Thailand and the Southeast Asian Networks;* Bradley, *Imagining Vietnam and America,* 158–160; Lockhart, *Nation in Arms,* chap. 7.

35. Patricia M. Pelley, *Postcolonial Vietnam: New Histories of the National Past* (Durham, N.C.: Duke University Press, 2002).

36. Ibid., 82.

37. Ibid., 13.

38. Ibid., 59–60.

39. Besides Pelley and Ninh's work, see Shaun Kinsley Malarney, *Culture, Ritual and Revolution in Vietnam* (Honolulu: University of Hawaii Press, 2002), and Shawn McHale, "Vietnamese Marxism, Dissent and the Politics of Postcolonial Memory: Tran Duc Thao, 1946–1993," *Journal of Asian Studies 61* (February 2002): 7–31.

40. See, for instance, Georges Boudarel, *Cent fleurs éclosés dans la nuit du Vietnam:*

Communisme et dissidence, 1954–1956 (Paris: Jacques Bertoin, 1991), and Hirohide Kurihara, "Changes in the Literary Policy of the Vietnamese Workers' Party, 1956–1958," in Takashi Shiraishi and Motoo Furuta, eds., *Indochina in the 1940s and 1950s* (Ithaca, N.Y.: Cornell University Southeast Asia Program, 1992), 165–196. For an account of these issues drawing on newly available archives from Eastern Europe, see Balazs Szalontai, "Political and Economic Crisis in North Vietnam, 1954–1956," *Cold War History* 5 (November 2005): 395–426.

41. Ninh, *A World Transformed,* 184

42. Ibid., 236. For a more sustained analysis along these lines for the period after 1954, see Benedict J. Tria Kerkvliet, *The Power of Everyday Politics: How Vietnamese Peasants Transformed National Policy* (Ithaca, N.Y.: Cornell University Press, 2005).

43. Ninh, *A World Transformed,* 74, 82, and 68–82 passim.

44. Truong Chinh, "Chu nghia Mac va van hoa Viet Nam" (Marxism and Vietnamese Culture), 1948, in *Ve Van hoa va nghe thuat* (Culture and Thought), vol. 1 (Hanoi: Van Hoc, 1985).

45. To view To Ngoc Van's *Two Young Girls and a Child* and *Militia Woman,* see www.iapone.org/Pages/To_Ngoc_Van.html (accessed Jan. 19, 2006).

46. Nora A. Taylor, "Framing the National Spirit: Viewing and Reviewing Painting under the Revolution," in Hue-Tam Ho Tai, ed., *The Country of Memory: Remaking the Past in Late Socialist Vietnam* (Berkeley: University of California Press, 2001), 109–134. See also Hue-Tam Ho Tai, *Painters in Hanoi: An Ethnography of Vietnamese Art* (Honolulu: University of Hawaii Press, 2004).

47. Ninh, *A World Transformed,* 126–141.

48. Ibid., 139.

49. Taylor, "Framing the National Spirit," 123–124. See also Bui Xuan Phai, *Viet duoi anh den dau* (Hanoi: Nha Xuat Ban My Thuat, 2000). To view representative images of Phai's Hanoi streetscapes, see www.iapone.org/Pages/Phai_SITES.html (accessed Jan. 19, 2006).

50. Jane Bradley Winston, *Postcolonial Duras: Cultural Memory in Postwar France* (New York: Palgrave, 2001). For nuanced discussions of French public opinion drawing on the regular polling by the Institut français d'opinion publique, see Paul Clay Sorum, *Intellectuals and Decolonization in France* (Chapel Hill, N.C.: University of North Carolina Press, 1977), 5–12, and Serge Tignères, *La guerre d'Indochine et l'opinion publique française entre 1954 et 1994: mémoire et histoire* (Toulouse: Université de Toulouse–Le Mirail, 1999).

51. Winston, *Postcolonial Duras,* 46.

52. Stephen J. Whitfield, "Limited Engagement: *The Quiet American* as History," *Journal of American Studies* 30 (April 1996): 65–86. See also Jonathan Nashel, "Fictions of Quiet and Ugly Americans" in his *Edward Lansdale's Cold War* (Amherst, Mass.: University of Massachusetts Press, 2005), 149–186.

53. Whitfield, "Limited Engagement," 72.

54. Michael Adas, *Dominance by Design: Technological Imperatives and America's Civilizing Mission* (Cambridge, Mass.: Harvard University Press, 2006). See also James Scott, *Seeing Like at State: How Certain Schemes to Improve the Human Condition Have Failed* (New Haven, Conn.: Yale University Press, 1998).

55. Dipesh Chakrabarty, *Provincializing Europe: Postcolonial Thought and Historical Difference* (Princeton, N.J.: Princeton University Press, 2000), 8.

56. Matthew Connelly, *A Diplomatic Revolution: Algeria's Fight for Independence and*

the *Origins of the Post–Cold War Era* (New York: Columbia University Press, 2002). For a similarly complex and suggestive rethinking of the Cold War in Latin America, see Greg Grandin, *The Last Colonial Massacre: Latin America in the Cold War* (Chicago: University of Chicago Press, 2004).

3. Vietnamese Historians and the First Indochina War

1. Vietnamese scholarship refers to the First Indochina War as the "Cuoc khang chien chong thuc dan Phap" or the Resistance Struggle against Colonial France. I will refer to the conflict as the "French war" in order to differentiate it from the Second Indochina War against the United States and Republic of Vietnam and from the Third Indochina War against the People's Republic of China and Democratic Kampuchea.

2. The fiftieth anniversary of Dien Bien Phu is the most recent example of the importance of the French War's legacy in Vietnam today. Party and state efforts to commemorate the battle included the inauguration of "Dien Bien Phu Tourism Year 2004," a month-long exhibition at the Vietnam Military History Museum; the May 7 celebration at Dien Bien Phu stadium; and scores of new and revised scholarship including Vo Nguyen Giap's own memoir of the event. The official goals of the commemoration ceremonies were "to promote patriotism, educate historical tradition and introduce significance and broad impact of Dien Bien Phu victory." See *Nhan Dan* (The People), 4 March 2004.

3. For the purposes of this chapter, studies from the former Democratic Republic of Vietnam or North Vietnam (1955 to 1976) and from the Socialist Republic of Vietnam (1976 to the present) are included. Works published in the Republic of Vietnam (South Vietnam, 1955 to 1975) and from diasporic presses are not included.

4. There exist numerous memoirs and writings by key figures of the French war, including Ho Chi Minh, General Vo Nguyen Giap, Pham Van Dong, Truong Chinh, Le Duan, Hoang Van Thai, Le Trong Tan, Chu Van Tan, and Dang Van Viet, many of which have been translated into English. Since these texts constitute primary sources, I did not include them in the survey of the historiography.

5. For regional and provincial studies, see *Mien Nam bo khang chien, 1945–1975* (The Southern Struggle, 1945–1975) (Hanoi: Quan Doi Nhan Dan, 1990); Dang Van Bat, ed., *Ha Tay: Lich Su Khang Chien Chong Thuc Dan Phap* (Ha Tay: History of the Resistance Struggle against Colonial France) (Hanoi, Quan Doi Nhan Dan, 1998); Phan Thanh Son, ed., *Lich Su Dang Bo Quang Tri* (History of the Communist Party of Quang Tri) (Hanoi: Chinh Tri Quoc Gia, 1996); *Lich Su Dang Bo Tinh Quang Ngai, 1945–1975* (History of the Communist Party of Quang Ngai Province, 1945–1975) (Hanoi: Chinh Tri Quoc Gia, 1999); *Lich Su Khang Chien Chong Phap Khu Ta Ngan Song Hong, 1945–1955* (The History of the Resistance War against Colonial France in the Red River Delta) (Hanoi: Chinh Tri Quoc Gia, 1999); *Lich Su Dang Bo Tinh Hung Yen, Tap 1:1929–1954* (The History of the Communist Party in Hung Yen Province, vol. 1: 1929–1954) (Hanoi: Chinh Tri Quoc Gia, 1998).

6. On December 22, 1946, the Viet Minh government issued a proclamation that it intended to adopt what was essentially the Chinese model of warfare. By 1947, General Secretary Truong Chinh, in a series of articles published

between March and August, made explicit the Vietnamese revolution's appropriation of Mao's model to suit Vietnamese conditions. These essays were later published in a single volume. See Truong Chinh, *Khang chien nhat dinh thang loi* (The Resistance Will Win) (Hanoi: Su That, 1948).

7. In November 1945, Ho Chi Minh made the controversial decision to dissolve the ICP, although the Party apparatus continued to exist, due to the presence of the Chinese nationalist troops and the need to appeal to non-communist nationalists in northern Vietnam. In southern Vietnam, the situation was more dire for the communists due to armed clashes not only with freed French troops and General Douglas Gracey's British soldiers, but also the violent jockeying for power with the sects, Trotskyites, and urban nationalists. Moreover, commanders in the southern region, including first Tran Van Giau and later Nguyen Binh, often exceeded or disregarded orders from the party.

8. See "Nghi quyet cua Hoi nghi Toan quoc lan thu ba" (Resolution of the Third National Party Conference), January 21–February 3, 1950 in *Van Kien Dang* (Party Documents), comp. Dang Cong Sang (Communisty Party), 39 vols. (Hanoi: Chinh Tri Quoc Gia, 2004), Vol. 11 (1950). See also *Chien Tranh Cach Mang Viet Nam, 1945–1975* (Vietnam's Revolutionary War, 1945–1975) (Hanoi: Chinh Tri Quoc Gia, 2000), 125.

9. Tran Huy Lieu, "Diem lai thuyet 'Ba Giai Doan' cua chung ta" (Reanalysis of Our Three-Stage Theory), *Nghien Cuu Lich Su (NCLS)*, vol. 34, November 1957, 1–5.

10. Lieu served as minister of propaganda during the French war and after 1954, and he remained a high-level party member and influential historian. His interpretation could be considered as the *revised* official view rather than a challenge to the party interpretation.

11. The offensives include: Tran Hung Dao campaign at Vinh Phuc in early 1951, the Ha Nam Ninh and Hoang Hoa Tham campaigns of 1951, the Hoa Binh operations from the end of 1951 to early 1952, and the Tay Bac (Northwest) campaign at the end of 1952 and in early 1953.

12. Lieu, "Diem lai thuyet 'Ba Giai Doan' cua chung ta," 5. Lieu's argument that the French war never witnessed a general counteroffensive was most likely part of a burgeoning trend to divert attention southwards after nation-wide elections failed to materialize in 1956. Following a violent land reform and organizational rectification campaign that greatly damaged the party's prestige in the eyes of the people, Le Duan's 1957 manifesto, entitled "The Path to Revolution in the South," constituted the first declaration that reunification would be a long-term goal, marking the start of an agenda shift from northern development to southern war in the party. Lieu's article on the French war, appearing on the heels of Le Duan's influential publication, must be read in the context of these events.

13. *Tong ket cuoc khang chien chong thuc dan Phap* (Summary of the Resistance Struggle Against Colonial France) (Hanoi: Chinh Tri Quoc Gia, 1996).

14. Like Lieu's articles, the 1996 study constitutes the reconceptualized official line rather than a challenge to the "revisionist" view. By the mid-1990s, the party needed to balance the task of liberalizing the economy and of maintaining ideological and political power. The official survey which represents a compromise interpretation can be read as the application of this balancing policy to the writing of history.

15. Tran Huy Lieu,"De ra viec lich su khang chien" (On the subject of writing the history of the Resistance), *NCLS*, vol. 45, December 1962, 1–2.
16. Ibid., 1.
17. By 1962, Secretary General Le Duan and his faction promoted revolutionary war over peaceful coexistence. Urging academics to study how the home-front aided the battlefront during the French war, Lieu's 1962 article supported Le Duan, who wanted to relegate northern development (home-front) to supporting southern war (battlefront).
18. See figures in *Tong ket cuoc khang chien chong thuc dan Phap*, 190.
19. See Bui Dinh Thanh, Ngo Tien Chat, Luu Trac, and Le Gia Xung, *Am muu cua de quoc Phap-My trong chien dich Dien Bien Phu* (The French-American Imperialist Plot during the Dien Bien Phu Victory) (Hanoi: Su Hoc, 1963), 5.
20. "Ky niem 25 nam ngay toan quoc khang chien chong thuc dan Phap" [25th Anniversary of the Total Victory over the Colonial France], *NCLS*, vol. 141, November and December 1971, 2.
21. Pham Quang Toan, "Tim hieu vai tro cua nhan to chinh tri-tinh than trong cuoc khang chien chong Phap va trong cuoc khang chien chong My hien nay" (Understanding the Role Played by the Political-Intellectual Factor in the past French war and the present American War), *NCLS*, vol. 111, June 1968, 3–14.
22. Ngo Tien Chat, "Vai net ve truyen thong dau tranh anh dung cua nhan dan cac dan toc Viet Bac trong cuoc khang chien chong Phap, 1945–1954" (Few Aspects Concerning the Tradition of the Struggle of Great Fortitude of the People of All Ethnicities in Viet Bac during the French war), *NCLS*, vol. 122, May 1969, 4–13.
23. Following Le Duan's handling of the "General Offensive-General Uprising" of 1968 with its disastrous second and third waves, scholarship needed to boost confidence in party leadership and maintain popular support for the new stage of fighting after the Tet Offensive and with the initiation of peace negotiations at Paris.
24. In 1973, armed clashes took place at the Sino-Vietnamese border that increased to approximately 200 clashes in 1974. In Cambodia, Pol Pot's forces began attacking North Vietnamese arms depots, hospitals, and base camps in 1974.
25. The Chinese offensive in 1979 took place in the same region as Vietnam's 1950 Border Offensive against the French. See Phan Huy Thiep's 1980 article, "Buoc dau tim hieu mot so van de ve su chi dao nghe thuat quan su cua dang trong chien dich bien gioi thu-dong 1950" (The Initial Understanding of Aspects Regarding the Military Operatics of the party during the Border Campaign of the Fall and Winter, 1950), *NCLS*, vol. 2 (191), March–April 1980, 7. The author states that on the thirtieth anniversary of the Border Campaign, the Chinese aggression in the area took on another meaning. It is also interesting to note that in listing the nations that recognized the DRV in 1950, the author does not mention the very first nation to do so, the People's Republic of China.
26. Nguyen Anh Thai, "Am muu cua Trung Quoc tu Dien Bien Phu den Gio Ne Ve" (The Chinese Plot from Dien Bien Phu to Geneva), *NCLS*, vol. 6 (213), 1983, 32.
27. See Chou En Lai's comments made on October 8, 1953, to Beijing Press Agency.

28. The PRC went to Geneva with the largest delegation of 200 representatives. See Nguyen Anh Thai, "Am muu cua Trung Quoc," 33.

29. Ibid., 33.

30. See *Su that ve quan he giua Viet Nam-Trung Quoc trong 30 nam qua* (The Truth About Sino-Vietnamese Relations over the past 30 years) (Hanoi: Ministry of Foreign Affairs, 1979), 18–23.

31. See Nguyen Hao Hung, "Chien thang Dien Bien Phu: chien thang chung cua lien minh doan ket chien dau Viet Nam-Lao-Campuchia" (The Dien Bien Phu Victory: The Allied Victory of the Resistance of Vietnam, Laos and Cambodia), *NCLS,* vol. 1 (214), 1984, 45.

32. Pham Duc Thanh, *Lich Su Campuchia* (Cambodian History) (Hanoi: Van Hoa Thong Tin, 1995), 203.

33. Hoang Van Thai, *Lien minh doan ket chien dau Viet Nam, Campuchia, Lao* (Hanoi: Su That, 1983), 20–21.

34. In addition, Do Muoi replaced Pham Van Dong as prime minister. However, the shift was not extremely radical since Nguyen Van Linh, Do Muoi, Vo Chi Cong, Vo Van Kiet, and others who rose in 1986 were all protegés of Le Duan and/or Le Duc Tho. Events, rather than personalities, would force the significant changes in Vietnamese foreign and domestic policies.

35. According to Hanoi's foremost diplomatic historian, Luu Van Loi, the Soviet Union opposed the presence of the revolutionary parties of Cambodia and Laos at Geneva since Moscow "wanted to avoid issues where its interests were at stake" while China continued to help the Pathet Lao and the Khmer Issarak even though it had recognized the royal governments in both countries. See Luu Van Loi, "45 nam nhin lai: hiep dinh Gio-Ne-Ve ve Viet Nam, phan 1" (45 years in retrospect: the Geneva Accords regarding Vietnam), *Lich Su Quan Su (LSQS),* part 1 in 4 (118) 7&8/1999; part 2 in 5 (119) 9&10/1999.

36. See *Tong ket cuoc khang chien chong thuc dan Phap,* pp. 209–217; Luu Van Loi, *Nam muoi nam ngoai giao Vietnam (1945–1995), Tap 1* (50 Years of Vietnamese Diplomacy, 1945–1995, vol. 1) (Hanoi: Cong An Nhan Dan, 1996). However, see a recent editorial in *Quan Doi Nhan Dan* (People's Army Daily) on March 28 2004 by General Giap's interpreter, Hoang Minh Phuong, on Giap's relations with CMAG and the decision-making behind Dien Bien Phu. The editorial states that although Giap had been advised by Chinese advisors to attack French units fast and hard, Giap changed plans at the last minute to undertake a slow and steady ambush.

37. See Phan Ngoc Lien and Trinh Vuon Hong, "Quan he Viet-My trong nhung nam 1945–1954" (Vietnam-U.S. relations in the period from 1945–1954), *NCLS,* vol. 273 (1994), 29–35.

38. See "Ky niem 25 nam," 2.

39. See Bui Dinh Thanh, "Chien thang Dien Bien Phu—mot cung hien to lon vao phong trao giai phong dan toc trong the ky XX" (The Dien Bien Phu Victory: A Grand Dedication to the Peoples' Liberation Movement of the Twentieth Century), *NCLS,* vol. 2(273), Issues 3&4, 1994, 1–8. See also Cao Van Luong, "Y nghia lich su va tam voc thoi dai cua cuoc khang chien chong thuc dan Phap" (The Historical Meaning of the Great Stature of the Resistance Against the Colonialist French), *NCLS,* 5(230), 1986, 5–6.

40. Mai Ly Quang, ed., *The 30-Year War, 1945–1975,* vol. 1 (Hanoi: The Gioi Publishers, 2002), 224.

41. Luong, "Y nghia lich su," 4.
42. Le Kim Hai, *Ho Chi Minh voi quan he ngoai giao Viet-Phap, Thoi ky 1945–1945* (Ho Chi Minh and diplomatic relations between Vietnam and France, 1945–1946) (Hanoi: Dai Hoc Quoc Gia, 1999).
43. See Nguyen Phuc Luan, ed., *Ngoai Giao Vietnam Hien Dai, 1945–1975* (Modern Vietnamese Diplomacy) (Hanoi: Chinh Tri Quoc Gia, 2001), 104–106.
44. Ibid., 110.
45. Phan Ngoc Lien, "Cuoc khang chien chong thuc dan Phap cua nhan dan Vietnam: trong sach giao khoa lich su cac nuoc phuong Tây" (The Vietnamese Peoples' Resistance against Colonial France in Western Textbooks), *LSQS*, vols. 3 and 4, 1988, 9–13.
46. Ibid, 11.
47. See Nguyen Thanh, "Tap thu muc gan day du ve cuoc chien tranh Viet-Phap 1945–1954" (A nearly complete bibliographic study regarding the Vietnamese-French War 1945–1954), *LSQS*, vol. 4 (118), July and August 1999, 46–47.

4. Franklin Roosevelt, Trusteeship, and Indochina: A Reassessment

1. The chapter builds on Stein Tønnesson, *The Vietnamese Revolution of 1945: Roosevelt, Ho Chi Minh, and de Gaulle in a World at War* (London: Sage Publications, (1991). Portions from the chapter "Interpretations of Roosevelt's Policy" reprinted in revised from by permission of Sage Publications Ltd.
2. See Russell H. Fifield, "American Policy toward Indochina during the Second World War: Some Tentative Conclusions," in James E. O'Neill and Robert Krauskopf, eds., *World War II: An Account of Its Documents* (Washington, D.C.: Harvard University Press, 1976), 59–70; Donald Cameron Watt, "Britain, America, and Indo-China, 1942–1945," in Watt, ed., *Succeeding John Bull, America in Britain's Place, 1900–1975* (Cambridge: Cambridge University Press, 1984), 194–219; Watt, "Britain and the Historiography of the Yalta Conference and the Cold War," *Diplomatic History* 13, no. 1 (winter 1989): 67–98.
3. Bernard Fall, *Last Reflections on a War* (New York: Doubleday, 1967), 133, and Arthur M. Schlesinger Jr., *The Bitter Heritage: Vietnam and American Democracy 1941–1966* (London: Andre Deutsch, 1967), 11.
4. Senator Mike Gravel, ed., *The Pentagon Papers: The Defense Department History of United States Decisionmaking on Vietnam* (Boston: Beacon Press, 1971), vol. 1, 2.
5. Edward R. Drachman, *United States Policy toward Vietnam, 1940–1945* (Cranbury, N.J.: Fairleigh Dickinson University Press, 1970), 93–94, 161–162.
6. Gary R. Hess, "Franklin Roosevelt and Indochina," *Journal of American History* 59 (September 1972): 356, 363, 367ff.
7. Christopher Thorne, "Indochina and the Anglo-American Relations 1942–45," *Pacific Historical Review* 45 (February 1976): 95–96.
8. William Roger Louis, *Imperialism at Bay, 1941–1945: The United States and the Decolonization of the British Empire* (Oxford: Clarendon Press, 1977), 27–28, 41.
9. Walter LaFeber, "Roosevelt, Churchill, and Indochina: 1942–45," *The American Historical Review* 80 (December 1975): 1288, 1291.
10. Fifield, "American Policy toward Indochina," 61–63.
11. George C. Herring, "The Truman Administration and the Restoration of French Sovereignty in Indochina," *Diplomatic History* 1 (1977): 97.
12. George C. Herring, *America's Longest War: The United States and Vietnam, 1950–1975* (New York: Wiley and Sons, 1979), 6.

13. Robert Dallek, *Franklin D. Roosevelt and American Foreign Policy, 1932–1945* (New York: Oxford University Press, 1979), 512–513; George McT. Kahin, *Intervention: How America Became Involved in Vietnam* (New York: Knopf, 1986), 4; Robert J. McMahon, "A Strategic Perspective on U.S. Involvement," in McMahon, ed., *Major Problems in the History of the Vietnam War* (Lexington, Mass.: D. C. Heath, 1995), 104; McMahon, *The Limits of Empire: The United States and Southeast Asia Since World War II* (New York: Columbia University Press, 1999), 18.

14. Minutes of Roosevelt-Stalin meeting, Feb. 8, 1945, *FRUS, 1945, The Conferences at Malta and Yalta* (Washington, D.C.: U.S. Government Printing Office, 1955): 770.

15. Gary R. Hess, *The United States' Emergence as a Southeast Asian Power, 1940–1950* (New York: Columbia University Press, 1987), 141, 144, 149, 153, 158.

16. Lloyd C. Gardner, *Approaching Vietnam: From World War II through Dienbienphu, 1941–1954* (New York: Norton, 1988), 50–52.

17. Robert A. Divine, *Roosevelt and World War II* (Baltimore, Md.: Johns Hopkins University Press, 1970), 57–65.

18. This is LaFeber's principal argument in "Roosevelt, Churchill, and Indochina."

19. Mark Philip Bradley, *Imagining Vietnam and America: The Making of Postcolonial Vietnam, 1919–1950* (Chapel Hill, N.C.: University of North Carolina Press, 2000).

20. Tønnesson, *The Vietnamese Revolution*, 163–167, 214–215, 260–261.

21. Roy E. Appleman, et al., *Okinawa: The Last Battle* (Washington, D.C.: U.S. Department of the Army, 1948), 428.

22. Note from Leahy to "AJM," Oct. 17, 1944, Combined Chiefs of Staff, 401 (10–11–44), RG 218, NARA.

23. Joint Logistics Plans Committee Directive, "Indo China as a Substitute for the Burma Supply Route," Oct. 21, 1944, CCS 401 (10–11–44), RG 218, NARA; memo by Joint Chiefs of Staff Secretary with enclosure "Indochina as a Substitute for the Burma Supply Route, Report by the Joint Staff Planners" and draft "Memorandum for the President from Admiral Leahy," Oct. 30, 1944, CCS 401 (10–11–44), RG 218, NARA.

24. President Roosevelt to Edward Stettinius, Jan. 1, 1945: *FRUS, 1945*, 6:293.

25. Protocol of Proceedings of the Crimea Conference, Feb. 11, 1945, *FRUS, The Conferences at Malta and Yalta, 1945:* 977.

26. Herring, *America's Longest War*, 5–6; Drachman, *United States Policy*, 51–52, 91.

27. Protocol of Proceedings of the Crimea Conference, Feb. 11, 1945, *FRUS, The Conferences at Malta and Yalta, 1945:* 977.

28. Roosevelt-Stalin meeting, Feb. 8, 1945, *FRUS, The Conferences at Malta and Yalta, 1945:* 770.

29. George Marshall to General MacArthur, Feb. 7, 1945, box 89, Leahy Files, RG 218, NARA.

30. Joint Planning Staff memo, Feb. 27, 1945, "Integration of China Theater Operations with Campaign in the Pacific," box 1537, RG 332 (China Theater), NARA.

31. Minutes of Roosevelt-Stalin meeting, Feb. 8, 1945, *FRUS, The Conferences at Malta and Yalta, 1945:* 770.

32. David Stafford, *Roosevelt and Churchill: Men of Secrets* (London: Abacus, 2000), 118–120.

33. Report based on Magic intercepts, SRH-200, RG 457, NARA.

34. "Recent Political Developments in French Indo-China," April 6, 1945, SRH-095, RG 457, NARA.

35. The present author has failed to find evidence that Roosevelt had anything to do with preparing for the raid.

36. Summary of Magic intercepts, SRS 306, Jan. 20, 1945, Magic Far East Summaries, box 4, RG 457, NARA.

37. Summary of Magic intercepts, no. 1053, Feb. 11, 1945, box 13, Diplomatic Magic Summaries, RG 457, NARA.

38. "Recent Political Developments in French Indo-China," April 6, 1945, SRH-095, RG 457, NARA.

39. Summary of Magic intercepts, no. 1063, Feb. 21, 1945; no. 1068, Feb. 26, 1945; no. 1070, Feb. 28, 1945, box 13, RG 457, NARA.

40. Summary of Magic intercepts, no. 1071, March 1, 1945; no. 1073, March 3, 1945; no. 1075, March 5, 1945, box 13, RG 457, NARA.

41. Intercepted document (Magic), Doc. H-171612, March 3, 1945, quoted in "Recent Political Developments."

42. Summary of Magic intercepts, no. 1079, March 9, 1945, box 13, RG 457, NARA.

43. Michael Schaller, *The U.S. Crusade in China, 1938–1945* (New York: Columbia University Press, 1979), 216–217.

44. Jim Bishop, *FDR's Last Year: April 1944–April 1945* (New York: William Morrow, 1974), 491; Albert C. Wedemeyer, *Wedemeyer Reports!* (New York: Henry Holt, 1958), 340; Drachman, *United States Policy*, 84.

45. James M. Merrill, *A Sailor's Admiral: A Biography of William F. Halsey* (New York: Thomas Y. Crowell, 1976), 210.

46. Memcon, Charles Taussig with Roosevelt, March 15, 1945, *FRUS, 1945,* 1: 124.

47. Minutes of SWNCC Subcommittee, Far East Meeting, March 23, 1945, film T 1198, RG 353, NARA.

48. Bishop, *FDR's Last Year,* 516. Bishop does not give any source for this information.

49. Joint Planning Staff document, JPS 687/D, May 30, 1945, Section 1-B, American-British Cooperation 384 Indo-China (Dec. 16, 1944), RG 165, NARA.

50. Patrick Hurley to Truman, May 28, 1945, box 3, Map Room Files, HSTL.

51. British Chiefs of Staff memo, March 30, 1945, with draft telegram from Churchill to Roosevelt, CAB 122/1171, PRO.

52. Hollis to Churchill, March 31, 1945, PREM 3/178/2; Churchill to Hollis, March 31, 1945, PREM3/178/3, PRO.

53. Churchill to Brigadier L. C. Hollis, April 3, 1945, PREM 3/178/3, PRO.

54. Churchill to Roosevelt, April 11, 1945, in Warren E. Kimball, ed., *Churchill and Roosevelt: The Complete Correspondence* (Princeton, N.J.: Princeton University Press, 1984), vol. 3, 626–627; William Leahy to George Marshall, with copy of the telegram from Churchill, April 11, 1945, Section 1-B, ABC 384 Indochina (Dec. 16, 1944), RG 165, NARA.

55. Henri Bonnet to Stettinius, April 14, 1945, Section 1-B, ABC 384 Indo-China (Dec. 16, 1944), RG 165, NARA.

56. Edward Stettinius to Truman, "Policy Manual," April 16, 1945, box 159, President's Secretary's Files, HSTL. The source for the paragraph on Indochina is Roosevelt to Stettinius, Nov. 3, 1944, *FRUS, 1944,* 3:780.

57. *Causes, Origins and Lessons of the Vietnam War: Hearings before the Committee on*

Foreign Relations, United States Senate, 92nd Congress, second session, May 9–11, 1972 (Washington, D.C.: U.S. Government Printing Office, 1973), 167, 175–176.

58. Note on WDSCA 334 State-War-Navy Coordinating Committee by Hilldring, April 21, 1945; memo by Chief of Staff, U.S. Army, undated (probably April 23, 1945), Section 1-B, ABC 384 Indo-China, Dec. 16, 1944, RG 165, NARA; Joints Chiefs of Staff memo, "Policy with Respect to Indo-China," April 27, 1945; unsigned note, May 4, 1945, all in Section 5, CCS 370 France (8-5-44), RG 218, NARA.

59. Drachman, *United States Policy,* 56.

60. Joseph Grew to Jefferson Caffery, May 9, 1945, *FRUS, 1945,* 6:307, and Joseph Grew to Patrick Hurley, June 2, 1945, *FRUS, 1945,* 6:312.

61. Patrick Hurley to Roosevelt, May 28, 1945, Box 3, Map Room Files, HSTL.

62. Albert Wedemeyer to George Marshall, May 28, 1945, French Indo-China, Book-1, box 1562, China Burma India Theater, RG 332, NARA.

63. Cordell Hull to Albert Wedemeyer, June 4, 1945, Section 1-B, ABC 384 Indochina, Dec. 16, 1944, RG 165, NARA.

64. Truman to Patrick Hurley, June 4, 1945, box 4, Map Room Files, HSTL.

65. Patrick Hurley to Joseph Grew, June 6, 1945, box 3, Map Room Files, HSTL.

66. Joseph Grew to Patrick Hurley, June 7, 1945, Section 1-B, ABC 384 Indochina (16 Dec 44), RG 165, NARA.

67. Archimedes L. Patti, *Why Vietnam? Prelude to America's Albatross* (Berkeley: University of California Press, 1980), 120.

68. Russell D. Buhite, *Patrick J. Hurley and American Foreign Policy* (Ithaca, N.Y.: Cornell University Press, 1973), 247, 252.

69. Joseph Grew to Henry Stimson, "Policy Paper Prepared in the Department of State," June 28, 1945, *FRUS, 1945,* 6:568.

70. The author has sought, without complete success, to establish the following chain: If it had not been for Roosevelt's Indochina policy, those U.S. actions that led Japan to fear an Allied invasion of Indochina would not have been carried out. If Japan had not feared a U.S. invasion, it would not have carried out the March 9 coup. If it had not been for the March 9 coup, there would not have been a power vacuum in Indochina, and then the Viet Minh would not have seized power and proclaimed an independent republic in August. Attempts to establish the chain may be found in Stein Tønnesson, *The Vietnamese Revolution of 1945.*

5. Creating Defense Capacity in Vietnam, 1945–1947

1. *Co Giai Phong* (Hanoi), no. 16 (Sept. 12, 45).

2. Philippe Héduy, ed., *Histoire de l'Indochine,* vol. 2 (Paris: Société de Production Litteraire/Henri Veyrier, 1983), 285.

3. Tran Van Giau et al., *Lich Su Sai Gon—Cho Lon—Gia Dinh Khang Chien, 1945–1975* (History of Saigon, Cho Lon, Gia Dinh Resistance, 1945–1975) (Ho Chi Minh City: NXB TPHCM, 1994), 42.

4. Archimedes L. A. Patti, *Why Viet Nam?: Prelude to America's Albatross* (Berkeley: University of California Press, 1980), 349.

5. Tran Van Giau et al., *Lich Su Sai Gon,* 45. Texts of relevant north-south exchanges have never been published, nor has any memoir revealed the content of Hanoi deliberations from September 23 to 25.

6. Vien Lich Su Quan Su Viet Nam, *Phong Trao Nam Tien (1945–1946)* (Southern Advance Movement, 1945–1946) (Hanoi: QDND, 1997), 36. This will hereafter be referred to as the PTNT.

7. "Gui Dong bao Nam bo" (A Message to Southern Countrymen), published in *Cuu Quoc*, Sept. 29, 1945. *Ho Chi Minh Toan Tap* (Complete Works of Ho Chi Minh), vol. 4 (Hanoi: Su That, 1984), 25–60. This message, as well as daily reports of events in the south, reached localities most commonly by telegraph or Morse code radio transmissions, thence being transcribed quickly to newspapers and leaflets.

8. PTNT, 35, 140, 175. For the earlier Quang Ngai upheavals, see David G. Marr, *Vietnam 1945: The Quest for Power* (Berkeley: University of California Press, 1995), 102–103, 222–224, 350, 425, 427, 432, 433–435.

9. Chi Doi units varied considerably in size, from two hundred to two thousand men.

10. Vien Lich Su Quan Su Viet Nam, *Chi Doi 3 Giai Phong Quan Nam Tien* (The Liberation Army's Chi Doi 3 Advances South) (Hanoi: QDND, 1995), 10–17. Hereafter CD3.

11. Vien Lich Su Quan Su Viet Nam, *Chi Doi Vi Dan* (Hanoi: QDND, 1998), 28, 33–34, 49, 54. Hereafter CD Vi Dan.

12. PTNT, 124, 295; CD Vi Dan, 34, 61.

13. Not only Viet Minh units but also the Chinese Nationalist Army had political officers.

14. PTNT, 57.

15. Nguyen Viet, editor, *Nam Bo va Nam Phan Trung Bo trong hai nam dau Khang Chien (1945–1946)* (Southern and South Central Vietnam in the First Two Years of Resistance) (Hanoi: Van Su Dia, 1957), 49, 51; PTNT, 95–96, 140–143, 170–173, 182–183; CD 3. 113 Nguyen Phung Minh, editor, *Nam Trung Bo Khang Chien 1945–1975* (South-central Region Resistance, 1945–1975) (Hanoi: CTQG, 1995), 76–78. Hereafter NTBKC. Peter M. Dunn, *The First Vietnam War* (London: C. Hurst, 1985), 298, 307–308, 310.

16. CD Vi Dan, 56–59; PTNT, 76, 119, 129–135, 149, 163; CD 3, 120–122; Dunn, *The First Vietnam War*, 336; Ban Nghien Cuu Lich Su Quan Doi, *Luc Luong Vu Trang Cach Mang trong nam dau cua chinh quyen Nhan Dan* (Revolutionary Armed Forces in the First Year of People's Authority) (Hanoi: QDND, 1970), 27–28.

17. Philippe Devillers, *Histoire du Viet nam de 1940 à 1952* (Paris: de Seuil, 1952), 176. Adrien Dansette, *Leclerc* (Paris: Flamarion, 1952), 194. PTNT, 78–80, 143–144, 173–174; CD 3, 122–125, 146g. NTBKC, 83–84.

18. Vo Nguyen Giap, *Unforgettable Months and Years* (Ithaca, NY: Cornell Southeast Asia Program, 1975), 75–77. Translation by Mai Elliot.

19. Ban Nghien Cuu Lich Su Quan Doi, *Lich Su Quan Doi Nhan Dan Viet Nam* (History of the Vietnam People's Army) (Hanoi: QDND, 1974), 134–138. Marr, *Vietnam 1945*, 225–227.

20. *Cong Bao* 1945, 2; Marr, *Vietnam 1945*, 504–505.

21. Tran Ngoc Ngon, *Lich Su Bo Doi Thong Tin Lien Lac,* (History of Communication and Liaison Units), vol. 1: 1945–1954 (Hanoi: QDND, 1985), 14.

22. The following examples are taken from: d. 85 Quoc Phong (linh tinh) 1945, Van Phong, GF 38; AOM (Aix); and early issues of the *Cong Bao*.

23. Again these examples come from d. 85, Quoc Phong (linh tinh) 1945, Van Phong, GF 38, AOM (Aix).

24. Truong Ban Quan Su Tan Thuat (Hung Yen) to Truong Ban Quan Su Ha Noi; Sept. 13, 1945, and Uy Ban Nhan Dan Bac Bo to Uy Ban Nhan Dan Hung Yen, Oct. 8, 1945, in d. Hung Yen, GF 67, AOM (Aix). I have not seen a general policy statement on such matters.

25. Tran Ngoc Ngon, 10–11, 15–16, 18. D. 85, Quoc Phong (linh tinh) 1945, Van Phong, GF 38 AOM (Aix).

26. Tran Ngoc Ngon, 27, 30–34, 36–37.

27. Oct. 20, 1945 pass issued to Haiphong People's Committee, d. Giay phep ve viec linh tinh, GF 45 AOM (Aix).

28. Tran Minh Hong et al., *Lich Su Hau Can Quan Doi Nhan Dan Viet Nam, 1944–1954* (History of People's Army Logistics), vol. 1. (Hanoi: Tong Cuc Hau Can, 1985), 80–83; Hoang Chi et al., *Bien Nien Su Kien Lich Su Hau Can Quan Doi Nhan Dan Viet Nam* (Historical Chronology of People's Army Logistics) (Hanoi: Tong Cuc Hau Can, 1986), 56–57, 63–64; Pham Nhu Vuu et al., *Lich Su Quan Gioi Viet Nam Thoi Ki Khang Chien Chong Thuc Dan Phap (1945–1954)* (Vietnam Arms History during the Resistance against French Colonialists, 1945–1954) (Hanoi: Lao Dong, 1990), 20–22.

29. Nov. 26, 1945 UBNDBB to Hanoi distillery; and Dec. 6, 1945 QP to O Kiem Soat Nha May Ruou, both in d. 85, Quoc Phong (linh tinh) 1945, Van Phong, GF 38 AOM (Aix).

30. Le Dinh Cam, et al., *Lich Su Truong Si Quan Luc Quan Tran Quoc Tuan* (History of the Tran Quoc Tuan Army Officer Academy) (Hanoi: QDND, 1985), 20–37.

31. Le Dinh Cam, et al., 40–43.

32. Patti, *Why Viet Nam?*, 291–292.

33. Patti, *Why Viet Nam?*, 346; Peter Worthing, *Occupation and Revolution: China and the Vietnamese August Revolution of 1945* (Berkeley: Institute of East Asian Studies, 2001), 74–75.

34. René Charbonneau and José Maigre, *Les parias de la victoire: Indochine-Chine 1945* (Paris: Editions France-Empire, 1980), 382–397; Worthing, 117–219; reports by Lt. Col. Robert Quilichini between January and June 1946, in AOM, Laos, carton Q4; Nguyen To Uyen, 190–192, 202–204, 207; Vien Lich Su Quan Su Viet Nam, *Lich Su cuoc Khang Chien chong Thuc Dan Phap 1945–1954* (History of Resistance to French Colonialism 1945–1954), vol. 1, (Hanoi: QDND, 1994), 108–109. Hereafter LSKC-1. General Leclerc's staff had estimated that 50,000 troops would be necessary to storm the Haiphong-Hanoi-Nam Dinh triangle, a force he had no hope of mobilizing in early 1946. Alain Ruscio, *La guerre Française d'Indochine* (Brussels: Editions Complexe, 1992), 57–60.

36. Worthing, *Occupation and Revolution*, 120–124, 135–169; Stein Tønnesson, "La paix imposée par la Chine: l'accord franco-vietnamien du 6 mars 1946," in Charles-Robert Ageron and Philippe Devillers, eds., *Les guerres d'Indochine de 1945 à 1975* (Paris: Institut d'Histoire du Temps Présent, 1996); Ministère de la France d'Outre-Mer, *Bulletin Hebdomadaire*, no. 67 (March 18, 1946). These triangular diplomatic efforts did not prevent a violent altercation in Haiphong harbor between Chinese and French forces on the morning of March 6.

37. Devillers, *Histoire*, 237–238; Claude Paillat, *Dossier secret de l'Indochine* (Paris: Presses de la Cité, 1964), 66–67; Jean Julien Fonde, *Traitez à tout prix* (Paris: Robert Laffont, 1971), 157–162; film batch no. FUB/5/635. By earlier Sino-French agreement, twelve French planes were also to land at Gia Lam airport

in the hours just preceding French arrival by road from Haiphong. Worthing, *Occupation and Revolution*, 143–144.

38. Fonde, *Traitez*, 159. Photos of Leclerc driving his own Jeep amidst ecstatic French civilians confirm the flags on each side.

39. SL 71 May 22, 1946, in *Cong Bao* 1946, 437–441. This decree was held back from publication for three months, presumably for security reasons. When published, the first portion of the section on organization was deleted.

40. LSKC-1, 152. Curiously, no intelligence bureau is listed.

41. LSKC-1, 150–151. These were antiaircraft guns converted into field guns.

42. Doan Tue, Song Hao, et al., *Voi Xung Kích* (Assault Elephants) (Hanoi: Phong Chinh Tri-Bo Tu Lenh Phao Binh, 1966), 5–15.

43. Tran Dai Nghia, "The First Days of the Armaments Service," *Vietnam Courier* (Hanoi), no. 12/1980, pp. 23–24; Pham Nhu Vuu, 23, 36.

44. Hoang Chi, et al., *Bien nien*, 80–81.

45. Christopher E. Goscha, "Le contexte asiatique de la guerre franco-vietnamienne: réseaux, relations et économie (d'août 1945 à mai 1954)," Ph.D. thesis, Ecole Pratique des Hautes Études, 2000, 359–360.

46. Fonde, 179, 188–189, 204, 223, 242–248, 270; Jean Valluy, "Indochine: octobre 45-mars 47," *Revue des Deux Mondes*, Nov-Dec 1967, 201–202, 206, 216.

47. Sep. 19, 1946 UBNDBB to all provinces, Tu Ve xung dot voi nhan vien nha thue quan dossier, GF 24, AOM (Aix). However, another file deals with a tax official sacked after being arrested locally. Hoa Binh (viec hien hanh) dossier, GF 11, AOM (Aix).

48. Nov. 11, 1946, Giam Doc Nha Thue Quan va Thue Giam Thu to Chu Tich UBNDBB, attaching copy of Oct. 14, 1946 incident report. Nov. 21, 1946, UBNDBB to all provinces, Tu Ve xung dot voi nhan vien nha thue quan dossier, GF 24, AOM (Aix).

49. Cao Hung and Nguyen Hoai An, *Binh Dinh: Lich Su Chien Tranh Nhan Dan 30 nam (1945–1975)* (Binh Dinh: History of 30 Years of People's War (1945–1975) (np: Bo Chi Huy Quan Su tinh Binh Dinh, 1992), 86–87; LSKC-1, 140–142; NTBKC, 90–91; Nguyen Viet, 92–94. Nguyen Kim Dung and Nguyen Van Khoan, *Tuong Nguyen Son* (General Nguyen Son) (Hanoi: Lao Dong, 1994), 82.

50. Cao Hung and Nguyen Hoai An, *Binh Dinh*, 87–89.

51. Goscha, "Le contexte asiatique," 375–384, 399–402.

52. The June 1, 1946, ceremony opening the Academy is described in *Chien Si* (Hue) no. 29 (June 19, 1946).

53. Goscha, "Le contexte asiatique," 370–371, quoting from the notebook of a dead Japanese instructor.

54. Nguyen Viet, *Nam Bo*, 94.

55. Gilbert Bodinier, compiler, *La guerre d'Indochine 1945–1954: Textes et documents, Vol. 1: Le retour de la France en Indochine 1945–1946* (Vincennes: Service historique de l'Armée de Terre, 1987), 67–71. Besides "partisans," the French recruited native "supplétifs" and civilian "auxiliaires." By July they also had brought from the metropole about 10,000 Indochinese replacements for "Europeans" ending tours-of-duty. Half of these were "Annamites."

56. Report for August 1946, Directeur de la Police et de la Sûreté Federales en Indochine, CP 186, AOM (Aix).

57. Martin Shipway, *The Road to War: France and Vietnam, 1944–1947* (Oxford: Berghahn Books, 1996), 239–240.

58. Report for November 1946 (distributed December 17), Directeur de la Po-

lice et de la Sûreté Federales en Indochine, CP 186, AOM (Aix). Even at this late date, the Sûreté admitted that the "rebels" had generally respected the cease-fire.

59. Devillers, *Histoire*, 318.

60. Shipway, *The Road to War*, 240; Bodinier, *La guerre*, 313–317. Stein Tønnesson, *1946: Déclenchement de la guerre d'Indochine* (Paris: l'Harmattan, 1987, 1987), 65–70.

61. Nghi quyet hoi nghi can bo Trung Uong tu ngay 7/31–8/1, 1946, *Van Kien Dang ve khang chien*, vol. 1, 57–74.

62. Tønnesson, "The Outbreak," 105. Vo Nguyen Giap, *Unforgettable Days*, (Hanoi: FLPH, 1975), 319, compliments Morlière as "someone who meant well and desired peace."

63. Nghi quyet Hoi nghi Quan Su Toan Quoc cua Dang ngay 10-19-1946, *Van Kien Dang ve khang chien*, vol. 1, 75–78.

64. Vo Nguyen Giap, *Unforgettable Days*, 357–365. Nguyen Kien Giang, *Viet Nam nam dau tien sau Cach Mang Thang Tam* (Vietnam in the First Year following the August Revolution) (Hanoi: Su That, 1961, 230–234.

65. Nguyen To Uyen, *Cong cuoc Bao Ve va Xay Dung Chinh quyen Nhan Dan o Vietnam trong nhung nam 1945–1946* (Protecting and Building People's Government in Vietnam 1945–1946) (Hanoi: KHXH, 1999), 267, 269, 272. The outbreak of full-scale war in December made it impossible to conduct elections for the "People's Assembly."

66. Nguyen To Uyen, *Cong cuoc*, 261–262.

67. "Cong viec khan cap bay gio," *Ho Chi Minh Toan*, vol. 4, 179–181. The two sections are written very differently, perhaps as speech notes for two different audiences.

68. Ngo Vi Thien, et al., *Tran Dang Ninh: Con Nguoi va Lich Su* (Tran Dang Ninh: Character and History) (Hanoi: Chinh Tri Quoc Gia, 1996), 24.

69. Ngo Vi Thien, et al., 326–327; *Lich Su Quan Doi Nhan Dan Viet Nam*, 246.

70. Tønnesson, "The Outbreak," 131, 137–149; Vo Nguyen Giap, *Unforgettable Days*, 373–380; Shipway, 240–242.

71. Vo Nguyen Giap, *Chien dau trong vong vay*, (Fighting while Encircled) (Hanoi: QDND and Thanh Nien, 1995), 35. LSKC-1, 151, adds that 82,000 men represented an increase of 32,000 over the end of 1945.

72. LSKC-1, 150. No date is attached to this list, but the context suggests August or September 1946.

73. Oct. 10, 1946, "Note sur l'armée vietnamienne," 10H 530 SHAT, as cited by Goscha, "Le contexte asiatique," 58.

74. Bodinier, *La guerre*, 84. Three-quarters of these French forces were "Européens" and one-quarter "Autochtones."

75. Vuong Thua Vu, *Truong Thanh trong Chien Dau* (Growing up in Battle) (Hanoi: QDND, 1979), 85–86.

76. Ibid., 99–101.

77. Tønnesson, "The Outbreak," 178–209, discusses these Franco-Vietnamese interactions in exquisite detail. See also Vo Nguyen Giap, *Unforgettable Days*, 390–413.

78. LSKC-1, 168–169; Tønnesson, "The Outbreak," 203–205.

79. Ho Chi Minh, realizing the significance of Léon Blum becoming prime minister, had sent Blum a long message via Sainteny, which however was held up in Saigon and did not reach Blum until December 20. Tønnesson, "The Outbreak," 198–200.

80. Vu Ky, "Nhung chang duong truong ky khang chien nhat dinh thang loi" (Stages in the Protracted Resistance Certain of Victory), *Tap chi Lich Su Quan Su* (Hanoi), no. 36 (12-1988), 81. Vu Ky, as Ho's personal secretary, had carried the letter to Giam and brought back the bad news.

81. Vo Nguyen Giap, *Chien dau*, 26; LSKC-1, 169, reprints this message, which appears to have been sent in the clear, but disguised as a commercial instruction requiring the receiver to add and subtract numbers to get the correct time of 2000.

82. Tønnesson, "The Outbreak," 214–221, offers further interesting speculations.

83. Vo Nguyen Giap, *Chien dau*, 43. By contrast, LSKC-2, 20, states that it was only the local Hoan Kiem lighting facility (nha may den Bo Ho) which was sabotaged.

84. Vuong Thua Vu, *Truong Thanh*, 111–115. Vien Lich Su Quan Su Viet Nam, *Lich Su cuoc Khang Chien chong Thuc Dan Phap 1945–1954* (History of Resistance to French Colonialism 1945–1954), vol. 2 (Hanoi: QDND, 1994), 23–28.

85. Vuong Thua Vu, *Truong Thanh*, 116–121; LSKC-2, 28–33. A. Teulieres, *La guerre du Vietnam 1945–1975* (Paris, 1979), Annex 1 "Bataille d'Hanoi."

86. Vuong Thua Vu, *Truong Thanh*, 122–146; LSKC-2, 32-45; Vo Nguyen Giap, *Chien dau*, 50–68.

87. LSKC-2, 98–102.

88. Vo Nguyen Giap, *Chien dau*, 91.

89. Ibid., 100.

90. LSKC-2, 102–103.

91. Vo Nguyen Giap, *Chien dau*, 101.

92. Ibid., 107.

93. Ibid., 150–161.

94. Vuong Thua Vu, *Truong Thanh*, 148–168.

6. Forging the "Great Combination": Britain and the Indochina Problem, 1945–1950

1. George C. Herring and Richard H. Immerman, "Eisenhower, Dulles, and Dienbienphu: 'The Day We Didn't Go to War' Revisited," *Journal of American History* 71 (September 1984): 355, 357, 360.

2. For this transformation, see especially Robert M. Blum, *Drawing the Line: The Origin of the American Containment Policy in East Asia* (New York: Norton, 1982); Lloyd C. Gardner, *Approaching Vietnam: From World War II to Dienbienphu* (New York: Norton, 1985); Mark Atwood Lawrence, *Assuming the Burden: Europe and the American Commitment to War in Vietnam* (Berkeley: University of California Press, 2005); Andrew J. Rotter, *The Path to Vietnam: Origins of the American Commitment to Southeast Asia* (Ithaca, N.Y.: Cornell University Press, 1989); and Michael Schaller, "Securing the Great Crescent: Occupied Japan and the Origins of Containment in Southeast Asia," *Journal of American History* 69 (September 1982): 392–414.

3. For analysis of Britain's postwar struggle to preserve its empire amid straightened circumstances, see especially John Darwin, *Britain and Decolonisation: The Retreat from Empire in the Post-War World* (London: Macmillan, 1988), especially chap. 4. For studies that have suggested the importance of studying policymaking toward Indochina within the context of British imperial decline,

see especially Lloyd C. Gardner, *Approaching Vietnam;* Walter LaFeber, "Roosevelt, Churchill, and Indochina, 1942–1945," *American Historical Review* 80 (December 1975): 1277–1295; Wm. Roger Louis, *Imperialism at Bay: The United States and the Decolonization of the British Empire, 1941–1945* (New York: Oxford University Press, 1978); Rotter, *The Path to Vietnam;* John J. Sbrega, *Anglo-American Relations and Colonialism in East Asia, 1941–1945* (New York: Garland, 1983); and Christopher Thorne, *Allies of a Kind: The United States, Britain, and the War against Japan, 1941–1945* (Oxford: Oxford University Press, 1978).

4. For the best study of British behavior in this period, see Fredrik Logevall, *Choosing War: The Lost Chance for Peace and the Escalation of War in Vietnam* (Berkeley: University of California Press, 1999).

5. The analysis here builds on my treatment of British policymaking in my book, *Assuming the Burden.* This chapter provides additional detail and sets the shift in British thinking across the 1945–1950 period within the context of British imperial decline.

6. Minute by Alexander Cadogan, Feb. 2, 1944, FO371/41723, PRO.

7. Foreign Office Report for Dominions Prime Ministers' Conference, April 5, 1944, FO371/41931, PRO.

8. Prime minister's briefing paper for Quebec conference, September 1944, FO371/41720, PRO.

9. Minute by Victor Cavendish-Bentinck, Oct. 26, 1944, FO371/41720, PRO.

10. Franco-British scheming to send Blaizot to SEAC headquarters is traceable in a mass of documents in both Paris and London. See especially M. Massigli to Foreign Ministry, Oct. 2, 1944, Asie/Indochine/45, MAE; "Extract from SACSEA's Eighteenth Meeting," Oct. 25, 1944, WO203/5068, PRO: SEAC to Foreign Office, Oct. 27, 1944, FO371/41720, PRO.

11. Force 136 report, "Future Plans," Dec. 28, 1944, WO203/5559, PRO; Massigli to Bidault, Nov. 29, 1944, Asie/Indochine/45, MAE.

12. Christopher Thorne, *The Issue of War: States, Societies, and the Far Eastern Conflict of 1941–1945* (New York: Oxford University Press, 1985), 211–212, and Darwin, *Britain and Decolonisation,* 65–66.

13. Sterndale Bennett to Eden, "Brief for Secretary of State's Interview with M. Massigli," March 12, 1945, FO371/46305, PRO.

14. WP (44) 111, "The Future of Indo-China and Other French Pacific Possessions," CAB66, vol. 47, PRO.

15. Ibid.

16. Sterndale Bennett to Eden, "Brief for Secretary of State's Interview with M. Massigli," March 12, 1945, FO371/46305, PRO.

17. For a review of this scholarship, see Stein Tønnesson's chapter in this volume.

18. Lord Louis Mountbatten to COS, Sept. 23, 1945, FO371/46308, PRO.

19. Darwin, *Britain and Decolonisation,* 71.

20. Rita Hindon, "Imperialism Today," April 1945, Fabian Colonial Bureau Papers/31, Rhodes House, Oxford University.

21. *Parliamentary Debates* (Hansard), Fifth Series, vol. 414 (London: His Majesty's Stationary Office, 1945), 398, 1151–1154, 1863–1864; vol. 415, 1727–1729.

22. Kenneth O. Morgan, *Labour in Power, 1945–1951* (Oxford: Oxford University Press, 1984), 63.

23. "Pacific Intervention Condemned by Laski," *New York Times,* Nov. 15, 1945, 5.

24. Quoted in D. R. SarDesai, *Indian Foreign Policy in Cambodia, Laos, and Vietnam, 1947–1964* (Berkeley: University of California Press, 1968), 10.
25. Commander in Chief, India, to War Office, Sept. 18, 1945, WO203/2235, PRO.
26. Lord Louis Mountbatten to COS, Oct. 2, 1945, FO371/46309, PRO.
27. Dening to Foreign Office, Sept. 10, 1945.
28. Statement by Ernest Bevin, Oct. 24, 1945, FO371/53960, PRO.
29. "Minutes of SACSEA's Twenty-eighth Miscellaneous Meeting," Sept. 23, 1945, WO203/2173, PRO.
30. Gracey to Mountbatten, Sept. 28, 1945, WO203/4431, PRO.
31. Brain to Mountbatten, Sept. 25, 1945, WO203/4431, PRO; Brain to Dening, Sept. 25, 1945, WO203/5023, PRO; Dening to Foreign Office, "A Report on Political and Economic Conditions in Saigon Region," Oct. 26, 1945, FO371/46309, PRO.
32. Saigon to Mountbatten, Oct. 1, 1945, WO203/2173, PRO.
33. "Minutes of SACSEA's Twenty-seventh Miscellaneous Meeting," Sept. 22, 1945, WO203/4453, PRO.
34. Joint Planning Staff paper no. 201, "Handover of FIC to French," Sept. 21, 1945, WO203, 2151.
35. Mountbatten to COS, Oct. 2, 1945, FO371/46309, PRO.
36. Mountbatten to COS, Sept. 24, 1945, WO203/4431, PRO.
37. Memcon, Sterndale Bennett with John Allison, Feb. 6, 1946, FO371/54052, PRO.
38. Report by Joint Planning Staff, "SACSEA's Plan for Reduction of Forces to Peacetime Strengths," Feb. 5, 1946, FO371/54038, PRO.
39. Cabinet Office to John Wilson-Young, Dec. 17, 1945, FO371, file 46310, PRO; Ernest Meiklereid to Ernest Bevin, Feb. 1, 1946, FO371, file 53959, PRO.
40. London to State Department, Jan. 29, 1947, RG59, Central Decimal File, 851G.00/1–2947, NARA.
41. Singapore to Foreign Ministry, Feb. 3, 1947, Asie/Indochine/373, MAE.
42. Tokyo to Foreign Ministry, Feb. 16, 1947, Asie/Indochine/373, MAE.
43. Dening to Foreign Office, Feb. 7, 1947, FO371/63547, PRO.
44. J. E. Coulson to John Anderson, Jan. 14, 1947, FO371/63459, PRO.
45. Air Headquarters (India) to Air Attaché (Paris), Feb. 4, 1947, FO371/63460, PRO.
46. Minute by Anderson, Jan. 31, 1947, FO371/53970, PRO.
47. Bevin to Hicks, Feb. 25, 1947, FO371/63453, PRO.
48. Killearn to Foreign Office, Jan. 26, 1947, FO371/63542, PRO; draft minute by Bevin for Attlee, Feb. 10, 1947, FO371/63542, PRO.
49. Minute by Anderson, Jan. 23, 1947, FO371/63459, PRO.
50. MacDonald to Bevin, Feb. 2, 1948, FO959/23, PRO.
51. Foreign Office report, "Communist Strategy in S. E. Asia," Nov. 8, 1948, FO371, file 69695, PRO.
52. Memcon, Bevin and Georges Bidault, Dec. 17, 1947, Europe/Grande Bretagne, 38, MAE.
53. Rotter, *The Path to Vietnam,* especially, 49–69.
54. Foreign Office to British embassy in Washington, April 14, 1948, FO371/69654, PRO.
55. Bangkok (Thompson) to Foreign Office, Dec. 14, 1948, FO371/69684, PRO.
56. Hanoi to Saigon, June 7, 1948, FO959/19, PRO.
57. Minute by Gerard Mackworth-Young, May 13, 1948, FO371/69656, PRO.

58. SarDesai, *Indian Foreign Policy in Cambodia, Laos, and Vietnam,* 16–18.

59. London to Foreign Ministry, Dec. 11, 1949, Etats-associés/Indes, 1954–1955, MAE.

60. Paper by Foreign Office Research Department, May 15, 1949, FO371/76036, PRO.

61. Cabinet memo, "Sir William Strang's Tour in South East Asia and the Far East," March 17, 1949, CAB129/33, PRO.

62. Foreign Office to British embassy in Washington, April 14, 1948, FO371/69654, PRO.

63. Minute by Graves, Feb. 23, 1949, FO371/76003, PRO.

64. Minute by Lloyd, June 11, 1949, FO371/76033, PRO.

65. Bangkok to Foreign Office, Dec. 14, 1948, FO371/69684, PRO.

66. British Information Service release, "Mr. Bevin at the National Press Club," April 1, 1949, FO371/74184, PRO.

67. Gibbs to Foreign Office, March 16, 1950, FO371/83651, PRO.

68. Brief for Bevin's talks with Robert Schuman, March 6, 1950, FO371/83600, PRO.

69. Scott to Graves, April 26, 1950, FO371/83644, PRO.

70. Foreign Ministers' Conference memo, "Minute No. 1," Asie/Indochine, file 278, MAE; M. Massigli to Foreign Ministry, May 3, 1950, Asie/Indochine, file 278, MAE; "Compte-Rendu de la Cinquième réunion des Ministres," May 13, 1950, Secrétaire Général, vol. 8, Conférence Tripartite de Londres, MAE.

71. Total amounts are extremely difficult to calculate based on available documentation. It is likely that the figures are included in material that remains classified.

72. Graves (Saigon) to Foreign Office, Nov. 24, 1952, FO371/101077, PRO.

73. Quoted in Graves to Foreign Office, Dec. 23, 1952, FO371/101077, PRO.

74. Note by Strang, Jan. 6, 1953, FO371/106787, PRO.

75. James R. Arnold, *The First Domino: Eisenhower, the Military, and America's Intervention in Vietnam* (New York: Morrow, 1991), 78.

76. Conclusions of cabinet meeting, July 6, 1953, C. C. (53), Thirty-ninth Conclusions, CAB128, PRO.

77. Conclusions of cabinet meeting, May 3, 1954, C. C. (54), Thirty-first Conclusions, CAB128, PRO.

78. See, for example, Bruce R. Kuniholm, *The Origins of the Cold War in the Near East: Great Power Conflict and Diplomacy in Iran, Turkey, and Greece* (Princeton, N.J.: Princeton University Press, 1980), especially chap. 6, and Melvyn P. Leffler, *A Preponderance of Power: National Security, the Truman Administration, and the Cold War* (Stanford, Calif.: Stanford University Press, 1992), 121–127, 142–144.

7. French Imperial Reconstruction and the Development of the Indochina War, 1945–1950

1. D. Bruce Marshall, *The French Colonial Myth and Constitution-Making in the Fourth Republic* (New Haven, Conn.: Yale University Press, 1973); Andrew Shennan, *Rethinking France: Plans for Renewal, 1940–1946* (Oxford: Oxford University Press, 1989), chap. 6; C.-R. Ageron, "La survivance d'un mythe: La puissance par l'empire colonial (1944–1947)," *Revue française d'histoire d'outre-mer,* 77 (1985): 388–397.

2. Tony Smith, "The French Colonial Consensus and People's War, 1946–58,"

Journal of Contemporary History 9 (1974): 217–247; Alain-Gérard Marsot, "The Crucial Year: Indochina 1946," *Journal of Contemporary History* 19 (1984): 337–354; James I. Lewis, "The French Colonial Service and the Issues of Reform, 1944–48," *Contemporary European History* 4 (1995): 157–169; and "The MRP and the Genesis of the French Union, 1944–1948," *French History* 12 (1998): 276–314.

3. Martin Shipway, "Reformism and the French 'Official Mind': The 1944 Brazzaville Conference and the Legacy of the Popular Front," in Tony Chafer and Amanda Sackur, eds., *French Colonial Empire and the Popular Front* (London: Macmillan, 1999), 146.

4. Smith, "The French Colonial Consensus," 217–221.

5. Frédéric Turpin, "Le RPF et la guerre d'Indochine (1947–1954)," in *De Gaulle et le Rassemblement du peuple français (1947–1955)* (Paris: Armand Colin, 1998), 530–531.

6. Stein Tønnesson, *1946: Déclenchement de la guerre d'Indochine* (Paris: Harmattan, 1987), 136–196 passim; Philippe Devillers, *Paris-Saigon-Hanoi: Les archives de la guerre, 1944–1947* (Paris: Gallimard, 1988), 285–325; Martin Shipway, *The Road to War: France and Vietnam, 1944–1947* (Oxford: Berghahn, 1996), 260–267; William J. Duiker, *The Communist Road to Power in Vietnam,* 2nd ed. (Boulder, Colo.: Westview Press, 1996), 130–131.

7. Ministère des Affaires Etrangères (MAE), Paris, Série Asie-Océanie 1944–1949, vol. 255, no. 4145/CAAP3, Pignon to COMININDO, Nov. 19, 1946.

8. Ibid,; Pierre Brocheux and Daniel Hémery, *Indochine: La colonisation ambiguë* (Paris: Découverte, 2001), 164–171.

9. Jean-Pierre Rioux, *The Fourth Republic 1944–1958* (Cambridge: Cambridge University Press, 1987), 120.

10. Tony Smith, "A Comparative Study of French and British Decolonization," *Comparative Studies in Society and History* 20:1 (1978): 79–80, 85–86.

11. Pierre Letamendia, *Le Mouvement républicain populaire: Histoire d'un grand parti français* (Paris: Beauchesne, 1995), and Emile-François Callot, *Le Mouvement républicain populaire: Origine, structure, doctrine, programme et action politique* (Paris: Marcel Rivière, 1978).

12. Christian Bougeard, *René Pleven: Un français libre en politique* (Rennes: Presses universitaires de Rennes, 1994), 168.

13. Archives Nationales, Paris, Archives de l'UDSR, 412AP/1, Secrétariat Général de l'UDSR, "circulaire commune aux responables régionaux et départmentaux du MLN, Libération Nord, de l'OCA et de ceux de la Résistance," July 27, 1945; Letamendia, *Le Mouvement républicain populaire*, 161–164, 179–180.

14. François Bédarida and Jean-Pierre Rioux, eds., *Pierre Mendès France et le mendèsisme: L'expérience gouvernementale et sa posterité, 1954–1955* (Paris: Fayard, 1985); Janine Chêne, Edith Aberdam, and Henri Morsel, eds., *Pierre Mendès France: La morale en politique* (Grenoble: Presses universitaires de Grenoble, 1990); René Girault, ed., *Pierre Mendès France et le rôle de la France dans le monde* (Grenoble: Presses universitaires de Grenoble, 1991).

15. Raymond Poidevin, *Robert Schuman: Homme d'état 1886–1963* (Paris: Imprimerie National, 1986), 340–344; Danièle Zéraffa-Dray, "Le Mouvement républicain populaire et la communauté européenne de défense 1950–1954," in Serge Berstein, Jean-Marie Mayeur, and Pierre Milza, eds., *Le MRP et la construction européenne* (Paris: Complèxe, 1993), 182–193.

16. William I. Hitchcock demonstrates the success of French diplomacy in post-

war Europe in *France Restored: Cold War Diplomacy and the Quest for Leadership in Europe, 1944–1954* (Chapel Hill, N.C.: University of North Carolina Press, 1998). That success found no echo in colonial policy.

17. The term "colonial myth" is used in different, although complementary, ways by D. Bruce Marshall and Charles-Robert Ageron; see note 1.

18. Odile Rudelle, "L'année 1946: Les stratégies d'intervention du général de Gaulle," in *Cahiers de la Fondation Charles de Gaulle,* no. 4, *La genèse du RPF* (Paris: Fondation Charles de Gaulle, 1997), 179–197.

19. Serge Berstein, "De Gaulle, l'état, la république," in Fondation Charles de Gaulle, Actes du collogue, *De Gaulle et le Rassemblement du people français (1947–1955)* (Paris: Armand Colin, 1998), 386–388.

20. Irwin M. Wall, *French Communism in the Era of Stalin* (Westport, Conn.: Greenwood Press, 1984), chap. 3.

21. PRO, FO 371/67688, Z2248/312/17, Embassy record of Henri Laurentie speech, Feb. 27, 1947.

22. NARA, RG 59, Lot file 53D246, box 1, "Review of United States' Policy toward French Colonial Areas," Feb. 15, 1950.

23. AN, Papiers MRP, 350AP/71, Dossier 3MRP8/Dr2, Secrétariat-Général note, "Les aspects politiques du fédéralisme," July 6, 1948, Georges Le Brun Keris note, Feb. 1, 1949; Lewis, "The MRP," 276–314; R. E. M. Irving, *Christian Democracy in France* (London: Allen and Unwin, 1973), 199–205.

24. AN, Georges Bidault papers, 457AP, box 112, MRP Centre National report to Bidault's ministerial secretary, April 2, 1946.

25. Philip M. Williams, *Crisis and Compromise: Politics in the Fourth Republic,* 3rd. ed. (London: Longman, 1964), and Duncan MacRae, *Parliament, Parties, and Society in France, 1946–1958* (London: Macmillan, 1967).

26. AN, Archives de l'UDSR, 412AP/1, "Réflexions sur l'UDSR," July 8, 1946.

27. Williams, *Crisis and Compromise,* 174–175.

28. Earlier frictions between MRP, Socialist, and PCF ministers peaked after de Gaulle's January 1946 resignation. See AN, Papiers MRP, 350AP/76, 4MRP8/Dr4, Francisque Gay to Félix Gouin, Feb. 28, 1946.

29. Letamendia, *Le Mouvement républicain populaire,* 89, 98–101.

30. Bruno Béthouart, "Le MRP, un nouveau partenaire," in Serge Berstein, Frédéric Cépède, Gilles Morin, and Antoine Prost, eds., *Le parti socialiste entre résistance et république* (Paris: Publications de la Sorbonne, 2000), 257–258.

31. Jean-Jacques Becker, "L'anticommunisme de l'SFIO," in Serge Berstein, ed., *Paul Ramadier: La république et le socialisme* (Paris: Complexe, 1990), 199–201.

32. B. D. Graham, *Choice and Democratic Order: The French Socialist Party, 1937–1950* (Cambridge: Cambridge University Press, 1994), 369–372; Christine Sellin, "Paul Ramadier et l'Indochine en 1947," in Berstein, *Paul Ramadier,* 377–385; Edward Rice-Maximin, *Accommodation and Resistance: The French Left, Indochina and the Cold War, 1944–1954* (Westport, Conn.: Greenwood Press, 1986), 42–48.

33. PRO, FO 371/67680, Z170/58/17, Duff Cooper memo., Dec. 30, 1946.

34. Bernard Chantebout, "Le partage des responsabilités de la défense entre politiques et militaires de 1945 à 1962," in Olivier Forcade, Eric Duhamel, and Philippe Vial, eds., *Militaires en république 1870–1962* (Paris: Publications de la Sorbonne, 1999), 84–85.

35. Bruce D. Graham, "Le choix atlantique ou troisième force internationale?," in Berstein, *Paul Ramadier,* 160.

36. Alain Bergounioux, "La perception de la puissance par la S.F.I.O. de 1944 à 1947," in René Girault and Robert Frank, eds., *La puissance française en question!*, 1945–1949 (Paris: Publications de la Sorbonne, 1988), 358–359.

37. AN, Bidault Papers, 457AP, box 112, MAE Secrétariat-Générale note, Jan. 10, 1947; MAE, série Afrique-Levant 1944–1959, sous-série Algérie, vol. 5, General Frandon to general staff, June 3, 1947.

38. PRO, FO 371/67688, Z312/312/17, Paris Chancery to FO, Jan. 6, 1947.

39. AN, Bidault papers, 457AP, box 115, tel. 460, Juin to Bidault, June 4, 1947; Martin Thomas, *The French North African Crisis: Colonial Breakdown and Anglo-French Relations, 1945–1962* (London: Macmillan, 2000), 34. In February 1947, Juin turned down the government's offer of the Indochina High Commission. See Philippe Vial, "La Quatrième et son maréchal: Essai sur le comportement politique d'Alphonse Juin, 1947–1956," in Forcade, Duhamel, and Vial, *Militaires*, 157–158.

40. Jacques Tronchon, "La nuit la plus longue . . . du 29 au 30 mars 1947," and Jean Fremigacci, "Bilan provisoire de l'insurrection de 1947: Nécessité de nouvelles recherches," in F. Arzalier and J. Suret-Canale, eds., *Madagascar 1947: La tragédie oubliée* (Paris: Le temps des cerises, 1999), 118–126, 177–189; Francis Koerner, *Madagascar: Colonisation française et nationalisme malgache vingtième siècle* (Paris: Harmattan, 1994), 329–341. The government admitted to eighty-nine thousand deaths.

41. Marc Michel, "L'Empire colonial dans les débats parlémentaires," in Serge Berstein and Pierre Milza, eds., *L'année 1947* (Paris: Presses de la Fondation nationale des sciences politiques, 2000), 191–201 passim; Jacques Dalloz, *The War in Indo-China, 1945–54* (Dublin: Gilland Macmillan, 1990), 83.

42. Charles-Robert Ageron, "L'opinion publique face aux problèmes de l'Union française," in Ageron, ed., *Les chemins de la décolonisation française 1936–1956* (Paris: CNRS, 1986), 37. Opinion split 35 to 37 percent.

43. AN, Bidault Papers, 457AP, box 57, dossier Asie-Océanie 1947–1948, "Résumé des événements politiques en extrême-orient, juin 1947."

44. PRO, FO 959/14, FO to Saigon Consulate, Feb. 10, 1947; MAE, série Asie-Océanie, vol. 255, Valluy to COMININDO, June 28, 1947; Saigon Bureau fédéral, "Etude sur les activités américaines en Indochine," Sept. 11, 1947.

45. Dalloz, *The War in Indo-China*, 87–88, 96.

46. MAE, série Asie, vol. 255, MAE Secretariat note, Sept. 15, 1947.

47. MAE, série Nations Unies et Organisations Internationales, vol. 573, Cabinet Diplomatique (Rabat), "La question marocaine à l'ONU," Aug. 27, 1947; Robert J. MacMahon, *Colonialism and Cold War: The United States and the Struggle for Indonesian Independence, 1945–1949* (Ithaca, N.Y.: Cornell University Press, 1981).

48. Irwin M. Wall, *The United States and the Making of Postwar France, 1945–1954* (Cambridge: Cambridge University Press, 1989), 236–237; Marc Michel, "De Lattre et les débuts de l'americainisation de la guerre d'Indochine," *Revue française d'histoire d'outre-mer* 77 (1985): 322–323.

49. Hugues Tertrais, "L'emergence de la guerre civile dans le conflit d'Indochine (1945–1954)," *Relations internationales* 105 (2001): 46–49.

50. On Moutet, see Chafer and Sackur, *French Colonial Empire*.

51. Sellin, "Paul Ramadier et l'Indochine," 379.

52. Duiker, *The Communist Road*, 124–125; Shipway, *The Road to War*, 164.

53. Centre des archives d'outre-mer (AOM), Papiers Marius Moutet, carton

3/D82: Cochinchina 1946–1947, Moutet reply to d'Argenlieu letter of Aug. 3, 1946; Shipway, *The Road to War*, 180–188; Jacques Valette, "La conférence de Fontainebleau (1946)," in Ageron, *Les chemins*, 240–242.

54. CAOM, Affaires Politiques, C2116/D2, EMGDN, Section Afrique, "Note sur le statut d'Algérie," May 1947.

55. Valette, "La conférence," 236–237.

56. Devillers, *Paris-Saigon-Hanoi;* Tønnesson, *1946: Déclenchement de la guerre;* Shipway, *The Road to War*, chaps. 7–8.

57. AOM, Papiers Marius Moutet, C3/D81, Robert Lascaux letter to Moutet, Nov. 19, 1946; "SFIO section de Pnom Penh, motion votée à l'unanimité— réunion de 3 juillet 1947."

58. Mark Atwood Lawrence, "Transnational Coalition-Building and the Making of the Cold War in Indochina, 1947–1949," *Diplomatic History* 26:3 (2002), 458.

59. AOM, Papiers Robert Delavignette, PA 19, C3/D29, Paul Coste-Floret to the *directeur des affaires politiques*, April 23, 1948.

60. PRO, FO 371/72946, Z1738/6/17, Harvey (Paris) to FO, March 1, 1948.

61. Frédéric Turpin, "Le Gaullisme et les négociations entre Bao Dai et la Quatrième République (1947–1949)," *Revue d'Histoire Diplomatique*, 111:2 (1997), 143–144.

62. Dalloz, *The War in Indo-China*, 89–91.

63. MAE, Asie, vol. 255, Henri Bonnet to Foreign Ministry, Sept. 8, 1948.

64. USNA, RG 59, Decimal files 890.00, Box 7174, minutes of Southeast Asia Conference (Bangkok), June 21–26, 1948.

65. Jacques Dalloz, "Alain Savary, un socialiste face à la guerre d'Indochine," *Vingtième siècle* (January 1997), 42–54; Rice-Maximin, *Accommodation*, 70–71.

66. Annie Lacroix-Riz, "Puissance ou dépendance française?: La vision des 'décideurs' des affaires étrangères en 1948–9," in Girault and Frank, *La puissance*, 58–59.

67. Antoine Daveau, "Le poids de la guerre d'Indochine," *Revue d'histoire diplomatique* 103 (1993): 339–340; Hugues Tertrais, "Le poids financier de la guerre d'Indochine," in Maurice Vaïsse, ed., *L'armée française dans la guerre d'Indochine* (Paris: Complexe, 2000), 39. During 1948 and 1949, High Commissioners Emile Bolleart and Léon Pignon pushed French ministers to seek a reversal of the ban on the disbursement of Marshall aid funding in Indochina: MAE, Asie, vol. 255, Saigon High Commission, "Participation de l'Indochine au Plan Marshall," April 9, 1949.

68. PRO, FO 371/89166, WF1011/1, "France: Annual Review for 1949."

69. MAE, sous-série Grande-Bretagne, vol. 39, "Compte rendu des conversations entre M. Schuman et M. Bevin," Jan. 13, 1949.

70. Dalloz, *The War in Indo-China*, 116–118; Frank Giles, *The Locust Years: The Story of the Fourth French Republic, 1946–1958* (New York: Carroll and Graf, 1991), 115–120.

71. Maurice Vaïsse, "Ramadier et les problèmes de défense nationale (1947–1949)," in Berstein, *Paul Ramadier*, 276–278; Rice-Maximin, *Accommodation*, 85–88.

72. Turpin, "Le RPF," 532.

73. USNA, RG 59, 890.00, Box 7174, FEA memo, "Indochina," Nov. 7, 1949.

74. PRO, F0 371/69654, F6302/255/86, Ashley Clarke to Grey, April 22, 1948; entry for Feb. 12, 1948, *Vincent Auriol: Journal du septennat, 1947–1954*, tome 2: 1948, (Paris, 1978), 89–90.

75. Ageron, "L'opinion publique," 47; Alain Ruscio, *Les communistes français et la guerre d'Indochine, 1944–1954* (Paris: Harmattan, 1985).

76. Williams, *Crisis and Compromise*, 91–93, 106–107. The SFIO's departmental federations reasserted their power over the party executive once the party was reconstituted, see Graham, *Choice and Democratic Order*, 263–266, 274–289.

77. AN, Fonds MRP, 350AP7, dossier: 1MRP6/Dr. 2, Secrétariat-Général, "Note sur l'organisation du M.R.P." no date.

78. AN, Fonds MRP, 350AP7, dossier: 1MRP6/DR1, André Colin letter regarding Secrétariat Equipes, Nov. 22, 1951.

79. Jacques Dalloz, "L'opposition M.R.P. à la guerre d'Indochine," *Revue d'Histoire Moderne et Contemporaine*, 43:1 (1996), 106–118.

80. PRO, FO 371/89170, WF1017/4, Sir Olive Harvey to FO, Jan. 26, 1950.

81. Alain Ruscio, "L'Opinion publique et la guerre d'Indochine: Sondages et témoignages," *Vingtième siècle* 1 (1991): 35–46.

82. Bougeard, René Pleven, 199–202; Williams, *Crisis and Compromise*, 174–176.

83. Jean-Pierre Rioux, "Varus, Qu'as-tu fait de mes légions?" in Vaïsse, ed., *L'armée française*, 21–31.

84. Pierre Mendès France, *Oeuvres complètes*, tome 2: *Une politique de l'économie 1943–1954* (Paris: Gallimard, 1985), 297–303.

85. Ibid., 304–307.

86. Dalloz, *The War in Indo-China*, 134–136.

87. AN, Papiers René Mayer, "Note sur les effectifs engagés en Indochine," n.d. (1953), and Jean Letourneau letter to Mayer, May 15, 1953.

8. Ho Chi Minh and the Strategy of People's War

1. The statement is printed in *Van kien Dang* (Party Documents), 1945–1954, vol. 2, pt. 1 (Hanoi: Ban Nghien cuu Lich su Dang Trung uong xuat ban, 1979), 11–16.

2. Vo Nguyen Giap's most famous treatise on strategy during the Franco–Viet Minh conflict is *People's War, People's Army* (New York: Praeger, 1962).

3. For further information about Ho Chi Minh's early years, see my *Ho Chi Minh: A Life* (New York: Hyperion, 2000), chap. 1.

4. See Ho Chi Minh, "The Path Which Led Me to Leninism," translated in Bernard B. Fall, ed., *Ho Chi Minh on Revolution* (New York: Praeger, 1967), 24.

5. Nguyen Ai Quoc, "Some Considerations on the Colonial Question," in *L'humanité*, May 25, 1922, cited in Fall, *Ho Chi Minh on Revolution*, 26.

6. Ho Chi Minh's remark about the "voice in the wilderness" is cited in A. Neuberg, ed., *Armed Insurrection* (London: NLB, 1970), 22. Ho shared the view of the Indian communist M. N. Roy, who had unsuccessfully argued at the Second Comintern Congress in 1920 that the Asian revolution was a necessary prerequisite to the overthrow of world capitalism. See my *Ho Chi Minh*, 95.

7. The article, entitled "The Party's Work among the Peasants," is contained in Neuberg, *Armed Insurrection*, 255–271. Some observers question Ho Chi Minh's authorship of this piece, which has never been definitively established. In any event, it appears to reflect his views on the strategy and tactics to be applied in the Vietnamese revolution.

8. Ho himself was skeptical about the prospects for the uprising, popularly known as the Nghe Tinh revolt, but he felt that it must receive support from

the ICP to preserve its reputation among the masses. See my *Ho Chi Minh,* 183–184.

9. One such pamphlet is contained in *Ho Chi Minh Toan tap* (The Complete Writings of Ho Chi Minh), 1st ed., vol. 3 (Hanoi: Su that, 1980), 163–209.

10. He had apparently used the name Ho Chi Minh for the first time during the course of his visit to South China in 1942. The name became familiar to millions of his compatriots after the establishment of the DRV in September 1945.

11. Ho's comment is cited in several Vietnamese accounts of the period, including Hoang Van Hoan's *A Drop in the Ocean: Hoang Van Hoan's Revolutionary Reminiscences* (Beijing: Foreign Languages Press, 1988), 187–188.

12. See "Nghi quyet cua Toan quoc Hoi nghi Dang Cong san Dong duong" (Resolution of the National Conference of the Indochinese Communist Party), in *Van kien Dang* (1930–1945), vol. 3, (Hanoi: Ban Nghien cuu Lich su Dang Truong uong, 1977), 415–417, cited in my *Ho Chi Minh,* 328–329.

13. An English translation of the tract is contained in *Truong Chinh: Selected Writings* (Hanoi: Foreign Languages Press, 1977), 85–216. In an interview with me in Hanoi on December 5, 1990, Chinh's son Dang Xuan Ky declared that his father had written his treatise at the request of President Ho Chi Minh and that the ideas contained therein reflected the overall view of the party leadership. As the party's general secretary and its chief ideologue at the time, Truong Chinh was a natural choice to author the piece.

14. Truong Chinh, *Selected Writings,* 188. Mao later retracted this view. See *Selected Military Writings of Mao Zedong* (Peking: Foreign Languages Press, 1972), 186n.

15. Truong Chinh had drawn much of his material from Mao's treatise "On Protracted War," composed at Yan'an in 1938. That same year, Ho Chi Minh had briefly visited Yan'an but evidently did not meet with Mao at the time.

16. Yves Gras, *Histoire de la guerre d'Indochine* (Paris: Denoël, 1992), 196.

17. Truong Chinh, *Selected Writings,* 175–176.

18. Ngo Tien Chat, "Notes on the Tradition of Heroic Struggle of Nationalities in the Northwest from the August Revolution to the Present Resistance Against America," in *Nghien Cuu Lich Su* (Historical Research), no. 95 (February 1967), cited in Joint Publication Research Service No. 9609 (Translations on North Vietnam), no. 151, 6. See also *The Outline History of the Vietnamese Workers' Party* (Hanoi: Foreign Languages Press, 1972), 56. There has been some disagreement among Vietnamese historians over the date of the beginning of the second stage. Vo Nguyen Giap once commented to a Cuban journalist that it was difficult to pinpoint an exact date, as there was no firm demarcation between the two stages.

19. Giap, *People's War, People's Army,* 92. For the quote, see *Cuoc Khang chien Than thanh cua Nhan dan Viet Nam* (The Sacred War of the Vietnamese People), vol. 1 (Hanoi: Su that, 1958), 239.

20. For a discussion of Ho's visit to Moscow and relevant sources, see my *Ho Chi Minh,* 420–423.

21. For Liu Shaoqi's speech, see Melvin Gurtov, *The First Vietnam Crisis: Chinese Communist Strategy and United States Involvement, 1953–1954* (New York: Columbia University Press, 1967), 7–8.

22. See Georges Boudarel, "L'idéologie importée au Vietnam avec le Maoisme,"

in Boudarel, et al., eds., *La bureaucratie au Vietnam* (Paris: Harmattan, 1983), 31–106.

23. Truong Chinh, *Ban ve Cach mang Viet Nam* (On the Vietnamese Revolution) (Hanoi, 1956), 6.

24. It is curious that he did not attend the conference in the winter of 1949–1950 that adopted these changes. At the time he was en route to Beijing. See my *Ho Chi Minh*, 429.

25. Truong Chinh's speech is cited in *Van kien Dang* (1945–1954), vol. 2, pt. 2, 265–338.

26. Vo Nguyen Giap, *Nhiem vu Quan su truoc mat chuyen sang Tong phan cong* (On the Military Task of Preparing the General Counteroffensive) (Hanoi, 1950).

27. See Qiang Zhai, "Transplanting the Chinese Model: Chinese Military Advisers and the First Vietnam War, 1950–1954," in *Journal of Military History* (October 1993), 700–703, and *Chen Geng Riji* (Chen Geng's Diary), vol. 2 (Beijing: Liberation Army Publishing House, 1984), 38–39.

28. In his *People's War, People's Army*, Vo Nguyen Giap later wrote that the revolution "had to move" to a third stage and that the concept was "a general law of a revolutionary war such as Vietnam," since such a war could be victorious only when it could liberate land and annihilate a substantial proportion of the enemy's military forces. See page 88. He felt that mobile warfare would play the primary role in the final phase of the conflict, however, because it could most effectively utilize the spiritual advantage of the revolutionary forces, while positional war should be avoided because it magnified the enemy's material superiority on the battlefield. Giap, *Nhiem vu*, 33.

29. See *Liu Shaoqi Nianpu* (Liu Shaoqi's Chronicle) (n.p.: Central Documents Press, 1996), telegram of December 8, 1950, 265. The role of Chinese advisers in planning the general offensive is discussed in *Zhongguo junshi guwentuan fang Ywe kang fa douzheng shishi* (The Chinese Military Advisery Group in Vietnam during the Anti-French War) (Beijing: Liberation Army Publishing House, 1990), 27.

30. See Ho's political report to the Second Party Congress in *Ho Chi Minh: Selected Writings* (Hanoi: Foreign Languages Press, 1977), 114–117.

31. The quote is from Bui Dinh Thanh, "Nghien cu cac giai doan cua cuoc khang chien" (Studying the Stages in the War of Resistance) in *NCLS*, no. 45 (December 1962), 14.

32. Giap, *People's War, People's Army*, 148.

33. Report to the Sixth Plenum of the VWP, July 1954, translated in *Ho Chi Minh: Selected Writings*, 181–183.

34. Vo Nguyen Giap made his own contribution to the Vietnamese version of revolutionary war, but the record suggests that his role was primarily tactical in nature, to carry out grand strategic decisions made by the party leadership as a whole. After the conflict was over, he became one of the chief spokesmen for the Vietnamese revolution and a popularizer of the concept of people's war.

35. After the fall of Saigon in spring 1975, Hanoi's mythmakers clung to the fiction that the final "Ho Chi Minh campaign" against South Vietnamese troops had been a successful application of the "general offensive and uprising" format, which had been formally adopted by party leaders in the early 1960s and was designed to combine political and military forms of struggle in the final stages of the campaign. In reality, it was a conventional military offen-

sive that relied almost exclusively on military operations by main-force units from North Vietnam.

9. The Declining Value of Indochina: France and the Economics of Empire, 1950–1955

1. Jacques Marseille, "L'investissement français dans l'empire colonial: L'enquête du gouvernement de Vichy (1943)," *Revue historique* 512 (October-December 1974): 408–432.

2. Catherine Hodeir, *Le grand patronat colonial français face à la décolonisation*, PhD diss., Université de Paris 1, 1999, 327–329.

3. Hugues Tertrais, *Le coût de la guerre d'Indochine 1945–1954*, PhD diss., Université de Paris 1, 1998, 419.

4. Paul Bernard, "La mise en place du plan de modernisation et d'équipement de l'Indochine," *Marchés coloniaux du monde*, June 12, 1948, 967–969.

5. François Bloch-Lainé, ed., *La zone franc* (Paris: Presses universitaires de France, 1956), 486–487.

6. Ibid., 351, 486, 487.

7. Nguyen Kiem, *Le Sud-Vietnam depuis Dien Bien Phû* (Paris: Maspero, 1963), 150.

8. "Note pour M. le Ministre des Affaires étrangères," December 1955, MAE, Asie-Océanie, 1944–1955, Indochine, file 268.

9. Bousch report, March 25, 1954, Paris, Archives du Ministère des Finances, box B 33540, folder 2. Among the several official estimates of the cost of the Indochina war, this report by a French senator gives the lowest figures.

10. Bousch report; Jean-Marcel Jeanneney, *Tableaux statistiques relatifs à l'économie française et à l'économie mondiale* (Paris: Armand Colin, 1957), 157; Michael Louis Martin, *Warriors to Managers: The French Military Establishment since 1945* (Chapel Hill, N.C.: University of North Carolina Press, 1981), 54.

11. Georges Bidault in cabinet meeting, Dec. 2, 1953, in Vincent Auriol, *Journal du septennat*, vol. 7 (Paris: Armand Colin, 1970–1978), 538.

12. Tertrais, *Le coût de la guerre d'Indochine*, 124, 140, 256, 257, 449.

13. Etat-major combiné des forces armées, Troisième Division, fiche pour le Ministre, March 17, 1953, AN, René Pleven papers, series 560AP, box 48.

14. Ibid.

15. John S. Duffield, *Power Rules: The Evolution of NATO's Conventional Force Posture* (Stanford, Calif.: Stanford University Press, 1995), 97.

16. Secrétariat-général permanent de la défense nationale, "Résumé d'une étude de M. Leroy-Beaulieu . . . sur la contribution financière à la défense de l'Allemagne," Oct. 10, 1952, AN, 560AP48; Gerd Hardach, "The Marshall Plan in Germany, 1948–1952," *Journal of European Economic History* 16, no. 3 (winter 1987): 433–485.

17. Memo, "Assistance fournie par les Etats-Unis à la France pour l'équipement de ses forces armées," March 15, 1953, AN, Georges Bidault papers, series 457AP, box 44, folder 2.

18. Britain, France, and Italy all took advantage of offshore procurements to develop their own independent arms industries. They shunned the national specialization of armaments, which the United States recommended to NATO members.

19. "Note générale sur la politique française en Indochine" (unsigned), July 21, 1953, AN, René Mayer papers, series 363AP, box 31.

20. Alphonse Juin to René Pleven, Nov. 19, 1952, AN, 560AP48.

21. Pierre Rocolle, *Pourquoi Dien Bien Phû?* (Paris: Flammarion, 1968), 21.

22. Quotations in Auriol, *Journal du septennat,* vol. 7, 812n., and 813n.

23. "Comité de défense nationale," March 11, 1954, AN, 560AP50.

24. Ivan M. Lombardo (Paris), telegram to Ministry of Foreign Affairs, May 22, 1954, quoted in Michel Dumoulin, ed., *La Communauté Européenne de Défense: Leçons pour demain?* (Brussels: Peter Lang, 2000), 200.

25. Memo by Jean Laloy, "Entretien avec le conseiller de l'ambassade de l'URSS," March 26, 1954, MAE, Asie-Océanie, 1944–1955, Dossiers généraux, file 194.

26. Louis Joxe (Moscow) to Foreign Ministry, no. 1121–1130, April 14, 1954, MAE, Asie-Océanie, 1944–1955, Dossiers généraux, file 196.

27. "Note du Ministre des Etats Associés," Sept. 30, 1954, *Documents diplomatiques français, 1954 (21 juillet–31 décembre),* 489–492.

28. Walter Bedell Smith to John Foster Dulles, Sept. 30, 1954, *FRUS, 1952–1954,* vol. 13, pt. 2, 2100–2101.

10. "The Same Struggle for Liberty": Korea and Vietnam

1. Jacques Soustelle, "Indo-China and Korea: One Front," *Foreign Affairs* 29, no. 1 (October 1950): 56, 61, 64, 65, 66.

2. Quoted in *The US Government and the Vietnam War: Executive and Legislative Roles in Relationships,* pt. 1, 1945–1961 (Washington, D.C.: U.S. Government Printing Office, 1984), 68.

3. John F. Melby, "Memoir, Vietnam—1950," *Diplomatic History* 6, no. 1 (Winter 1982): 108.

4. George W. Allen, *None So Blind: A Personal Account of the Intelligence Failure in Vietnam* (Chicago: Ivan Dee, 2001), 20.

5. Ibid., 22.

6. "Substance of Statements Made at Wake Island Conference on 15 October 1950," *FRUS, 1950,* 7: 957–958. Truman referred specifically to the trip Philip Jessup had just completed: a fourteen-country tour of Asia in March 1950. Jessup had found the French sadly wanting in Indochina. They were "failing to put over their viewpoint" on Indochina and Asia. They are conspicuously lacking in a sense of public relations." They were making "somewhat the same mistakes that the British General Braddock made in the French and Indian Wars." Bao Dai's government "would be deficient in competent personnel even if all elements rallied to his side." *FRUS, 1950,* 6, April 3, 1950: 69, 71.

7. "Substance of Statements Made at Wake Island Conference on 15 October 1950," *FRUS, 1950,* 7:957–958.

8. Ibid. According to MacArthur, it wasn't much of a problem to begin with: "He contrasted the Indochinese situation sharply with Korea and left the impression that our problem in Korea was more difficult from a military point of view than the problem faced by the French in Indochina." Rusk, perhaps recalling Radford's offhand comment, asked MacArthur "how seriously popular opinion should be weighed as a military factor in such operations as Indochina and Korea." Would, for example, a hostile population have interfered with the landing at Inchon? "He replied that a hostile population could, of course, have made the task more difficult but it would not have been a decisive factor," because "armed men passing through a village in Asia

are treated with the highest respect." It was more of an annoyance than anything else, due to the "logistic support which it gives the enemy" such as
"food, water, care of wounded and, particularly, intelligence." The plain talk
and cold turkey Truman promised French prime minister, René Pleven
turned out to be rather mild so far as the French were concerned but very
tough about the Chinese. There would be no recognition of the communist
regime. "They have been very mean to all Americans," Truman informed
Pleven. "They have mistreated our people every time they had a chance, and
we have been their friends ever since the Open Door Policy, and a long time
before that. I don't appreciate that." Pleven acknowledged that France had
been slow to see the Chinese as aggressors, but once they crossed the thirty-
eighth parallel into South Korea, "we reached the same conclusion about the
Chinese communists that you did." France would, therefore, support a U.S.
resolution on Chinese aggression in the United Nations. Memorandum for
the President, January 30, 1951, Secretary's File, Harry S. Truman Library, Declassified Documents Research Service. As Washington braced for the opening of hearings on General MacArthur's recall, a leak to the *New York Times*
made public not only the general's doubts about the possibility of China entering the Korean War but also his strictures on the quality of French troops
in Indochina. The reporter added, in brackets: "The French there have made
considerable progress since." See Anthony Leviero, "Wake Talks Bared," *New
York Times,* April 21, 1951, 1. The following week, Tillman Durdin reported
on the "pained surprise" with which the report was read in Hanoi. "Americans here [in Hanoi]," Durdin wrote, "are inclined to agree with the French
reactions." An American officer attached to French troops ranked the French
soldier in Indochina above his American counterpart. Tillman Durdin,
"M'Arthur Report Pains Frenchmen," *New York Times,* May 1, 1951, 6.

9. Tillman Durdin, "De Lattre Cheers French in Vietnam," *New York Times,*
Jan. 11, 1951, 4. De Lattre returned the compliment. "De Lattre Credits U.S.
Aid in Tongking," read a headline in the *New York Times* shortly after his appointment. "French Chief Says American Supplies Played Big Part in Successful Defense," January 24, 1951, 6. Hardly a week went by without a puff
piece on de Lattre by Durdin. See, for example, "French Are Heartened by
Gains in Indo-China," *New York Times,* Jan. 28, 1951, E-4. Durdin was cautious.
In careful subjunctive clauses he pointed out that it was necessary to "emphasize that many basic realities of the situation might well continue to war-
rant a contrasting mood of gloom and pessimism." These included the
increased strength of the Viet Minh and the possibility of Chinese intervention. For Durdin's profile, see "Fighter on a Mission," *New York Times* February 18, 1951, 152.

10. Durdin, "Fighter on a Mission," 152.

11. "Far East General is 'D. D. T.' to French," *New York Times,* Aug. 19, 1951, 23.
Irwin Wall observed that only "the pressures of war and desperation over the
possibility of losing both Korea and Vietnam can explain the American in-
fatuation with the general, who had previously been highly regarded in
Washington, but also suspected for his alleged flirtation with Communism."
Wall, *The United States and the Making of Postwar France, 1945–1954* (New York:
Cambridge University Press, 1991), 243.

12. Michael James, "De Lattre of Rhine, Danube and Tonkin," *New York Times
Magazine,* Aug. 26, 1951, 59.

13. Hanson Baldwin, "The Crisis in Indo-China," *New York Times Magazine,* Jan. 5, 1951, 4. Baldwin described de Lattre as a man of "much temperament and little tact . . . He proved to be one of the most difficult French officers with whom Americans had to deal during the last war."

14. Memorandum, Charlton Ogburn to Dean Rusk, August 18, 1950, *FRUS, 1950,* 6:863–864. In the same memorandum, Ogburn pointed to the central contradiction, one which would not change over the entire course of the French war in Indochina: "the French, who have been telling us every few days for many months that the French Army cannot be expected to fight for Vietnamese independence, have now decided that we should build up a Vietnamese Army to fight for the French Union." Ogburn's prescience—and his open contempt for the quality of many of his fellow State Department officers—was apparent in an earlier memorandum. In March he noted the absence in Saigon of anyone who knew anything about the country. It was not, therefore, surprising that the legation should imagine that American aid would have much of an impact on the military situation. "My hunch is that Ho Chi-minh's cohorts having stood off 130–150 thousand French colonial troops for four years (during which time they must have conceived a blazing hatred for France and France's friends), are not going to wilt under the *psychological* impact of American military assistance. They might on the other hand give way under the *physical* impact of American weapons—if we send enough. Should things get too hot for them, they will, I suppose, do what the Indonesian Republicans used to tell us they would do—i.e., go underground until a more propitious occasion presented itself. So unless the French are prepared to police Vietnam indefinitely or are enabled by the magnitude of our assistance actually to kill off a hundred thousand of the more ardent Vietnamese rebels, it may well be that a military decision now—even if it can be achieved—will be followed a couple of years hence by a take-over by Ho's party." Ogburn to Walton Butterworth, March 21, 1950, *FRUS,* 6:767 (italics original).

15. John Ohly to Dean Acheson, November 20, 1950, quoted in *The US Government and the Vietnam War: Executive and Legislative Roles in Relationships,* pt. 1, 1945–1961 (Washington, D.C.: Government Printing Office, 1984), 84.

16. Durdin, "M'Arthur Report Pains Frenchmen."

17. Donald Heath to Secretary of State, May 15, 1951, *FRUS,* 6, pt. 1: 419. Heath called the general's tone "impertinent."

18. Heath to Secretary of State, June 14, 1951, *FRUS,* 6, pt. 1: 425–428.

19. This charge was immediately refuted in a telegram from Ambassador David Bruce to the Secretary of State, 19 June 1951, *FRUS,* 6, pt 1: 428–429.

20. Ibid.: Heath to Secretary of State, June 14, 1951, *FRUS,* 6, pt. 1: 425–428. Acheson's response to French complaints was acerbic. One of USIE's main functions was to teach English; the Vietnamese wanted it and, if they were to make use of American aid, needed it. Of course French should continue to be Vietnam's second language, but teaching it was hardly a USIE task. Similarly, it was "entirely appropriate" that the first book USIE had translated was on U.S. history. "If the Viets 'know nothing or little' of their own history or that of France, this is a problem for the Ministry of Education and incidentally one which should have been taken up long ago." It was not an American problem. Acheson to Heath, July 13, 1951, *FRUS,* 6, pt. 1: 453.

21. Heath to Secretary of State, June 14, 1951, *FRUS,* 6, pt. 1: 425ff.

22. The U.S. consul in Hanoi thought there were additional explanations for de

Lattre's angry mood: "De Lattre looked old and worn-out, spoke very low, almost in reverie but very bitterly." The cause was the death of his son Bernard in combat. "What price all this sacrifice," de Lattre had asked, "if those ostensibly on our side refuse to believe in our sincerity? If this constant sacrificing of our youths' flower does not prove us sincere in desire to give Vietnam independence, what further is necessary to drive the idea home?" In a "bona fide war," he would have had the consolation of knowing Bernard had died a hero's death. Instead, his son had "been offered up on behalf of an ungrateful people," who not only had not warned the French unit there were Viet Minh in the area, but had "booed and hissed *'vendus'* (sold out)" at the Vietnamese soldiers accompanying them." There was no comment on this indication that French sincerity was widely in doubt, nor on the "typical first reaction" of Vietnamese officials to the news—fear that de Lattre would order napalm reprisal raids. Bao Dai was also worried, telling Heath he feared that de Lattre "might now conceive war as one of revenge." Wendell Blancke to Secretary of State, May 31, 1951, *FRUS,* 6, pt. 1: 424, 425.

23. Heath to Secretary of State, June 29, 1951, *FRUS,* 6, pt. 1: 433–439.

24. Bruce to Secretary of State, July 5, 1951, *FRUS,* 6, pt. 1: 443.

25. Blum was also a CIA agent. See *The US Government and the Vietnam War,* 91.

26. Robert Blum to Secretary of State, July 12, 1951, *FRUS,* 6, pt. 1: 450, 451.

27. Jonathan B. Bingham to Secretary of State, July 12 1951, *FRUS,* 6, pt. 1: 448, 449.

28. Donald Heath to Secretary of State, July 20, 1951, *FRUS,* 6, pt. 1: 457–459.

29. Livingston Merchant to Dean Rusk, July 27, 1951, *FRUS,* 6, pt. 1: 462–464.

30. Ibid.

31. In August, Heath left for consultations in Washington, Paris, and London, and the chargé, Edmond Gullion, took over. Gullion to Secretary of State, Aug. 18, 1951, *FRUS,* 6, pt. 1: 480–484.

32. "The French MacArthur," *Time,* Sept. 24, 1951, 32. "Africa is a good place to stay away from," Bogart told the press, "but I suppose that statement will burn up all the Africans."

33. Ibid.

34. "The French MacArthur," *Time,* Sept. 24, 1951, 32, 35; Michael James, "De Lattre Cites Indo-China Peril," *New York Times,* Sept. 14, 1951, section 3, 5.

35. Editorial, "De Lattre and His Message," *Life,* 31, no. 13, Sept. 24, 1951, 52.

36. Ibid.

37. "The French MacArthur," *Time,* Sept. 24, 1951, 32, 33, 34, 35. For all its adulation of de Lattre and, in particular, his appeals to the Vietnamese to fight for their country, *Time* admitted that according to U.S. observers, "half the Indo-Chinese would still vote for Ho rather than French-supported Bao [Dai]" in free elections.

38. *New York Times,* Sept. 15, 1951, 2.

39. De Lattre made the same point at a National Press Club luncheon: "Once Tongking is lost there is really no barrier before Suez, and I will leave to your imagination how defeatism and defeat would swell up as time passes, how Communist fifth columns would get into the game in every country as strong external Communist forces apply pressure on their frontiers." "Asia Called Stake of Indo-China War," *New York Times,* Sept. 31, 1951, 3.

40. Minutes to meeting at the Pentagon, Sept. 20, 1951, *FRUS,* 6, pt. 1: 517–521.

41. Memorandum of conversation by William M. Gibson, Office of Philippines

and Southeast Asian Affairs. Members of de Lattre's staff confided to a reporter that while the talks had been cordial enough, they felt the United States had "a tendency to underestimate the Viet minh forces. 'They do not seem to fully understand the problems of guerillas,' this officer asserted. 'You have to fight in Indo-China to know about that kind of Communist.'" Michael James, "U.S. Asked to Assay Indo-China's Peril," *New York Times,* Sept. 16, 1951, 5.

42. *U.S.-Vietnam Relations: 1945–1967: Study Prepared by the Department of Defense* (Washington, D.C.: U.S. Government Printing Office, 1971), book 8, Nov. 6, 1951, 459.

43. Henry R. Lieberman, "Report on the 'Little Wars' of Southeast Asia," *New York Times,* Sept. 9, 1951, B-4.

44. Robert Allen Griffin to Richard Bissell, Nov. 30, 1951, *FRUS,* 6, pt. 1: 549.

45. Donald Heath to Secretary of State, Dec. 9, 1951, *FRUS,* 6, pt. 1: 558–559.

46. Substance of discussions of State–Joint Chiefs of Staff meeting at the Pentagon building, Dec. 21, 1951, *FRUS,* 6, pt. 1: 569–570. When asked if France could hold on in Indochina if the Chinese stayed out, General Collins answered that they could, "but there is no chance that they really can clean up the situation." Nitze then wondered what it would take, and Collins responded, "a lot." Two things worried him: the lack of able native leadership and the fact that "as of now the Indochina thing is clearly a one man show. If anything should happen to De Lattre, it might all go to pieces."

47. Geoffrey Warner, "Britain and the Crisis over Dien Bien Phu, April, 1954: The Failure of United Action," in Laurence S. Kaplan, et al., *Dien Bien Phu and the Crisis of Franco-American Relations, 1954–1955* (Wilmington, Del.: SR Books, 1990), 56.

48. "Asia Called Stake of Indo-China War," *New York Times,* Sept. 21, 1951, 3.

49. Memorandum of the discussion at the 177th Meeting of the National Security Council, December 24, 1953, 13 (DDRS).

50. Ibid., 19. Nixon hoped the United States could convince the Indochinese that independence within the French Union was indeed possible.

51. Robert S. McNamara et al., *Argument without End: In Search of Answers to the Vietnam Tragedy* (New York: Public Affairs, 1999), 53.

52. Ibid., 82. Luu Doan Huynh, a Vietnamese historian, reflected that American after American explained that the United States did not intend to attack Vietnam in the mid 1950s. "But really," he said, "your bullets are the killers of our people. We see that this is America's gift to Vietnam—allowing the French to kill our people. This is the most convincing evidence we have of America's loyalties in this affair . . . please try to understand me when I say: *Blood speaks with a terrible voice!*"

11. Assessing Dien Bien Phu

1. Jacques Valette, *La guerre d'Indochine 1945–1954* (Paris: Armand Colin, 1994), 183–192.

2. Jacques Thobie, Gilbert Meynier, Catherine Coquery-Vidrovitch, and Charles-Robert Ageron, *Histoire de la France coloniale, 1914–1990* (Paris: Armand Colin, 1990), 380.

3. General Henri Navarre, *Agonie de l'Indochine, 1953–1954* (Paris: Plon, 1956),

62–88. On French government attitudes see Jules Roy, *The Battle of Dien Bien Phu* (New York: Pyramid Books, 1966), 41–43.

4. Memorandum of discussion at 161st Meeting of the National Security Council, Sept. 9, 1953. Department of State, *Foreign Relations of the United States, 1952–1954,* vol.13, *Indochina* (Washington, D.C.: U.S. Government Printing Office, 1982), 782, 785.

5. The best account of the siege in English remains Bernard B. Fall, *Hell in a Very Small Place: The Siege of Dien Bien Phu* (New York: Lippincott, 1966). More recently see Howard R. Simpson, *Dien Bien Phu: The Epic Battle America Forgot* (Washington, D.C.: Brasseys, 1994). The definitive battle account in French may be Roger Bruge, *Les hommes de Dien Bien Phu* (Paris: Librairie académique Perrin, 1999). The definitive operational account that bears the fruits of documentary research remains Pierre Rocolle, *Pourquoi Dien Bien Phû?* (Paris: Flammarion, 1968). Also see Captain Jean Pouget, *Nous etions à Dien Bien Phû* (Paris: Presses de la Cité, 1954). The paragraphs in this chapter that center on the battle are based on these sources.

6. See John Prados, *Operation Vulture* (New York: ibooks, 2002).

7. Allan W. Cameron, ed., *Vietnam Crisis: A Documentary History,* vol. 1: *1940–1956* (Ithaca, N.Y.: Cornell University Press, 1971), 218.

8. On Geneva, see Jean Lacouture and Philippe Devillers, *The End of a War: Indochina 1954* (New York: Praeger, 1969), from which the "two of clubs" quote is drawn. Also see Robert Randle, *Geneva, 1954* (Princeton: Princeton University Press, 1969).

9. CIA, NIE 63–54, "Consequences within Indochina of the Fall of Dien Bien Phu," April 30, 1954, *FRUS, 1952–1954,* 13: 1451.

10. Prados, *Operation Vulture,* 156–160.

11. "Indochina: American Style," *Time,* June 14, 1954, 33.

12. National Security Council, "Memorandum of Discussion at the 196th Meeting of the National Security Council," May 8, 1954, *FRUS, 1952–1954,* 13: 1505.

13. Alexander Zervoudakis, "Nihil mirare, nihilcontemptare, omnia intelligere: Franco-Vietnamese Intelligence in Indochina, 1950–1954," *Intelligence and National Security* 13, no. 1 (spring 1998): 195–229.

14. Quoted in Simpson, *Dien Bien Phu: The Epic Battle America Forgot,* 174–175.

15. "Indochina: Concentrate! Reinforce!" *Time,* May 31, 1954, 22.

16. State Department cable 4194, May 21, 1954, *FRUS, 1952–1954,* 13: 594.

17. General Paul Ely, *Memoires I: L'Indochine dans la tourmente* (Paris: Plon, 1964), 181–189.

18. Georges Fleury, *La guerre en Indochine 1945–1954* (Paris: Plon, 1994), 359–374.

19. Thobie, et al., *Histoire de la France coloniale,* 381–382.

20. NSC-124, "Draft—Indochina Section of NSC Paper," Feb. 13, 1952, *FRUS, 1952–1954,* 82–91.

21. Department of Defense study, *United States–Vietnam Relations 1945–1967* (Washington, D.C.: Government Printing Office, n.d. [1972]), book 8, 520–534.

22. *Public Papers of the Presidents of the United States: Dwight D. Eisenhower, 1954* (Washington, D.C.: Government Printing Office, 1960), 381–390.

23. Department of State draft, "Joint Resolution," April 2, 1954, *FRUS, 1952–1954,* vol. 13, 1211–1212.

24. *Treaties and Alliances of the World: An International Survey Covering Treaties in*

Force and Communities of States (New York: Charles Scribner's Sons, 1974), 195–198.

25. Dwight D. Eisenhower, *The White House Years: Mandate for Change, 1953–1956* (Garden City, N.Y.: Doubleday, 1963), 347.

26. Enlightening on this point is Paul R. Kattenburg, *The Vietnam Trauma in American Foreign Policy, 1945–1975* (New Brunswick, N.J.: Transaction Books, 1980).

27. Cameron, *Vietnam Crisis*, 350–351.

28. David L. Anderson, *Trapped by Success: The Eisenhower Administration and Vietnam* (New York: Columbia University Press, 1991), passim.

29. See Robert H. Ferrell, ed., *The Eisenhower Diaries* (New York: Norton, 1981).

30. Eisenhower, *The White House Years*, 351, 364.

31. Quoted in ibid, 351, 364.

32. This and the previous quotes are from Arthur M. Schlesinger Jr., *A Thousand Days: John F. Kennedy in the White House* (New York: Fawcett, 1967), 300.

33. *Washington Star*, May 10, 1954.

34. Chalmers Roberts, "The Day We Didn't Go to War," *Reporter*, Sept. 14, 1954.

35. Prados, *Operation Vulture*, 116–129.

36. Robert A. Caro, *The Years of Lyndon Johnson: Master of the Senate* (New York: Knopf, 2002), 488–570.

37. Department of State, "Memorandum for the Secretary's File," April 5, 1954, DDEL, Dulles papers, Subject series, box 9, folder: "Indochina 1954 (2)."

38. Lyndon B. Johnson, "Your Senator Reports," April 15, 1954, LBJ Library, Johnson papers, Senate papers, constituent newsletters. All the quotes that follow are taken from the same source, from issues dated as given in the text.

39. LBJ Library, Johnson papers, Senate papers, constituent mail for March and April 1954.

40. Fredrik Logevall, *Choosing War: The Lost Chance for Peace and the Escalation of War in Vietnam* (Berkeley: University of California Press, 1999).

41. Richard M. Nixon, *RN: The Memoirs of Richard Nixon* (New York: Warner Books, 1978), vol. 1, 190.

42. Lewis Chester, Godfrey Hodgson, and Bruce Page, *An American Melodrama: The Presidential Campaign of 1968* (New York: Dell, 1969), 761.

12. China and the Indochina Settlement at the Geneva Conference of 1954

1. Among new Chinese sources on the Geneva Conference of 1954, the most notable are the documents declassified in summer 2004 and made available to researchers at the Foreign Ministry Archive (hereafter FMA) of the People's Republic of the China.

2. See *Foreign Relations of the United States, 1952–1954*, 16: 415.

3. *FRUS, 1952–1954*, 16: 415.

4. Li Ping and Ma Zhisun et al., *Zhou Enlai nianpu, 1949–1976* (A Chronological Record of Zhou Enlai) (Beijing: Zhongyang wenxian, 1998), vol. 1, 355; Shi Zhe, *Zai lishi juren shenbian: Shi Zhe huiyilu* (At the Side of Historical Giants: Shi Zhe's Memoir) (Beijing: Zhongyang dangxiao, 1998), 480.

5. Li, *Zhou Enlai nianpu*, 355; Xiong Huayuan, *Zhou Enlai chudeng shijie wutai* (Zhou Enlai's First Appearance on the World Stage) (Shenyang: Liaoning renmin, 1999), 5–6.

6. Li, *Zhou Enlai nianpu*, 356–357; Jin Chongji, et al., *Zhou Enlai zhuan, 1949–1976* (A Biography of Zhou Enlai) (Beijing: Zhongyang wenxian, 1998), 154–156.

7. For a more detailed discussion of Beijing's changing policies toward Taiwan in 1953 and 1954, see Chen Jian, *Mao's China and the Cold War* (Chapel Hill, N.C.: University of North Carolina Press, 2001), 167–170.

8. Wang Bingnan, *Zhongmei huitan jiunian* (Recollections of Nine Years of Sino-American Talks) (Beijing: Shijie zhishi, 1985), 5–6; Zhou Enlai, "Report on Diplomatic Issues," Aug. 12, 1954, Fujian Provincial Archive, 101–5–5, 54.08.12.

9. Mao's relationship with Zhou Enlai and his "peace initiative" in 1954 and 1955 was a complicated one. Although Mao supported the "peaceful coexistence" foreign policy at that time, he regretted it in summer 1958, when the Great Leap Forward was emerging in China. For a more detailed discussion, see Chen Jian, *Mao's China and the Cold War*, 343.

10. For definition and discussion of Chinese "victim mentality," see Chen Jian, *Mao's China and the Cold War*, 12–13.

11. See Chen Jian, *Mao's China and the Cold War*, chap. 5; see also Zhai Qiang, *China and the Vietnam Wars* (Chapel Hill, N.C.: University of North Carolina Press, 2000), chaps. 1–2.

12. Li, *Zhou Enlai nianpu*, 358; Xiong, *Zhou Enlai chudeng shijie wutai*, 12–13.

13. Xiong, *Zhou Enlai chudeng shijie wutai*, 13; Li Lianqing, *Da waijiaojia Zhou Enlai: shezhan rineiwa* (Great Diplomat Zhou Enlai: The Geneva Debate) (Hong Kong: Tiandi tushu, 1994), 86.

14. See Ilya V. Gaiduk, *Confronting Vietnam: Soviet Policy toward the Indochina Conflict, 1954–1963* (Washington, D.C., and Stanford, Calif.: Woodrow Wilson Center Press and Stanford University Press, 2003), chap. 2.

15. Zhou to CCP Central Committee, concerning meetings with Malenkov, Molotov, and other Soviet leaders, April 23, 1954, 206–00048–08, FMA; Shi Zhe, *Zai lishi jüren shenbian*, 480–486; see also Li, *Zhou Enlai nianpu*, 360; Xiong, *Zhou Enlai chudeng shijie wutai*, 13. For an account of Moscow's handling of the meeting based on Russian documents, see Gaiduk, *Confronting Vietnam*, 22–24.

16. Zhou to Mao, Liu and CCP Central Committee, April 28, 1954, cited from Li, *Zhou Enlai nianpu*, 363; see also Zhou to CCP Central Committee, April 26 and 30, 1954, concerning the first meeting of the Geneva Conference and the meetings of April 28 and 29, 1954, 206–00045–01 and 206–00045–02, FMA.

17. Telegram, Zhou to CCP Central Committee, concerning conversation with Eden, May 1, 1954, 206–00005–03, FMA; see also Li, *Zhou Enlai nianpu*, 364.

18. Xiong, *Zhou Enlai chudeng shijie wutai*, 81–82; see also *FRUS, 1952–1954*, 16, 755–756.

19. Li, *Zhou Enlai nianpu*, 365–366.

20. Zhou to Wei Guoqing and report to CCP Central Committee, May 13, 1954, Li, *Zhou Enlai nianpu*, 367.

21. Minute, meeting between Chinese, Soviet, and Vietnamese delegations, May 15, 1954, Institute of Contemporary China under the Chinese Academy of Social Science, comp. *Zhongsu guanxi dangan wenjian xuanbian, 1945–1989*

(Selected Archival Documents of Sino-Soviet Relations, 1949–1989) (Beijing: Dangdai zhongguo yanjiu suo, 1997), 69–72; Li, *Zhou Enlai nianpu*, 367–368; see also Zhou to CCP Central Committee, concerning the first secret session on Indochina, May 18, 1954, 206–00045–12, FMA.

22. Minutes, Zhou's meetings with Eden, May 14, 20, and 27, 1954, 206–00005–01, 206–00005–02, 206–00005–03, FMA; Li, *Zhou Enlai nianpu*, 367, 368–369, 370.

23. Zhou to Mao, Liu, and CCP Central Committee, May 17, 28, and 29, 1954, Li, *Zhou Enlai nianpu*, 368, 370–371.

24. Ibid., 371–372.

25. Zhou to Mao, Liu, and CCP Central Committee, Jin, *Zhou Enlai zhuan, 1949–1976*, 168–169.

26. CCP Central Committee to Zhou, May 31, 1954, Li, *Zhou Enlai nianpu*, 372.

27. Zhou to Mao, Liu, and CCP Central Committee, June 8, 1954 (two telegrams were dispatched on the day), Li, *Zhou Enlai nianpu*, 377–378.

28. Zhou to Mao, Liu, and CCP Central Committee, June 12, 1954, Li, *Zhou Enlai nianpu*, 380.

29. Qu Xing, *Zhongguo waijiao wushi nian* (Fifty Years of Chinese Diplomacy) (Nanjing: Jiangsu renmin, 2000), 118.

30. Xiong, *Zhou Enlai chudeng shijie wutai*, 90–91; Li, *Zhou Enlai nianpu*, 383–384.

31. Li, *Zhou Enlai nianpu*, 383–384; Xiong, *Zhou Enlai chudeng shijie wutai*, 90–91; Qu, *Zhongguo waijiao wushi nian*, 121.

32. Minute, Zhou's meeting with Eden, June 16, 1954, 206–00005–05, FMA; see also Li, *Zhou Enlai nianpu*, 385–387.

33. Li, *Zhou Enlai nianpu*, 383; Jin, *Zhou Enlai zhuan, 1949–1976*, 169; see also *FRUS, 1952–1954*, 16:1158.

34. Minute, Zhou's meeting with Bidault, June 17, 1954, 206–00006–02, FMA; Li, *Zhou Enlai nianpu*, 387.

35. *FRUS, 1952–1954*, 16:1204–1205.

36. Zhou to Mao, Liu, and CCP Central Committee, Xiong, *Zhou Enlai chudeng shijie wutai*, 98.

37. Ibid., 91; Li, *Zhou Enlai nianpu, 1949–1976*, 385–386.

38. CCP Central Committee to Zhou, June 20, 1954, 206–00049–01, 6–7, FMA; CCP Central Committee to Wei Guoqing and Qiao Xiaoguang for delivery to VWP Central Committee, June 20, 1954, 206–00049–01, 8–9, FMA.

39. Zhou to Mao, Liu, and CCP Central Committee, June 19, 1954, cited from Xiong, *Zhou Enlai chudeng shijie wutai*, 91.

40. Minute, Zhou's meeting with Mendès France, June 23, 1954, 206–00006–06, FMA; see also *FRUS, 1952–1954*, 16:1233–1234.

41. Minute, Zhou's meeting with Phoui Sananikone, June 21, 1954, 206–00007–03, FMA; Zhou to CCP Central Committee, concerning meeting with Cambodian and Laotian delegates, June 24, 1954, 106–00046–29, FMA; Li, *Zhou Enlai nianpu*, 388–389; Li, *Da waijiaojia Zhou Enlai*, 306–314.

42. The five principles, or *Pancha shila*, include (1) mutual respect for sovereignty and territorial integrity, (2) nonaggression, (3) noninterference in another country's internal affairs, (4) equal and mutual benefit, and (5) peaceful coexistence.

43. Zhou to CCP Central Committee, 13:00, July 3, 1954, 206–00019–03, 22, concerning meetings with Ho Chi Minh and other Vietnamese leaders, FMA; see also Li, *Zhou Enlai nianpu*, 394; Xiong, *Zhou Enlai chudeng shijie wutai*, 140.

44. Qu, *Zhongguo waijiao wushi nian,* 127; Zhou to CCP Central Committee, 13:00, concerning meetings with Ho Chi Minh and other Vietnamese leaders, July 3, 1954, 206–00019–03, 22, FMA.
45. Ibid.
46. Zhou to CCP Central Committee, 18:00, July 4, 1954, 206–00019–03, 23–24, concerning meetings with Ho Chi Minh and other Vietnamese leaders, FMA; Qu, *Zhongguo waijiao wushi nian,* 127–128, and Xiong, *Zhou Enlai chudeng shijie wutai,* 141–142.
47. Xiong, *Zhou Enlai chudeng shijie wutai,* 142.
48. Ibid., 143–144.
49. Li, *Zhou Enlai nianpu,* 394–395; Wang, *Zhongmei huitan jiunian,* 13.
50. Ho Chi Minh, "Report to the Sixth Meeting of the VWP Central Committee," July 15, 1954, *Hu Zhiming xuanji* (Selected Works of Ho Chi Minh, Chinese language edition) (Hanoi: Foreign Language Press, 1962), 2:290–298.
51. Xiong, *Zhou Enlai chudeng shijie wutai,* 145; Li, *Zhou Enlai nianpu,* 395.
52. Xiong, *Zhou Enlai chudeng shijie wutai,* 145–146; Li, *Zhou Enlai nianpu,* 395.
53. Li, *Zhou Enlai nianpu,* 395; Xiong, *Zhou Enlai chudeng shijie wutai,* 147.
54. Zhou to Mao, Liu, and forward to Ho Chi Minh, July 11, 1954, cited from Xiong, *Zhou Enlai chudeng shijie wutai,* 147–148; see also Li, *Zhou Enlai nianpu,* 396–197.
55. Xiong, *Zhou Enlai chudeng shijie wutai,* 148.
56. Ibid., 150.
57. Xiong, *Zhou Enlai chudeng shijie wutai,* 151–152; Li, *Da waijiaojia Zhou Enlai,* 352–358; Qu, *Zhongguo waijiao wushi nian,* 131–132; Li, *Zhou Enlai nianpu,* 397.
58. Xiong, *Zhou Enlai chudeng shijie wutai,* 154.
59. Minute, Zhou's meeting with Eden, July 13, 1954, 206–00005–07, FMA.
60. Li, *Zhou Enlai nianpu,* 398–402. According to Chinese sources, Zhou, Molotov, and Dong reached an agreement to accept the seventeenth parallel as the demarcation line at a meeting on July 19. For an account of Molotov's role in the last stage of the negotiation, see Gaiduk, *Confronting Vietnam,* 43–49.
61. Although the agreement was signed at 3:00 AM on July 21, it was dated July 20, so that Mendès France could still allege that his deadline had been kept.

13. After Geneva: The French Presence in Vietnam, 1954–1963

I would like to thank Kenneth Osgood for his helpful comments on earlier drafts of this essay.

1. See Nicola Cooper, *France in Indochina: Colonial Encounters* (Oxford and New York: Berg, 2001), chaps. 1–3, for a detailed analysis of French motivations and methods in colonizing Indochina.
2. See, for example, Seth Jacobs, "'Our System Demands the Supreme Being': The U.S. Religious Revival and the 'Diem Experiment,' 1954–1955," *Diplomatic History* 25 (fall 2001), 596; and George McT. Kahin, *Intervention: How America Became Involved in Vietnam* (New York: Anchor, 1986), 66.
3. Memo, July 10, 1954, SHAT, Ely papers, vol. 40; Laurent Cesari, "La France, les Etats-Unis, et l'Indochine, 1945–1957," Diss., Université de Nanterre, 1991, 812.
4. Alain Ruscio, *La guerre française d'Indochine* (Brussels: Complexe, 1992), 229.

Many French officials doubted Diem's chances for success, preferring to work with pro-French elements such as former premiers Tran Van Huu, Nguyen Van Tam, Buu Loc, or Dr. Phan Huy Quat. See also William Duiker, *U.S. Containment Policy and the Conflict in Indochina* (Stanford: Stanford University Press, 1994), 198; de Jean to MAE, Sept. 10, 1954, *DDF, 1954,* 320–321; foreign ministry memo, July 29, 1954, MAE, Cabinet du Ministre, Cabinet Pineau, vol. 18.

5. Meetings in Saigon, Aug. 21 and 24, 1954, SHAT, Ely papers, vol. 37; Baudet to MAE, Aug. 13, 1954, MAE, Asie, 1944–1955, Indochine, vol. 157.

6. Minute of understanding between Bedell Smith, La Chambre, and Faure, Sept. 27–29, 1954; Smith to Saigon, Sept. 28, 1954, *FRUS, 1954,* 13:2080–2081; memcon, Mendès France, Eden, and Dulles, Oct. 23, 1954, MAE, Asie 1944–1955, Indochine, vol. 194. See also Frank Costigliola, *France and the United States: The Cold Alliance 1940–1990* (New York: Twayne, 1992), 109; telegram Dillon to State Department, Jan. 6, 1955, *FRUS, 1955–1957,* 1:19; Achilles to State Department, Jan. 18, 1955, *FRUS, 1955–1957,* 1:45; and summary of tripartite meetings, Dec. 18, 1954, MAE, Asie 1944–1955, Indochine, vol. 157.

7. Young to State Department, March 25, 1955, *FRUS, 1955–1957,* 1:147.

8. LaForest to Ely, March 31, 1955, *DDF, 1955,* 373–374.

9. Dillon to DOS, April 13, 1955, NARA, RG 59, microfilm, C0008, reel 2; Pinay to Couve de Murville, April 21, 1955, *DDF, 1955,* 484–486; Gibson to Roux, April 13, 1955, MAE, Asie 1944–1955, Indochine, vol. 196. See also Roux to MAE, April 14, 1955, MAE, Asie 1944–1955, Indochine, vol. 87; LaForest to Ely, April 13, 1955, *DDF, 1955,* 437–439; Dulles to Saigon, NARA, RG 59, microfilm LM071, reel 15.

10. Couve de Murville to MAE, April 28, 1955, *DDF, 1955,* 523–524.

11. See David Anderson, *Trapped by Success: The Eisenhower Administration and Vietnam, 1953–1961* (New York: Columbia University Press, 1991), 110–113, for detail on the sect crisis. For a first-hand account, see Edward Lansdale, *In the Midst of Wars: An American's Mission to Southeast Asia* (New York: Harper and Row, 1972), 244–312. For a summary of Franco-U.S. discussions, see Pinay to Couve de Murville, April 29, 1955, *DDF, 1955,* 541–543.

12. Ely to MAE, April 21, 1955, SHAT, Ely papers, vol. 39.

13. See Daniel P. O'C. Greene, "John Foster Dulles and the End of the Franco-American Entente in Indochina," *Diplomatic History* 16 (fall 1992): 511–549; Ely to MAE, May 6, 1954, SHAT, Ely Papers, vol. 39; Ely to MAE, May 15, 1955, SHAT, Ely papers, vol. 40.

14. MAE to Hoppenot, Aug. 2, 1955, MAE, Papiers d'Agents, Henri Hoppenot Papers, vol. 15.

15. Article 14a of the Agreement on the Cessation of Hostilities in Vietnam and Point 7 of the Final Declaration of the Geneva Conference on Indochina, July 21, 1954, in Frank Weinstein, *Vietnam's Unheld Elections: The Failure to Carry Out the 1956 Reunification Elections and the Effect on Hanoi's Present Outlook* (Ithaca, N.Y.: Cornell University Press, 1966), 10–12.

16. Duiker, *U.S. Containment Policy,* 213, 217, and Weinstein, *Vietnam's Unheld Elections,* 20. For discussion of the legal obligations that the United States and South Vietnam incurred under the Geneva agreements, see Robert Randle, *Geneva 1954;* Richard Falk, ed., *The Vietnam War and International Law* (Princeton, 1968), 543–573; and Weinstein, *Vietnam's Unheld Elections,* 11–13.

17. Anderson, *Trapped By Success*, 123–124.

18. See, for example, George Herring, *America's Longest War: The United States and Vietnam, 1950–1975* (New York: Knopf, 1986), 55–56; Robert Scigliano, *South Vietnam: Nation under Stress* (Boston: Houghton Mifflin, 1964), 134; Kahin, *Intervention*, 89; Stanley Karnow, *Vietnam: A History* (New York: Viking, 1983), 24; Laurent Cesari, "La France, les Etats-Unis, et l'Indochine," 891–892, 913, 968, 1074–1075.

19. Memo by division d'Asie-Océanie, "French Policy in Vietnam," Feb. 11, 1956, *DDF, 1956*, 190–192; memo for the Minster, Feb. 16, 1956, MAE, CLV, SV, 40; Pineau to Minister of National Defense, Feb. 17, 1956, MAE, CLV, SV, 40; *The Pentagon Papers: The Defense Department History of the United States Decision-Making on Vietnam*, vol. 1, Gravel ed. (Boston: Beacon Press, 1971), 217; Ronald Spector, *Advice and Support: The Early Years of the United States Army in Vietnam, 1941–1960* (New York: Free Press, 1985), 238.

20. Hoppenot to Pinay, Jan. 18, 1956, *DDF, 1956*, vol. 1, 55–56.

21. Hoppenot to MAE, March 2, 1956, MAE, CLV, SV, vol. 38; Hoppenot to MAE, March 19, 1956, CLV, SV, vol. 38. Of the Vietnamese to be trained abroad in 1955, 729 were sent to France and 166 to the United States; in 1956, 450 were sent to France and 881 to the United States. Furthermore, the United States ended funding for six hundred Vietnamese officers who were training at various French military schools, and in June 1956 Diem suspended the training of all Vietnamese officers in France. Hoppenot to MAE, March 6, 1956, MAE, CLV, SV, vol. 38; Hoppenot to MAE, June 15, 1956, MAE, CLV, SV, vol. 38; July 1956 memos, MAE, CLV, SV, vol. 38; and Hoppenot to Minister, top secret, Aug. 13, 1956, MAE, CLV, SV, vol. 73. Hoppenot claimed he had a letter from General Williams, dated March 16, 1956, that proved that the idea of closing the EMS was an American initiative.

22. Dulles to Paris and Saigon, Aug. 15, 1956, NARA, RG 59, 651.00/3–2455 to 651.51G9/1–12–55, Box 2618.

23. Couve de Murville to MAE, Feb. 25, 1956, MAE, CLV, SV, vol. 44.

24. Hoppenot to MAE, Feb. 28, 1956, MAE, CLV, SV, vol. 44.

25. Memo for the minister, Feb. 27, 1956, MAE, CLV, SV, vol. 44.

26. See memo for the minister, Feb. 29, 1956, MAE, CLV, SV, vol. 44; memcon, Couve de Murville and Dulles, February 28, 1956, *FRUS, 1955–1957*, 1:648.

27. Memo to Eden and Molotov, May 14, 1956, MAE, CLV, SV, vol. 69; Hoppenot to Pineau, July 14, 1956, *DDF, 1956*, vol. 2, 99–107.

28. Hoppenot to Pineau, Aug. 13, 1956, MAE, CLV, SV, vol. 73.

29. Pineau to Payart, Aug. 29, 1956, *DDF, 1956*, vol. 2, 316–324.

30. Jacques Dalloz, *The War in Indochina, 1945–1954* (Dublin: Gill and Macmillan, 1990), 196.

31. Memo on aid mission to Vietnam, Feb. 18, 1956, MAE, CLV, SV, vol. 87.

32. The French share of Vietnamese imports fell from 66.7 percent to 27.4 percent from July 1955 to July 1956. Saigon embassy to MAE, April 24, 1956, MAE, CLV, SV, vol. 55.

33. Memo on aid mission to Vietnam, Feb. 18, 1956, MAE, CLV, SV, vol. 87.

34. See Pierre Journoud, "Face-à-face culturel au Sud-Vietnam, 1954–1965," *Entre rayonnement et réciprocité: Contributions à l'histoire de la diplomatie culturelle*, ed. Pierre Journoud (Paris: Publications de la Sorbonne, 2002), 139–166, for a detailed account of French cultural diplomacy in South Vietnam after Geneva.

35. Memo on Franco-Indochinese cultural problems, July 3, 1953, AN 457AP/52; memo, 1954, MAE, Asie 1944–1955, Indochine, vol. 83.

36. Memo of French working group discussion in Saigon, Dec. 3, 1954, SHAT, Ely papers, vol. 37; minutes of Franco-American working group meeting, Dec. 15, 1954, MAE, CLV, SV, vol. 47.

37. Hoppenot to Pinay, Feb. 11, 1956, MAE, CLV, SV vol. 51.

38. Dannaud to the Commissariat of the Republic, March 24, 1956, CLV, SV, vol. 48.

39. D'Andurain de Maytie to MAE, May 9, 1957, MAE, Cabinet du Ministre, Cabinet Pineau, vol. 17.

40. Memo, Aug. 12, 1958, MAE, CLV, SV, vol. 33.

41. Dannaud to minister of education, Sept. 4, 1956, MAE, Etats-Associés, 1945–1957, section iv, vol. 191.

42. Memo, June 18, 1956, MAE, CLV, SV, vol. 87.

43. Hoppenot to minister, Aug. 3, 1956, MAE, CLV, SV, vol. 125.

44. Hoppenot to minister, Aug. 13, 1956, MAE, CLV, SV, vol. 73.

45. Payart to minister, Oct. 3, 1956, secret, MAE, CLV, SV, vol. 87; Payart to minister, Nov. 21, 1956, MAE, CLV, SV, vol. 87.

46. Sainteny to MAE, Jan. 29, 1957, MAE, CLV, RDVN, vol. 32.

47. French Consulate in New York to MAE, Jan. 30, 1957, CLV, SV, vol. 71.

48. See Collins to Dulles, Jan. 20, 1955, *FRUS, 1955–1957,* 1:54.

49. Hoppenot to minister, Aug. 13, 1956, MAE, CLV, SV, vol. 73.

50. Dalloz, *The War in Indochina,* 195–196; Bernard Fall, "Indochina Since Geneva," *Pacific Affairs,* vol. 28, no. 1 (March 1955), 20; Jean Sainteny, *Ho Chi Minh and His Vietnam: A Personal Memoir* (Chicago: Cowles Book, 1972), 108.

51. Roux to Washington, Aug. 20, 1954, MAE, Asie 1944–1955, Indochine, vol. 84.

52. Aurillac to Director of Division d'Asie-Océanie and Chief of Economic and Financing Affairs Services, Feb. 7, 1956, MAE, CLV, RDVN, vol. 44; memo for the President of the Council, June 7, 1958, MAE, CLV, RDVN, vol. 35.

53. Memo, Oct. 1, 1959, MAE, CLV, RDVN, vol. 45.

54. Sainteny, *Ho Chi Minh and His Vietnam,* 153.

55. The North Vietnamese seized the initiative regarding the 1956 elections in declarations, one on June 6 and the second on July 9, 1955, in which they stated that they were ready to consult. When it became clear the South Vietnamese would not begin consultations, and the July 20 deadline passed without action, Hanoi protested to the co-chairs on August 17 and continued to protest periodically thereafter. Historians disagree about the extent of North Vietnamese sincerity in pursuing elections. For arguments that the DRV wanted the elections to take place, see Scigliano, *South Vietnam,* 133; Carlyle Thayer, *War By Other Means: National Liberation and Revolution in Vietnam* (Sydney: Allen and Urwin, 1989), 6–7; and Duiker, *Sacred War: Nationalism and Revolution in a Divided Vietnam* (Boston: McGraw-Hill, 1995), 99–100.

56. Hoppenot to MAE, March 1, 1956, MAE, CLV, SV, vol. 23.

57. MAE to Chambon, Dec. 22, 1959, MAE, CLV, RDVN, vol. 12; *Ho Chi Minh and His Vietnam,* Sainteny, 115. Only about one hundred French nationals still lived in the North at this point.

58. Chambon to MAE, May 16, 1960, MAE, CLV, RDVN, vol. 37; memo, October 1960, MAE, CLV, RDVN, vol. 45.

59. Memo, Jan. 14, 1958, MAE, CLV, SV, vol. 9.

60. Dalloz, *The War in Indochina,* 109.

61. Payart to Minister, June 30, 1958, MAE, CLV, SV, vol. 129.

62. Lalouette to Murville, March 31, 1959, MAE, CLV, SV, vol. 131.

63. Lalouette to Couve de Murville, May 15, 1959, MAE, CLV, SV, vol. 48.

64. Lalouette to Murville, Sept. 30, 1959, MAE, CLV, SV, vol. 133.

65. Fifty-three French-operated or -subsidized schools existed in Vietnam with twenty-four thousand pupils. The University of Saigon employed more than forty French professors. Memo by R. Benoit, 1959, MAE, CLV, SV, vol. 47.

66. Lalouette to Couve de Murville, Dec. 31, 1960, MAE, CLV, SV, vol. 136.

67. Ruelle to Manac'h, April 11, 1960, *DDF, 1960,* vol. 1, 455–462.

68. Manac'h to Ruelle, April 12, 1960, MAE, CLV, SV, vol. 87.

69. Memo, May 28, 1960, MAE, CLV, SV, vol. 71.

70. Lalouette to Murville, Sept. 17, 1960, MAE, CLV, SV, vol. 75.

71. Lalouette to MAE, Oct. 1, 1960, CLV, SV, vol. 69.

72. Chauvel to MAE, Oct. 11, 1960, MAE, CLV, SV, vol. 69; Manac'h to Lalouette, Oct. 15, 1960, MAE, CLV, SV, vol. 11.

73. Lalouette to Couve de Murville, Oct. 24, 1960, MAE, CLV, SV, vol. 11.

74. Lalouette to MAE, Nov. 18, 1960, MAE, CLV, SV, vol. 136.

75. For discussion of neutralization, see Fredrik Logevall, "De Gaulle, Neutralization and American Involvement in Vietnam, 1963–1964," *Pacific Historical Review* 61, no. 1 (February 1992), and Logevall, *Choosing War: The Lost Chance for Peace and the Escalation of War in Vietnam* (Berkeley: University of California Press, 1999), 13–15, 68, 129–133, and 187–188.

76. When Lalouette met with Diem in early February 1962, Diem, for the first time, indicated he was willing to consider an exchange of views with Hanoi. Lalouette to Murville, Feb. 1, 1962, *DDF, 1962,* vol. 1, no. 33.

14. Chronicle of a War Foretold: The United States and Vietnam, 1945–1954

1. Fredrik Logevall, *Choosing War: The Lost Chance for Peace and the Escalation of War in Vietnam* (Berkeley: University of California Press, 1999), 298–299.

2. Robert S. McNamara, *In Retrospect: The Tragedy and Lessons of Vietnam* (New York: Times Books, 1995), 32.

3. Tim O'Brien, *Going After Cacciato* (New York: Dell, 1975), 273.

4. John White, *A Voyage to Cochin China* (Kuala Lampur and New York: Oxford University Press, 1972), 38, 41, 219, 231.

5. Mark Philip Bradley, *Imagining Vietnam and America: The Making of Postcolonial Vietnam, 1919–1950* (Chapel Hill, N.C.: University of North Carolina Press, 2000), 47–51.

6. William J. Duiker, *Ho Chi Minh: A Life* (New York: Hyperion, 2000), 289, 300; M. C. Latta to Secretary of State, Oct. 17, 1945, in Dennis Merrill, ed., *Documentary History of the Truman Presidency,* vol. 32 (Bethesda, Md.: University Publications of America, 2001), 1; Ronald Spector, *Advice and Support: The Early Years, 1941–1960* (Washington, D.C.: Center of Military History, U.S. Army, 1983), 42.

7. Bradley, *Imagining Vietnam and America,* 167.

8. Ibid., 168.

9. William Conrad Gibbons, *The U.S. Government and the Vietnam War: Executive and Legislative Roles and Relationships: Part I: 1945–1960* (Princeton, N.J.: Princeton University Press, 1986), 143.

10. Ibid., 230.

11. Spector, *Advice and Support*, 9.

12. Policy Information Committee, Department of State, "Weekly Review," Aug. 30, 1950, in Merrill, *Documentary History*, 504.

13. Gibbons, *The U.S. Government*, 107.

14. Duiker, *Ho Chi Minh*, 50.

15. SEA Conference–Communist Activities in Southeast Asia, French Indo-China, June 22, 1948, in Merrill, *Documentary History*, 52.

16. Allen Griffin, "United States Objectives and Opportunities in Southeast Asia," Aug. 8, 1950, in Merrill, *Documentary History*, 420.

17. Herbert S. Parmet, *JFK: The Presidency of John F. Kennedy* (New York: Penguin, 1983), 328.

18. George C. Herring, *America's Longest War: The United States and Vietnam, 1950–1975*, 3rd ed. (New York: McGraw-Hill, 1996), 129.

19. George McT. Kahin, *Intervention: How America Became Involved in Vietnam* (New York: Anchor Books, 1986), 339.

20. Doris Kearns, *Lyndon Johnson and the American Dream* (New York: Harper and Row, 1976), 330.

21. Kahin, *Intervention*, 5.

22. Gibbons, *The U.S. Government*, 88.

23. Kahin, *Intervention*, 9.

24. Gibbons, *The U.S. Government*, 100.

25. Ibid., 97.

26. Duiker, *Ho Chi Minh*, 421.

27. Andrew J. Rotter, *The Path to Vietnam: Origins of the American Commitment to Southeast Asia* (Ithaca, N.Y.: Cornell University Press, 1987), 119–121.

28. Gibbons, *The U.S. Government*, 158.

29. Ibid., 202.

30. Kearns, *Lyndon Johnson*, 252.

31. Larry Berman, *Lyndon Johnson's War: The Road to Stalemate in Vietnam* (New York: Norton, 1989), 152.

32. See William S. Borden, *The Pacific Alliance: United States Foreign Economic Policy and Japanese Trade Recovery, 1947–1955* (Madison, Wis.: University of Wisconsin Press, 1984); Michael Schaller, *The American Occupation of Japan: The Origins of the Cold War in Asia* (New York: Oxford University Press, 1985); Rotter, esp. 35–48, 127–140. See also Robert M. Blum, *Drawing the Line: The Origin of American Containment Policy in East Asia* (New York: Norton, 1982).

33. Rotter, *The Path to Vietnam*, esp. 49–69, 141–164.

34. Ibid., 168–169.

35. Ibid., 94.

36. Report of the Military Survey Group in Southeast Asia: Indochina, State Department Report, Aug. 5, 1950, in Merrill, *Documentary History*, 483.

37. Kahin, *Intervention*, 39.

38. Gibbons, *The U.S. Government*, 120.

39. Yuen Foong Khong, *Analogies at War: Korea, Munich, Dien Bien Phu, and the Vietnam Decisions of 1965* (Princeton, N.J.: Princeton University Press, 1992), 93.

40. Ibid., 92.

41. Logevall, *Choosing War*, 276–77.

42. Khong, *Analogies at War*, 97–147. See also Ernest R. May, *"Lessons" of the Past: The Use and Misuse of History in American Foreign Policy* (New York: Oxford University Press, 1973), 105–110.

43. Stanley Karnow, *In Our Image: America's Empire in the Philippines* (New York: Random House, 1989), 341–345.

44. Ibid., 246–255. See also Robert J. McMahon, *The Limits of Empire: The United States and Southeast Asia Since World War II* (New York: Columbia University Press, 1999), 56–59.

45. Edward Geary Lansdale, *In the Midst of Wars: An American's Mission to Southeast Asia* (New York: Harper and Row, 1972), 126.

46. Herring, *America's Longest War*, 175.

47. Telegram from Acheson to Consulate in Hanoi, May 20, 1949, in Gareth Porter, ed., *Vietnam: A History in Documents* (New York: Meridian, 1979), 79.

48. Gibbons, *The U.S. Government*, 132.

49. Ibid., 255; Dwight David Eisenhower, *Mandate for Change, 1953–1956* (Garden City, N.Y.: Doubleday, 1963), 372.

50. Gibbons, *The U.S. Government*, 92; Robert Shaplen, *The Lost Revolution: The U.S. in Vietnam, 1946–1966* (New York: Harper, 1966), 65; Philip E. Catton, *Diem's Final Failure: Prelude to America's War in Vietnam* (Lawrence, Kans.: University of Kansas Press, 2002), 64.

51. Duiker, *Ho Chi Minh*, 330. "If the Americans had been our masters, they would now be giving us our freedom," Ho told Major Archimedes Patti of the OSS in late 1945. Karnow, *In Our Image*, 323.

52. Kearns, *Lyndon Johnson*, 373.

53. Herring, *America's Longest War*, 181.

54. Summary Report No. 1 of the Military Group Joint MDAP Survey Mission to Southeast Asia, Aug. 5, 1950, in Merrill, *Documentary History*, 462.

55. Gibbons, *The U.S. Government*, 99.

56. Joint State-Defense MDAP Survey Mission to Southeast Asia, Dec. 6, 1950, in Merrill, *Documentary History*, 620.

57. Herring, *America's Longest War*, 33.

58. Melanie Billings-Yun, *Decision against War: Eisenhower and Dien Bien Phu, 1954* (New York: Columbia University Press, 1988), 95.

59. Gibbons, *The U.S. Government*, 220.

60. In addition to Billings-Yun, see David Anderson, *Trapped by Success: The Eisenhower Administration and Vietnam, 1953–1961* (New York: Columbia University Press, 1991); Lloyd Gardner, *Approaching Vietnam: From World War II through Dien Bien Phu* (New York: Norton, 1988); and George C. Herring and Richard Immerman, "Eisenhower, Dulles, and Dien Bien Phu: 'The Day We Didn't Go to War' Revisited," *Journal of American History*, 71 (Sept. 1984), 343–363.

61. George W. Ball, *The Past Has Another Pattern* (New York: Norton, 1982), 400–402.

62. Gibbons, *The U.S. Government*, 103.

63. Ibid., 206.

64. Ibid., 245.

65. Gardner, *Approaching Vietnam*, 266.

66. Ibid., 355.

67. McNamara, *In Retrospect*, 306–309; Ball, *The Past Has Another Pattern*, 408–409; Herring, *America's Longest War*, 226.

68. Gibbons, *The U.S. Government*, 238.

69. Ibid., 129, 150.

70. Ibid., 97, 119, 131.

71. Ibid., 26; A. L. Moffat to John Carter Vincent, Aug. 9, 1946, in Porter, *Vietnam*, 46–48.

72. Rotter, *The Path to Vietnam*, 95, 173–174, 213.
73. Logevall, *Choosing War*, 350.
74. Gibbons, *The U.S. Government*, 153.
75. Ibid., 191.
76. Gabriel García Márquez, *Chronicle of a Death Foretold*, transl. Gregory Rabassa (New York: Knopf, 1983), 9.

Contributors

MARK PHILIP BRADLEY
Associate Professor of History,
Northwestern University

LAURENT CESARI
Professor of Contemporary History,
University of Artois

CHEN JIAN
Professor of History,
Cornell University

WILLIAM J. DUIKER
Emeritus Professor of History,
Penn State University

MARK ATWOOD LAWRENCE
Associate Professor of History,
University of Texas at Austin

FREDRIK LOGEVALL
Professor of History,
Cornell University

DAVID G. MARR
Emeritus Professor,
Research School of Pacific and Asian Studies,
Australian National University

LIEN-HANG T. NGUYEN
Assistant Professor of History,
University of Kentucky

JOHN PRADOS
Senior Fellow,
National Security Archive, Washington, D.C.

ANDREW J. ROTTER
Professor of History,
Colgate University

KATHRYN C. STATLER
Associate Professor of History,
University of San Diego

MARTIN THOMAS
Reader,
Department of History,
University of Exeter

STEIN TØNNESSON
Director, International Peace Research Institute,
Oslo

MARILYN B. YOUNG
Professor of History,
New York University

Index